LESLIE DIENES
Department of Geography

THE WEST EUROPEAN CITY

The West European City:
A Social Geography

PAUL WHITE
Lecturer in Geography
at the University of Sheffield

LONGMAN
London and New York

Longman Group Limited
Longman House, Burnt Mill, Harlow
Essex CM20 2JE, England
Associated companies throughout the world

Published in the United States of America
by Longman Inc., New York

First published 1984

British Library Cataloguing in Publication Data

White, Paul
The West European City.
1. Cities and towns – Europe – History
I. Title
940'. 09173'2   HT131

ISBN 0-582-30047-9

Library of Congress Cataloging in Publication Data

White, Paul, D. Phil.
The West European City.

Bibliography: p.
Includes index.
1. Cities and towns – Europe. 2. Rural-urban migration – Europe.
3. Anthropo-geography – Europe. I. Title.
HT131.W54 1984   307.7'64'094   83-9382
ISBN 0-582-30047-9

Set in 11/12 pt VIP Garamond Roman No. 3.
Printed in Singapore by
Selector Printing Co (Pte) Ltd

For my parents, Cyril and Ethel White

Contents

List of Figures ix
List of Tables xi
Preface xii
Acknowledgements xvi
Maps – location of cities mentioned in the text xvii

One	The Legacy of History	1
	Introduction	1
	Controlling interests and the pre-industrial legacy	3
	Urban demography before 1800	14
	The nineteenth century: the industrial city	16
	City walls	22
	Haussmannization, planning and the twentieth century	27
	Conclusions	31
Two	Housing in the Western European City	35
	Housing classes	36
	Dwelling types and housing densities	47
	A summary of housing	54
Three	Demography	57
	Components of change	57
	Fertility	62
	Mortality	63
	Age-structures	68
	The distribution of the sexes	72
Four	Domestic Migration and the City	74
	Structural determinants and correlates of migration	74
	Mass domestic migration in Northern Europe	77
	Post-war domestic migration in Southern European cities	82
	Belgium and Switzerland: domestic migration and cultural cleavage	91
	Contemporary Northern European cities	94

Five International Migration and the City 97
     The evolution of international migration 97
     The size of the migrant groups 101
     The migrants: origins, characteristics and occupations 108
     Migrants in the housing market 115
     Segregation 120
     Conclusions 131

Six Intra-urban Migration 134
     The volume of movement 135
     The movers and their motives 137
     Patterns of movement 139

Seven The Residential Kaleidoscope 151
     Social structures 152
     Residential segregation and housing variables 155
     Social class and location 160
     Social dimensions and spatial patterns 170
     Behaviour in social space 182
     Conclusions 187

Eight Change in the Inner-City 191
     Demographic and social composition 191
     City-centre depopulation 198
     Renewal and redevelopment: restoration and rehabilitation 204

Nine The Suburbs and Beyond 212
     The history of suburban growth 212
     Types of suburb 215
     The journey-to-work 226
     Alternatives to suburban growth 229

     Appendix – Data sources for figures and tables 233
     Notes on further reading 235
     References 238
     Index of authors 258
     Index of places 264
     Index of subjects 268

List of Figures

1.1	The expansion of Nancy, sixteenth to eighteenth centuries	8
1.2	Karlsruhe in the middle of the eighteenth century	9
1.3	Street-plan of north-eastern Madrid	24
1.4	Vienna in 1844	25
1.5	Second World War damage in the Ruhr cities	30
2.1	Population size and single-household residential buildings, 1968–75	49
2.2	Persons per dwelling, 1968–75	54
3.1	Two models of urban demographic development	58
3.2	Rates of population change, Zürich, 1924–78	60
3.3	Model of the influences on morbidity and mortality	64
3.4	Selected causes of death, Paris, 1900–4 and 1960–4	65
3.5	Standardized mortality rates by *arrondissements* of Paris, 1900–4 and 1960–4	66
3.6	Infant mortality in Rome, 1958–61	67
3.7	Proportions of resident population aged 0–14 years, Bologna, 1968 and Lyon, 1975	69
4.1	Migrant birthplaces and places of residence in Paris, 1911	80
4.2	Turin, proportion of newly-arriving migrants originating in Southern Italy, 1957	84
4.3	Sub-populations defined by birthplace, Barcelona, 1970	88
4.4	Resident domestic migrants in Brussels, 1961: origins and changes in importance, 1947–61	93
5.1	Foreigners in cities, 1970–5	104
5.2	Non-Austrian populations in Vienna, 1947–79	106
5.3	Dominant foreigner nationalities, 1970–5	109
5.4	Foreign migrants in Antwerp, Brussels, Paris, West Berlin and Zürich	124
5.5	Foreigner clusters on the basis of indices of dissimilarity, Brussels, 1970	127
5.6	Distributions of Moroccans and British in Brussels, 1970	128
6.1	External and internal migration in Zürich, 1978	140

ix

6.2	Net intra-urban migration, Rome 1964, Cologne 1978	142
6.3	Gross intra-urban migration rates, Amsterdam 1977, Stockholm 1978	143
6.4	Intra-urban migration and distance, Bonn	145
6.5	Intra-urban migration districts in Brussels	147
6.6	Nodal flows in intra-urban migration – Rome, 1964	148
6.7	Nodal flows in intra-urban migration – Vienna, 1978	149
7.1	Industry and high-status areas, Turin	165
7.2	Social areas in Rome, 1951	172
7.3	Residential districts in Vienna, 1961	179
7.4	Residential districts in Copenhagen, 1965	181
7.5	Electoral patterns and social areas, Paris	183
7.6	A model of the Western European city	188
8.1	The location of Belleville, Paris	193
8.2	Population decline in inner Bergen, 1960–75	200
8.3	Population change in central Amsterdam, 1869–1977	200
8.4	Proportion of total floor space in residential use – central Aarhus, 1963	204
9.1	Industrial areas in Paris	216
9.2	Commuting in the Green Heart of the Randstad	228

List of Tables

1.1   Dates of removal of fortifications – selected cities   23

2.1   Owner-occupied dwellings as percentage of all occupied private dwellings – selected cities   36

2.2   Privately-rented dwellings as percentage of all occupied private dwellings – selected cities   39

2.3   Publicly-rented dwellings as percentage of all occupied private dwellings – selected cities   43

2.4   Estimates of shanty-towns etc. – Portuguese and Spanish cities   46

2.5   Dwelling types – selected cities, 1970   48

2.6   Housing age – selected cities   51

3.1   Components of population change – selected West German and Italian cities, 1978   58

3.2   In-migration and fertility – selected cities   61

4.1   Segregation of domestic migrants, Barcelona, 1970   86

5.1   Foreign-born populations – selected Southern European cities, 1971   101

5.2   Resident foreign citizens – selected Northern European cities, 1970–5   103

5.3   Evolution of foreigner populations, 1970–9 – selected cities   105

5.4   Origins of foreign residents – selected cities, 1970–5   110

5.5   Segregation indices for foreign nationalities, Brussels, 1970   127

6.1   Intra-urban migration – selected cities   135

6.2   Migration within urban administrative sub-units   144

7.1   Social composition of four Western European cities   154

7.2   Segregation of social classes, Brussels 1970   157

7.3   Social dimensions derived from multivariate analyses – selected cities   174

8.1   Inner-city population declines – selected cities   199

Preface

Most of the published work in English on urban geography inevitably deals with cities of the English-speaking world. This feature, although perhaps a little short-sighted, posed no problems while the subject was in an empiricist phase, describing individual cities and their evolution. When urban geographers began increasingly to search for generalizations, and these positivist trends first made themselves felt in North America and the United Kingdom, their models and general laws of behaviour were drawn from a limited set of cases taken from a limited number of historical, social, cultural, economic and political contexts.

The primary objective of the present volume is to broaden the range of material that is put before English-speaking students of urban, social and population geography. The book aims to demonstrate that cities in Western Europe have evolved, and continue to evolve, in circumstances which do not reproduce those of North America, Australasia or even, in certain repects, the British Isles. The standard English-language textbooks deal with the urban structures of these latter groups of cities admirably, but Western Europe, with some of the longest urban traditions anywhere, is generally largely ignored. The result is that the vast majority of English-speaking students, and especially the dismaying number with no foreign language capabilities whatsoever, at present study an urban geography that fails to encompass a major geographical region of profound urban distinctiveness. The present volume is designed to be used as a supplement to the standard urban geography texts and especially by students of urbanism, society or population who already have some background or understanding of established ideas on urban social geography as currently practised in the English-speaking world.

This volume is thus a supplementary text serving both for those interested in systematic sub-disciplines (such as urban geography or migration study) and those looking at human geography in a particular empirical context (such as students taking courses on Western Europe). It is not designed as a 'state-of-the-art' summary of current developments in urban geography within Western Europe; nor is it intended as a basic textbook of urban geography illustrated with European examples. The discussion in the book draws heavily from the published works of Western European scholars (and others writing about the region), but considerable use has also been made of census figures and other published governmental statistical series (see Appendix).

The final structure of the book represents a personal view of the significant points of interest in Western European cities. In particular, considerable emphasis is placed upon migration to cities (Ch. 4 and 5) because it is felt that these migration patterns are of prime importance for the evolution of social behaviour and structure within the cities. Migration to Western European cities has occurred via an evolutionary scenario that is unique to the region, whereby domestic migrants have, through time, been replaced by international migrants, at least in Northern Europe, with the resultant creation of distinct migrant minority groups in the cities. The historical legacy of Western European cities is stressed in Chapter 1, again because of the uniqueness of that legacy: the historical background of these cities is vastly different and more complex than for the urban societies of the New World which were foundations of a period of incipient capitalist development in a context of free market economies and democratic institutions. Chapter 2 outlines the complexity of urban housing markets in Western Europe, again showing several individualistic features of housing traditions. Chapters 7, 8 and 9 consider social distributions and changes within cities. The book does not make any concerted attempt to examine the development of urban planning in the twentieth century, this topic having been dealt with in Sutcliffe's (1981) *Towards the Planned City* and in the work by Burtenshaw et al. (1981).

The present volume does not contain any detailed discussion of cities in the British Isles for two reasons. Firstly there is the pragmatic reason that British cities are well covered in existing English-language urban textbooks. Secondly, at a more substantive level, urban society in the British Isles is organized in ways that differ from the European mainland in several key respects. For example, the housing market in British cities contains a far more important owner-occupier sector than is the case elsewhere (see Ch. 2) and this has considerable repercussions on the distributions of social classes within the city. Other differences concern the location of high status districts, deriving from various cultural effects on locational desirability (Ch. 7) and the generally low levels of occurrence of single-family housing in cities of the European mainland. Many of the features distinguishing British cities and making them exceptions to general European patterns result from the separate paths of historical evolution they have followed.

However, it should not be imagined that all Western European cities are structured in the same way in terms of social geography. To supplement the crude belief that all cities in the world are like Chicago with the idea that all Western European cities are like Paris would scarcely constitute progress. A repeated theme of the material in this volume is that, although various general features emerge, the Western European region is notable for a diversity of city types with classifications possible on a variety of bases, the most useful being Northern versus Southern Europe, and old cities versus those that are creations of nineteenth-century industrial growth. These are, of course, extremely broad divisions but they help in the understanding of evolutionary processes – for example in the discussion of migration to cities (see Ch. 4 and 5).

The definition of Western Europe adopted here includes all countries to the west of the block of state socialist societies: in other words, the mainland European Community countries with the addition of Portugal, Spain, Switzerland, Austria, Norway, Sweden and Finland. Inevitably, in a defined region of such linguistic diversity, almost insurmountable problems are presented to anyone attempting the ambitious task of synthesizing the works of authors writing in their native languages. It is my regret that original work in several languages does not appear in the reference list for this book, but that is, I hope, excusable. No doubt much valuable material has been published in such languages as Finnish, Swedish or Greek but I am unable to read it!

The preparation of this book took three years, from 1979 to 1982, and the volume is very much a child of that period. With few exceptions (such as France) the most recent censuses available were taken in 1970 or 1971. Wherever possible (such as on the question of foreign migrants – Ch. 5) use has been made of statistical yearbooks to update this information to the late 1970s. Inevitably, however, the major data base remains that of the earlier censuses. The 1970s, with the general onset of recession, will surely prove to have been an extremely interesting decade in the evolution of Western European cities, but analysis of that evolution must await the publication of the censuses of the early 1980s.

It is my great regret that, in a book of this scope, it is not possible to convey the real flavour or sense of place of the cities mentioned and discussed. The traveller in Western Europe is likely to be immediately struck by the particular building styles, urban morphology and ways of life of individual cities, a variety that I have constantly observed in my journeys around the Continent. To convey the real atmosphere of urban living in different Western European city neighbourhoods would, however, require the evocative prose of a Richard Cobb or a Georges Simenon and these are descriptive skills and powers of detailed observation that few geographers possess. Anyway, I find, on counting them, that, despite being relatively well-travelled in Western Europe, I have personal experience of only just over one-quarter of the cities mentioned in this book. Whilst paying its respects to the humanistic approaches, the present volume stays with a more aggregated approach to urban social life.

Finally, certain points of detail must be clarified. Several of the illustrations in the text are of individual cities, the objective being to demonstrate the existence (or non-existence) of overall spatial patterns rather than as a basis for ideographic description. On these maps a single point is indicated as the 'city centre' simply for the purpose of orienting the resulting pattern. Throughout the book, anglicized spellings have been used of place-names except where these are now archaic, obscure or pedantic. Maps of the cities mentioned in the text will be found immediately preceding Chapter 1.

A large number of people have been of immense help in bringing this book to the light of day. Sections of the manuscript have been read by Ron Johnston, Peter Jones, Philip Ogden, Gwyn Rowley, Tony Sutcliffe, George Taylor and

Bob Woods, all of whom made valuable comments: all blame for the shortcomings of the volume must, of course, lie with the author. Bob Woods in particular has been a constant source of advice and help.

It would be literally true to say that the book could not have been written without the efforts of Julia Dagg and the Inter-Library Loans service of Sheffield University Library in obtaining for me many obscure foreign items, often borrowed from abroad. The staff of the Office of Population Censuses and Surveys Library in London, and of the Bibliothèque Nationale in Paris, have also been of assistance.

The figures were almost entirely the work of Rosemary Duncan and I am delighted to thank her for her willing help. Among those who turned my handwriting into neat typescript were Karen Bellamy, Joan Dunn, Carole Elliss, Penny Shamma and Ann Tester.

I would also like to acknowledge the help and support of my wife Elizabeth in the production of this book. She has willingly put up with many meal-time monologues from me as I have tried out on her the frameworks for various topics, and she has still had the patience and interest to read and comment on substantial sections of the manuscript. I have also benefited from her personal knowledge of several parts of Europe that I have never visited. Finally, however, I would like to thank my parents for the early encouragement they gave me: it is to them that this book is dedicated.

PAUL WHITE
Sheffield
December 1982

Acknowledgements

We are grateful to the following for permission to reproduce copyright material:

The American Sociological Association for our Fig 7.2 (after D. C. McElrath 1962); Der Aufbau for our Fig 7.3 (after M. Sauberer & K. Cserjan 1972); Bevolking en Gezin for our Fig 6.5 (after B. Meeus 1975); Geographische Institut der Universität Bonn for our Fig 6.4 (after H. Böhm et al 1975); Geografisk Magasin 'Kulturgeografi' for our Fig 8.4 (after W. Taubmann 1969); Geografisk Tidsskrift for our Fig 7.4 (after Matthiessen 1973); The Institute of British Geographers for our Fig 4.1 (after P. E. Ogden & S. W. C. Winchester 1975); Norsk Geografisk Tidsskrift for our Fig 8.2 (after M. Helvig 1976); Revue Française de Science Politique for our Fig 7.5 (after J. Ranger 1977); Utrechtse Geografische Studies for our Fig 9.2 (after J. A. Van Ginkel 1979)

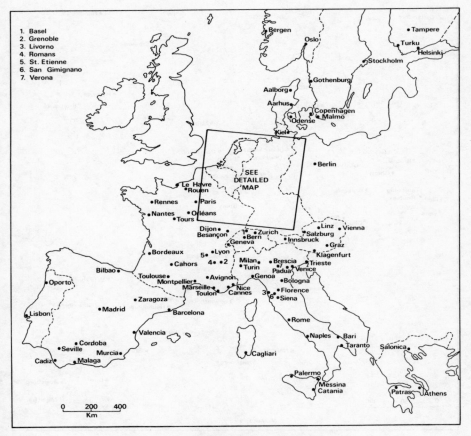

1. Basel
2. Grenoble
3. Livorno
4. Romans
5. St. Etienne
6. San Gimignano
7. Verona

Map 1   Location of cities mentioned in the text

1. Bochum
2. Düsseldorf

Hamburg

Bremen

Amsterdam

Hanover

The Hague
Utrecht
Rotterdam

Brunswick

Münster
Bielefeld

Gelsenkirchen
Duisburg
1 Dortmund
Essen
2 Wuppertal
Mönchengladbach

Bruges
Antwerp
Dunkirk
Ghent

Brussels
Cologne

Tourcoing
Roubaix
Lille
Lens

Liège
Bonn

Namur
Charleroi

Wiesbaden
Frankfurt
Mainz

Trier
Würzburg

Ludwigshafen
Mannheim
Nuremberg
Heidelberg

Karlsruhe

Nancy
Stuttgart

Strasbourg

Ulm
Augsburg
Munich

0   50   100
Km

Freiburg

Mulhouse

Map 2   Location of cities mentioned in the text

CHAPTER ONE

The Legacy of History

INTRODUCTION

The cities of Western Europe display a dazzling diversity of courses of historical evolution, but there are sufficient common elements to justify the derivation of certain generalizations applying to Western European cities as a whole.

Whilst some cities can trace their origins back over millennia, others were founded only within the last couple of centuries. Some that were once mighty have now become backwaters out of the mainstream of modern social and economic development; others have never slipped from a position of eminence. Some cities have always been dominated by tertiary and quaternary economic activities; some have, on the other hand, taken the lead as the industrial powerhouses of nations. It is not the place here to attempt to reduce the urban history of Western Europe to a few thousand words; many distinguished historians have spent their lives in such undertakings and European urban history has been well covered in books such as Lewis Mumford's *The City in History* (1961) or, from a more geographical perspective, Vance's *This Scene of Man* (1977). Nor is it intended here to *précis* the thesis and arguments concerning Sjoberg's *The Pre-Industrial City* (1960), nor to attempt to revise Dickinson's *The West European City* (1961) with its historical – morphological approach.

Instead, the objective of the present chapter is to indicate the extent to which the history of Western European cities has influenced the social geography of urban life at the present day. The relevant salient features of urban history are thus not the great political struggles, the patronage of the arts or the construction of monumental buildings, but the accumulated circumstances and events of the day-to-day – the structures of population composition, the nature of housing, the degree of economic and social specialization within different city districts, the overriding cultural attitudes of society and of sub-classes. Throughout this book it will time and again be demonstrated that in much of the contemporary urban social geography of Western Europe an understanding of the past is a vital key to the elucidation of the present-day. This chapter sketches that historical legacy up to the end of the nineteenth

1

century: the detailed picture of more recent (and certain older) developments will be presented wherever relevant in succeeding chapters.

With a relatively limited number of exceptions, the main thrust of spatial theory concerning the city in the developed world has been based either on empirical evidence or on reasoning derived deductively from the Anglo-American world and, in particular, from the axioms of North American urban life. However, the theories and models thus produced may not be universally applicable for two reasons. Firstly, they are tied to a particular model of culture, and secondly, the evolutionary strands in these models are few since they are founded on urban experiences that lack the historical complexities of urban social, economic and political relationships such as are found in European cities. Certainly there are cities of the New World which owe their origin to colonial foundations, or to trading requirements dictated by the colonial power in Europe; but the vast majority of New World urban structures are the creation of the last 150 years, of a period of incipient and later burgeoning free-market capitalist economic activity based, politically, on concepts of democracy and a relatively egalitarian spirit. This period of New World urban growth lies almost entirely within the time-span of the development of modern communications systems, a fact that influences life within cities and that has also facilitated inter-urban movements to the extent that such cities have, from the outset, formed part of developing city-systems set within the context of rational market economies.

The contrasts with the cities of Western Europe are profound. Certainly most European cities have grown since the start of the nineteenth century through industrial expansion in a growing capitalist production mode, but for very few cities (and those largely confined to coalfields) has this been the only structural influence on urban growth. The majority of European cities have histories in which other socio-economic structures, never significantly present in the New World, have played a major role. Indeed, it is through these non-economic determinants of urban structure that European cities have acquired some of their most distinctive features (Lichtenberger 1972). Feudalism, paternalism, symbolism, mercantilism, absolutism and municipal socialism have played a variety of roles in different cities. Many urban places were for centuries intimately connected with local rural life rather than evolved urban social entities in their own right. Autocratic powers in the hands of kings, princes, nobles and bishops have stamped their mark not just on the morphology but also on the way of life in cities as different as Stockholm and Lisbon, Vienna and Liège, whilst other cities have enjoyed periods of dominion over city-states. Finally, the continued turbulence of European international (and even domestic) politics, in some cases well into the present century, has left its marks in the legacies of urban fortification systems which remain of great significance in many cities.

The historical antecedents of modern patterns of daily living in European cities are thus rich in the diversity of influences represented. The waves of historical change have washed through the European city, often radically remodelling and redefining the overall shape and the details; but in often

2

important respects these successive waves have rarely managed to obliterate completely the traces of their predecessors. These successive layers of sequent occupance have made their mark not just on urban morphology, which has concerned many urban geographers (Dickinson 1961), but also on the social geography of the city. The complex set of influences and processes that have gone to make up the socio-spatial patterning of the Western European city thus distinguish the cities in this part of the world from almost all others.

CONTROLLING INTERESTS AND THE PRE-INDUSTRIAL LEGACY

The origins of most European cities are unknown and cannot be dated. Few cities have been created as urban places on virgin territory: most have evolved from rural settlements through long processes of economic and population growth and the accretion of new functions. Certain Western European cities were in existence before the growth of the Roman Empire: apart from their own city-states the Ancient Greeks were responsible for the foundation of other Mediterranean cities such as Naples, Bari (which was an Illyrian settlement before Greek colonization), Marseille, Nice and Valencia. Other pre-Roman settlements include Seville, Barcelona, Toulouse, Milan, Palermo, Bologna and Trieste. By the end of the Roman Empire a high proportion of Western Europe's largest present-day cities were already in existence. In Italy only Venice, of the major cities, is a post-Roman creation whilst in Spain only Bilbao and Madrid, the latter fortified by the Moors, were not Roman towns of some note. In Northern Europe the boundary of the Roman Empire marked the limit of urban experience so that the only German cities claiming Roman ancestry are Cologne, Trier, Wiesbaden and Augsburg whilst, in the Netherlands, Utrecht was a Roman creation but the other modern cities were not. The cities of Northern Europe and Scandinavia are much younger than those of Southern Europe, many not growing to any prominence until the Middle Ages. Amsterdam appears to have been founded as a town only in 1275, The Hague after 1250, Bremen after 965 and Munich in the latter half of the twelfth century.

The actual foundation of the city is, however, far less important to the historical legacy than are the circumstances of the control over city evolution exerted by various urban interest-groups or by powers external to the cities such as national rulers. As Curl (1970: 1) puts it:

the political climate is determined by the dominant members of a society, that is, by the ruling classes and . . . the political climate thus created in turn influences the design of urban settlements profoundly.

Similar arguments have been put forward by Mumford (1961), Lichtenberger (1972: 219) and by Burtenshaw et al. (1981: 5–11). The thrust of this viewpoint is that the nature of power within the city and the manner in which it is exercised are vital influences on overall urban form and internal morphology, particularly in the arrangement of formal spaces within the city (such as markets, churches and squares) and their relationships to residences and neigh-bourhoods. Political and social conditions also formed the context for archi-tectural design with vernacular architecture being no less affected than more grandiose projects. In these ways the control of a city by a dominant interest becomes reflected in the day-to-day life of the ordinary citizen.

These dominant interest-groups were of various types and from the early medieval period on it is possible to discern a series of incipient conflicts between different groups within many cities, conflicts that were to colour urban growth for centuries. On the one side were the urban representatives of feudal power – barons and various other landowners generally deriving their privileged positions and their wealth from their ownership of rural land in the urban hinterland. Allied with this group were generally the judiciary and the clergy. On the other side were the growing ranks of the commercial interests comprised of merchants and artisans: these formed the basis of what was later to develop into the *bourgeois* class, the city burghers, with, below them and with little political power, their subservient employees and the general labourers.

As urban economies grew, the numbers of the commercial group tended to grow faster than those of the feudal party with the result that the physical expansion of the urban area could create segregation between the two groups (Claval 1981: 248). Lyon is a case in point: here the orginal post-Roman city of the barons, their retinues and the priests was on the right (west) bank of the Saône whilst the merchant and artisan quarter – the commercial city – grew to prominence on the 'peninsula' between the Saône and the Rhône. By the later fourteenth century the population of the commercial city outweighed that of the aristocratic city and the 'peninsula' had become the real city-centre (Fédou 1980).

Class interests were generally not, however, so clear cut as this simple example suggests for, as time progressed, the aspiring merchant class – the growing *bourgeoisie* – became more divorced from the lower artisans and labourers and, with hopes of ennoblement, could move into the 'opposing' camp, often demonstrating their new status by purchases of rural land. Where the merchant class came to overwhelm the feudal interest, as in parts of Germany, the castles originally built by the urban barons were sometimes pulled down as reminders of a bygone age (Curl 1970: 72), but in many other cities the position of the merchant *bourgeoisie* was a somewhat ambivalent one. Nor did the feudal landowners always stay aloof from commerce: many saw its potential benefits, as in Marseille where they became involved in the admin-istration of the port (Vieille 1978: 83–6).

Whilst it can be accepted that the social structure of the medieval town was thus extremely complex, it is perhaps permissible to put forward the general-ization that, whilst feudal and burgher interests co-existed in almost all cities, one of these generally took the lead and gave form to the urban area. Some of the city-states of central Italy such as Siena might be accepted as polar exem-plars of the ascendancy of the feudalist interest, whilst the North German cities of the Hanseatic League would be examples of cities dominated by merchant interests.

4

The feudal city

Braudel (1981: 515–19) has suggested that three basic types of city are recognizable in pre-industrial Europe: the feudal city, the burgher city and the absolutist or subjugated city. In the first of these the city was an adjunct to the countryside and was intimately linked to it. A high proportion of the more wealthy citizens were rural landlords whilst such a city housed a significant agricultural labour force alongside the guild structure of the artisan classes (Waley 1978: 9–15). An important section of the urban population was thus held in semi-serflike bondage to their landlords and the feudal controlling families reproduced in the city the conditions of inter-group hostility that had previously marked their existence in the countryside, thus producing a 'city of factions' (Vance 1977: 131–2). Siena is a classic example of a city fitting this description, but it is important to note that some of these features could obtain even within a burgher city. Medieval Florence, for example, with its vitally important trading interests in textiles, was nevertheless subject to internal divisions based largely on the feudal interests of some of the leading families.

Sjoberg's (1960) book, *The Pre-Industrial City*, has been important in conditioning current thinking on the internal structure of medieval cities. Sjoberg would not recognize Braudel's (1981) division of the pre-industrial city into three categories, but in practice Sjoberg was basically discussing the feudalist case: in his view city society was made up of three groups – an upper class, a lower class and a group outside mainstream society. The city was controlled by the *élite* of the upper class who derived their positions of power from non-urban sources. The lower class formed the bulk of the population whilst the outcaste section included minority ethnic groups (such as the Jews) and others who, whilst necessary to the functioning of the urban economy, took no role in urban society (Radford, 1979). In such a city, Sjoberg postulated that the *élite* would live at the centre, close to the religious, ceremonial and political core, attended by their retinues. The lower class would live in more peripheral locations with the outcaste groups at the very edge or living in segregated communities within the urban structure.

Sjoberg's model does have many points of congruence with the feudal city of medieval central Italy. The definition of the three classes is acceptable, with the *élite* being urban in location but not in origin or spirit, and with the Jewish outcaste group living in segregated neighbourhoods, and other marginal groups eking out a fragile existence outside the city walls. Medieval ghettos existed in many European cities of the past, some of the clearest examples being in Naples, Rome, Venice, Bologna, Cordoba, Bordeaux, Vienna and Antwerp. The role and composition of a feudal *élite* has survived into relatively recent centuries. In eighteenth-century Madrid many of the controlling noble families derived their wealth and prestige largely from their ownership of huge flocks of sheep in the Castilian countryside (Soubeyroux 1978: 48). The position of the Prince of Salina within Palermo society in Lampedusa's novel *The Leopard*, set in the Sicily of the 1860s, also springs to mind.

However, the congregating of the *élite*, the powerful and the wealthy at the centre, suggested by Sjoberg, was by no means the normal pattern. Claval (1981: 252) has shown the scattering of the richest residents throughout the French town of Cahors, whilst Le Roy Ladurie's (1981) analysis of the neighbourhoods of Romans similarly demonstrates that whilst certain districts were dominantly populated by artisans or farm labourers, the controlling *élite* were relatively ubiquitous. In the earliest feudal cities the localization of each feudal faction to a separate district was common. Even as late as the sixteenth century, the construction of new noble palaces in Bologna saw families build in the district of the city facing their rural places of origin and landholding (Ricci 1980: 109) – an early example of sectoral bias in rural–urban movement. Similarly in Renaissance and then Spanish-dominated Naples, baronial residences were scattered throughout the city with many built on the edge of the centre rather than within it (Döpp 1968: 140).

The result was the creation of an urban morphology dominated by the palaces of the nobles, these palaces often being fortified and equipped with towers, a townscape still partially observable in several Italian cities but best seen now in the small Tuscan town of San Gimignano. Each palace in these cities dominated a limited district of the city within which a particular clan held sway and from which it could attack other clans – factional rivalry was extremely common and heightened by the existence of Guelph versus Ghibelline struggles in the thirteenth century, which also affected burgher cities of some importance such as Florence and Bologna. The importance of clan districts is retained in certain smaller Central Italian cities, the best-known case being the *contrade* of Siena, the organizers of the annual bare-back horse-races around the central square. One political result of the existence within such feudal cities of distinct warring factions was the practice of filling certain important local offices only by foreigners who would be outside local clan rivalries (Hook 1979: 26; Waley 1978: 32–4), a practice also followed, for similar reasons, in Marseille (Vieille 1978: 90).

The *élite* dominance of the feudal city was maintained, then, despite various power struggles within the *élite*. Although city constitutions often appear to have embraced municipal ideals, the feudal element in institutions and way of life remained dominant, whilst certain key families commonly controlled city government for long periods. In the long run landownership triumphed, at least in Italy, and at times of crisis the city's fortunes were put in the hands of one family (Waley 1978: 128–39), providing a basis for later absolutism at the hands of such as the Medici in Florence, the Viscontis and the Sforzas in Milan, and the Scaligers in Verona.

The mercantile city

Whilst in Southern Europe the feudal interest tended to prevail over the commercial in terms of control over the city, in Northern Europe the reverse tended to be the case. That is, of course, a sweeping generalization. Venice stands out as a Southern European city lacking any feudal element, dependent entirely on trade; but Venice, of course, was a maritime republic with no important mainland possessions until the fifteenth century, this absence of feudalism enabling her to evolve a system of government that was part monarchy, part commercial aristocracy and part republicanism (Cosgrove 1982).

Trading and commercial interests were organized through the guild system. Each guild grouped together all those involved in a particular trade or activity, from the humblest apprentice to the most wealthy merchant, and where a city had a particularly specialized economic structure the role of the guilds in city administration could be important. The mercantile city tended to be a relatively exclusive organization in which citizenship was difficult to achieve and membership restricted – the burgher city of Braudel's classification (p. 5 above). Given the absence of a feudal *élite*, this type of city was much more distinct from the surrounding countryside. Power in the purely mercantile city was exercised through the guilds and through the most successful and prosperous merchants and master craftsmen taking the positions of administrative responsibility of the city as a whole. In terms of the internal zoning of the city, Vance (1977: 146–53) has pointed out that occupational districts developed with different trades dominating different city districts, no doubt for what would now be called reasons of industrial linkage. The burgher house served as workshop, store and residence for the merchant or master craftsman and for his employees and apprentices, with the result that there was little in the way of significant spatial separation of social classes

In the mercantile city the *élite* derived their power from urban activities rather than from rural landownership. There was a social mixture within urban space and no great tendency for concentric zoning around the centre. The mercantile city and the feudal city are thus independent types of pre-industrial structure, neither providing a good match to Sjoberg's model. However, as described here, they were polar types on a continuum that stretched between them, involving a variety of gradations in the relative strengths of the different interests: Florence, for example, with its feudal aristocracy and its wool guilds co-existing together, might be placed near the centre of the continuum.

The *absolutist city*

The absolutist city forms the third of Braudel's pre-industrial city types: what he called the 'subjugated' city. In such a city power was wielded not by a feudal group nor by merchant interests but by a single individual or family, sometimes even an absentee ruler. In Italy it has already been described how the feudal city developed into the absolutist city dominated by individual family dynasties. In Germany, with its pattern of political fragmentation, many cities became the seat of ruling dukes, princes and electors from an early period. Berlin was the residence of the Hohenzollerns from 1470, Munich of the Wittelsbachs from 1255, Düsseldorf was a ducal city from the thirteenth century and Brunswick from the twelfth.

It was not, however, until the sixteenth and seventeenth centuries that the dominance of cities by monarchical authority became of real significance in shaping urban space and determining the course of urban development. In particular, the absolutist power of the monarch began to play an important role in city planning. Three illustrative examples will demonstrate the sorts of city evolution that occurred.

In Nancy in Eastern France three great periods of urban expansion were instigated and planned by three of the rulers of Lorraine – Charles III (1545–1608), Duke Leopold (1698–1729) and King Stanislas (1737–66). The city had, in fact, been created as a ducal residence in the eleventh century. Charles III decided that continuous ring-like accretion on to the old urban nucleus (Fig. 1.1) was inefficient because of the constant need for expansion of the fortifications. Instead he created a new town, with its own walls, to the south, an extension which gradually became fully built up during the seventeenth century (Dion 1974). Duke Leopold, at the start of the eighteenth century, amalgamated the old and new towns by creating a single wall around the whole and permitting building where the old separating wall had stood. Later in that century, King Stanislas rebuilt some of the quarters of the old town and embellished the centre to the glory of the state, but keeping urban development still within the fortifications. It was not until well into the nineteenth century, indeed not until 1830, that Nancy witnessed what might be termed free market urban expansion with the development of new urban areas outside the walls of the older city.

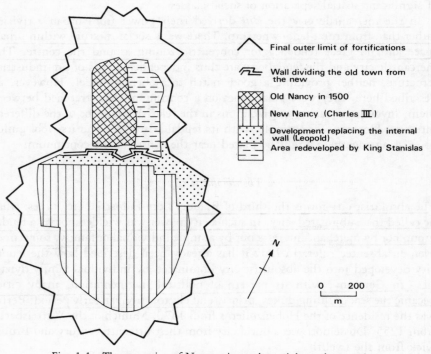

Final outer limit of fortifications

Wall dividing the old town from the new

Old Nancy in 1500

New Nancy (Charles III)

Development replacing the internal wall (Leopold)

Area redeveloped by King Stanislas

N

0   200
        m

Fig. 1.1 The expansion of Nancy, sixteenth to eighteenth centuries.
(*Source*: redrawn from Dion 1974)

Stockholm will serve as a second illustrative case (Råberg 1979). By the early seventeenth century the Swedish kings had succeeded in turning Sweden into a European power, and deliberate efforts were then made at urban expansion. The period saw the foundation of Gothenburg and the creation, in 1625, of a detailed plan for the rebuilding and urban growth of Stockholm to a geometrical design with the royal palace at the exact centre. However, the plan was not completed because, although building activity was intense during the later seventeenth century, Sweden's eclipse as a power led to the decline of Stockholm and population expansion there did not resume until the middle of the eighteenth century.

The pivoting of Stockholm's city plan on the royal palace is interesting as a reflection of one view of the theoretical role of kingship, with the monarch at the centre of his subjects. <u>An alternative view is that manifest in Karlsruhe</u> (Fig. 1.2), arguably the most complete and best-known monarchically planned

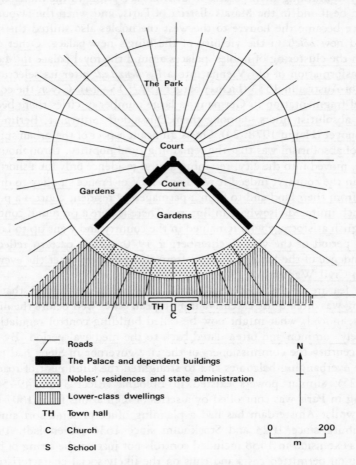

Fig. 1.2   Karlsruhe in the middle of the eighteenth century.
(*Source*: redrawn from a contemporary print by Christian Thran)

city of Western Europe (Abele and Leidlmair 1968; Traband 1978). Karlsruhe was founded in 1715 because the Margrave Karl-Wilhelm disagreed with the citizens of a nearby small town about its rebuilding after destruction by the French during the War of the Spanish Succession. (It was the same war that, by destroying Heidelberg, led to the creation of Mannheim by the Palatine Electors.) In Karlsruhe the Margrave planned his new town on the shape of a triangle with, at its apex, the princely residence – a *château* with three storeys. Building styles and densities were carefully laid down: the residences in the centre of the triangle were to be for the nobles and state officials whilst the base of the triangle was composed of labourers' dwellings of a limited size and height. The princely city was constructed for the display of power and spatial relations in the city were arranged to maintain an appropriate hierarchical structure.

With the evolution of absolute monarchy and the translation of the role of the nobles from feudal barons to courtiers, the *élite* started to congregate together in building their palaces in districts accessible to the monarch. Examples can be found in the Marais district of Paris, and when the favoured royal residence became the Louvre to the west the nobles also shifted their location to build new *hôtels* in the vicinity of the king's new palace. Other examples occur in the clustering of nobles' palaces around the royal palace in Madrid and the transformation of old Vienna into a *Residenzstadt* after its selection as the capital of Austria in 1533 (Lichtenberger 1977: 13–14). Given the continuing political fragmentation in Germany, a large number of cities there became the seats of absolutist rulers – among them Düsseldorf, Stuttgart, Berlin, Munich and Hanover (Hajdu 1978: 24). One significant aspect of the urban spirit of the period of absolutism was that the remaining rural nobility, throughout most of Europe, moved into the city, retaining a rural residence only for a short summer season in the country: indeed it was Louis XIV of France's policy to divorce his nobles from their land and to form a permanently resident court – a policy that was much imitated elsewhere in Europe. There is here a profound contrast with the English aristocracy who remained in the country and went up to London for a short period of the year (Lichtenberger 1970: 49), a pattern reflecting the independence of the landed interests from the monarchy after the events of the English Civil War and of 1688.

One feature of the absolutist period that needs stressing is that detailed planning was often quite extensive in European cities well before the nineteenth century; indeed, what might now be called building control regulations were extremely common and often dated back to the medieval period. By the thirteenth century the commissioners of the city governor in Siena had powers to remove overhanging balconies and to straighten the alignment of roads (Hook 1979: 25); similar powers existed in Bologna (Ricci 1980: 49–50). New building in Paris was controlled by a series of regulations from 1607 (Evenson 1979) whilst Amsterdam has had a planning office of some sort since 1617, Gothenburg since 1623 and Stockholm since 1636 (Sidenbladh 1975: 27). Nancy's extension in 1588 included controls not just on the siting of buildings but also on permitted costs and thus on the likely social characteristics of the occupants (Dion 1974: 253–4).

Efficacious planning control was aided by notions of the ultimate prerogatives of royal landownership which meant that the royal authorities could use powers of expropriation to further their purposes in a manner that had not been open to earlier systems of political power. Expropriatory powers were used for a variety of purposes, for example to acquire land for schemes of city prestige, monuments or parks. Such powers were invoked in the construction of fortifications, such as in the case of Barcelona where the Bourbons demolished 1,350 houses in 1717 to build a citadel, the evicted inhabitants becoming the nucleus of the first extramural settlement (Wynn 1979: 185–6). A policy was followed in Stockholm in the seventeenth century whereby all land likely to be affected under the development plan was taken into state ownership, a precursor of the land policy of the city in the twentieth century (see Ch. 9).

Of course it would be erroneous to imply, by concentrating on planning and control in the absolutist city, that mercantile cities of the same period were unfettered in development. Building regulations of some kind were in force in virtually all major towns for the sake of maintaining some elements of light and air in crowded city-centres and to aid fire-prevention, with regulations of road width and building height being most common. Indeed, Lichtenberger (1972: 220) and others have argued that it has been the traditons of height regulations stretching through from the seventeenth century to the present day that have limited skyscraper construction in the centre of the European city.

The ecclesiastical interest

Whilst in the pre-industrial city the major power sources lay with the nobility, the merchant interests or with the monarchy, it is necessary to remember that ecclesiastical powers were of no small importance in the evolution of many Western European cities. In certain cases the church provided secular leadership in the person of a prince-bishop (as in Liège and Basel) or, in the case of Rome itself, through the pope.

Everywhere in pre-Reformation Europe, and in many Catholic countries into more recent times, the church was a major force in urban landownership whilst the clerical population formed a significant proportion of the cities' total inhabitants. Soubeyroux (1978), for example, has shown that in the eighteenth century the numbers of the 'religious' may have totalled between one-seventh and one-fifth of Madrid's total population. At the same period in Bologna 6 per cent of the population were priests, monks, nuns and other clericals whilst one-sixth of the intra-mural land was in use for churches, monasteries, convents and other religious institutions (Ricci 1980: 117). For an earlier period, Lichtenberger (1977: 34) has estimated that the 1450 population of Vienna of 25,000 included 2,000 (8 per cent) ecclesiastics.

Given the extent of these religious interests, the extinction of religious landownership could be of considerable benefit to growing cities. In the countries of the Reformation, such as England and Sweden, the confiscation of much ecclesiastical land occurred in the sixteenth century, and whilst in England the bulk of monastic property quickly passed to private interests, in Sweden the state (through the monarch) retained these estates which formed a useful addition to the stock of available land for controlled urban growth (Råberg 1979: 13).

Even in Catholic countries the power of ecclesiastical (or more especially monastic) interests has been in decline for at least the last two centuries. In France the Revolution brought the transfer of church property to the public authorities and thence the sale of much monastic land to private interests: in Paris these changes affected especially the left (south) bank of the Seine where residential development had always been closely linked to the fortunes of the large numbers of religious houses (Sutcliffe 1970: 3). In Barcelona, monastic rights were extinguished in 1835, bringing new land at the city-centre into potential urban use (Ferras 1977a: 347). Monastic property in Vienna had been brought under state control in 1782 by Joseph II, allowing the secular use of religious buildings (Lichtenberger 1977: 147). In Rome the problem of the insertion of the functions of a modern capital into an established city after 1870 was met by the expropriation of religious houses: as these had been on the Quirinale hill in the eastern district of the city this area became, and has remained, the governmental quarter (Regni and Sennato 1973: 903–7). In many cities the eventual development of ex-monastic property and land took on specific characteristics of urban estate growth as a result of the possibilities afforded for planned development within a short time-period: such was the case, for example, in Madrid (Capote 1976).

The interplay of interests

Whilst it is possible to suggest a categorization of the pre-industrial Western European city into three types – feudal, mercantile and absolutist – reality was not usually as simple as this. Certainly these models have their value – the feudal city of factions and heterogeneous districts, the mercantile city of occupational quarters, and the monarchical city of social rank and hierarchy. But many cities today bear the influences of all three of these urban paradigms, whilst the ascendancy of any one set of powers was rarely complete in any single city.

Elisabeth Lichtenberger's detailed study of the old city of Vienna provides a useful example of the interplay of interests over time in a single pre-industrial city (Lichtenberger 1977). From the middle of the twelfth century onwards, Vienna maintained dual roles as both a mercantile town and the residence of a feudal nobility. The indigenous mercantile element was reinforced by an important group of resident foreign merchants, whilst a further complicating factor (existing also in several other medieval European cities) was the university, founded in 1365. Lichtenberger suggests that throughout the later Middle Ages the mercantile interest was in the ascendancy, certainly demographically but also in terms of urban control. In 1450 the city's population was composed of 8,000 merchants, master craftsmen and their dependents, 10,000 labourers, 3,000 nobles and their retinues (the feudal element), 2,000 clergy and 2,000 connected with the university. The city's residential structure derived from the mercantile interest. The burghers tended to own their own houses (85 per cent did so in 1563) but 80 per cent of these houses had occupants other than the owner and his family, these being his employees and sometimes others who rented rooms.

In 1533 Vienna became the Habsburg capital and the 'ennoblement' of the city began, producing strong social segregation between the old inner-city and areas outside it where previously there had only been district differentiation on commercial grounds. The nobles acquired a steadily increasing proportion of the property of the inner-city until, by 1779, they were, in ownership terms, in a position of equality with the burghers, a position that was maintained until the start of rapid urban growth in the mid-nineteenth century.

Vienna was therefore a city in which the pattern of political dominance swung from commerce to aristocracy and monarch, accompanied by changes in the residential structure of the city. Vertical social segregation between master and man within burgher houses was to some extent replaced by spatial segregation, yet with the peripheral commercial areas retaining a strong element of social status arrangement by housing storey whilst the compact urban palaces of the nobles also segregated the servants to the upper floors. The connection of workplace and residence thus remained strong, a relic of the mercantile dominance: as late as 1869, 72 per cent of the city's apprentices and 23 per cent of the full employees lived in the houses of their employers, and in that year 22 per cent of the working population was effectively self-employed and likely to be living above their workshops (Bobek and Lichtenberger 1966: 35–7).

Relatively few European cities escaped the influence of the absolutist period entirely, perhaps the most important ones to do so being those of the Netherlands and Switzerland where there was a smoother transition from pre-industrial mercantile interests to modern capitalism without progressing through despotism; another example, already mentioned, is that of Venice which nevertheless stagnated through the seventeenth and eighteenth centuries. Mumford (1961: 339–40) has observed that London was one of the few mercantile cities powerful enough to stand up to the state on equal terms and avoid urban subjugation to the designs of absolute monarchy.

The interplay of the various institutional and class interests outlined in this section obviously occurred differently in every city, but general patterns emerge in a clear enough light to provide some tentative conclusions. Feudal and mercantile interests dominated Western European urban history for much of the pre-industrial period with ecclesiastical power playing a minor and steadily diminishing role. Feudal interests held sway for longer in Southern Europe, whilst north of the Alps city power became progressively more strongly commercially based in societies which were less encumbered with large numbers of petty nobles. In neither case, however, is the model of the pre-industrial city developed by Sjoberg of great relevance to reality. The spatial hierarchy from a central *élite* downwards and outwards to the peripheral outcastes was more nearly approached from the sixteenth century onwards as absolutism subverted urban structures and forms to its own desires and brought stricter controls on free development. These general patterns of the pre-industrial evolution of European cities thus owe much to the structure of power in society and to the ways in which the *locus* of power had repercussions for city growth, for spatial patterns in the city and for urban ways of life.

URBAN DEMOGRAPHY BEFORE 1800

Early cities in Europe were generally small settlements limited in population size by the low levels of urban economic activities and thus of urban demand, and also by the possibilities of supplying such centres with foodstuffs, given the prevailing agricultural technology, the organization of marketing or expropriation, and the availability of transport. Athens at its heyday may have reached a population of 150,000 and Rome in the later Empire at least 300,000 but these were truly exceptional cases (Davis 1955: 431–2). Other Roman *civitates* were very small – Bordeaux possibly had a population of 25,000 (Papy 1972: 518), Bologna 15,000 (Ricci 1980: 19).

After the fall of the Roman Empire, towns declined drastically in population, and even in the flourishing medieval period few cities counted more than 20,000 inhabitants. In 1300, Bordeaux's population was about 30,000 (Papy 1972: 521), Siena had 52,000 (Hook 1979: 36) and Bologna about 50,000 (Ricci 1980: 66). The only medieval cities to achieve 100,000 inhabitants were Paris (which reached 200,000 by 1320), Milan, Venice and Florence. In Northern and Central Europe, Nuremberg housed no more than 20,000, Cologne, the largest German city, 40,000, Basel 8,000, Brussels (in 1450) 40,000 and Bruges 70,000 (Mumford 1961: 314). In Christian Spain, Barcelona was the largest city, a census return of 1363 showing the population as 34,339 (Ferras 1977a: 199). Urban populations of the later medieval period generally fell in the wake of the Black Death, which was particularly damaging in Italy where Florence, for example, may have lost 60 per cent of its population.

In succeeding centuries, urban population growth evolved in response to a variety of influences, important among them being national and regional population trends, fluctuations in economic fortunes, variations in the presence and virulence of epidemics, and with oscillations in local rural conditons. This last factor was of especial importance in Southern Europe, given the feudal nature of the city there, and is a reminder of how small the cities were and how dependent on their immediate hinterland for provisioning and for economic well-being (Ponsot 1980): indeed, in many cities agricultural activities were carried on within the walls which were deliberately built beyond the housing limit to contain garden land of use for provisioning in times of siege (Braudel 1981: 486–7). Southern European cities have often retained intimate connections with the countryside well into the present century: D. H. Lawrence (1944: 27) just after the First World War lay in his hotel room in Palermo in Sicily before dawn and heard

the thrilling tinkle of innumerable goat-bells as the first flock enters the city.

The countryside has only recently retreated from the southern city.

By the end of the eighteenth century the general increase in population that was being experienced all over Europe, coupled with a measure of genuine economic and social advance in some areas, had created Europe's first large modern cities. Indeed, already by the year 1600 the list of cities with populations of 100,000 or more included Lisbon, Madrid, Seville, Rome, Palermo, Milan, Naples (probably the largest at 240,000), Paris, Antwerp and Amsterdam (Mumford 1961: 355).

Vienna's population reached 160,000 by 1770 (Bobek and Lichtenberger 1966: 24–5) and grew very rapidly thereafter. Madrid stood at 150,000 in 1723 and had grown to about 235,000 by 1797 (Soubeyroux 1978). In 1783 Berlin housed 141,000, of whom a staggering 23 per cent were soldiers and their families – a reflection of the role of the city for the absolutist Hohenzollern monarchy (Braudel 1981: 531). Amsterdam had reached 200,000 by this period whilst by 1800 the populations of Brussels, Bordeaux and Barcelona all stood at about 100,000 (Verniers 1958: 18; Guillaume 1972: 232; Ferras 1977a: 199). The earliest trustworthy census for Paris puts the population in 1817 at 714,000 (De Bertier de Sauvigny 1977: 156) whilst Chevalier (1973: 183) estimates the city's population at about 525,000 in 1789 on the eve of the Revolution. Paris was unquestionably the largest city in continental Europe with Naples as the second largest, its population being about 440,000 in 1800 (Döpp 1968: 23). Copenhagen was the largest city in Scandinavia, achieving a population of 133,000 by 1840 (Hyldtoft 1979: 50).

It has generally been argued that population growth, or even stability, in the pre-industrial European city was possible only through net in-migration because urban mortality was high and certainly exceeded fertility (Grigg 1980: 66–8; Keyfitz 1980): the cities were thus important consumers of rural population surpluses (Wrigley 1967). Sharlin (1978) has questioned the assumption that high urban mortality was a result of poor urban hygiene and overcrowded conditions by examining data from certain German and Austrian cities for the seventeenth and eighteenth centuries. He suggests that in fact there was generally net natural increase among the permanent residents of the cities and that it was simply the level of temporary adult migrants to urban areas who created the surplus of deaths, since such migrants were often unavailable for marriage and thus unlikely to produce births. Unfortunately, it is not easily possible to produce evidence to test these ideas further.

Certainly the level of mortality was the key factor in determining natural increase. Epidemics could have a severe effect in crowded urban conditons and almost all cities were affected from time to time by plague, the last major European outbreak being in Marseille in 1720 when 50,000 died. Too rapid a rate of population increase could also bring the threat of famine resulting from poor harvests if the possibilities of provisioning the city did not keep pace (Hook 1979: 19). However, evidence for some cities suggests that they were not really, in normal years, graveyards for their populations. Soubeyroux (1978: 21–7) has calculated that in 1797 Madrid had a natural growth rate of 4.6 per thousand resulting from a crude birth rate of 23.5 and a crude death rate of 18.9 per thousand. Nevertheless the major role in population growth was played by in-migration and it was this that gave the city its population structure, deficient in those aged less than 16 and with a median age that was higher than that of Spain as a whole. On the other hand Rome, situated in the midst of the degraded Campagna, suffered frequent epidemics and was unable to sustain itself by natural change for 1,400 years from the fall of the Roman Empire to the elevation of the city to the status of Italy's capital in 1871 (Rossi 1959: 3). The pre-industrial European city, therefore, generally depended heavily on continuous in-migration for its population stability or growth.

THE NINETEENTH CENTURY: THE INDUSTRIAL CITY

It was the nineteenth century that saw the real development and flowering of industrial capitalism in Europe, bringing with it a new set of influences on urban form and living to overlay the pre-industrial legacies of feudalism, mercantilism and authoritarianism. The century saw rapid urban population growth almost everywhere, resulting both in the manifold enlargement of many historic cities and also the growth to prominence of certain new industrial centres, although few of these latter were in fact completely new urban creations. The development of large-scale industrial capitalism spread from Britain to Belgium and thence to Germany and France, to the Netherlands, Scandinavia and the Alpine countries, whilst Southern Europe industrialized much later and maintained more traditional social and economic systems throughout the century with nascent industrialism affecting only a limited number of cities, such as Barcelona and Milan, before the end of the century. So whilst in Northern Europe urban growth was largely fuelled by industrial requirements for labour leading to large-scale rural–urban migration (see Ch. 3), in Southern Europe urban growth was more often associated with overpopulation in the countryside (Ponsot 1980).

The rapid growth of the industrial Northern European cities and the emergence of a new type of city structure can best be exemplified by the case of the Ruhr in Germany. Large-scale industrial development in the Ruhr did not start until about 1840, but growth was then extremely rapid. In 1843 the population of the district as a whole was 237,000; by 1895 it had multiplied almost six-fold to total 1.5 million (Steinberg 1978: 4). In 1840, Bochum was still an agricultural country town with a population of 4,200, including a small textile-manufacturing sector (Crew 1979: 11–14; Wolcke 1968: 21–2): the town largely remained within its medieval walls until the middle of the century (Wolcke 1968: 22–4). In Duisburg the first house outside the walls was not built until 1820, but then from 1848 to 1904 the town's population grew from 9,000 to 107,000 (Jackson 1981: 204–6; 1982: 248).

The leading industrial sector in the growth of the Ruhr was coal with iron and steel production following; diversification into lighter manufacturing and engineering did not start to occur until the end of the century. The number of miners in the Ruhr rose from 9,000 in 1840 to 229,000 in 1900 (Steinberg 1978: 3–4). This sort of rapid economic and employment growth had several very major effects, three of which stand out as meriting discussion here. The first was the implication for housing such rapidly-growing populations; the second concerns the in-migration needed to sustain growth; and the third relates to the changes in social structure brought about.

Where large industrial enterprises were added to small towns, there were great problems in the provision of sufficient accommodation through the existing housing market and employers increasingly found it necessary or desirable to provide their own accommodation for their employees (Niethammer and Bruggemeier 1978: 112–13). The first *cités ouvrières* appeared in Belgium and France by the middle of the century and the idea quickly caught on elsewhere. In the Ruhr the earliest employer-provided housing was generally single storey but later construction (and provision increased rapidly after 1880) was of more substantial property, although the vast tenement blocks characteristic of Berlin were never part of normal building practice in the Ruhr (Achilles 1969: 122; Jackson 1981: 204–6). As early as 1873, 16 per cent of married miners in the Ruhr lived in a works dwelling, and by 1913 this proportion had risen to 40 per cent (Steinberg 1978: 35–7). The rapid growth of employer-provided housing and of other rented property reduced the level of owner-occupation drastically: in 1850 most Ruhr miners owned their own homes with small gardens but by 1876 no more than 10 per cent did so (Crew 1979: 152, 172).

Population growth in the Ruhr was fuelled by massive in-migration from surrounding areas and generally less than half the cities' resident populations had been born there: indeed in 1871 only 33 per cent of Bochum's population was native to the city (Wolcke 1968: 38); by 1907 only 23 per cent of the city's workforce was native (Crew 1979: 59–61). However, there was a considerable turnover of the population with total annual migration rates (in-migrants plus out-migrants, ignoring intra-urban migrants) reaching extremely high levels – 45 per cent per annum in Duisburg in the first decade of the twentieth century (Jackson 1982: 248) – so that there was considerable fluidity in the actual composition of the population. The general youthfulness of the population, reinforced by young adult in-migrants, brought significant natural increases to the Ruhr cities and natural growth commonly occurred at a rate of 2 per cent per annum during the second half of the nineteenth century (Steinberg 1978: 61–2). In fact, during the period from 1875 to 1895, natural increase actually accounted for 71.5 per cent of Bochum's population growth, 61.9 per cent in Dortmund, 66.2 per cent in Duisburg and 70.4 per cent in Essen, whereas as late as the early 1870s net in-migration had been the more important growth component in three of the four cities, the exception being Essen (Steinberg 1978: 52–8). Undeniably, however, the level of natural increase had been conditioned by the selective age-structures of the earlier in-migrants.

Towards the end of the century the possible pool of local rural–urban migrants began to dry up and the Ruhr increasingly started to draw labour from further afield – from East Prussia, Poland and Austria-Hungary so that by 1910 Poles constituted 8.9 per cent of the population in Gelsenkirchen and 4.6 per cent in Bochum (Wolcke 1968: 38–40; Steinberg 1978: 75–82). The continued development of the Ruhr was shown by the very high rates of in-migration that continued into the twentieth century: in Bochum the annual in-migration rate varied between 166 and 288 per thousand residents between 1880 and 1900 (Crew 1979: 60–1). Such migration rates were higher than occurred elsewhere: whilst in 1890 in-migration in Essen was 193 persons per thousand residents, in Cologne the rate was 136 and in Berlin 117 (Niethammer and Bruggemeier 1978: 119).

The rise of industrial capitalism, in particular the development of the factory system and of large production units leading to rapid population growth, not just in the Ruhr but also in the Belgian and French coalfields and other indus-trializing cities, also led to the production of a new working-class or proletarian population, reducing or even eliminating the old social and economic rela-tionships of artisan and master craftsman. The new populations of the industrial cities were almost exclusively employed in secondary activities and in unskilled or semi-skilled processes. The skilled artisan class often found itself in a posi-tion of downward social mobility as it was drawn into the factory system through the competition between factory-produced and artisan-produced commodities which led to the ascendancy of the former. As late as 1858 one in ten of Bochum's working population owned businesses but within thirteen years this proportion had halved, and Crew (1979: 17–19) has estimated that by 1907, 78 per cent of the city's working population could be categorized as dependent manual workers with the true capitalist dominant group amounting to only 6 per cent, the middle group of civil servants and other white-collar employees or smaller independent businessmen together making up the remaining 16 per cent.

The Ruhr was no doubt somewhat extreme in the size of the proletarian element in its population, largely because the urban base had been limited at the outset. In Northern France, where Lille and other towns had an important urban history stretching back centuries, the middle groups were more evenly represented: in the middle of the nineteenth century they formed about 32 per cent of Lille's population with the class of larger capitalists at 8 per cent and the working class at 59 per cent. As in the Ruhr, the provision of housing by employers became a very important feature (Trenard et al. 1977: 342, 360) as later described by Zola in *Germinal*.

Poverty and squalor generally characterized the conditions for the new industrial classes, especially in the heavy industrial cities where (unlike the textile towns) there was relatively little female employment. In Bochum in the 1870s and 1880s, three-quarters of the working population lived at or near the level of subsistence and under the constant threat of layoff in times of economic slump; company housing only exacerbated these problems by locking the workers into a paternalistic relationship with their employers and discouraging the mobility between firms that might have forced wage-levels up (Crew 1979). Residential building generally followed a cyclical pattern in all the industrial cities of Europe, with the years of fastest industrial growth (and therefore the greatest returns on industrial investment) being years of lower building activity, just at the time when in-migrants to the cities were likely to be at their most numerous, creating severe housing shortages and overcrowded conditions (Hammarström 1979; Hyldtoft 1979; Wolcke 1968: 44–6). It is difficult, then, to disagree with Crew's conclusion, (1979: 22), based on the Ruhr, that in Northern Europe, where the degree of integration between master and man in the mercantile city had historically been relatively high,

industrialization intensified the extremes of wealth and poverty, power and impotence, and increased the social distance between strata.

The industrialization of the Ruhr, although perhaps extreme in its extent, was not atypical in its effects, particularly on housing, population growth and social evolution. In many of the older and larger cities there was less need for employer provision of housing since existing properties could be subdivided whilst the established speculative building industry could expand to provide new types of rented accommodation. In Paris the growing working class was housed through the former method with the recently-arrived in-migrants being particularly susceptible to finding themselves in lodging houses or even renting rooms by the night. Whilst the early years of the nineteenth century saw the creation of new *bourgeois* quarters, principally in the north-western districts of the city, the growing working class were left to fend for themselves in the crowded *arrondissements* of the inner city and in the growing eastern inner suburbs (Chevalier 1973).

In Berlin the rapidly rising working-class population was accommodated, in the later part of the century, in purpose-built tenement blocks constructed by private speculators using cheap but substantial materials. These rented tenement apartment blocks (*Mietskasernen* – 'rented barracks') were usually five storeys high with a complex series of internal courtyards rendering many apartments dark and unhealthy from the moment of construction. Apartment sizes were minimal – in 1900, 50 per cent of all low-income dwellings in Berlin consisted of only one room plus a kitchen, and such apartments housed 44 per cent of the city's population (Liang 1970). Rents, nevertheless, were high because of the constant tendency towards housing shortage, and householders in the smallest and poorest accommodation often took in lodgers to help to pay the rent – in 1875, 21 per cent of all Berlin households did so (Liang 1970: 106).

NB

Proletarianization was a general feature of nineteenth-century economic developments, even in cities of Southern Europe where industrial growth was rather slower. The possibilities of upward social mobility were relatively restricted (Crew 1979: 80; Sewell 1976: 218), and downward mobility was more common; a substantial sector of the new industrial working class was composed, in fact, of ex-agricultural workers and peasants. In Marseille, in mid-century, only 7 per cent of the sons of unskilled or semi-skilled fathers had achieved non-manual jobs by the date of their marriage but, interestingly, upward social mobility was higher for peasants' sons, who were in-migrants to the city, than for the indigenous population. The Marseillais tended to stay within the familial occupational environment, suggesting that the appearance of class consciousness in nineteenth-century European cities was not just a reaction to blocked aspirations and to the situation of the moment but also owed something to a more long-standing corporatist cultural tradition among the labouring population (Sewell 1976).

It was not only the great industrial cities that experienced rapid population growth in the nineteenth century: the capital cities of speedily evolving international and imperial powers also saw large-scale population growth but without the domination of a few large enterprises that was found in the industrial cities. Paris and Berlin have already been mentioned; another example is Vienna where by 1840 the urban agglomeration as a whole housed 440,000 inhabitants, a figure that grew to 2 million by 1910 (Bobek and Lichtenberger 1966). As in the industrial cities, such population increase was largely determined through net in-migration which consistently exceeded natural growth during the period. Indeed, fertility decline occurred throughout the century, largely brought about by a fall in illegitimacy from 50 per cent of all births in 1810 to 28 per cent in 1914. Given the high levels of in-migration, it is not surprising that the proportion of Vienna's resident population that had been born elsewhere rose from 37.5 per cent in 1840 to 65.5 per cent in 1890 (Bobek and Lichtenberger 1966: 32–4).

Brussels was another large city where the rapidity of in-migration and the youthfulness of the migrants helped to maintain the natural increase in the city throughout the nineteenth century. Here the population grew from 100,000 at the turn of the century to 898,000 in 1900, with the majority of the migrants coming from the nearest Flemish-speaking parts of Belgium (Verniers 1958: 18, 371–2).

The detail of natural population change in the nineteenth century is made more complex by the continuation of high urban mortality rates from the pre-industrial period, and by certain practices regarding the nursing of infants. That urban mortality was high is attested by the figures for life expectancy at birth calculated by Preston and Van de Walle (1978) for France for 1846–50. Life expectancy in the *département* of the Seine (dominated by Paris) was 29.5, in the Rhône (Lyon) 34.5, and in Bouches-du-Rhône (Marseille) 32.2, while for France as a whole the figure was 40.4. These differentials remained of some significance throughout the century, demonstrating that even now natural growth in the city was likely to be less than in the countryside, unless urban fertility was particularly high.

The other demographic complication arises from the practice of sending newborn infants out to rural areas for wet-nursing, the children surviving this practice not returning to their parents until the ages of five to ten. In Paris in the years of the Restoration (1815–30), between a half and two-thirds of all the newborn were thus sent *en nourrice* to the countryside, this serving to reduce the overall Parisian mortality rate by translating infant mortality elsewhere (De Bertier de Sauvigny 1977: 157–67). Even as late as 1897, 33 per cent of newborn Parisian children were sent out of the city, and the rate was even higher (47 per cent) in Lyon (Rollet 1982: 577). These practices of the rural nursing of urban infants also existed elsewhere such as in Hamburg (Lindemann 1981) and Madrid (Soubeyroux 1978: 24).

The nineteenth century did not see rapid urban population growth everywhere. Cities which did not industrialize rapidly and which had no power of attraction through administrative or commercial growth often underwent relative stagnation for at least part of the century, remaining dominated by artisanal and traditionalist structures at a time when other cities were moving into capitalist, industrialist and bureaucratic dominance. Bordeaux, for example, remained a colonial trading port for the first half of the century and only experienced population growth on a substantial scale when certain industries processing imported products were established there (Papy 1972: 529–31). Throughout the century, Bordeaux retained a traditional social structure with a considerable landed interest and the absence of a modern industrial capitalist class. Migration to the city involved large numbers of females from local rural areas arriving for domestic service, and this almost certainly contributed to the high illegitimacy rate which lay at around one-third of all births throughout the century and was still as high as 25.8 per cent (France's highest urban rate) on the eve of the First World War. Until about 1850 natural change was positive, but thereafter deaths exceeded births so that the population increase of the later years of the century was entirely fuelled by in-migration (Guillaume 1972).

Bordeaux was not alone in displaying this pattern of slow growth and the dominance of female migration; other non-industrial cities of Southern Europe experienced a very similar evolution, for example Bologna, where the population remained stable at about 70,000 from the middle of the sixteenth century to 1860, a stability only sustained by continuous net in-migration. It was not until the unification of Italy and the creation of the railway network centred on the city that Bologna lost its appearance of being stranded in the wrong century and began to experience growth (Ricci 1980). In many other Southern European cities the significance of the in-migration of female domestic servants has continued to the present day (see Ch. 4).

Summarizing the nineteenth-century evolution of the Western European city, it is possible to see the creation, in this period, of a new urban form, that of industrial capitalism operating in relatively free-market conditions. In social terms the salient effect of this was the creation of the new urban working class and the increased social distance between the upper and lower echelons of society, an increased social distance that went hand in hand with a tendency for spatial segregation with the creation of new forms of housing specifically for the working class. The population growth involved in these developments was largely brought about by large-scale migration. Whilst in certain cases nineteenth-century urban industrialism effectively created new cities, in most instances the new developments were meshed into existing settlements so that the new urban model was laid over the social and morphological relics of earlier structures of social and economic relationships.

It is important to recognize, however, that the old was not swept away completely. The urban morphology of earlier centuries may have been modified but it was not eliminated and replanned. Older housing units continued (and continue) in use. In particular, the legacy of the burgher city and its small commercial or artisan enterprise remained significant: indeed, in many societies, particularly of the South, this was the dominant mode of urban economic organization. Even in Germany and Belgium, the mainsprings of the continental European industrial revolution, the small shopkeeper and self-employed craftsman are still important components of urban life and their importance increases as one travels southwards. Retailing, especially, has not been penetrated by large-scale capitalism. The intimate connection between workplace and residence, characteristic of mercantile cities, is thus still important for many European citizens (see Ch. 7 and 9).

Thus the nineteenth century heralded a new model of social and economic organization, but one which was fitted into existing structures and which affected some areas more profoundly than others.

CITY WALLS

The nineteenth century was also the period during which, largely as a result of urban expansion, the old fortification systems around European cities were at last removed. Defences played an important role in European cities in the past, both in defining the city in contrast to the surrounding countryside and in limiting the scope for the spatial expansion of the built-up area. At least until the seventeenth century, virtually all settlements with any pretensions to urban status possessed some kind of fortifications (The Hague was one of the few significant exceptions) – indeed walls and gates were a *sine qua non* for the recognition of town or city status in most cases.

The simple walls of the medieval period could be easily extended or rebuilt as towns grew, but with the invention of gunpowder and the development of artillery in the sixteenth century the old walls became obsolete and were replaced by highly complex sets of fortifications often involving a series of walls, earthworks and ditches complete with bastions and surrounded by an area in which construction was prohibited in order to maintain a clear line of fire for the defenders: such fortifications were extremely costly and could not be easily extended (Curl 1970: 95). The result was increasing urban density within the defences, exemplified by Strasbourg where the medieval walls were extended four times between 1200 and 1450 but where the fortifications of 1580 remained in place until 1870 despite a three-fold increase in the intra-mural population (Mumford 1961: 359). Such restrictions on urban spatial expansion have often been adduced as reasons for European urban traditions of building upwards rather than outwards, creating high-density tenement housing instead of lower-density single-family dwellings (Curl 1970: 95).

Within Western Europe it was in England that town defences first lost their significance, owing to the generally pacific nature of England's domestic politics after the end of the Wars of the Roses (except for the Civil War when town defence regained some importance). English towns were thus almost never equipped with the straitjackets of artillery-proof fortifications. Elsewhere the major urban civilizations that were without fear (and thus without walls) at this time were those of the Turkish Empire (except in Hungary) and in Japan (Braudel 1981: 491–5). Throughout mainland Europe, defences continued to play a major role in restricting urban expansion, often well into the nineteenth century. Table 1.1 gives the dates of the removal of the fortifications in certain cities. It was not until after the Napoleonic Wars (which had resulted in numerous cities being besieged) that the momentum grew for the removal of the defences. The case of Stockholm (Table 1.1) is rather exceptional, for the medieval walls there were removed in the early seventeenth century to make way for the extension of the city, and a new set of fortifications was envisaged but never built (Råberg 1979: 18–19).

Table 1.1   Dates of removal of fortifications – selected cities

City	Date
Stockholm	1620s
Brussels	1830s
Geneva	1851
Barcelona	1854
Vienna	1857
Basel	1860–67
Madrid	1868
Bologna	1902
Paris	1926–32

One of the commonest and most important features accompanying fortifications was a military *glacis*, the unbuilt area outside the walls retained to give an uninterrupted line of fire. The military value of such an area could still be demonstrated during the Napoleonic Wars, but by the later years of the nineteenth century the whole defensive system had become obsolete: in the siege of Paris in 1870–1 the German attackers remained at least 3 km beyond the fortifications and simply fired into the city over them (Horne 1965). Nevertheless the one-time existence of the *glacis militaire* has left profound imprints in many cities.

An outstanding example is Madrid where the defensive system was built in 1630 under the command of Philip IV (Soubeyroux 1978: 35). Until the last years of the eighteenth century, Madrid had no extra-mural suburbs whatsoever, unlike most other cities where suburbs had been permitted to grow beyond the unbuilt *glacis* (De Terán 1961). During the 1840s and 1850s, large-scale plans were formulated for the expansion of the city and some small schemes were initiated, but the major trigger was the demolition of the walls in 1868 when permission was given for the planned growth of a specified zone (the *Ensanche* – literally 'the expansion') around the old fortification lines. The

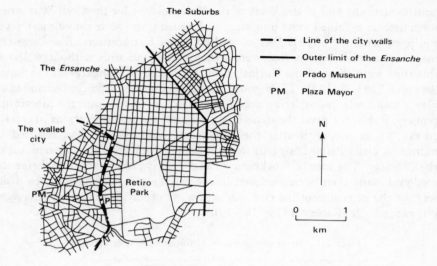

Fig. 1.3   Street-plan of north-eastern Madrid.

old walled city, the planned *Ensanche* beyond the walls, and the unplanned, unco-ordinated and unrestricted growth zone beyond stand out clearly as distinctive and separate urban morphological zones of the city's street-plan (Fig. 1.3). The effect of regulated planning in the *Ensanche* was to keep this area for more substantial and expensive residential development with lower-cost housing pushed out to the unplanned areas. A very similar scenario developed in the *Ensanche* of Barcelona which grew under the plan of Cerdà to the north of the old walled city after the demolition of the fortifications (Lowder 1980). In many other cities the rapid construction of new areas contemporaneous with the demolition of the walls has produced areas of distinct and contrasted morphologies, Bilbao (in Spain) and Bari (in Italy) being particularly clear cases.

Vienna provides another interesting example of the effect of the circumvallating *glacis* (Fig. 1.4). Until the later eighteenth century there was relatively little extra-mural suburban growth because of the perceived continuance of a Turkish threat: in 1779 there were only 3,832 houses outside the walls (Bobek and Lichtenberger 1966: 24—5) although the first serious suggestion for the removal of the walls had already come in 1777 (Breitling 1980: 34). By 1840, population growth had led to the extensive growth of suburbs beyond the walls although the unbuilt defensive zone was retained and protected from construction. Indeed, the social segregation between the wealthy in the city centre and the new proletariat in the suburbs led to military arguments after the 1848 revolution for the retention of the *glacis*, not as a defence against a foreign enemy, but as a way of protecting the centre from attack by the suburban working class (Schorske 1980: 27—9). Nevertheless the ascendancy of liberal democracy brought new confidence among the ruling powers and the demolition of Vienna's walls was accompanied by the filling-in of the unbuilt area

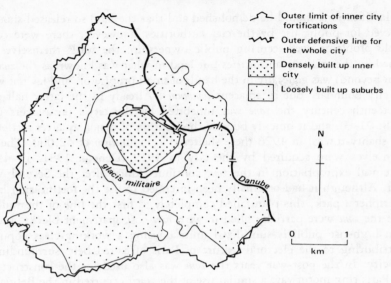

Outer limit of inner city fortifications

Outer defensive line for the whole city

Densely built up inner city

Loosely built up suburbs

Fig. 1.4 Vienna in 1844.
(*Source*: redrawn from a contemporary plan reproduced in Schorske 1980)

from 1857 onwards. This became the area of the Ringstrasse, a circular road around the centre, lined with monumental buildings (such as the City Hall, various museums, the parliament building and so on) and by substantial apartment blocks built by private enterprise under strict building regulations, designed as residences for the new industrial and commercial *élite* of the Austrian Empire. As Schorske (1980: 33) has put it:

what had been a military insulation belt became a sociological isolation belt,

limiting the city centre from the suburbs just as the wall and *glacis* had done. Geneva was another city which saw similar developments in the *glacis* (Lerch et al. 1972: 16), and the same occurred in Copenhagen (Lichtenberger 1970: 53).

In many cities the creation of spacious new apartment blocks along the *boulevards* that replaced the walls encouraged the middle classes to move out of the crowded centres (Niethammer and Bruggemeier 1978: 110; Verniers 1958: 20), this process inevitably tending to reduce the previous heterogeneity of population and social composition that had been found within the walled cities (Olives Puig 1969: 46–7).

A final major example of the effect of fortifications systems is provided by Paris. Paris had had several walls, the effects of these on urban morphology being still noticeable in many places (Sutcliffe 1970: 1–4). The final set of defences was built after 1845, beyond the then limit of continuous physical urbanization. They were 35 km in length and 130 to 135 metres wide, and beyond was a *glacis* of 250 to 300 metres in which permanent buildings were prohibited (Evenson 1979). After the *débâcle* of 1870–1 it was proposed that the fortifications should be demolished and that the land so released should be reserved for public use by the city authorities. However, there were considerable problems over securing public ownership: the walls themselves were owned by the military authorities but land in what was known as the *zone* (the *glacis* beyond) was generally in the hands of small proprietors and lay not within the city boundary but in adjacent *communes*. Already in the latter half of the nineteenth century the *zone* was inhabited by the city's rag-pickers (Faure 1978: 91–3), and it quickly became the location of major squatter settlements and shanty-towns: in 1926 these sheltered a population of 42,000. The walls themselves were acquired by the city in 1919 (Deneux 1981: 43–4), but piecemeal expropriation in the *zone* continued until after the Second World War. Although it had originally been intended to use the fortification land as a peripheral park, this plan failed completely as first the line of the walls and then the *zone* were partially filled in with low-cost apartment blocks, much of it in high-rise publicly-subsidized units housing a working-class population contributing to the electoral feature of Paris of a 'red belt' surrounding the old city. In the post-war years the *zone* was also used for the construction of the Paris ring motorway; a similar use of the *glacis* occurred in the Belgian city of Antwerp where the fortifications remained almost intact until after the Second World War.

Apart from their physical existence, city walls often played an important role as a tax threshold, with special taxes (in French the *octroi*) payable on goods transported into the city from outside. This had the effect of raising the cost of living in the walled area (also affected, often, by higher property taxes) and also raising industrial costs. Larger-scale industry therefore stayed outside the city (Sutcliffe 1970: 147–8), and the working-class population, especially recent in-migrants, was encouraged to seek residence just outside the *octroi* limits. Thus in Paris certain workers' quarters actually lost population during the period from 1817 to 1831 at a time when increase was the norm, the suggested explanation being removal beyond the tax line (De Bertier de Sauvigny 1977: 158). Paris retained the *octroi* in various forms until 1900 (Sutcliffe 1970: 268); in Brussels abolition came only in 1860 although the ramparts had been removed in the 1830s (Bogaert-Damin and Maréchal 1978: 36–7); whilst in Milan such taxes existed in a modified form until 1893 (Lyttelton 1979: 255–6).

For a variety of reasons, therefore, the line of old city fortifications often remains one of the best-marked internal boundaries within the present-day city, whether one is looking at land use, housing development, urban morphology or urban social space. Whilst the boundary is no longer a wall or a tax fence, it still often has a morphological expression. One of the commonest of all features has been the replacement of the defensive line by a road ringing the city-cenre. Another example has been the replacement of the defences by a set of linear parks, perhaps ringed by a set of *boulevards*. Where water defences were a vital part of the general system these remain important, although now demilitarized, aspects of the urban landscape. In many cities the railway station (or stations) lies against the line of the walls.

Very few European cities retain more than limited sections of their walls (Nuremberg, Toulon, Florence and Verona being examples of cities where important sections of wall still exist), but the legacy of the defences remains as a barrier between the suburbs and the city-centre. In many cities, to cross the line of the walls is to enter a different environment, this being especially so in cities where the line is preserved as a major *boulevard*: cities of this type include Seville, Bordeaux, Bologna, Cologne, Brussels and Aarhus. Water defences mark part or all of the boundaries of the inner-city in Amsterdam, Utrecht, Copenhagen, Bremen and Zürich. Examples of parks replacing fortifications occur in Hamburg, Münster and Frankfurt. The legacy of the city walls is the separation of the inner-city from the suburbs in a manner that is generally much less clear in English cities and almost non-existent in the new developed world.

HAUSSMANNIZATION, PLANNING AND THE TWENTIETH CENTURY

In the nineteenth century the period of most rapid urban growth occurred in the era of the increasing substitution of the capitalist mode of production in place of more traditional patterns. It brought about the removal of old fortifications to permit further expansion and it saw, in many countries, the accession of liberal democratic ideals with imperialist ambitions in some cases. It was an era of a belief in the market-place and in free trade. All these features were part and parcel of the evolution of a new economic and social system within Western Europe which ultimately affected all aspects of life.

Within the city the rise to power of new capitalist and industrialist classes and their self-perception as municipal *élites* led to initiatives for the replanning and reconstruction of city-centres with a view to greater 'efficiency', however defined, and to the beautification of cities and the provision of modern amenities. Such projects can be seen as more democratic equivalents of the autocratic schemes of the seventeenth and eighteenth centuries: indeed, in capital cities the driving forces were inspired by central government, sometimes working outside the channels of local democracy. In provincial cities the motivation came from groups of private individuals within municipal authorities. In Europe it has become common to term all such projects 'Haussmannization' after Baron Haussmann, the Prefect of the Seine *département* of France from 1853 to 1870, who set about transforming Paris into a new city. It is, however, worth noting that, both in Paris and elsewhere, many of the prestige schemes associated with Haussmannization can be traced back to unfulfilled plans of the Napoleonic period when Bonaparte's Prefects set about redesigning many of their subject cities (Regni and Sennato 1973: 899–901; Ricci 1980: 121). In addition, a sort of proto-Haussmannization had occurred two centuries earlier with the creation of roads designed to take the newly-designed horse-drawn carriages (Braudel 1981: 498).

In his memoirs, Baron Haussmann (1893) produced a detailed discussion of the projects he masterminded in Paris. Most significant for social considerations were the creation of new roads and their imposing flanking buildings, but of great importance also were lighting schemes, new parks, a new water-supply, cemeteries, a new sewerage system and the reorganization of the city's public transport services. With his streets, Haussmann created new routes through the medieval core of the city by demolishing existing housing; the new streets were then lined with regular imposing apartment blocks for the middle classes, with retailing and commercial activities on the ground floor. The objectives were many and varied, including the easing of communications within the city, the beautification of the urban environment (or at least the creation of imposing vistas), the redevelopment of slum areas, the alleviation of unemployment through public works (Sutcliffe 1970: 27), and the creation of a more defensible urban morphology. Napoleon had long ago realized the utility of wide straight avenues for troop movements (Curl 1970: 121) and, as in Vienna, the year of revolutions (1848) led the authorities to see the threat to their power as lying as much with the urban proletariat as with external forces.

The cutting of Haussmann's new streets destroyed many erstwhile working-class neighbourhoods within the city, speeding up the process of decline in other places (Mallet 1967: 20–1). Lower-income families were forced to move out of the centre to more peripheral locations (Bastié 1975: 58) and were replaced, in the commodious new apartments, by a wealthier population. The supply of new working-class housing in the centre was grossly insufficient, especially as the public works programmes encouraged the migration to the capital of large numbers of new labourers (Evenson 1979: 12).

Haussmann's works in Paris were quickly emulated elsewhere, within France in cities such as Lyon and Toulouse (Burtenshaw et al. 1981: 14), in Montpellier (Lacave 1980; Vidal 1978) and Marseille. Neither in Paris nor in the provinces were the schemes always a financial success for the private capital drawn in (Dubois 1980; Sutcliffe 1970: 40), but everywhere urban morphology was altered and new middle-class residences were created in, and on the edge of, city centres. Emulation also occurred elsewhere in Europe, with new streets often being created to provide access from the centre to the new peripheral railway stations. In Rome the Piazza Venezia was created as a new central square with radial roads running eastwards towards the station and westwards towards the Tiber and the Vatican (Regni and Sennato 1973), although the final link to the Papal city was not completed until Mussolini's days in power. In Brussels, King Leopold II encouraged legislation in 1867 permitting land expropriation for the public interest, these powers then being used to create new roads driven through the heart of the city (Verniers 1958: 41–3). Stockholm similarly saw the preparation of Haussmann-inspired street-plans during the 1860s and 1870s although many of these schemes did not come to fruition, largely because of their prohibitive cost (Råberg 1979: 23; Sidenbladh 1975: 28). Everywhere the general effect was to disrupt existing inner-city neighbourhoods and to replace a relatively heterogeneous or lower-class population by one drawn almost exclusively from the more wealthy who were able to afford the prestigious new apartments.

28

Haussmannization was, of course, but one facet of the general development of municipal concern with both restrictive and positive urban planning that occurred during the nineteenth century throughout the Continent. Objectives for the improvement of public health facilities led to interventionist powers in most countries (Calabi 1980: 57). Expropriation powers became available generally. Building regulations were revised to permit apartment blocks to rise higher but at the same time to maintain air and sunlight in the newly-widened streets below. The construction of the *Ensanche* in both Madrid and Barcelona are obvious examples of the products of such controls, as also is the Ringstrasse in Vienna. In Greater Berlin, where building regulations differed markedly from parish to parish within the suburbs of the city, housing differentiation developed according to the building codes applicable in each district, separating areas of five-storey apartments from villa areas and so on (Müller 1976: 144–5; 1978).

A clear example of detailed early modern planning exists in Helsinki (Åström 1979) where city plans of 1812–17 established building regulations and requirements for brick or stone constructions in certain areas of the centre with cheaper wooden working-class housing only permitted at the edge of the city. Upper-class central-city housing was to be grouped around squares copied from Georgian London, the whole arrangement being designed to create an imposing administrative city with a distinctive pattern of social zoning (effected through building regulations) that has effects on Helsinki's urban structure to the present day.

Thus varieties of modern urban planning came relatively early to many of the cities of Northern Europe but within a context dictated by free enterprise and by the investment of private capital in urban development, even to the extent of the provision of services such as gas and electricity by private companies. In particular, the housing market in the nineteenth century remained devoid of any municipal involvement except through building regulations, which were far from being in existence in all cities. Even in Germany, where such regulations were introduced relatively early on, it was not until the 1890s that they could be said to be enforced in most cities (Sutcliffe 1981). Nevertheless, wherever building regulations existed they were instrumental in generating social segregation between areas of different house types.

It is in the twentieth century that the *milieu* of Western European urban development has shifted from that of liberal capitalism to much greater governmental involvement – to the 'municipal socialism' of Vienna or Bologna, to large-scale public authority involvement in housing, to slum clearance and rehabilitation projects initiated by local government, to national policies for urban conservation, and to the production of new models of guided urban growth such as Stockholm's satellite suburbs or the New Towns around Paris. These are the policies of social welfare as they affect urban areas (Lichtenberger 1970: 47, 51). Not all parts of Western Europe have moved into this new age at the same speed. Arguably Vienna led the way, whilst at the opposite end of the time continuum lie the cities of Portugal or Greece where free-market forces are still almost unchallenged in their influence on urban life. Nevertheless, the twentieth century can be characterized as a period of increasing public interventionism, even though most of the roots of such intervention lie in the nineteenth century (Sutcliffe 1981). Twentieth-century urban developments, and their social effects, are indicated and discussed at greater length in successive chapters of this book, and especially in Chapters 2, 8 and 9.

One special feature of the twentieth century must, however, be mentioned here – the topic of urban destruction and reconstruction. Many cities have, in the more distant past, been subjected to disastrous events. The wooden cities of medieval and early modern Europe were susceptible to fire of which that in London in 1666 stands out; Stockholm was similarly destroyed in 1625, while part of Hamburg shared the same fate in 1842. Other cities have suffered earthquake damage – the destruction of Lisbon in 1755 and of Messina in both 1783 and 1908 (Ioli Gigante 1980) are obvious examples together with the less severe effects of the 1980 earthquake in Naples.

But the most important causes of destruction in recent years have been the two world wars, especially the second in which all German cities were bombed whilst many cities elsewhere, such as Le Havre and Marseille in France, Rotterdam in the Netherlands, and Turin and Messina in Italy, were also damaged to a greater or lesser degree. Paris only escaped razing by the retreating German troops acting on Hitler's own orders because of the effective insubordination of his ground commanders who 'neglected' to put his orders into effect (Evenson 1979: 279). In Berlin, 34 per cent of the housing stock had been totally destroyed by the end of the war, 54 per cent damaged and only 12 per cent left completely intact (Trebbi 1978: 16). But it was in the Ruhr (Fig. 1.5) that some of the most severe and concentrated destruction occurred; within West Germany only Cologne and Würzburg suffered worse (Steinberg 1978: 112). In Rotterdam, 280 hectares of urban buildings were razed after bombing in 1940 and 1943. Of the French cities, Le Havre was

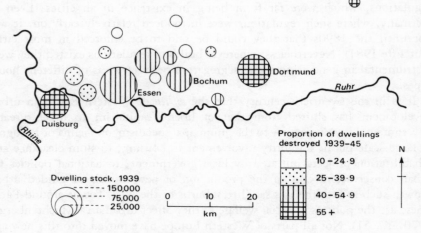

Fig. 1.5   Second World War damage in the Ruhr cities.
(*Data source*: Steinberg 1978)

perhaps the most badly affected with 9,900 dwellings destroyed and 9,700 damaged.

Destruction brought opportunities for the total replanning of urban morphology, but in relatively few cases has this actually occurred. Certainly the centre of Lisbon was completely redesigned by Pombàl after the earthquake (Gaspar 1976: 51), but the 1783 destruction of Messina in Sicily did not produce any significant change to the internal morphology of the city. After the 1908 earthquake it was briefly suggested that the site should be abandoned, but instead the city was quickly brought back to life with its original street-plan intact, although the housing problem was given insufficient attention and resulted in the perpetuation of *barrache* (shanty-towns) for years afterwards (Ginatempo and Cammarota 1977: 166; Ioli Gigante 1980).

After the Second World War, Dortmund, Le Havre and Rotterdam were rebuilt to new street-plans but in most other cities rebuilding followed traditional lines, in some cases (such as in Rouen and Nuremberg) even involving reconstructing the old buildings bit by bit. Restoration of the old was a significant aspect of the post-war planning policies of cities such as Cologne and Stuttgart, and where large-scale planned remodelling of city-centres was perhaps envisaged it was sometimes not fully implemented because of the fragmented nature of landownership in the historic cores. These pres-ervationist tendencies have surprised many non-European observers who, with cultural myopia, expected post-war reconstruction to involve new approaches to urban traffic management and to functional segregation within the inner-city, the latter in particular being against the whole tenor of European urban life (Holzner 1970: 316–17). Nevertheless, although wartime destruction changed the inner-city less than might have been expected, the severe housing shortages everywhere experienced after the war led to the general adoption of the suburban publicly-financed large-scale apartment estate (the *grand ensemble*) throughout most of Europe, and that has transformed city peripheries out of all past recognition.

The history of post-war reconstruction clearly displays the continuing importance of the past in the modern Western European city. By both popular sentiment and municipal decision the general response was to revive the legacy of the past and modify it, as necessary, for modern needs. Thus the economic and social structures of the past, having determined much of the urban morphology and image of the city, leave their marks even on present-day developments.

CONCLUSIONS

The influence of the past is felt in all aspects of modern-day Western European city life, as will be shown time and again in succeeding chapters of this book. To walk the streets of central Turin is to step into the Roman gridiron street pattern. The newly-arrived migrant from the provinces climbing from the train in a Paris station and seeking a room in a nearby residential hotel is reproducing the actions of countless migrants from the past. The craftsman or small shop-keeper locking up for the night in the side-streets of Brussels or Hamburg or Athens and then climbing the stairs to his apartment above is part of a traditon of the mixed residential and commercial use of property that goes back centu-ries. This chapter has explored some of the more pervasive legacies from the past and has shown how the contemporary pattern of Western European urban life has developed under a variety of influences ranging from feudalism through trading interests, absolutism and industrial capitalism to the modern welfare state. It is virtually impossible to draw up a satisfactory list of influences from the past that are still of importance at the present. Nevertheless, the following items may be accepted as a tentative statement, some of them relating to topics which, although not having been accorded detailed discussion in the present chapter, are dealt with later in the volume.

1. The major landmarks of the Western European city are generally non-economic in origin and date, by and large, from the constructions of the controlling interests of the past (Lichtenberger 1970: 46). The dominant urban features are not banks, shopping areas or central business districts but churches, palaces, castles, monumental squares and other symbols of non-economic power. Thus while the citizen of New York may perceive the city-centre as the sky-scrapers of Manhattan, the citizen of Milan sees his city's centre as the cathedral square.

2. A significant proportion of urban land, even in city-centres, serves multiple purposes: single-use areas are relatively few and confined more to the periphery (Georgulas and Markopoulou 1977: 73). In particular, many buildings have commercial, administrative or even industrial uses at ground level or in interior courtyards with residential accommodation in the upper storeys. This is a type of urban building use that dates back to the earliest days of trading interests and is sometimes still being created in urban redevelopment schemes of the present day (see Ch. 8, p. 208). It is, however, noticeable that this long tradition of mixed land uses is generally now being diluted, especially in the cities of Northern Europe, as single-use zoning becomes more common.

3. Much urban European manufacturing and commercial activity is still on a relatively small scale, more especially in Southern Europe, another throwback to the past. This small-scale activity accords well with the possibilities afforded by the tenement house of several storeys and perpetuates the mixed urban land uses mentioned above (Lichtenberger 1970: 57–8). One result of this feature is the existence, especially in Southern Europe, of a significant class of the self-employed artisans and shopkeepers, a social class that is much reduced in importance in some other urban societies (see Ch. 7).

4. The large tenement house with its high density of dwellings, and high urban population densities as a whole, are in part a legacy of the old restrictions on urban spatial expansion dictated, up to the middle of the nineteenth century in most cases, by the existence of peripheral fortifications systems and of rapid urban growth in the years before the development of efficient mass transpor-

tation systems. European cities built upwards rather than outwards, but the existence of detailed building regulations prohibited the ultimate solution of the skyscraper and maintained regularity on the urban skyline.

5. The removal of the defences did not eliminate what had often already become (and what elsewhere became) a distinct social, functional and economic gradient from the centre to the suburbs. The city-centres of Western Europe remain, in most cases, sharply delineated from surrounding more recent developments both in the perception of the citizens and in the composition of the residents of old and new areas.

6. Two housing traditions have emerged over the last five centuries: the first sees the whole city as the context for urban life and the housing units as small private enclaves (the Mediterranean tradition); the second sees the dwelling as the essential setting with urban space being interstitial between dwellings (the North-West European tradition). These two traditions, described by Rapoport (1969: 349), will be examined in more detail in the next chapter. It is not inconceivable that the Mediterranean tradition owes its origins to the high urban densities of enclosed Southern cities whilst the North-West European tradition, centred on England (but not Scotland), results from the more spacious urban traditions of the British Isles which lacked defensive considerations.

7. Western European cities have, since pre-industrial times, had relatively strong representations of the wealthy and the *élite* at or near the city-centre. Such traditions were reinforced in the nineteenth century by Haussmannization and, as shall be seen in Chapter 8, more recently urban renewal in inner-city areas has once more led to gentrification. NB

8. The Western European city has always to some extent depended, for its demographic stability or growth, on continuous processes of in-migration. As will be seen in Chapters 4 and 5, the sources of the migrants may have changed through time but their importance has not diminished.

9. The expansion of cities has often led to their absorption of surrounding settlements, villages or small towns, which often retain certain of their own distinctive social and demographic features and thus add complexity to the overall map of the social geography of the city (Lichtenberger 1970: 46). This is a phenomenon that obviously makes itself most clearly felt in suburban areas (see Ch. 9).

10. Urban morphology is rarely simple. In most cases urban growth has occurred over centuries in a piecemeal and unplanned manner under a variety of influences. Housing of markedly different types may be closely juxtaposed whilst expansion into areas of long-settled farmland may lead to the perpetuation, as city roads, of centuries-old field boundaries.

11. Western European society has not developed the anti-urban ethos that characterizes English or much North American culture. It was pointed out NB earlier (p. 10) that the *élites* in Europe took up permanent residence in the city whilst in England they visited their urban properties only for a 'season'. The cultural evaluation of urbanism in Western Europe is thus rather different from that in the rest of the developed world. This point will be further explored

in Chapter 7 in connection with the continued preferences of *élites* in Western Europe for city-centre living.

Because of the length of the continuous urban history of Western Europe, and because of the complexities of the processes of evolution that have occurred, these historical legacies of the Western European city are unique and divide such cities from those in all other parts of the globe. Within Western Europe there are certainly variations in urban history – between North and South, between industrial and non-industrial cities, and between capitals and provincial centres for example – but elements of the phenomena listed above are of significance in all cases. An appreciation of the marks of the past is essential as a background to the analysis of contemporary urban social geography.

CHAPTER TWO

Housing in the Western European City

It is not the intention of this chapter to provide an exhaustive discussion of all aspects of housing type, structure and methods of occupation throughout the cities of Western Europe. Indeed, if the Western European housing situation can be characterized in a single word that word must be 'diversity.' The cardboard and corrugated iron shanty-towns around Lisbon are a far cry from the trim tree-lined middle-class suburbs of Zürich with their squat *bourgeois* blocks of modern flats. There is a world of difference between the massive *grands ensembles* built around Paris since the Second World War and the seventeenth-century inner-city town houses of Amsterdam.

Nevertheless, certain unifying themes inevitably run through any examination, however brief, of housing in Western European cities. The objective here is to bring out some of those themes by considering the various housing 'classes' identifiable, and by focusing upon certain key variables such as dwelling types and levels of overcrowding. These themes therefore accord with Robson's (1975: 19) claim that a study of:

the characteristics of the stock of housing is a vital preliminary to any study of social areas since it provides the set of housing opportunities which facilitate or frustrate a household in its attempt to match its needs and aspirations with its housing space.

This chapter may therefore be regarded as the essential preamble to the later discussion of migration and of social areas within the city. In this chapter, analysis and discussion of housing markets are concentrated at the level of the individual city rather than at the national level. Whilst this inevitably reduces the volume of data available, it also reduces some of the problems of misinterpretation that are likely to occur from the use of national data to infer the structures of cities' housing markets, such misinterpretations arising from the inclusion, in national data, of rural areas and small urban places where housing situations may be very different from those of the cities.

HOUSING CLASSES

The concept of the housing class was first put forward by Rex and Moore (1967) in their study of ethnicity in Birmingham, but it has quickly become an established concept and has been reformulated by others (Johnston 1980a: 197–8; Robson 1975: 43). A housing class may normally be identified as a group of people with 'similar' opportunities and constraints to housing occupation, usually distinguished by type of housing tenure. Although used here as the basis for the discussion of European urban housing, it is important to note at the outset that the implicit ordering of the classes in a descending hierarchy from most desirable (owner-occupation) to least desirable (lodgers) used by British authors is not of equal applicability in Western Europe. In particular, owner-occupation is less commonly found in Western European cities and is often not as 'desirable' as it appears to English eyes.

Owner-occupation

Certainly owner-occupation can be singled out as a first distinct housing class in Western Europe, included within this category being the occupation of mortgaged properties as a step towards ownership. The proportions of dwellings in this class are everywhere lower in mainland European cities than in the British Isles where commonly one-half of urban housing is owner-occupied (Bassett and Short 1980). Table 2.1 illustrates this point with an example chosen from each country where suitable data are available. Of the sixty large cities for which the proportion is known (no cities in Portugal, Spain or Greece come in this category), the maximum rate of owner-occupation was in Turku, Finland (51.4 per cent) and the minimum in Geneva (2.0 per cent). Overall,

Table 2.1   Owner-occupied dwellings as percentage of all occupied private dwellings – selected cities

City	Country	Date	Percent owner-occupied
Tampere*	Finland	1970	45.2
Bologna	Italy	1971	33.3
Bordeaux	France	1975	29.3
Brussels	Belgium	1970	27.0
Düsseldorf	W. Germany	1968	13.0
Oslo	Norway	1970	12.1
Malmö	Sweden	1970	10.1
Copenhagen/Frederiksberg	Denmark	1970	7.4
Rotterdam†	Netherlands	1971	7.0
Zürich	Switzerland	1970	6.6
Vienna	Austria	1971	5.1

*Owner-occupying households as percentage of all households
†Owner-occupied dwellings as percentage of all dwellings

Data source: see Appendix

some 45 per cent of dwellings in Finnish cities were owner-occupied, one-third in Italian cities, 30 per cent in French and 25 per cent in Belgian cities. At the lower levels of the scale are the cities of the Netherlands, Switzerland and Austria. However, the inapplicability of national figures to individual cities may be illustrated by these cases. In Amsterdam only 4.4 per cent of dwellings are owner-occupied, in Rotterdam 7.0 per cent and in Utrecht 19.5 per cent, but in the newly built inner areas of the Randstad between these cities (thus in their commuter belts) 43 per cent of dwellings are owner-occupied (Van Ginkel 1979: 97–100). Kaufmann et al. (1978: 84–5), in a study of Austria's six largest urban areas (Vienna, Graz, Linz, Klagenfurt, Salzburg and Innsbruck), found that a total of 9.1 per cent of housing units in the six cities were in owner-occupation but that in the rural areas surrounding each city owner-occupation was in the majority.

Owner-occupied dwellings have come into existence in European cities in a variety of ways. Some, the oldest city-centre properties, have retained a tenurial type that was dominant in the mercantile period (Ch. 1, pp. 12–13). Often such dwellings form only part of a building, the owner-landlord occupying one apartment with the others being rented from him (Lowder 1980: 6). In Northern Europe a large number of small owner-occupied properties (generally single-family units) originate in co-operative housing associations founded at the turn of the century or in less formal self-help clubs and societies. Many of these properties have poor amenities and are today subject to steady deterioration. The inter-war years witnessed the rapid and unplanned growth of such housing areas around the peripheries of many cities (see Ch. 9).

House construction by a builder specifically for sale is rendered more complex in Western Europe than in Britain by the lesser importance of major financial institutions specializing in the provision of mortgage finance. House purchase has, in the past, generally been supported by borrowing on the open money market on relatively short repayment periods, although in many countries governmental initiatives have been made in the last fifteen years with a view to smoothing the way towards housing ownership (Boleat 1980). Only in West Germany and the Netherlands have mechanisms existed, as in the United Kingdom building societies, for transforming liquid savings into mortgage loans (Duclaud-Williams 1978: 231). In Spain it has been government policy in recent years to ease the possibilities of financial institutions lending for house purchase (King, J. C. 1971), but in a recent study of new building for sale in Madrid it was found that a deposit of 46 per cent of purchase cost was the average required, with mortgages commonly running for only five or ten years (Gago Llorente 1979: 125).

In the post-war period some countries have encouraged building for sale by various forms of direct subsidization of construction or by governmental financing of the borrowing requirements of construction companies. Such has been the case in France where a special financial agency (the *Crédit Foncier*) was set up in 1950 to handle these matters (Duclaud-Williams 1978: 17–18). Such policies shade into other forms of property construction whereby government-supported public or semi-public housing authorities have been empowered or even encouraged to build subsidized-cost housing for sale. In Italy it was specific governmental policy during the Fascist period to support the construction of middle-income housing through the allocation of grants to the public housing authorities. During the post-war period, too, there has been encouragement of home ownership in Italy through the setting of ratios of housing for rent and for sale built by the national housing management (*Ina-Casa*), a continuation of Fascist policies (Sbragia 1979). Similarly in Spain, much housing built under the auspices of the public authorities has been for sale but, given the limited provision of mortgage finance already mentioned, access to even this subsidized-construction property is difficult and costly whilst the desirability of home ownership in the poorly-equipped and inconvenient tower-block estates is low (Ferras 1977a: 283–6). In France in recent years around one-fifth to one-third of all new housing completions by the HLM societies (agencies providing low-cost properties – *habitation à loyer modéré*) have been built for direct sale (Duclaud-Williams 1978: 142–51): in the new towns around Paris the proportion has been as high as 36.5 per cent (Goursolas 1980: 420). On the other hand, sales of HLM dwellings to sitting tenants, possible since 1964, have generated very little increase in the stock of owner-occupied dwellings (Duclaud-Williams 1978: 142).

Owner-occupation in the British Isles and much of the rest of the English-speaking world is largely confined to single-family dwellings, with almost all apartments being rented in some form. In Western Europe the picture is very different, with high proportions of owner-occupied property in fact being in the form of flats, although unfortunately the necessary cross-tabulations of housing tenure against dwelling type are unavailable. Nevertheless an impression can be gained from the fact that in Düsseldorf in 1968, 14 per cent of dwellings were owner-occupied yet only 5 per cent of all dwellings were in buildings housing only one dwelling. In Marseille in 1975 the owner-occupation rate was 37 per cent but the proportion of dwellings in single-dwelling buildings was only 13 per cent. Thus owner-occupation in Western European cities often involves apartments in large blocks whilst owner-occupation is generally of lesser importance as a tenure type than in Britain.

Privately-rented property

The renting of properties on the open market is an extremely broad and complex type of housing tenure in Western European cities. Such tenure commonly involves both the highest and the lowest income categories, occurs in properties of all ages and types (single-family housing as well as apartments), and includes a very wide range of landlords. Indeed, the distinction between privately-rented and publicly-rented property is very blurred in the many cases where non-profit-making organizations and housing co-operatives with some state backing are involved. The definition of privately-rented housing used here is of properties where the landlords' prime motivations are economic in nature, either through the securing of profit from rent or where a large manufacturing or commercial enterprise offers housing to its own employees at a low or

Table 2.2 Privately-rented dwellings as percentage of all occupied private dwellings – selected cities

City	Country	Date	Percent privately-rented
Basel	Switzerland	1970	84.7
Bern	Switzerland	1970	83.1
Vienna	Austria	1971	69.9
Rotterdam*	Netherlands	1971	65.0
W. Berlin		1968	63.0
The Hague*	Netherlands	1971	60.1
Stockholm*	Sweden	1970	54.1
Cologne	W. Germany	1968	52.2
Hamburg	W. Germany	1968	44.0
Gothenburg*	Sweden	1970	39.5

*Privately-rented as percentage of all dwellings

Data sources: see Appendix

minimal rent with the idea of stabilizing the work-force. In Helsinki in 1970, for example, almost 7 per cent of households lived in dwellings provided by employers, whilst this type of accommodation is of particularly great importance throughout Western Europe in the housing of foreign migrant workers (Ch. 5).

This definition based on economic objective is, however, by no means uniformly applied. For example, in Italy the definition of privately-rented accommodation normally excludes ownership by corporate private institutions, such as banks and insurance companies, which are regarded as public landlords (Dandri 1978: 139). Many national censuses do not permit the isolation of private renting as a separate housing class. Nevertheless, Table 2.2 gives some of the information that is available. As with levels of owner-occupation, the proportions of privately-rented dwellings appear to be relatively specific to each country, with Swiss cities very high (80 per cent or more with Geneva at 90 per cent), Dutch cities at around 60 per cent and German and Swedish cities rather lower. In Italian cities, approximately one-third of dwellings are privately-rented (Dandri 1978: 139) whilst in Paris in 1970 approximately 69 per cent of households were in this class (Madge and Willmott, 1981: 66). Thus throughout Western Europe the proportion of privately-rented properties tends to be higher than the 16 per cent recorded in England and Wales in 1975 (Bassett and Short 1980: 82–3).

The history of tenanted accommodation is a long one and the mercantile period already showed the importance of rented property for the dwellings of those who were not the artisan-masters or the merchants (Ch. 1, p. 13). Subsequent increases in the numbers of the urban aristocracy could only be accommodated, in crowded walled cities, by the development of apartment blocks designed for a more prestigious population with individual apartments being rented from a private owner who often lived in one of the apartments himself. The nineteenth century gave a fillip to the growth of private renting, both through industrial urban growth and the crowding of migrants into the cities, and through Haussmannization schemes and the 'reconquest' of city-centres by the middle classes. In the former case, private capital from both the small investor and the larger speculative interests was drawn into the construction sector; in the latter case, only the larger suppliers of finance were involved. Nevertheless, even relatively large schemes often counted significant numbers of private individual investors; for example, the development of Vienna's Ringstrasse belt (Ch. 1, pp. 24–5) involved much construction where the new owners were the titled nobility, although only a minority of these lived in their own property there (Schorske 1980: 56).

Private investment in housing for rent was generally viewed as a viable means of securing a satisfactory profit, albeit that such investment fluctuated alongside booms and slumps in the general economic situation. In the newly-industrializing fringes of the growing cities the landlords were often the old rural landowners, but urban groups such as lawyers, small businessmen and other entrepreneurs also saw residential property as a good investment. The types of property constructed covered both multi-family housing (such as the *Mietskasernen* of Germany – the tenements of Berlin for example) and smaller house types such as reproductions of the regional style of historical vernacular architecture (Müller 1976: 134–6.).

In certain Southern European countries such as Portugal, Spain and Greece, large-scale free-market construction of privately-rented property has continued to the present day. Indeed, the lack of any form of control of the free market may be evidenced in many cities by the chaotic nature of urban fringe development where speculative building continues apace with little reference to any overall development plan or to amenity provision (Naylon 1981: 245–7). However, one distinct problem of the privately-rented sector in the economically poorer urban societies of Southern Europe has been that inflation in building costs in recent decades has not been matched by increases in the abilities of the lower-income urban residents to pay; this especially applies to recently-arrived migrants. The consequence has been that the privately-rented sector has ceased to build specifically for lower-income groups and has concentrated instead on more prestigious developments for the middle classes. Thus, as Ferras (1977a: 258) has pointed out in Barcelona, new housing provision has been aimed too high up the social scale: housing is not overall in short supply, but cheap housing is unavailable. Similar features occur throughout the Mediterranean world where *de luxe* rented housing stands empty whilst the poor turn to shanty-towns and marginalized properties as a cure to their problems of access to the normal market (Ginatempo and Cammarota 1977).

In Northern and Central Europe the twentieth-century history of the privately-rented sector has been one of public control. Indeed, Lichtenberger (1970: 54) has gone so far as to suggest that the most important cause of the present-day complexity of the housing markets in Western Europe was the introduction of rent control legislation for private properties at the time of the First World War. It is worth examining the effects of such legislation in two well-documented cases – those of Vienna and Paris.

Rent protection legislation was first promulgated in Vienna in 1917 (Lichtenberger 1977: 253) and extended in 1922 (Bobek and Lichtenberger 1966: 28), the intention being to maintain the existing levels of housing cost at a period when increasing inflation and high unemployment could have squeezed the poorer tenants severely. Already in the last years before the First World War the supply of new low-income privately-rented dwellings had dried up as a result of processes of rising cost very similar to those outlined above for Southern Europe. Land speculation involved many small interests and, with rising land values and the need to secure a profit on investments, new property was aimed higher in the market (Bobek and Lichtenberger 1966: 50–6). With the strict control of rents, the proportion of household income that went to pay for accommodation fell drastically as inflation raised all other prices: by 1932, rent accounted for only 4 per cent of the worker family's expenditure. The result was a total cessation of private building for rent and, with inflation, many of the larger institutional landlords went bankrupt through debt charges on their older properties. A further effect was to cut back intra-urban migration to exceptionally low levels. The inevitable accompaniment to rent control came in the increased provision of municipal housing which occurred between the wars when rent control was at its height.

The situation in Paris was very similar. By 1914, as elsewhere,

rising costs has outstripped the workers' capacity to pay an economic rent for new accommodation (Sutcliffe 1970: 124)

and rent control was introduced at the outbreak of the war. Although it was originally intended that the controls should be removed in 1922, this did not happen. Controls did not apply to new properties but there was general fear that they would be extended (as indeed they were in 1941) so that, as in Vienna, new private building for rent effectively stopped. By 1937, rents accounted for only 6 per cent of household income and this proportion fell even lower by the end of the Second World War (Sutcliffe 1970: 256–7). Since 1949, rent controls have been steadily reduced, even on older property, but this has only been possible via a massive increase in the availability of publicly-rented property. As late as 1974 in Paris, 68 per cent of unfurnished privately-rented dwellings still had controlled rents, although in the post-war years these rents have been steadily brought more into line with open-market conditions (Duclaud-Williams 1978: 56–8).

Rent control legislation has made its mark on most Northern European societies and has become a recent policy in some Southern European countries, especially in Italy where the 1963 extension of rent control to all post-war dwellings has been blamed for the steady decline in new housing starts since that year (Dandri 1978: 139). Sweden operated a rent control policy from 1942 to 1975 allied with a 1945 declaration that housing should take no more than 20 per cent of the average worker's wages (Burtenshaw et al. 1981: 122–3). In West Germany, rent controls were abolished in the later 1960s (Lichtenberger 1976: 92).

Although the progressive reduction of rent controls in much of Western Europe in recent years has once again made it a reasonable investment to build for the privately-rented market, it would be true to say that the existing stock of such housing is generally of two kinds: firstly, older (pre-First World War) properties with a heavy over-representation of both low-income and high-income groups reflecting the diversity of social class use associated with privately-rented accommodation for well over a century; and secondly, new properties almost exclusively aimed at the better-off.

Finally it is necessary to point out that the association of small investors in the past with the privately-rented sector has meant that, even at the present time, a significant proportion of the urban population can be classed as *rentiers*, deriving their income in part from their ownership of small amounts of property. This class, however, is an ageing and declining one with little entrepreneurial initiative in the operation of the modern-day urban housing market, where the tendency runs towards larger owning interests (Aust 1980).

Before turning to the third major variety of housing tenure, it is necessary to reiterate the importance of employer-provided accommodation in certain specialized cases. Reference was made in Chapter 1 (pp. 17–19) to the considerable significance of such housing in many nineteenth-century industrial cities. Recent economic problems and the de-industrialization of society have reduced the number of these dwellings but they remain of some importance here and there – for example in Wuppertal in West Germany in 1969 employer-provided housing formed up to one-third of the total housing stock in some city sub-districts (Weise 1973: 45).

The public sector

The public rented housing market, like the equivalent private sector, is of great complexity with many important variations from one country to another. According to the definition given above (p. 38), the publicly-rented sector encompasses all properties where the prime motive is not the achievement of profit. However, this distinction is blurred by the fact that in some countries, particularly in Southern Europe, the public sector has, from time to time, been encouraged to show a healthy return on capital investment. Elsewhere, particularly in Northern Europe, a large number of private organizations provide non-profit housing. For example, in West Germany one-sixth of such accommodation is provided through trades union sponsorship (Burtenshaw et al. 1981: 126–7), whilst in Scandinvia a variety of co-operative housing associations exist, some (see above, p. 37) creating owner-occupied housing and others catering for the rented market. In Vienna in 1971, 7.5 per cent of all dwellings were rented from non-profit-making housing associations, and similar co-operatives accounted for 12.1 per cent of housing in Stockholm in 1970, 13.6 per cent in Gothenburg and 31.6 per cent in Malmö.

Elsewhere the operation of public housing varies from country to country. In general, housing is not a direct responsibility of the local authority (as in Britain) but of separate housing agencies in which funds from central government and local government are often supplemented by borrowing on the open financial market and by investment by private companies and large employers:

Table 2.3   Publicly-rented dwellings as percentage of all occupied private dwellings – selected cities

City	Country	Date	Percent publicly-rented
Hanover	W. Germany	1968	36.0
Cologne	W. Germany	1968	32.8
Vienna	Austria	1971	26.0
Amsterdam*	Netherlands	1971	25.8
Stockholm*	Sweden	1970	25.0
The Hague*	Netherlands	1971	23.1
Copenhagen/Frederiksberg	Denmark	1970	16.1
Zürich	Switzerland	1970	5.4
Basel	Switzerland	1970	3.5

*Publicly-rented dwellings as percentage of all dwellings

Data sources: see Appendix

indeed, in France employers have, since 1953, been obliged to contribute a sum equivalent to 1 per cent of their salaries bill to the public housing authorities. Similar requirements exist in some other countries. Much public sector building in these circumstances has in fact been carried out by private companies.

Table 2.3 illustrates the levels of publicly-rented housing in selected cities for which data are available, once again an incomplete list. Those cities of Southern Europe, of which no example is given here, would certainly fall at the lower end of the scale whilst in French cities around one-quarter of dwellings are generally rented from public or quasi-public authorities. The figure for Stockholm includes a substantial element of housing rented from semi-public bodies supervised by the local authority.

The origins of public housing in much of Europe lie at the turn of the century, at the period when, as discussed above (p. 41), the provision of new low-income housing in the privately-rented sector was slowing down. In Italy the first national housing law was passed in 1903, establishing local agencies to administer housing for low-income people (Sbragia 1979: 135). Public housing authorities were first set up in France in 1912 (Sutcliffe 1970: 258): this was the same year that the first municipal housing was made available to tenants other than municipal employees in Vienna (Bobek and Lichtenberger 1966: 56). In Belgium it was the housing shortage of the years immediately after the First World War that resulted in the creation of the national housing agency (Verniers 1958: 63).

Progress in public house-building in the inter-war period was variable from country to country and city to city. Vienna led the way, the city council buying up cheap land and by 1934 constructing 63,000 new dwellings, virtually all in large apartment blocks: during the inter-war period public construction accounted for 70 per cent of all housing completions (Bobek and Lichtenberger 1966: 137–45). In Paris between 1921 and 1940, 27,000 government-sponsored new dwelling units were built (Evenson 1979: 219), with important construction occurring in the *zone* around the old fortifications (Deneux 1981; see Ch. 1, pp. 25–6). The inter-war years also saw tentative moves towards public housing in Switzerland (Lerch et al. 1972) and 1939 was the year of the first relevant legislation in Spain (King, J. C. 1971: 385).

It was, however, the years after the Second World War that saw the most massive growth of the public housing sector in response to grave housing short-ages that affected most of Western Europe after the economic recession of the 1930s and wartime destruction (including the Civil War in Spain). The general result, visible in almost every city, is the monolithic apartment block built to factory production methods at low cost, generally on greenfield sites at city peripheries where land acquisition costs were also low. This type of construction has generally become known by its French name – the *grand ensemble*. The scale of operations involved has often led to the reform and enlargement of the orig-inal housing agencies, such as occurred in France in 1947 (Duclaud-Williams 1978: 19) or in Italy in 1949 (Sbragia 1979: 140), and to the formation of new agencies as in Spain in 1957 (Ferras 1977a). In West Germany, generous governmental credits were made available to encourage public authority construction as quickly as possible to replace lost wartime housing stock (Riquet 1960: 129–30), whilst in France central government support was at levels of up to 90 per cent between 1951 and 1973 – the years of the construc-tion of the *grands ensembles*. Further detailed discussion of the *grands ensembles* will be found in Chapter 9.

Policies of family allocation to publicly-rented accommodation differ between countries. For example, in the Netherlands the rules are not dissimilar to those of the United Kingdom: in Amsterdam, municipal housing allocation requires the new tenant to have been in the city for a minimum of two years (Cortie 1972a: 47). In Barcelona the supply of new public-sector housing (and some of it is anyway for sale – see above, p. 38) has scarcely kept pace with the need to absorb population from the cleared squatter settlements, so access for the 'normal' household from a non-slum dwelling is virtually non-existent (Ferras 1977a: 270–7). In Italy, length-of-stay qualifications have been intro-duced in northern cities to prevent recent southern migrants jumping the queue by virtue of their poor urban housing (Sbragia 1979: 141–2). On the other hand, in France the contributions made by employers to the funds of the housing agencies permit those employers to nominate tenants, a feature which increases the geographical mobility of those moving into publicly-subsidized properties who need not necessarily be of immediately local previous address (Duclaud-Williams 1978: 137; Bentham and Moseley 1980: 68).

One final feature of the publicly-rented sector is noteworthy and deserving of comment. In general (and there are variations from country to country and between agencies within individual countries) the publicly-rented sector enjoys considerable governmental financial support in its construction but does not benefit from rent subsidy. Once constructed, there is a general requirement to balance costs against revenue and in many instances, particularly in inner-city locations, the result is a rent level that militates against the occupation of publicly-rented property by those at the lowest end of the income scale:

indeed, the proportions of lower-middle class and white-collar tenants are sometimes considerable. Periodically there have been attempts in many countries to drive out wealthy tenants from the publicly-rented sector but they have not been greatly successful (Duclaud-Williams 1978: 139). Thus, as in Britain, the poorest households may be limited to privately-rented accommodation rather than being catered for by the public authorities (Robson 1979: 73).

The one major exception to this generalization concerns accommodation purpose-built to absorb populations direct from shanty-towns or squatter settlements. In France these dwellings are in the *cités de transit* which quickly became a segregated housing class for immigrants only (see Ch. 5, pp. 119– 20), whereas in Italy the short-term answer has been to construct 'minimal housing' (*case minime*) as a half-way stage to more regular accommodation, such minimal housing being, in practice, little more than a more formally planned shanty-town (Erminero and Peruzzi 1962). Similar accusations have been made about replacement housing for squatters in Barcelona (Ferras 1977a: 269). In West Germany, accommodation comparable to the French *cités* was provided for refugees from Eastern Europe in the early post-war years (Riquet 1960: 129–30).

Squatters and shanty-towns

It is, perhaps, inevitable that the range of illegal and unregularized housing tenures that can be collected together under the umbrella terms 'squatting and shanty-towns' are generally very difficult to identify in official censuses and reports, in part due to official attempts to ignore these housing phenomena. In the past, unofficial temporary accommodation was often the resort of the poorest and most recently-arrived migrants in the industrial cities of the north. In both Germany and Sweden in the later ninteenth century, periods of rapid in-migration to cities sometimes produced shanty-towns in places on the urban periphery but these were always shortlived (Niethammer and Bruggemeier 1978: 125–7). More recently in Northern Europe, illegal occupation of land or built property has been associated with squatting in inner-urban areas, often areas suffering planning blight in advance of redevelopment: such squatting has become of some importance in Amsterdam and West Berlin.

Foreign immigrant populations have also resorted to shanty-towns or *bidonvilles*, particularly in France. Here such illicit settlements around Paris have a long history, going back to the rag-pickers of the nineteenth century (Faure 1978) and continued by the residents of the Parisian fortification belt in the early years of the twentieth century (see Ch. 1, pp. 25–6). More recently, however, the *bidonvilles* have been almost exclusively populated by North Africans (see Ch. 5). It is in Southern Europe that 'irregular' settlements have made their biggest impact in recent years. Shanty-towns are a feature of the peripheral urban landscape of many cities, such as Rome, Barcelona, Madrid and Lisbon, whilst squatting in disused buildings has become almost institutionalized in Naples (Döpp 1968: 157–9). Table 2.4 shows both the official and unofficial estimates of the extent of squatting and shanty-towns in certain cities of Spain

Table 2.4   Estimates of shanty-towns etc. – Portuguese and Spanish cities

City	1970 census data		Unofficial estimates	
	A	B	A	B
Portugal				
Lisbon	5.9	6.4	n.a.	n.a.
Oporto	0.2	0.1	n.a.	n.a.
Spain				
Barcelona	1.0	n.a.	0.9 (1970)	1.5 (1970)
Madrid	1.1	n.a.	3.9 (1973)	4.1 (1973)
Malaga	1.4	n.a.	n.a.	n.a.
Seville	2.6	n.a.	n.a.	n.a.

A. Shanty-town households as percentage of total households
B. Shanty-town residents as percentage of total population
n.a. Not available

Data sources: see Appendix; Ferras 1977a; Montes Mieza et al. 1976

and Portugal. Definitions are often extremely complicated. Around Lisbon, for example, in addition to the shanties built of perishable materials there are also large numbers of substantial masonry properties built without permits. Construction by the user has evolved into a more organized market in which speculators are moving in and 'tenancies' increasing. Nevertheless, the largest illicit settlements (of up to 6,000 households) are still those of the classic shanty-towns. The existence of a substantial unregularized housing market is a virtual necessity in Lisbon where, as elsewhere, legal private building for rent in the inner-city is prohibitively expensive, whilst public authority housing amounts to no more than 5 per cent of completions each year (Salgueiro 1977). The census count of 49,000 living in shanty-towns in 1970 is certainly an underestimate.

The utility of the shanty-town is also shown in Madrid where an estimated 128,000 lived in a variety of types of illegal housing in 1973 (Montes Mieza et al. 1976: 161). Half of the households were tenants in some form. The official policy has been to try to assimilate the shanty-towns by providing basic amenities, but there have also been periodic drives for their demolition despite the fact that their replacement by publicly-subsidized housing is too costly.

Moves for the elimination of shanty-towns have been more successful in Barcelona. Here large-scale illicit housing dates back to the 1920s and by 1927 there were some 6,500 shanties (*barracas*) in the city (Lowder 1980: 6). The peak came in the 1950s when almost 15,000 shanties were in existence, housing nearly 70,000 people (Ferras 1977a: 266). Publicly-financed housing has been constructed to rehouse the shanty population but these new dwellings have often been substandard and have simply replaced the old sites with *barraquismo vertical*, huge apartment blocks of minimal services (Naylon 1981: 245).

One well-documented example of institutionalized shanty-towns is in Messina in Sicily where, indeed, many of the minimal-standard dwellings were built by the authorities after the 1908 earthquake and the bombardment of the Second World War. In the early 1970s an estimated 14 per cent of the city's residents were housed in such dwellings (Ginatempo and Cammarota 1977: 115).

Other housing classes

The squatter settlement is one possible response to a shortage of 'normal' housing and is particularly associated with in-migrants to cities. Other responses, such as the taking of sub-tenancies or the creation of collective households, have been resorted to at different times in different places.

The practice of taking in lodgers was extremely common in the industrial cities of Northern Europe in the past. The lodger benefited by getting a roof over his head whilst the household head obtained useful extra income. In Berlin in 1890, 23.1 per cent of households included lodgers whilst in Frankfurt the percentage was 24.6 (Niethammer and Bruggemeier 1978: 127). The pattern was for recently-arrived single migrants to become lodgers if they were male and domestic servants if they were female (Jackson 1982: 862). Lodgers were most commonly taken into the smallest and poorest accommodation where, because of the overall housing shortage and the accompanying high rents, their contributions to household budgets were most needed (Liang 1970: 106–7).

Sub-letting has continued to play a role everywhere in times of stress in the housing market (Bobek and Lichtenberger 1966: 135), and in the period after the Second World War it has become associated with the arrival in Northern European cities of large numbers of foreign labour migrants, reproducing the growth of lodging under the conditions of domestic rural–urban migration of the nineteenth century. In Southern Europe it is local rural–urban migration that conditions the state of the market in sub-letting to the present day. The collective household has, however, increased its importance in the contemporary situation in comparison with the past.

Finally there remains a small group of housing classes that are difficult to classify consisting, for example, of mobile homes (particularly boats in the cities of the Netherlands and Belgium), official residences and charity dwellings.

Overall a distinct feature of the housing scene in post-war Western Europe has been the keen governmental interest displayed in this aspect of life by governments of all shades in the political spectrum so that various government agencies at all levels have played important managerial roles in deciding the type of housing provision, its cost and allocation. This has been a topic that has received a great deal of attention in France (Castells 1977; 1978) where official measures for the promotion of public-sector housing in the *grands ensembles* have had a strong effect in determining new patterns of urban growth. Elsewhere, government initiatives have been equally influential (Elkins 1973: 57), for example in Sweden, the Netherlands and Austria.

DWELLING TYPES AND HOUSING DENSITIES

One of the most notable features of Western European cities is the great importance of apartment blocks in the urban landscape, certainly much greater

Table 2.5   Dwelling types – selected cities, 1970

City	Country	Percentage of all dwellings	
		In single-household buildings	In large apartment blocks
Antwerp	Belgium	20.8	63.5*
Aarhus	Denmark	19.9	72.6*
Madrid	Spain	4.8	88.3†
Oslo	Norway	10.8	69.9‡
Valencia	Spain	4.1	83.6†
Vienna ‖	Austria	6.1¶	89.2*

* In buildings housing three or more households
† In buildings housing five or more households
‡ In buildings of three or more storeys
¶ In buildings housing one or two households
‖ 1971

Data sources: see Appendix

than is the case in Great Britain. The traveller taking the train from Paris Gare du Nord to Charles de Gaulle airport will find it hard to spot any single-family dwellings along the route except for a few old cottages swallowed up by the progressive urban growth of large blocks of flats: on landing at London Heathrow and taking the Picadilly Line into central London, the same traveller passing through the suburbs of West London will, for much of the journey before the line plunges underground, find it as hard to identify any multiple-dwelling buildings. This is not to say that single-household buildings do not exist in mainland Western European cities, but that in general urban life in continental Europe is apartment life, often in very large apartment blocks (see Table 2.5). For example, in Spain it is possible to calculate, from census data, the average number of dwellings in apartment blocks of five dwellings or more: in 1970 the average for large cities varied from 11.6 in Seville to 15.7 in Madrid. In Vienna in 1971, 57 per cent of all dwellings were in buildings housing 21 or more dwelling units (Kaufmann et al. 1978: 77).

The story of the rise to prominence of the apartment house is a long one which has been discussed elsewhere. The established view (Lichtenberger 1970: 53–4; 1976: 88–90) is that the apartment house originated in Italy and spread into all areas from the sixteenth century onwards via France and Austria. In the medieval period, houses in Naples, for example, had been single two-storey dwellings, but later population expansion and pressure on land availability led to growing height and the development of true tenement blocks by the eighteenth century (Döpp 1968: 139–43; Lichtenberger 1970: 54). The growth of large apartment blocks in Northern Europe was stimulated by the need to house large numbers of industrial workers during the nineteenth century (Berry 1973: 126–7) but it is notable that employer-provided accommodation tended to be on a smaller scale, the tenement blocks being speculatively built by private landlords (Hammarström 1979; Bollerey and

Hartmann 1980: 140–1). In Northern Europe it is also possible to envisage the tenement block as being in some ways an evolution from the craftsman's house of the mercantile period in which parts of the accommodation had often been let (see Ch. 1, p. 13). England remained the bastion of the single-household building, evolving the Victorian terraced house as the 'appropriate' working-class housing. It is only in the other urban societies fringing the North Sea (such as in Northern Belgium and the Netherlands) that large apartment blocks have never become fully dominant (Lichtenberger 1976: 90). In Central Europe there was a short-lived battle over whether Vienna's Ringstrasse belt should be developed with 'English-style' houses or with apartments, but those advocating the latter won (Breitling 1980: 39).

One particularly significant feature of older apartment blocks in many European cities (including many blocks built as late as the 1930s) is the considerable variation in dwelling standards within blocks. Often the best accommodation, with the largest rooms and most spacious layout, was on the first floor (the *piano nobile* in Italian) with succeeding storeys having steadily diminishing standards whilst the ground floor housed the *concierge* along with retailing or commercial activities – a throwback to the mecantile house. Alternatively (and sometimes at the same time) there were great differences in the desirability of apartments between the front and back of a building, particularly where the back apartments opened only on to an internal courtyard. These variations are important in conditioning and creating the possibilities of social segregation within buildings and not just between them.

It is possible to hypothesize that, in the past, land values and pressures from

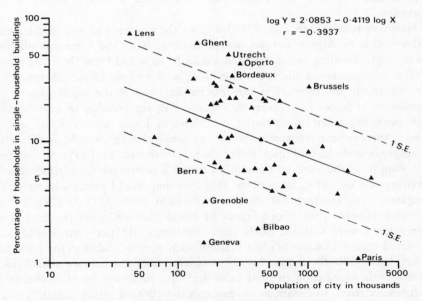

Fig. 2.1 Population size and single-household residential buildings, 1968–75. (*Data sources*: see Appendix)

competing land users have been highest at the centres of the most populous cities so that it was only by recourse to the construction of dwellings yielding very high population densities that developers could assure themselves of a profit in city-centres. This logic continues to work today as redevelopment schemes bring increases in building height in order to increase the numbers of apartments and maintain profitability (Lemay 1970: 56–7). Thus the largest cities might be expected to have the highest proportions of apartments. In practice, given the nature of the available census information, this question has to be examined from the opposite direction, by hypothesizing that smaller cities will have higher proportions of dwellings in lower density units – that is in single-household buildings. Figure 2.1 illustrates this relationship with data from 55 cities from all the major countries of Western Europe with the exception of Austria, Italy, Greece and Finland. The correlation coefficient of –0.39 (significant at the 0.01 level) demonstrates the general validity of the 'economic' hypothesis, but the level of explanation is not particularly high. Indeed, examination of the positive residuals suggests the relevance of Lichtenberger's ideas of a North Sea culture area of single-household buildings. One particular group of positive residuals involves the cities of Utrecht, Brussels, Ghent and Lens (on the French coalfield of the Nord). Much of the earliest industrial housing in this area, and in the Ruhr area of Germany, adopted the design of terraces of single-story buildings (a vernacular house-type of historic cultural dominance in Flanders). It was not until the latter half of the nineteenth century that these types of construction were augmented by apartment and tenement blocks in the smaller cities (Jackson 1981: 204–5) while the terraces and courts of the French *cités minières* are a lasting legacy in the landscape.

Negative residuals on Fig. 2.1 also show the existence of a second cultural realm – that of Alpine Europe, where Geneva, Bern and Grenoble all have fewer single-dwelling buildings than would be expected from their size alone.

The predominace of the apartment block well into the twentieth century is not necessarily the product of the free market, nor of the aspirations of the population at large. Governmental influences in the creation of new housing have been important in dictating the blend of house-types constructed. In France, surveys have repeatedly shown that urban residents would prefer to live in single-household buildings rather than apartments. In 1945, 56 per cent of a sample of the Parisian population stated a preference for a single-family dwelling and by 1964, 68 per cent said that they would prefer a house in the periphery to an apartment at the centre (Evenson 1979: 251). In Clerc's study of *grands ensembles* throughout France he found that whilst 88 per cent of his respondents were satisfied with their dwellings, 82 per cent would have preferred to live in an individual house if such were available at the same cost (Clerc 1967: 188–9): therein lay the problem, since the paucity of individual houses leads to inflation in their value and thus rationing by price (either for purchase or rent). In Besançon in France in the 1960s a survey found that only single people and childless households showed any favour for apartments and even then far from the majority of these groups was involved (Charles 1969: 226).

Because governmental agencies controlled, directly or indirectly, such a high proportion of housing finance in the early post-war period, managerial decisions were made at a high level. In West Germany, areas of single-household buildings destroyed in the Second World War were generally rebuilt with apartments (Böhm et al. 1975: 26), whilst the accommodation of growing urban populations and the solution to housing crises have also officially lain in large-scale highly-planned apartment-block estates (Trebbi 1978: 116–20), not just in Germany but throughout the continent. In Stockholm, for example, consumer desires were for single-family surburban dwellings, but the planning decisions contradicted these desires, going instead for high-density apartment-block surburban neighbourhoods (Popenoe 1977: 41–3). With the general reduction in housing shortages by the 1960s, increasing numbers of single-family dwellings have been completed and governments have begun to encourage their construction. Whereas in Stockholm in the 1960s, 70 per cent of newly-completed dwellings were apartments, by 1977, 70 per cent were houses (Burtenshaw et al. 1981: 118): the eclipse from power of the Social Democratic party between 1976 and 1982 further reduced the governmental feeling against single-family housing. In France, changes in governmental attitudes are evidenced in the New Towns around Paris: originally a limit of 30 per cent of total housing stock was placed on individual houses, but since 1976/7 this limit has been abolished and there is now official encouragement for private developers to build single-family housing units (Goursolas 1980; Tuppen 1979). The importance of the North Sea cultural area is shown in the fact that in the Netherlands, despite the construction of many new apartment-block estates, at least 30 per cent of new post-war housing completions in each year in the cities have customarily been of single-family dwellings (Jobse

Table 2.6 Housing age – selected cities

| City | Country | Percentage of housing stock built | |
		Pre-First World War	Post-Second World War
Antwerp	Belgium	42.0 (– 1919)	31.8 (1946–70)
Bari	Italy	8.6 (– 1919)	68.4 (1946–71)
Genoa	Italy	26.2 (– 1919)	51.1 (1946–71)
The Hague	Netherlands	20.2 (– 1906)	31.8 (1945–71)
Kiel	W. Germany	31.0 (– 1918)	48.0 (1949–68)
Malmö	Sweden	13.8 (– 1920)	63.1 (1941–70)
Marseille	France	32.7 (– 1914)	49.3 (1948–75)
Munich	W. Germany	21.0 (– 1918)	61.0 (1949–68)
Oslo	Norway	21.9 (– 1910)	46.4 (1946–70)
Paris	France	58.4 (– 1914)	19.6 (1948–75)
Rennes	France	14.9 (– 1914)	67.2 (1948–75)
Vienna	Austria	50.9 (– 1919)	28.2 (1945–71)

Data sources: see Appendix

1974: 356). Throughout Europe the recent recession has hit new public agency housing starts more than private building and it is the latter sector that is more likely to be building single-household units: for example in the province of Madrid, free-market housing starts amounted to 74 per cent of the total by 1977, with the publicly-supported sector much reduced (Gago Llorente 1979: 111).

Despite the great extent, almost everywhere, of post-war building and reconstruction, most cities retain a large proportion of their housing stock dating from before the First World War. Table 2.6 gives some comparative perspectives on this topic. Housing age varies markedly from city to city within the eight countries for which data are available. Towns and cities with low proportions of old houses include some badly affected by wartime destruction alongside others where rapid population growth and new construction have occurred since 1920: in this latter respect it is unfortunate that no data exist for the cities of Southern Europe except for those of Italy. On the other hand the urban cores of the largest cities, such as Paris and Vienna, retain large numbers of older properties and at the level of smaller sub-divisions the concentrations of old property are acute – for example in the second *arrondissement* of Lyon in 1968, 53 per cent of the dwellings had been built before 1871 and only 4 per cent were less than 25 years old (Bonneville 1974: 102).

Housing age is generally most important in conditioning the standards of housing amenities since many of the older properties, particularly those built as working-class tenements, have very poor access to internal lavatories, hot water, baths or central heating. The league table for the early 1970s of the worst-off cities in terms of households' access to baths within the dwelling includes (with more than 30 per cent lacking access) many of the large older cities of Northern Europe (Amsterdam, Brussels, Antwerp, Ghent, Paris, Lille, Copenhagen) as well as several of the more recently growing but poorer cities of the south (Naples, Catania, Messina, Athens, Salonica: data are lacking for Spain and Portugal). Cities with the best standards of housing amenities include all those in Switzerland, places such as Grenoble, Toulouse, Strasbourg and Nice in France, and Bologna, Milan and Verona in Italy. Within cities, poor housing particularly affects individual blocks or districts where, even after prolonged slum-clearance acitivity, conditions are still poor. In most large German cities, for example, areas of nineteenth-century workers' tenements with communal courtyard lavatories remain to be cleared (Achilles 1969: 121). Historically, poor housing has most often been identified via mortality levels, tuberculosis being a particular indicator (Sutcliffe 1970: 240–2), but recent slum-clearance schemes have used more multivariate definitions of housing deprivation.

Given the high proportion of dwellings in large apartment blocks, the dense use of available space in the intra-mural areas of the oldest cities, and relatively low levels of public open space, at least in the city-centres, mainland Western European cities generally display high residential population densities in comparison to British cities where inner-city wards rarely have a density in excess of 200 persons per hectare and where suburban levels are rarely above

100 per hectare. Measured at the minimum statistical areal unit, population densities in Western European cities usually exceed these figures. Döpp (1968: 242) quotes the peak densities for a variety of Italian cities in 1951 as being 825 persons per hectare in Naples, 348 in Turin, 442 in Venice, 698 in Rome, 607 in Palermo and 791 in Genoa. In Paris the densely-populated Marais district averaged 900 persons per hectare in 1969 (Evenson 1979: 315). The highest densities commonly occur in areas of old degraded tenements, often where individual dwellings have been sub-divided for sub-letting: Olives Puig (1969: 53–8) quotes such a district in Barcelona where the population density in 1945 was 1,361 persons per hectare. In Hanover the peak density in 1970 was 274 persons per hectare (Sprengel 1978: 128) whilst in Bonn, Böhm et al. (1975: 29–30) found densities of over 160 per hectare in substantial parts of the city including some inter-war suburban districts, with a peak density of 400 per hectare just outside the inner-city. High suburban population densities are attested in other cities such as Basel and Naples (Ettlin and Hafen 1978: 4; Bastano 1976). In relation to its population size, therefore, the Western European city is generally relatively compact.

The density of the occupation of individual dwellings, however, varies quite markedly with the differences being strongest between countries rather than between cities within any one country (see Fig. 2.2). It is clear that the occupancy densities in the cities of Southern Europe are higher than in more northerly cities – the averages for the cities of Portugal, Spain, Italy and Greece all exceed 3.0 persons per dwelling (in Spain the average exceeds 4.0): in Northern Europe, only the Netherlands produces densities at such a level. Italy and France both produce greater ranges of densities, suggesting an admixture of 'northern' and 'southern' cities within those countries. In Italy, for example, Milan, Turin, Bologna and Trieste all have less than three persons per dwelling whilst the southern cities of Naples, Palermo, Catania and Bari all have rates greater than 3.8.

It is noticeable from Fig. 2.2 that certain of the largest cities (often the capitals) have occupancy levels below those of smaller provincial cities. Such is the case in Vienna, Paris, Amsterdam, Oslo and Barcelona: each of these cities has the lowest density of occupation of its respective nation. The explanation for this lies in the inter-related phenomena of city-centre depopulation coupled with suburban growth beyond the city boundaries, accompanied by the ageing of city-centre residual populations. These phenomena have progressed much further in the largest cities. In Vienna the population diminished by 20 per cent between 1910 and 1961 but the number of private households rose by 45 per cent, the biggest increase being in one-person households which grew from being 6 per cent of all households to being 28 per cent: single people have stopped being lodgers and become householders in their own right such that the average household size fell from 4.4 persons in 1900 to 2.4 in 1961 (Gisser and Kaufmann 1972: 254). Because single-person households tend to be concentrated in inner-city areas, the numbers of persons per dwelling commonly rise from city-centre to periphery (Bellettini 1966: 15; Charles 1969: 223). And the trend of reducing average household size, noted in

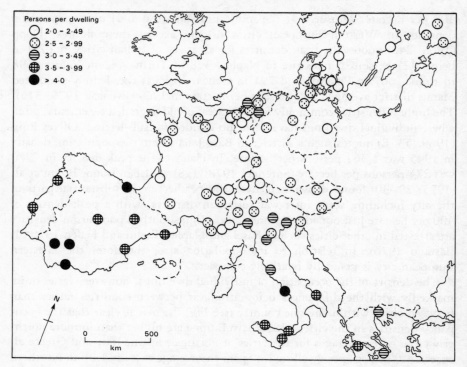

Fig. 2.2   Persons per dwelling, 1968–75.
(*Data sources*: see Appendix)

Vienna, is common throughout Europe, resulting from declining family sizes, increases in the potential for single-person household formation, and the general ageing of the population. Thus overcrowding as measured by persons per room, although still present to some extent everywhere, has similarly been reduced both through these changes in average household sizes and through decreases in the proportions of one- and two-roomed dwellings in post-war housing developments (Damais 1974: 284–5: Dandri 1978: 143; Talamo 1962: 206).

A SUMMARY OF HOUSING

The identification of housing classes and the delineation of broad trends of housing type and density throughout the cities of Western Europe should not obscure the fact that although these general patterns exist, when we turn to the level of individual city districts we shall find that housing is markedly differentiated, in all its possible variables, between quarters or zones of the city. It is, of course, this differentiation that forms a background to the demographic and social life of the city discussed in successive chapters. Chapter

7 contains a detailed consideration of the relationships between social status and housing variables in which it will be shown that few simple generalizations are, in fact, possible.

However, in summarizing the housing sector *per se*, without specific consideration of the occupants in detail, it is useful to return to the broad housing classes identified at the start of this chapter. Inner-city areas are the dominant location of the privately-rented housing stock, much of it dating back to the last century. As has been seen earlier, new building in this housing class has been retarded in many countries by rent control legislation which has also tended to militate against landlords spending on improvements. Hence it is in the privately-rented sector that the worst housing conditions often occur in the oldest property. In the industrial cities of Northern Europe, nineteenth-century rented property was build in inner-ring surburban areas to house the workers, and dwelling sizes have generally been small, almost always contained within either regular apartment blocks (the German tenements for example) or in more chaotic urban growth as in the industrial suburbs around Paris (see Ch. 8 and 9). On the other hand the privately-rented sector also constructed the prestigious apartment blocks of Vienna's Ringstrasse, the Haussmann *boulevards* in Paris, and the inner-city districts of many administrative and Southern European cities. Where, as in Madrid (Capote 1976) or Rome, these prestigious blocks remain in their original use, as upper-class residences, amenity standards are high and dwelling sizes are large. Rossi (1959: 48–9) in fact found that it was in just such inner-city areas that Rome's largest dwellings lay, with modern suburban housing, built on mass-production lines, being much smaller. However, contemporary developments in most cities are to some extent seeing the sub-division of large city-centre apartments for the use of low-status groups such as foreign migrants, and apartments which were in the vanguard of standards at the time of construction now often contain the poorest-quality housing (Killisch 1979: 85–9).

Owner-occupied property is a more suburban phenomenon and dominates significant areas of city peripheries except in cases, such as Switzerland, where owner-occupation scarcely exists and where privately-rented property of more recent vintage (in the absence of restrictive rent controls) fills the suburbs as well as the inner-city. The growth of owner-occupation in suburban areas in the inter-war period was often a case of self-help by the working class and the lower middle class via co-operative housing schemes and housing associations (Lichtenberger 1970: 54). More recent post-war developments have been inevitably rather more up-market, given the rather restrictive nature of mortgage financing in several European nations. It is, of course, important to note that government finance has, in many cases, been available to aid private developers or to provide financial support for purchasers. Owner-occupation does not solely exist in single-family dwellings: indeed, large numbers of owner-occupied properties are found in inner-city apartment blocks or even in surburban *grands ensembles* where public authority tenants have activated their right to purchase or have been effectively forced to do so. Nevertheless, overall owner-occupation levels throughout Western Europe are markedly lower than in Britain.

The suburban areas have increasingly been the scene of the growth of public-sector housing as rising land costs in the inner-city and the scale of housing schemes envisaged have forced public housing agencies to seek greenfield sites in peripheral areas for their operations. Public sector housing has consistently favoured the large apartment block, especially during the early post-war period when *grands ensembles* sprang up around most of Europe's major cities, and many of her smaller ones too. Although, as will be seen in Chapter 8, a limited number of high-cost public sector schemes sometimes accompany urban renewal projects, the inner-city has effectively been abandoned, in most cases to the private developer, sometimes with public support. Instead, the suburbs have been carved up into sectors of, in one area, publicly-rented apartments and, in others, privately-rented blocks or estates constructed for owner-occupation. In Lyon, for example, the eastern suburbs are the location of the low-rent public housing schemes, whilst to the west lie the dwellings for private rent or purchase (Bonneville 1974: 126). This development of spatial sectors matching housing classes has inevitable repercussions in the social geography of cities. Only in a few places, such as in Sweden and the Netherlands, have steps been taken by planning agencies to try to mix housing developments in peripheral areas in order to create a social diversity within neighbourhoods instead of the formation of homogeneous estates.

Finally, certain conclusions from within this chapter can be briefly restated. The first is that in continental Western Europe, owner-occupation is much less common than in Britain. The second is that, especially in Central and Northern Europe, government and governmental agencies have played a major role in housing provision in all housing classes, in many cases for periods of over seventy years. Thirdly, Western European city life is most commonly apartment life at high levels of residential density, yielding cities which are relatively compact in areal extent in comparison with cities of similar size in other parts of the developed world. Fourthly, there are certain clear spatial variations between countries, particularly between Northern and Southern Europe in terms of residential overcrowding, but levels of housing quality also vary between cities within individual countries. In total, Western European urban housing displays a rich cultural complexity which, as will be seen in successive chapters, both reflects and is reflected in wider spheres of urban social life and structure.

CHAPTER THREE

Demography

In Chapter 1 it was argued that in the pre-industrial period the demographic viability of most urban places in Western Europe was maintained only by continuous large-scale migration to the cities, since urban mortality was generally in excess of fertility. During the later nineteenth century, natural growth, in part fostered by changes in the age structure resultant upon massive rural–urban migration of young adults, became, for the first time, a truly significant feature in urban population growth (see Ch. 1, pp. 17–18). Nevertheless, in the twentieth century the key determinant of demographic change in the Western Europeon city has once more become migration and, of course, the social role of migration necessitates extended discussion of that topic in the three successive chapters. The present chapter is concerned with the other demographic elements – fertility, mortality and age and sex structures. First, however, it is necessary to examine the balance of importance between the natural and migration elements of population change.

COMPONENTS OF CHANGE

Many cities in Western Europe have, for varying periods of time, been undergoing population decline. By the later 1970s, amongst the largest cities generally only those in Southern Europe were experiencing population increase; cities such as Lisbon, Madrid, Barcelona, Bilbao, Athens, Salonica, Marseille, Toulouse, Rome and Palermo. In Northern Europe, population decline was the norm with exceptions occurring in certain smaller or middle-sized cities such as Tampere and Turku in Finland, Odense in Denmark, Bonn and Münster in West Germany, and Rennes, Le Havre, Strasbourg and Grenoble in France. It is, of course, important to stress that these are increases within city boundaries proper; if wider definitions of urban agglomerations are examined, growth is almost universal although even on such a wider definition Greater Copenhagen was losing population at the end of the decade. Throughout Western Europe the phenomena of city-centre depopulation and suburban growth are

Table 3.1   Components of population change – selected West German and Italian cities, 1978

| City | Country | Rates per thousand resident population | | |
		Net natural change	Net migration	Net total change
Rome	Italy	+3.2	+ 2.6	+ 5.8
Naples	Italy	+7.9	− 7.8	+ 0.1
Bonn	W. Germany	−3.0	+12.5	+ 9.5
Turin	Italy	+0.5	− 8.3	− 7.8
Frankfurt	W. Germany	−4.3	+ 3.2	− 1.1
Duisburg	W. Germany	−3.6	− 9.7	−13.3

Data sources: see Appendix

making their presence felt, even in the Mediterranean countries where overall city growth is still occurring.

Table 3.1 provides an example of each of the basic six types of population growth structure that can occur, limiting the examples to cities in West Germany and Italy. Growth by both natural and migration increase is relatively rare and, in these two countries, confined to the cities of Münster (West Germany), Rome, Palermo and Messina (Italy). Natural increase outweighing migration decline occurs, apart from in Naples, only in Bari. Migration gain outweighing natural loss is similarly rare, occurring only in Bonn and Wiesbaden. Frankfurt shares with West Berlin, Cologne and Florence the position of natural losses outweighing migration gains. But the commonest population structure is that exemplified by Duisburg which is shared by eighteen other major West German cities as well as six in Italy.

It can be suggested that the relationship between the components of change in the Western European city has passed through a variety of stages to give the present-day patterns: these can be represented as two models (see Fig. 3.1). Stage I in both models is the pre-industrial stage, already referred to, where population stability or growth is only assured by an excess of in-migration to balance the excess of mortality. Stage II is that of rapid population increase fuelled both by increased in-migration (or reduced return migration) and by natural growth. Selective in-migration of young adults would contribute to a higher crude birth rate and a reduction of the crude death rate, whilst mortality

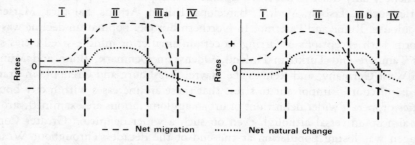

Fig. 3.1   Two models of urban demographic development.

anyway fell during the nineteenth century to create more favourable conditions for natural increase. It is possible to consider certain Southern European cities as still being in Stage II with high rates of rural–urban migration reinforcing high levels of natural population increase through the constant rejuvenation of the population.

This pattern of population increase, exemplified in Table 3.1 by Rome, can be broken in one of two ways. A reversal of natural growth preceding a decline in net migration (Stage IIIa) will produce a population structure of the types seen in Bonn and Frankfurt. The determining factor in such a scenario is likely to be a significant reduction in fertility levels such that, despite low mortality, the urban population cannot reproduce itself. Indeed, natural decline may create the conditions where a continuation of net in-migration is encouraged in order to maintain the urban labour-force. This interpretation could be applied to Vienna, where nineteenth-century natural population growth was reversed as early as 1914 (Holzmann 1971: 117), the birth rate in the 1930s being the lowest in Europe at 5.5. per thousand (Bobek and Lichtenberger 1966: 130). Vienna's demographic structure has been locked into Stage IIIa for over sixty years and remained, in the late 1970s, similar in type to that of Frankfurt.

The second way in which Stage II can be terminated is through a reversal of the migration pattern with natural change remaining relatively unaffected (hence Stage IIIb, Fig. 3.1). One way in which migration may cease to be a net provider of new population would be through the termination of economic growth in a city or the diversion of its traditional migrant streams to better opportunities elsewhere. The alternative, and certainly more common, scenario is of an increase of short-distance out-migration in the form of suburbanizing moves. The first of these possibilities may be suggested as an explanation for the population structures of Naples and Bari, whilst suburbanization is probably the explanation for Turin (Adamo 1969) and for similar structures in Northern European cities such as Helsinki, Aarhus and Gothenburg.

One distinct problem, of course, arises out of the customary position of urban administrative boundaries. The fact that cities themselves are losing population does not preclude population growth in their urban agglomerations once suburban municipalities or *communes* within the built-up limit are taken into account. In certain cities, such as Zürich or Amsterdam, the city boundaries have been partially adjusted from time to time to enclose newly urbanized areas but in other cities boundaries have become fossilized – Paris is a case in point where the city boundary is coincident with the line of the nineteenth-century fortifications. Probably the only Western European city where all built-up areas lie within the city boundary is Rome. Hence suburbanization is almost everywhere a force to be taken into account.

In Northern Europe, and increasingly in Southern Europe as well, fertility decline and suburbanization are occurring together and producing a fourth stage to the model in which urban depopulation is the overall tendency (Stage IV, Fig. 3.1). As Lowenthal and Comitas (1962) have pointed out, depopulation is normally brought about through selective migration and, as will be seen in later chapters, that is as true of Western European cities as in the general rural case. Selective out-migration from city-centres has been of those in the child-bearing stages of the life-cycle so that inner urban populations have seen increasing proportions of elderly residents whilst recently-arrived young migrants are single and contribute little to fertility. As suburbanization trends continue to develop, one might expect even more Western cities to progress into the fourth stage of the model.

Figure 3.2 is an illustration of the variations in natural and migration change rates in a single city – Zürich – over the period from 1912 to 1978. With the exception of the depression and war years, and certain post-war years of temporary slump, net migration increase outweighed net natural increase until the late 1950s. At that point the trend of suburban growth around the city, a trend that can be traced back several decades, took over and led to net migration loss. In-migration to the city remained at a high level, indeed higher throughout the 1960s than in all but two years of the 1950s, but it was out-migration that increased drastically, by 10,000 per year between the mid-points of the two decades. Zürich therefore entered Stage IIIb (Fig. 3.1) in 1961 and moved into Stage IV in 1969 as natural growth reversed. Amsterdam is another city with a similar recent population history (Gastelaars and Cortie

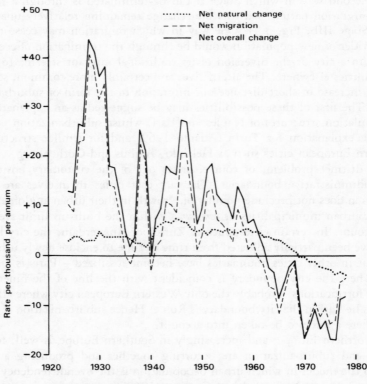

Fig. 3.2   Rates of population change, Zürich, 1924–78.
(*Data sources: Statistisches Jahrbücher der Stadt Zürich*, 1924–78)

Table 3.2   In-migration and fertility – selected cities

City	Country	Date	Rates per thousand resident population	
			In-migration	Births
Amsterdam	Netherlands	1978	42.3	9.8
Brussels	Belgium	1979	96.0	12.0
Copenhagen/				
Frederiksberg	Denmark	1978	76.0	9.3
Munich	W. Germany	1978	68.0	7.3
Oslo	Norway	1976	50.4	11.7
Stockholm	Sweden	1979	47.4	10.3
Turku	Finland	1975	44.7	14.9
Vienna	Austria	1978	67.8	8.5
Zürich	Switzerland	1978	86.1	7.6

Data sources: see Appendix

1973), as also is Stuttgart (Borris et al. 1977: 110). On the other hand, population evolution in the Belgian city of Liège has proceeded via fertility decline first, via Stage IIIa of the model (Sporck 1966: 43).

The case of Zürich (Fig. 3.2) along with the models already presented (Fig. 3.1) indicates that it is migration that is generally the dominant element in the population evolution of cities, certainly in creating new urban residents. This importance is, of course, reinforced when the social significance of migration is considered. Table 3.2 gives certain comparative data on in-migration rates and crude birth rates for cities of Northern and Central Europe in the later 1970s. In-migration rates vary from just over 40 per thousand per annum in Amsterdam to just under 100 per thousand in Brussels: in the later nineteenth century these rates would certainly have been much higher, as was definitely the case in Amsterdam for example (Anon. 1970: 43; see also Ch. 4). It is unfortunate that figures comparable to those in Table 3.2 do not exist for the cities of Southern Europe where fertility is almost certain to be at a higher level, although even here it is unlikely to exceed in-migration except in rare instances. Migration can therefore be accorded the prime role in urban demographic development in Western Europe.

So far the discussion in this chapter has been at the level of cities as a whole. Differences in the demographic components of change of course exist within cities between different sub-districts. City-centres are generally areas of depopulation through both net migration loss and net natural loss and this phenomenon, originally confined to Northern Europe, is becoming more common in the Mediterranean basin – during the 1970s parts of central Madrid, for example, started to witness natural decline for the first time (Ballesteros 1977). In general, therefore, the centres of cities have natural loss whilst suburban areas see natural increase. The centres often also have net migration loss, brought about by a high level of in-migration from outside the city more than compensated by losses via intra-urban migration and by moves to the suburban fringe. Suburban areas witness migration increase or stability coupled with natural increase. These demographic features of both city-centres and suburbs are both reflections of and causes of the age structures commonly found in such areas (see below, pp. 70–2).

FERTILITY

The topic of population fertility is not, today, of any major significance to the urban social geographer. Nevertheless, in the past the role of the city in general fertility decline has led to much discussion (Woods 1979: 136–52). Carlsson (1966) has examined the diffusionist argument, that urban centres were the innovators of controlled fertility for Sweden, but decided that although the fertility decline proceeded more quickly in Stockholm than elsewhere there was a similar starting date for the decline throughout Sweden so that diffusion was unlikely to be the main operative factor.

An alternative major role of urban areas may have been in creating cultural, social, religious and economic changes that lead to changes in prevailing attitudes towards marriage and childbearing. This prompts the question of whether migrants to the city from high fertility areas retain their high fertility for a significant period of time before being acculturated to prevailing urban norms. Ballesteros (1977: 430) has suggested, from a study of fertility in Madrid, that young rural in-migrants to the city do raise overall fertility levels but that because of their social and economic difficulties, such as access to satisfactory housing, the fertility of these migrants is quickly reduced to the general urban level. In the post-war period in Northern Europe the question of migrant fertility largely concerns foreign migrant populations, and the low average age-structures and high marital fertility of these groups have, in some cases, raised urban crude birth rates. In 1979, births to foreigners amounted to 45 per cent of all births in Geneva, 35 per cent in Basel, 33 per cent in Cologne and 29 per cent in Munich.

In the past, variations in urban fertility between towns have been largely explicable in terms of the occupational structures of the cities involved. Thus in late nineteenth-century Northern Germany, overall fertility (measured by Coale's indices) was highest in mining towns and non-textile manufacturing towns and lowest in administrative, retirement and university towns (Laux 1983). An important factor was probably the sex structure of the population, for in mining towns there were fewer females than males so that universal marriage for women was the norm: in administrative centres the proportions of women married were much lower because of the presence of large numbers of female domestic servants. Little work has been done on more recent periods so that the existence and causes of inter-urban fertility variations are generally a matter simply of speculation or of explanations couched in terms of known variations in the fertility associated with certain occupations at a national level.

Within cities, at the present day, crude birth rates may vary from district to district according to population age structures (Ballesteros 1977: 432) whilst more refined fertility indices may show relationships with local social or economic variables. Bellettini (1966), in a refined analysis of Bologna, found that general fertility rates were higher in areas of lower social class and in areas of high housing density but the levels of statistical explanation involved were low. When marital fertility alone was examined, the results were reversed with lower-class districts and high housing density producing lower fertility rates. Overall, Bellettini concluded that real differentials in fertility scarcely existed. This conclusion is in line with those emerging from national surveys in countries such as Sweden and France (Bernhardt 1972; Bastide et al. 1982: 873) that fertility does not, today, vary to any great extent according to such variables as occupation or household income. Urban fertility poses interesting problems to historical demographers but, apart from the fact that it generally remains below rural levels, it is today of little real significance in producing internal variations within the city.

MORTALITY

The same cannot be said about mortality where variations both in the past and at the present (although less now in scope) may be taken as important indicators of the conditions of urban life.

Within Western Europe the period of rapid urbanization and industrialization of the nineteenth century in many areas was marked by the perpetuation and even accentuation of differences in mortality between certain sub-sectors of the urban population at a time when national mortality levels were beginning to decline. A variety of factors can be called upon to explain these variations. Conditions of employment in certain trades were extremely poor and led to high occupational mortality. Low wage-levels and poverty resulted in poor dietary standards for sections of the urban working class. Residential over-crowding could lead to the rapid spread of contagious diseases whilst poor housing standards, particularly through dampness or darkness, encouraged ailments such as bronchitis and tuberculosis. Finally, conditions of water supply and sewage disposal played a major role in governing the spread of cholera and various intestinal infections. Woods (1978) has suggested that poverty reflected in poor housing standards was the most important cause of mortality variations in late nineteenth-century Birmingham, while Pyle and Rees (1971), looking at mortality in Chicago in more recent years, identified a distinction between causes of death (such as tuberculosis and infant mortality) that were related to poverty variables and others (such as certain infectious diseases) that were density-related and more directly linked to housing conditions. Figure 3.3 presents a model of the influences on morbidity and mortality. The three independent variables concern poverty, housing and sanitation, but there are likely to be, of course, intimate relationships between these. The well-off, for example, can afford less crowded accommodation at better levels of amenity provision. In the past (and to some extent still today

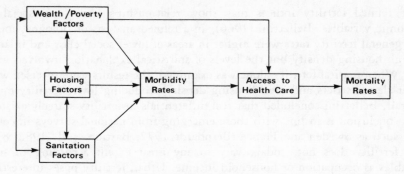

Fig. 3.3   Model of the influences on morbidity and mortality.

in some cases) family income was also a determinant of access to health care, such that for the poor, disease was more likely to result in death than was the case for the rich: case fatality rates for cholera in London in 1832 thus varied spatially from richer to poorer areas (Woods 1979: 90). From Figure 3.3 one might expect that through time the improvement in housing conditions and in public sanitation would produce a secular decline in the extent of spatial variations in mortality.

The existence of strong class differentials in urban mortality in the nineteenth century is attested by life expectation at birth figures for males for Barcelona during the period 1837–47 (Naylon 1981: 229–31). Strong socio-economic differences in mortality also existed in Paris (Chevalier 1973: 327–32), in Bordeaux (Guillaume 1972: 154) and in many other cities. Housing conditions arguably deteriorated in the most rapidly-growing cities, such as Paris, and this brought an increase in the importance of tuberculosis as a killer – the disease that above all others is related to housing standards (Chatelain 1969: 38–40; Evenson 1979: 210–1). Recent migrants to the city were particularly susceptible, given their concentration in areas of the poorest housing: for example, in Bordeaux in 1913 tuberculosis rates were twice as high among migrants as among the Bordeaux-born (Guillaume 1972: 154). According to McKeown's work in England (McKeown 1976), half the mortality decline there in the nineteenth century could be attributed to the reduction of tuberculosis: in contrast, in Northern France and other industrial areas of Northern Europe tuberculosis held its own or even increased in importance (Preston and Van de Walle 1978: 284). By the end of the century as other killers, notably infectious diseases, were in retreat in the face of improved sanitation and hygiene, tuberculosis stood out (Sutcliffe 1970: 104–9).

The importance of the reduction in tuberculosis deaths in the twentieth century is illustrated in Fig. 3.4 which deals with the case of Paris. Heart diseases and cancers have less environmental relationship, or even class relationship, than tuberculosis so that as these have become predominant as causes of death, spatial variations in mortality rates have weakened through time. Aubenque (1968) calculated mortality rates, standardized on the 1900–4 population age distribution, for the periods 1900–4, 1925–9, 1950–4 and

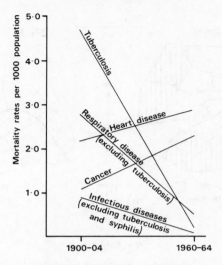

Fig. 3.4   Selected cause of death, Paris, 1900–4 and 1960–4.
(*Data source*: Aubenque 1968)

1960–4, thus controlling for the general ageing of the population over this period. When data for overall standardized mortality in the twenty *arrondisse-ments* of the city of Paris are examined, it can be calculated that the ratio of highest to lowest rates, which stood at 209 : 100 in 1900–4, had declined to 145 : 100 by the early 1960s, indicating a marked reduction in the spatial differentiation of mortality (Aubenque 1968: 102–3). Nevertheless, there was still a slight but noticeable tendency for the standardized mortality rates for 1960–4 to be lowest in the richer west of the city (Fig. 3.5), just as they were in 1900–4: indeed, for the twenty *arrondissements* the correlation between turn-of-the-century and early 1960s mortality is +0.55, significant at the 0.05 level, indicating general stability in the pattern.

These results in Paris are far from being unusual in their clarity. The decline in tuberculosis is recorded throughout Western Europe, even in Mediterranean countries where mortality has traditionally been controlled much more by intestinal infections. In Zaragoza in Spain, for example, tuberculosis fell from being the most important cause of death to being ninth in order between 1900 and 1960, being replaced by heart disease as the primary killer (Navarro Laguarta 1968: 41–2). The reduction in spatial variations in mortality is shown in Bologna where Bellettini, working on data from the early 1960s, found that when age-standardized mortality rates were calculated, apparent spatial differ-entials in crude death rates were eliminated, nor was there any significant relationship between standardized mortality rates and occupational or housing standard variables (Bellettini 1966: 35, 48). In Barcelona, Picheral (1969) found that tuberculosis was particularly important as a cause of death during the Spanish Civil War, but that its importance diminished sharply after 1950 when cancer overtook it as a killer, and by the mid-1960s even cirrhosis of the liver took more lives than tuberculosis. Nevertheless the reduction of tuber-

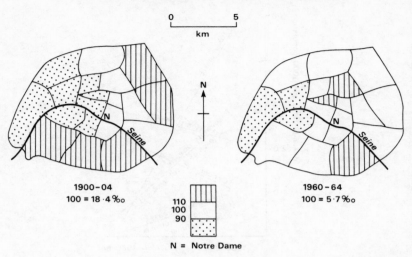

Fig. 3.5 Standarized mortality rates by *arrondissements* of Paris, 1900–4 and 1960–4. (*Data source*: Aubenque 1968)

culosis had been much slower in the oldest parts of the city-centre – densely-populated districts of poor housing and with a high proportion of recently-arrived in-migrants (Picheral 1969: 309–13).

A similar picture emerges in Dubesset's (1971) study of Lyon: there the highest incidence of tuberculosis morbidity is in the oldest quarters of the city-centre in areas characterized by overcrowded property, low wage-levels, high unemployment and high proportions of foreign immigrants. Whilst the French population of Lyon had a tuberculosis morbidity rate of 4.3 per ten thousand in 1968, that for foreigners was 24.9 (Dubesset 1971: 96–104). The link between tuberculosis, urban squalor and an immigrant population also exists in Marseille where the foreigner morbidity rate from the disease reached 32.4 per ten thousand in 1971 (Arnaud and Masini 1973: 9–11). An estimated 5–10 per cent of West African labour migrants in Paris suffer tuberculosis at some point during their stay (Bergues 1973: 72). Some of the links between poor housing and tuberculosis which were used as indicators of necessary slum-clearance areas in the inter-war years are thus still present (Evenson 1979: 212–16; Sutcliffe 1970: 240–1). It is, in fact, possible that post-war large-scale foreign immigration to many of Northern Europe's larger cities may have halted the reduction of spatial variations in mortality or even increased them once again. However, real evidence for this is hard to acquire since spatial variations in most causes of death, such as heart disease and cancer, are products of age-distributions rather than being 'real' spatial differentiations (Picheral 1969: 314–16): few studies have controlled for this by using standardized rates.

Whilst the overall reduction in tuberculosis deaths has been of great importance in reducing urban mortality rates, but with some spatial variations lingering on, so vestigial spatial differentiation may occur in the other type of mortality that has undergone a spectacular secular decline – infant mortality. Perinatal mortality (that between one day and one month after birth) is a reflection of congenital conditions in the newborn or of complications arising from childbirth, but mortality in the remaining eleven months of an infant's first year is more likely to be a reflection of exogenous factors such as poor housing conditions. Infant mortality rates do vary from district to district within cities. Herzog et al. (1977) found this to be the case in Rotterdam, although they found these variations resistant to the explanatory variables examined in their study. The link between high infant mortality and poor housing is shown in Roubaix (in the French northern coalfield) where in 1964, 25 per cent of the housing stock was still of the nineteenth-century courtyard type but these houses had 43 per cent of the city's infant mortality (Prouvost 1966: 52). In Vienna in 1976, infant mortality rates varied from 7 to 31 per thousand live births between the city's twenty-three administrative districts with the highest rates being found both in the old inner-city and in outer suburban areas, especially those of working-class populations built east of the Danube since the inter-war years. Infant mortality may thus be a reflection of both housing standards and social class, these 'independent' variables being, of course, closely connected.

The most detailed study of urban infant mortality is that by Federici (1964) on Rome, using data from the period 1958–61. Federici found the coefficient of variation, across fifty-one districts of the city, for mortality rates in the first month of life was 19.3 per cent, whilst for the remaining eleven months it was 38.9 per cent, indicating a much greater spatial variation. Federici noted the

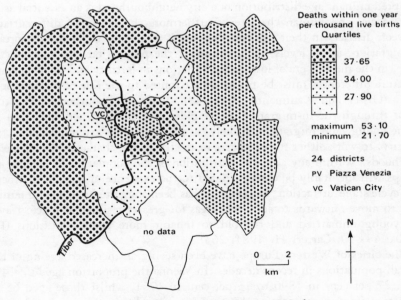

Fig. 3.6   Infant mortality in Rome, 1958–61.
(*Data source*: Federici 1964)

marked reduction in the overall infant mortality rate since the inter-war period but, grouping his data into twenty-four districts, demonstrated the existence of a spatial pattern in contemporary rates (Fig. 3.6). The highest rates were in the city-centre and in recent outer suburban areas, in both of which housing is, at least in sub-districts, poor. The inner area includes, amongst the generally well-to-do population (see Ch. 7, pp. 171–2), certain pockets of poor housing, whilst the outer suburbs are marked by the large apartment blocks of worker housing with low standards of amenities, including health care. Multiple-regression models, however, gave only a poor explanation of infant mortality rates, a conclusion similar to that arrived at by Bellettini (1966: 22–5) in Bologna. Variations in infant mortality therefore do exist in European cities but attempts at their explanation have been only partly successful.

However, it is necessary to underline the fact that present-day variations in mortality, although of some significance, and correlating with variables concerned with the urban environment or population composition, are now of much less importance than formerly. The institution of national standards of housing, of sanitation and of health care has gone far towards reducing earlier high levels of variation from district to district, the conquering of tuberculosis being particularly important in this respect. Nevertheless, mortality levels, because of their relationships with other social factors, remain of some interest in the urban social geography of Western Europe.

AGE-STRUCTURES

The predominant age distribution of a city neighbourhood is an essential aspect of its social and human character. Furthermore the extent of differentiation between districts in their age distributions is an indication of the importance of migration, at all levels, in determining the population structure of cities since, in the modern era of low spatial variations in fertility and mortality, age-structure differences must be primarily attributed to the role of migrant selectivity (Gisser and Kaufmann 1972: 248). 'Old' neighbourhoods may come about through the in-migration of the elderly or through net migration loss of the young, and migration is likely, as in other socio-geographic aspects of the city, to work either to perpetuate or to change the character of such neighbourhoods. Within any city the distribution of the population in specific age-groups will inevitably be closely related to the existence of areas of distinctive 'life-cycle stage' attraction. In general it has been suggested that young families tend to move outwards to suburban areas for greater residential space, leaving the young unmarried and the old to inhabit more central locations (Pahl 1970a: 48–50; Carter, H. 1981: 263).

The cities of Western Europe have been seeing an increased ageing of their overall populations in recent decades. In Vienna the proportion aged 0–14 fell from 27 per cent in 1890 to 13 per cent in 1961, whilst those aged 65 and over rose from 4 per cent to 17 per cent over the same period (Gisser and Kaufmann 1972: 247). In Bordeaux the proportion aged 65 and over rose

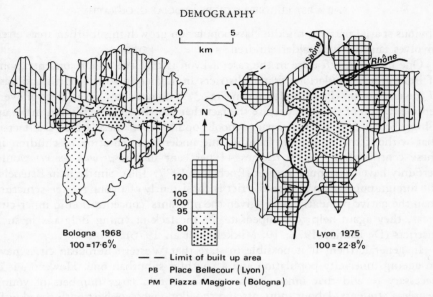

Fig. 3.7 Proportions of resident population aged 0–14 years, Bologna, 1968 and Lyon, 1975.
(*Data sources*: Bellettini 1969; Rochefort 1977)

from 13 per cent to 19 per cent simply between 1954 and 1975 (Pailhé 1978: 13). But it is at the intra-urban level that population ageing is most interesting, since the variations in this phenomenon from one area to another are generally profound.

Figure 3.7 present two examples of the spatial variations of an age-distribution component – that of children aged 0–14 years. The Bolognese pattern is a relatively simple one. The old densely-packed city-centre has a low proportion of young people – only 78 per cent of their normal representation for the city as a whole. Lower-than-average proportions of children are also observable in the older extensions of the city to the west, north and east. Surrounding these in a virtually complete semi-circle are districts with high proportions of children, these being areas affected by post-war housing developments. To the south of the city-centre are the steeply-rising foothills of the Appenines where suburban expansion has been slow and limited to middle-class villas. In total, therefore, Bologna presents a relatively simple picture of contrast between the old urban core and the newer peripheral districts, the former having few, and the latter many, children in the resident population.

The spatial pattern of the representation of children in Lyon (Fig. 3.7) is a little more complex but similar overall conclusions can be drawn. Once again the city-centre has a low proportion of children, but the distribution is more complex towards the periphery such that it is not possible to recognize a true suburban ring of over-representation of the young in the way that it was in Bologna. Certainly the effects of recent housing development in certain *communes* to the east and south are noticeable but to the west and north, where there has in fact been less, and more middle-class, growth there is less of an obvious spatial pattern; middle-class population growth in suburban areas often involves families with older children.

One interesting feature in the case of Lyon is that the major concentrations of immigrant populations in the districts immediately to the north and east of the city-centre (Place Bellecour on Fig. 3.7) do not show up as areas of over-representation of children despite the fact that North African children make up a high proportion of the primary-school population in these areas. The fact is that without the immigrant families the under-representation of children in these central areas (which reaches 41 per cent in one *arrondissement*) would certainly have been much greater (Rochefort 1977: 330). Similarly in Brussels, the foreign population in each district is consistently of a younger age-structure than the native population and, given the migrants' concentration in inner-city areas, they again help to compensate for the lack of young Belgians in such districts (De Lannoy 1978: 19; Mikkelsen et al. 1976).

In general, then, it is possible to state that Western European cities have an ageing inner-city population and a youthful suburban one. However, it is necessary to add that inner-city areas also contain large numbers of young people – students, labour migrants and the like – who co-exist with the elderly population but who are unmarried and therefore do not contribute to fertility or to the proportions of city-centre children. The extent to which the old may live in proximity to the young adults is indicated in those studies that have calculated indices of dissimilarity for the distributions of age-groups. For example, in the Austrian city of Linz in 1971, Kaufmann et al. (1978: 31) ascertained that the degree of separation between those of 60 and over and those aged 15–29 was less than between the old and those in the family-rearing life-cycle stages, aged 0–14 and 30–44. A very similar conclusion was arrived at in Bonn in a study using a complex classification involving age and household size: the old were most spatially separated from large households and least from one-person households aged 16–30 (Böhm et al. 1975: 110–11).

What is occurring in these and other cities is that the city-centre has become the location of a stable group of old indigenous city residents, declining slowly in number as they die off but increasing in proportionate importance as de-population occurs, coupled with a transitory or floating population composed largely of recently-arrived immigrants of one sort or another. This phenomenon has been shown in cities such as Barcelona, Madrid, Amsterdam and Brussels (Olives Puig 1969: 65; Abellan Garcia 1976: 310; Van Hulten 1968; De Lannoy 1978: 24): it doubtless occurs to some extent in at least some inner-city districts in almost all cities. The existence of large numbers of students in inner-city districts is common, given the general lack of halls of residence in European universities, the obvious link between students and old people being that both inhabit older, cheap, small apartments whilst family-rearing groups desire more modern accommodation (Laquerbe 1967; Charles 1969). The result may be that central city districts are more heterogeneous in both their demographic and their social composition than peripheral districts where family-rearing groups are heavily over-represented and where social composition is a direct reflection of housing variables, thus yielding relative homogeneity (Laquerbe 1967).

Large-scale peripheral housing construction in the post-war period around almost all cities has been concerned with solving the immediate shortage of low-cost accommodation for the lower-income population (see Ch. 2). Much of this new housing stock has been publicly-financed or subsidized and the allocation of new residents has been almost universally in favour of young and growing families. Thus in a new peripheral housing development outside Dijon in France in 1971, 43 per cent of the population was less than 20 years of age and only 1 per cent was over 65 (Doré 1972: 206): household sizes inevitably tended to be relatively large. These figures are similar to those that Clerc obtained from his massive survey of France's *grands ensembles* as a whole: he found (Clerc 1967: 120–44) that 42 per cent of their populations were aged 0–14 with 1 per cent aged 65 or more. Family-rearing households (married couples with children and no other household members) formed 71 per cent of all households. In Brussels the areas with the highest concentrations of children are those of most recent state-funded housing, and these areas similarly have the greatest numbers of large households (De Lannoy 1978: 22, 36). Even where state-financed housing has been less generally available, as for example in Madrid, peripheral areas have over-representations of children (Abellan Garcia 1976: 311), and thus relatively large households.

Such a situation, of young families in the periphery and both young adults and older households at the centre, coupled with the spatial distribution of housing variables described in the conclusion to Chapter 2 (pp. 54–6) results, not surprisingly, in correlations between age-structure, household size and certain housing variables. Everywhere the age of a public-sector apartment block is reflected in the age-structure of the families occupying it – new blocks with small children, older with teenagers or with more mixed ages as those moving beyond the family-rearing stages apply to be rehoused elsewhere, often nearer the city-centre given the peripheral nature of these housing developments (Putz and Prié 1975: 60). In general, the public housing sector contains a relatively young population, the owner-occupying sector a more representative cross-section of the city's age-structure whilst privately-rented property, generally being more central in location, displays some imbalances with some over-representation of the old. Housing age is an obvious control: in Vienna in 1961, 47 per cent of those living in areas built before 1919 were over 50, but only 25 per cent of those in areas built after the Second World War were in that age-group (Gisser and Kaufmann 1972: 248–50).

Privately-renting households tend, with notable exceptions amongst immigrant workers and other sub-groups, to be small, reflecting their age-structures, whilst households in publicly-rented property are large. As families have quit the inner-city, the increase in the number and importance of single-person households there has been rapid, largely due to the establishment of one-person female households occupied by an elderly spinster or widow (Van Hulten 1968: 100). The result is that falling household sizes, depopulation and the ageing of inner-city populations are closely connected. The only major exceptions to these comments on falling city-centre household sizes occur in Southern European cities where inner-city high-status neighbourhoods retain households with large numbers of domestic servants – in Madrid in the early 1970s, for example, cases of four or five servants to a family were not exceptional within the highest-status zones (Capote 1976: 340–1).

In general, then, the age distributions of the Western European city are relatively straightforward and can be summed up best in terms of the life-cycle with the age-groups associated with family-building over-represented towards the periphery whilst those life-cycle stages more commonly involving only one or two persons per household (young adults and the old) are more over-represented towards the city centre.

THE DISTRIBUTION OF THE SEXES

Historically there have often been imbalances between the numbers of males and females in Western European cities, brought about by differential employment possibilities and by selective migration rather than by demographic factors *per se*. This can be most clearly seen in the industrializing cities of Northern Europe during the later nineteenth century. In 1890 the number of men per 100 women was 112 in Bochum and Duisburg, 111 in Dortmund and 108 in Essen but less than 100 in many of the older administrative towns of Northern Germany such as Cologne and Düsseldorf. The female majority was greatest in the textile centres such as Elberfeld (now part of Wuppertal) where the ratio was 93 men per 100 women (Jackson 1982: 238–46; Niethammer and Bruggemeier 1978: 139). The existence of these imbalances between the sexes has been adduced earlier in this chapter (p. 62) as one explanation of overall fertility differentials between cities.

The varying employment possibilities that created sex imbalances in the past do still exist in various forms. Most notable for much of the post-war period until the 1970s was the male domination of international labour migrant flows to Northern European cities (see Ch. 5, p. 112). In Southern Europe, sex imbalances resulting from occupational structures still occur through the existence of large numbers of domestic servants in the privileged districts of some cities (Abellan Garcia 1976: 314–16; Capote 1976: 336–40). This was, of course, also the pattern in several Northern European cities of the past – differential female in-migration was generally brought about by opportunities for living-in servants and these jobs were almost exclusively the preserve of migrants, rarely of the locally-born (Niethammer and Bruggemeier 1978: 134).

In the contemporary situation, however, sex differentials at the level of the city as a whole in comparison with the rest of the country, or at the level of sub-districts within the city, can also be a function of the ageing of the population. In this respect the general experience is that peripheral city districts, dominated by family-rearing households, have demographic equality of the sexes (Abellan Garcia 1976: 316; Doré 1972: 206; Kaufmann et al. 1978: 21–3). Because of the ageing of urban populations, cities overall tend to have female predominance and this is most marked in the city-centres where over-representation of old people is also found.

In Brussels, for example, areas of female dominance are largely reflective of the map of areas of high proportions of the population over 65 (De Lannoy 1978: 38). The same is true in Vienna, but here the overall urban sex ratio is so skewed (in 1961, 77 men per 100 women) that female dominance occurs not just in the centre and not just in the old but in the inner suburbs and in the working age-groups as well (Gisser and Kaufmann 1972).

This example of Vienna demonstrates once again the importance of migration in generating and conditioning demographic structures. The sex imbalance typical of Vienna is a product of a net excess of females in the migration flows to the city. Throughout the cities of Western Europe the endogenous demographic variables of fertility and mortality have had some significance in producing urban growth, in affecting spatial variation within the city and in determining age-structures. But far more important, both for urban populations overall and for spatial differentiation within the city, have been the features of migration which have both demographic and social significance. It is those features that will be examined in the next three chapters.

73

CHAPTER FOUR

Domestic Migration and the City

In Chapter 3 it was repeatedly indicated that the demographic development of the Western European city generally owes much more to migration, of various sorts, than to the endogenous demographic processes of fertility, nuptiality and mortality. But the role of migration is much wider than its demographic effect: also of vital significance is the fact that migration always involves a selection process of the possible individuals involved (White and Woods 1980) and that in consequence migration never involves random cross-sections of the affected populations, whether at places of origin or of destination. Hence migrants may be distinguished from non-migrants in terms of demographic variables and also in terms of occupation, language, ethnicity, income level, religion and many other social and economic elements. Migration has been, and still is, of primary importance, not just in determining the overall population and social characteristics of cities, but also in conditioning the existence of distinctive sub-areas of the urban structure. In analysing these effects a distinction can be made between migration external to the city (movement to and from the urban area as a whole) and internal, or intra-urban, movements. In this and the next chapter a division will also be made between domestic and international migration although, as will be demonstrated, these are really part of one overall pattern of the structural evolution of the economies of Western Europe over the last two centuries.

STRUCTURAL DETERMINANTS AND CORRELATES OF MIGRATION

In Chapters 1 and 3 it has been argued that city-ward migration was essential in pre-industrial Western Europe to maintain demographic stability. Such migration was commonly over relatively short distances and was stabilizing in nature rather than producing radical urban growth or change – it was part of what might be described as a negative feedback system linking urban and rural areas, in which homeostasis or stability was the long-term norm. The localization of migrant origins can be seen in data produced by Soubeyroux

(1978: 119–21) for the origins of beggars arrested in Madrid in 1805. Despite the size and importance of Madrid it drew migrants from by no means all of the Spanish territory: indeed, 71 per cent of the migrant beggars came from Old and New Castile, immediately surrounding Madrid. The contributions from Aragon, Catalonia, Andalusia and Navarre – all populous parts of the kingdom – were each less than 1 per cent.

It was in the nineteenth century that migration to Western European cities took on a transformational character leading to rapid urban growth and social evolution in the manner outlined in Chapter 1 (pp. 17–20). Industrial and economic growth required large-scale inputs of labour which could not be provided by local urban sources. In the early years of urban economic growth, the demand for labour could to a large extent be met by migration from proximate rural areas where labour tended to be abundant as a result of high rates of natural population increase, and also through the displacement of traditional small-scale industries because of competition from goods manufactured in urban factories (White and Woods 1983). The commercialization of agriculture, accompanying the development of modern capitalism, also eroded traditional farming systems, replacing labour by capital and creating greater potential for rural-urban movement.

Johnston (1980a: 156–7) has argued that under the capitalist system of urban industrial development it was essential for the controllers of social and political power that the numbers of the urban working class should continue to increase rapidly so that these workers were always in a state of competition with each other and thus never able to produce the solidarity needed to press for higher wages or better social conditions. This argument can be developed to show how the continued arrival of migrants to occupy the lowest social and economic positions in urban societies permitted more established residents to enhance, consolidate or perpetuate their status at higher levels in the hierarchy, this being manifested in the poorer housing conditions of recent migrants and in their segregation from established citizens.

Large-scale labour migration in young industrializing societies throughout Western Europe (whether in Northern Europe in the nineteenth century or in Southern Europe more recently) involved the free-market transfer of rural populations to urban locations, initially over relatively short distances but later, as demand increased and local supply was diminished, from further afield as well. The dominance of short-distance moves applies whether we are examining nineteenth-century growth in Northern Europe, for example in Sheffield (Cromar 1980), or looking at urban industrial growth in Italy since the Second World War, such as in Bologna (Bellettini 1958: 531).

Urban development and early industrialization have national effects as well as local implications. It is largely through the social, political and attitudinal changes thus provoked that the integration of once disparate regions into a mass-consumer national social-economic system comes about. Urban industry, with its investment in large-scale production systems, requires a national (or wider) market and has the ability, both through competitiveness and through the political power wielded by the industrialist class, to ensure that such a market is indeed created. Within an individual country, therefore, the period of early urban industrialization is accompanied by the penetration of even the most peripheral regions by facets of the new economic order, leading towards greater inter-regional cohesiveness in a hierarchical situation headed by the industrial cities themselves. Alongside this economic integration goes a pattern of social change in which rural–urban migration itself acts as a catalyst, temporary migrants to the city being very important sources of information flow, stimulating rural awareness of alternative life-styles and of opportunities elsewhere (Corbin 1971). Thus the economic, political and social developments which accompany early industrialization tend to bring together the various pre-existing regional socio-economic systems and create an increasing degree of national cohesion and integration, a process that has been eloquently described for rural France by Weber (1977).

Before these homogenizing processes have worked themselves through, however, the early years of mass rural migration to newly-industrializing cities may bring in migrants who form a distinctive and separate group, recognizable perhaps through their dialect, their clothing, their eating habits or their attitudes which are those of their regions of origin. We might therefore expect to find great migrant distinctiveness in nineteenth-century Northern European cities or in Southern European cities of the present day where migrants originate from regions which retain a certain degree of cultural and social variation from the migrants' urban destinations.

It is, however, likely that the distinctiveness of these domestic migrant flows will be reduced through time as a result of the homogenizing processes described above. The present-day newly-arriving domestic migrant in Paris, wherever he originates from in France, is much more likely to conform to certain national norms of attitude and behaviour before migrating than did his forebears of 150 years ago who were socialized to new norms only after arriving in the city. Where this socio-economic modernization and homogenization process has not proceeded so far, or where regional cultures have been particularly resistant to assimilation and integration, domestic migrants from certain origins may remain a distinctive and significant sector of the urban population, for example in the cities of Eastern Spain or of Northern Italy.

A factor of equal importance in the post-war world has been the drying up of domestic rural sources of migrants. This is, of course, an extension of a process that has operated since the inception of urban industrial growth whereby the migration field for any particular city has constantly been widened to take in new areas for the supply of labour migrants to low-status jobs, in part as the spread of social modernization leads to fertility reductions in proximate areas and to an erosion of local labour reservoirs by creating conditions of full employment. Once this happens, domestic migrants arriving in the cities cease to be dominantly entering the lowest urban occupation levels and instead come from similar urban backgrounds, arriving with skills and aspirations that preclude menial employment.

The continuing need for proletarian in-migration, enhanced by the move towards a post-industrial society with its perceived range of undesirable jobs

(Böhning 1972), is now filled by the spreading of the migration net further afield to take in growing numbers of international migrants. The post-war period in Western Europe has seen this pattern, of international migrants in place of domestic migrants, operating on a large scale, dominantly in Northern and Central Europe but with some signs of international migration into Southern European cities in the 1970s. The international migrants in Northern Europe, whether from the Mediterranean Basin (Portugal, Spain, Italy, Yugoslavia, Greece, Turkey, the Maghreb – Tunisia, Algeria and Morocco), or from the ex-colonies of the European powers, are even more distinctive from their host societies – culturally, socially, behaviourally and ethnically – than was the case for domestic migrants in early industrializing societies. In addition, these new international migrants are open to governmental and official control (White and Woods 1983) in a way that was never applicable to domestic migrants on any scale: certainly Mussolini imposed restrictions (easily circumvented) on internal migration in Italy (Gabert 1958), and there have been occasional threats of governmental controls on Greek domestic migration to Athens (Carter, F. W. 1968: 100), but these have been the exceptions. It is because international migrants in the post-war period have been subject to controls and specific government policies that they are dealt with separately in Chapter 5.

Nevertheless it must be borne in mind that in structural terms international labour migration differs from domestic migration chiefly in timing, domestic migration becoming international migration once domestic sources of supply start to dry up. Both types of migrant fulfil similar roles on arriving in the city, at least during the phase of mass migration, fuelling the growth of the working-class urban population (Johnston 1980a: 156–8; White and Woods 1983).

In the light of this discussion of the overall system of migration to cities, the remainder of this chapter will consider the role of domestic migration in various situations. Firstly, attention will be paid to the domestic migrant in the Northern European city of the nineteenth century, concentrating on the example of Paris. Secondly, domestic migration to the industrializing city of Southern Europe in the post-war period will be considered, concentrating on Turin and Barcelona. Thirdly, it will be instructive to look at certain cities where, even in countries of reduced rural–urban domestic migration and large-scale international flows, local migration may still have some significance because of strongly-marked regional differences, Brussels being the obvious major example here.

MASS DOMESTIC MIGRATION IN NORTHERN EUROPE

Of all the cities of Northern Europe, that in which the role of domestic migrants in the nineteenth century has been most closely studied is Paris, notable being Chevalier's (1950) analysis of the formation of the Parisian population during that period.

The population of Paris proper (the area of the present-day twenty *arrondissements*) rose from 550,000 in 1801 to 2.9 million in 1921 in which year this growth ceased. During the later years of the period the city was experiencing a net migration gain of 10,000 per annum, the vast majority of whom came from other parts of France (Clerc 1964: 8–15). Chevalier has calculated that in the period 1837–46, 79.9 per cent of Parisian population growth was the direct result of the positive migration balance and that in the last years of the century 90 per cent of growth came from this source (Chevalier 1950: 49–52). It is also important to remember that because the in-migrants were dominantly young they tended to increase Parisian fertility rates whilst at the same time depressing mortality levels.

A major feature of migration in France in the early years of the nineteenth century was its temporary character for many of the participants. These were seasonal rural migrants who left the countryside for Paris in the spring, returning in October or November. In Paris they took a variety of occupations such as chimney-sweeps, cobblers, water-carriers and knife-grinders, but the most important group were employed in construction and public works – Chatelain (1970: 4) has estimated at 40,000 the number of seasonal migrants thus employed in Paris in 1840, dominantly from the eastern and western flanks of the Massif Central and from Lower Normandy to the west of Paris, all highly rural areas. By 1880, 40,000 seasonal migrants were moving from the single *département* of Creuse, one of the poorest in the Massif Central (Corbin 1971: 295). Within Paris such people lived frugally, often with fellow-migrants. Their objective was not initially to settle in Paris but to save as much money as possible to take back to their native villages: the migrants were thus not well integrated in Paris and remained a distinctive and cohesive group both occupationally and because of their regional loyalties (Corbin 1971: 312, 328). As seasonal building-workers they occupied a very low place in the urban social hierarchy.

Thus in the early nineteenth century, migration to Paris was, for a significant proportion, a seasonal or temporary activity, although inevitably some stayed on each winter to add to those who had intendedly made permanent moves to the city (De Bertier de Sauvigny 1977: 157). From the middle of the century, however, temporary migration began to diminish. By 1856, one in five Creusois were not returning to their villages at the end of the building season (Pinkney 1953: 4) and workers started taking their families with them. Temporary migration had paved the way for permanent migration by màking urban opportunities better known in rural areas, by introducing and strengthening the money economy, by encouraging an interest in education and in the use of French instead of *patois*, and by changing attitudes about the sanctity of the peasant holding (Corbin 1971). Chatelain (1970) has argued that in early nineteenth-century France temporary migration was essential to produce the awareness of national opportunities; only then could large-scale permanent migration occur. Resident in-migrants in Paris in the nineteenth century were therefore dominantly from rural backgrounds, often from areas with a history of temporary migration, with the normal pattern of distance decay in the migration field somewhat overlain by large contributions from distant *départements* (such as those of the Massif Central) that had taken part in these seasonal flows (Chatelain 1971: 30–4).

In terms of the distribution of migrants within Paris, Chevalier (1950) regarded immigrant segregation to be a function of occupation rather than origin, although others (Chatelain 1969: 35–6) have pointed out distinct regional groups in certain districts. Although in-migration was brought about by general economic development, migrants were concentrated in the construction industry and in a range of domestic and personal services. Consequently, map analysis of the 1872 census results shows a closer relationship between immigrant distributions and employment in domestic service or commerce than between immigrants and industrial workers (Chevalier 1950: 81–6). Nevertheless there was a notable tendency for migrants from certain French regions to enter specific occupations: in 1901, building workers were dominantly from Limousin on the northern flanks of the Massif Central, hotel and restaurant employees came from the *départements* of the southern edge of the Paris Basin, whilst metal-workers came especially from areas immediately around and to the north of the city (Chevalier 1950: 176–7). Because such occupations were themselves often localized within Paris, the migrants became concentrated in specific areas. Since relatively few migrants went into industrial employment, the industial areas of Paris were least infiltrated by provincials and these north-eastern city districts remained the most quintessentially Parisian in terms of their population origins (Cobb 1980a). Elsewhere migrant districts were easily identifiable, for example Bretons in the west of Paris where, being employed in domestic service, they lived in close proximity to upper-class Parisians. Mols (1968: 238) has indicated that similar features emerged in Brussels at the same period where the most industrial areas of the city had the same degree of under-representation of in-migrants.

Using data from 1911 for Paris as a whole, Ogden and Winchester (1975) have discovered a considerable extent of residential segregation in relation to migrant birthplaces. In particular, they concluded that the bigger the in-migrant group in Paris the less segregated it was likely to be, this presumably being the result of a process of secondary redistribution of the migrant population within Paris after the arrival of the initial migration streams which would have been strongly localized in destination as a result of the operation of chain-migration processes.

The most striking aspect of Ogden and Winchester's work is their use of principal components analysis to group migrant origins within France and destinations within Paris. The first three components extracted explained 64 per cent of the variance of the total data set. Mapping of the component loadings by French *départements* and of scores by Parisian *arrondissements* produced the interesting patterns of Fig. 4.1. The first component grouped together migrants from most of Western France along with those from certain areas in the Rhône corridor and Provence. The scores for this group show a distinct set of destinations in the western *arrondissements* of Paris – the upper-class area drawing in large numbers of domestic servants. The second component draws

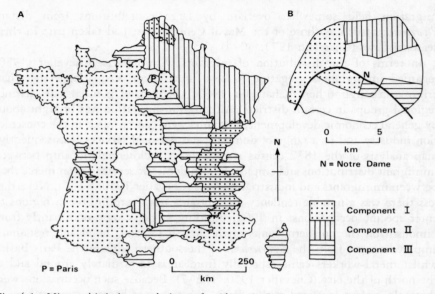

Fig. 4.1 Migrant birthplaces and places of residence in Paris, 1911. A: Component loadings for French *départements*, > + 0.5. B: Component scores for Parisian *arrondissements*, > + 0.75. (*Source*: redrawn from Ogden and Winchester 1975)

together migrants from the north and east who are localized within Paris in the more industrial areas of the north of the city, whilst the third component links migrants from much of the South of France with those from the Rhône–Saône–Seine axis and produces the highest component score in Paris for the *arrondissement* of the south-east containing the Gare de Lyon at which most of the migrants almost certainly arrived. Thus there is a marked similarity between the regional origins of migrants to Paris and their spatial distribution within the city, the role of railway termini being of obvious importance.

Few other nineteenth-century cities could possibly have produced such clear relationships between migrant origins and destinations, if only because all migrants arrived at the city at one station. A similar phenomenon has, however, been identified in Berlin where the Kreuzberg district was traditionally the residence of large numbers of migrants from areas to the east of the city, arriving at the Görlitzer Bahnhof within the district (Kouvelis 1979: 113). The station of arrival also seems to have had some importance in Brussels (Verniers 1958: 372–3). Elsewhere the segregation of migrants was much more likely to be the result of their occupations than of their origins.

Everywhere, however, the migrants tended to be found in the poorest accommodation. Building rarely kept pace with population growth and the increasingly overcrowded conditions worked to the greatest detriment of the newcomers (Chevalier 1973: 186–8, 199). Conditions were similar throughout Northern Europe, lodging houses and sub-tenancies being very common (Chevalier 1973: 228; Liang 1970: 106–7). Even in the last years of the nineteenth century it was common for urban housing markets to have to cater for large numbers of temporary migrants in the purely industrial cities, such as in the Ruhr, where the succession of boom and slump conditions led to high rates of migrant population turnover with recently-arrived migrants, the first to be thrown out of work in times of slump, setting off once more to look for opportunities elsewhere. Gross annual migration rates could be extremely high – around 45 per cent per annum moving in Duisburg in the Ruhr in the decade 1900– 10, excluding intra-urban movers (Jackson 1982: 248; Crew 1979). The migrant here was indeed part of an 'industrial reserve army', brought in during times of rapid economic growth and labour shortage, absorbed into the city with as little cost as possible, and laid off and sent away during recession (White and Woods 1983). Already by the end of the nineteenth century, however, the Ruhr was needing more distant, sometimes international, migrants, and the pattern was developing of local migrants concentrated in the more stable, skilled trades, whilst the distant migrants took jobs in the unskilled sectors or in unhealthy occupations and became the true proletarians (Crew 1979: 69). Building work was universally a migrant occupation: in Bordeaux around 95 per cent of employment in this sector was of migrants throughout the century, whilst female migrants were similarly dominant in domestic service (Guillaume 1972: 68–9). Similar phenomena occurred in Milan, one of Italy's few early industrial cities, where the usual overcrowding and sub-letting of migrants' accommodation are also recorded (Lyttleton 1979: 255).

The largest cities, such as Paris, Berlin or those of the Ruhr, drew their migrants from the whole of national territories. Paris was, perhaps, a little extreme because of its overwhelming dominance in a country with a poorly-articulated urban hierarchy, which meant that a higher proportion of the city's in-migrants were of rural origin than was the case in other large cities where some in-migrants came, if not originally from urban areas, at least via such environments. Smaller provincial cities tended to have more limited migration fields. Bordeaux's migrants, for example, came predominantly from south-west France with women coming from a more restricted area than men (Guillaume 1972: 56). Lyon's in-migrant population in 1891 was overwhelmingly drawn from Eastern France and, above all, from the Alps, whilst in Marseille the migrants came from a more limited coastal belt (Chatelain 1971: 35). In smaller cities, therefore, migrants were probably culturally more similar to their host populations, although with their rural origins singling them out as a separate group within the urban social and economic hierarchies. Thus it is possible to accept the nineteenth-century evidence from Northern Europe as being in accord with the general model of migration outlined at the start of this chapter: migration was rural-to-urban and fed labour into the lower end of the occupational hierarchy. Migrants were in several ways distinguished from the existing urban populations, not least through the positions of relative disadvantage that they suffered within the housing market.

It was in the inter-war years that these features of domestic migration began to weaken in Northern Europe. In some countries the early years of the twentieth century had already witnessed the institution of international migration streams as the release of rural labour in local areas became insufficient to keep pace with urban industrial demands for workers. The migration history of Northern European cities in the twentieth century has been of a steady reduction in the significance of the domestic migrant fed into low-skilled employment, and the increase in international migration for this purpose. It is a transformation that is immaculately recorded in the Maigret novels by Georges Simenon: in the early stories of the 1930s and 1940s the domestic servants of the wealthy Paris quarters are girls from Brittany or the Vendée, but in stories written in the late 1950s and early 1960s they are Spanish immigrant girls.

POST-WAR DOMESTIC MIGRATION IN SOUTHERN EUROPEAN CITIES

Large-scale industrial growth in Southern Europe is generally a post-war phenomenon. The years of the Italian 'miracle', although based on earlier foundations, were those of the 1950s: the same period saw the acceleration of growth in Spain, although the antecedents of industrial development in Bilbao and Barcelona date back to the last century. In Portugal and Greece it is perhaps inaccurate to talk of major industrial growth, but metropolitan urban expansion in Lisbon and Athens has been a significant post-war phenomenon.

The labour demand created in the expanding cities has been capable of drawing domestic in-migrants from well beyond local hinterlands and, given the existence of marked regional social and cultural differentiation, especially in Spain and Italy, the migrants have often been contrasted from their host populations in a manner that is more extreme than occurred even in nineteenth-century Paris. It is instructive to look at the resultant patterns of migration within two well-documented cases – Turin in the early 1960s after ten years of boom, and Barcelona in the mid-1970s.

In Turin the dominant interest lies in the role of Southern Italian migrants, especially during the 1950s when the first major migrant irruption occurred. The period from 1951 to 1960 saw the arrival in the city of an estimated 411,000 migrants (Fofi 1970) of whom Piedmontese from the local area around Turin certainly constituted the biggest single group by origin, but with southerners growing most rapidly in group size. If annual migrant numbers by region of origin are indexed at 100 in 1951, by 1960 the index for those from the north of Italy had risen to 216, from the centre to 261 and from the south to 818. In 1961, southern migrants for the first time outnumbered those from the north, the chief sending regions being Apulia in the 'heel' of Italy, Calabria in the 'toe', and Sicily.

The social and legal position of the southerners in Turin at this period deserves comment. Most newly-arrived migrants grouped themselves according to family or village connections and found work in the city through such connections or through illegal 'co-operatives' which contracted to major employers to provide labour at below recognized wage-levels. This system had grown up in response to the Fascist laws of 1931 and 1939 attempting to control rural–urban migration: workers had to have a residence permit before they could legally obtain a job, but they also had to have a job before a residence permit could be issued – a not untypical Italian 'Catch 22' situation which resulted in the massive southern migration being semi-clandestine in nature, leaving the migrants themselves open to potential exploitation. The construction industry in particular was largely operated with unregularized, and exploited, cheap southern labour (Gabert 1958). The employment exchange was used only to legitimize the position of the migrants once they had become established in the city. Fiat, the largest and most sought-after employer, was, despite the general labour shortage, in such demand from potential employees that the organization could afford to stay aloof from the unregularized migrants. The Fascist control system in fact fell into disuse by the early 1960s.

Even as early as 1951 the southern in-migrant population in Turin contained a higher proportion of illiterates and of the worst-educated than did the population of the city as a whole (Anfossi 1962). Even though migrants may be positively selected from the south, they may appear to be negative groups in the north – in the south they are innovators but in the north they are markedly traditional, a fact that reflects deep-seated cultural differences between the Italian regions (Galtung 1971). Anfossi (1962) reports an interesting piece of research in which samples of Piedmontese and southern men and women living in Turin were asked to rank the degree of censure to be given to certain social 'crimes'. The correlations were highest between Piedmontese men and women and southern men: southern women's opinions were only just correlated significantly to those of their menfolk and bore no statistical relationship to those of the Piedmontese. Anfossi argued that this showed that whilst southern men working in Turinese industry had become acculturated to local norms, southern women remained encapsulated in northern society with little contact outside the family and hence clung to traditional southern values – for example, placing great censure upon betrayal of a husband but viewing murder for motives of honour with relative indifference. In a similar test of rankings of the social status of certain occupations, southern women again stood out, for example allotting the parish priest a much higher rank than he was given by the other groups. Anfossi concludes that the stereotypes of southerners held in the minds of northerners have some elements of truth but are oversimplifications because they disregarded the differences in attitudes between southern males and females and also the probable differences between those of different southern origins (Anfossi 1962: 251–65). Beijer (1963: 20) suggests that in much rural–urban domestic migration throughout Europe the problems of integration are much greater for non-working women as a result of their high degree of isolation within the city.

As a result of their low position in the labour market and the importance of chain migration and regrouping within Turin, in-migration resulted in a distinctive distribution of southerners throughout the city in the early days of mass migration in the 1950s. New southern migrants formed a significantly high proportion of all migrants in two areas. The first, and dominant, area was

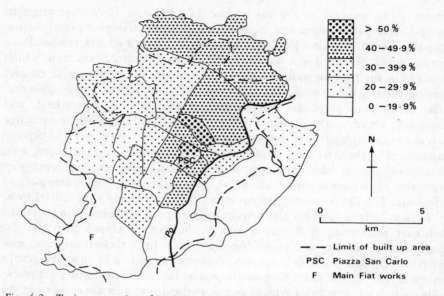

Fig. 4.2   Turin, proportion of newly-arriving migrants originating in Southern Italy, 1957. (*Source*: redrawn from Gabert 1958)

that of the city-centre (Fig. 4.2) where there was a tendency for migrants to displace a more upper-class population (Adamo 1969: 41), although even in the late 1950s the real *bourgeois* core, to the south-west of the Piazza San Carlo, had been scarcely affected (Gabert 1958: 42). From the start the centre housed a high proportion of the single and the youngest migrants, and the northern part of the centre of the city has remained the area of the densest concentration of southerners to the present day (Lusso 1978: 47). More peripheral areas of the city proper had smaller proportions of in-migrants directly from the south, especially in western districts of publicly-financed housing. The *bourgeois* area to the east of the Po, like that near the city-centre, received very small proportions of southerners, whilst in the southern suburbs around the Fiat works the relatively elevated rents of new housing precluded southerner in-migration.

The second area of southern migrant receipt was provided by the peripheral ex-villages of the outer fringe of the agglomeration where population growth took off during this period (Adamo 1969). Here family housing was more readily available at a cheaper rent than in the city itself: the area, however, constituted one of a transitory population with migrants aspiring to move into Turin itself to benefit from its better social amenities (Garbagnati 1962).

Within the city-centre, southern migrants lived in poor and overcrowded housing. In 1961 the mean ratio of persons per room for the city as a whole was 1.1, but 60 per cent of southern in-migrants were living in one or two rooms at an average density of 2.6 persons per room and one-third of the migrants lived at over 3 persons per room (Talamo 1962). Overcrowding was most prevalent in the very centre of the city where the migrants were effectively living on the margins of normal society. Migrants who had been in Turin longest tended to have better accommodation as a result of savings and intra-urban moves but they still lived at above-average housing densities (Talamo 1962: 187–216).

The general conclusion is that the first post-war wave of southern migration to Turin created a new marginal class within society; a class singled out by its low levels of educational attainment and skill, by its openness to exploitation within the labour market, its housing difficulties, its cultural distinctiveness and its spatial clustering. The southern migrants fuelled the boom of the Turin economy but it was not granted to them to benefit from that boom to any significant degree as a group. Even the rise of the Red Brigades in Turin in the 1970s owed its origin not to disaffected southern migrants but to elements of the urban intelligentsia.

Barcelona is the second great city of Southern Europe for which it is instructive to examine recent domestic in-migration. As in Turin, the history of industrial growth goes back well before the present century – in fact since 1910 the Barcelona-born have been in a minority in the city, except for the years of the Civil War. In the early inter-war years, migrants were already being drawn in from Valencia and Murcia, bringing the first major groups of non-Catalans to the city (Bolos y Capdevila 1959: 214–17). Between 1953 and 1970, official figures indicate that Barcelona received 498,000 migrants, with the origins of a great number being in Galicia, Andalusia or other southern and western regions of Spain, adding linguistic distinctiveness to the cultural mix inherent in all such migration from depressed rural areas to a growing industrial centre (Ferras 1977a: 200–1). By 1970, 35 per cent of the city's population had been born in non-Catalan-speaking areas, and an important proportion of the children born in Barcelona to non-Catalan parents could only speak Castilian. Thus in total, approximately 41 per cent of the population habitually used Castilian instead of Catalan: indeed, a survey of in-migrants arriving in Barcelona from outside Catalonia showed that 89 per cent did not believe it would be necessary to learn the local language (Esteva Fabregat 1975; 1977). Length of residence is an obvious variable in linguistic assimilation, only those migrants who have been present in the city for thirty years being completely assimilated in language use outside the home (Sostres 1966: 617–20). However, while there is some evidence of assimilation, for example in mixed marriages (Sostres 1966; Esteva Fabregat 1975), it is important to recognize the structural characteristics of the domestic migration to Barcelona to understand the patterns of insertion of the migrants within the city's urban structure.

Ever since the 1950s the dominant migration stream has been from Andalusia, with the provinces of Granada, Cordoba and Jaén being particularly strongly represented (Selva 1966: 551): each of these has very low levels of per capita income in comparison with Barcelona. Most migrants are of rural background and lack industrial skills: they have been drawn in to form a new industrial proletariat for the city (Ferras 1978: 179). Consistently high proportions of the migrants have been in the young adult age-groups and they have dominantly come alone, especially in the early post-war period (Bolos y

Capdevila 1959: 222–3). At first there were significant numbers of single females coming for domestic service, but such opportunities have steadily diminished so that by 1963 nearly 60 per cent of in-migrants were male and in in-migration districts masculinity of the population was the norm (Olives Puig 1969: 67). A significant proportion of the migrants were illiterate, a reflection of their poor agricultural origins, and their first urban occupations were dominantly in sectors designated as labouring and as public service (Selva 1966: 555–7).

Southern Spanish labour migrants are not, however, the only domestic migrant group affecting Barcelona. In addition, there is some middle-class migration of government and public officials from Castile. Linguistically these urban-originating middle-class migrants are more rigid in their ethnocentrism than the proletarian southerners and mix less with Catalan culture (Esteva Fabregat 1975: 42).

In total, therefore, Barcelona's social system is profoundly affected by domestic migration. Ferras (1977a: 211–12) has summarized that system in five classes. At the bottom is the labouring class composed of southern migrants. Above them lie the skilled workers who are dominantly Catalan, sometimes short-distance migrants to the city. The third class are the lower white-collar workers and self-employed, almost exclusively Catalan and, indeed, Barcelona-born. Above them are the upper white-collar, managerial and higher-ranking public employees composed of both Catalan and Castilian elements. The liberal professions and larger industrialists are made up of old Barcelona families, with some recent Castilian elements. Questions of class and status are thus intimately associated with place of origin.

Table 4.1   Segregation of domestic migrants, Barcelona, 1970

Region of origin	Total number	Percent of Spanish population of Barcelona	Index of segregation
Andalusia	202,680	11.8	20.1
Castile	146,223	8.5	6.4
Aragon	92,242	5.4	3.6
Valencia	56,123	3.3	9.4
Murcia	51,970	3.0	13.7
Galicia	46,918	2.7	7.7
Extremadura	29,909	1.7	18.0
Basque Provinces	17,962	1.0	12.0
Balearic Islands	7,187	0.4	18.8
Asturia	7,013	0.4	8.5
Canaries	2,400	0.1	12.4
Ceuta and Melilla	1,481	0.1	14.1
Catalonia	1,059,058	61.5	—
Total Spanish population	1,721,166		

Data source: Esteva Fabregat 1977

The distribution of recent domestic migrants within Barcelona can be examined using birthplace data from the 1970 census for the twelve administrative districts of the city (an inadequate number of statistical sub-divisions for a city of 1.75 million people). Segregation indices for populations born in twelve different regions of Spain are shown in Table 4.1. It should be noted that the generally low level of these indices is to be expected given the extremely coarse nature of the spatial units for which data are available (Woods 1976). If Ogden and Winchester's (1975) conclusions about Paris (see above, pp. 79–80) have a greater universal validity, we would expect to find that the magnitude of segregation is inversely proportional to the size of the migrant group. That is not, however, the case because the double-log correlation between the two variables yields a correlation coefficient of only −0.3, statistically insignificant. Certainly some small migrant groups, such as those from the Canaries and the Balearic Islands, show a high degree of segregation, but the highest segregation index of all is for the largest migrant group – the Andalusians – whilst the third largest group (from Aragon) have the lowest segregation of all. Two further controls on migrant segregation other than group size may be suggested – firstly, the age of the migration stream, whereby areas that have the longest traditions of movement to Barcelona (such as Aragon and Valencia) have lower degrees of migrant segregation; secondly, the urban or rural character of the migrant origins, so that rural Andalusians are highly segregated whilst urban Castilians or Asturians are not.

However, the dominant reason for the high degree of spatial segregation of the migrants from the south (Andalusia, Extremadura, Murcia) lies in their proletarian role in Barcelona society. For the newly-arrived southern in-migrant, two housing choices have traditionally been available (Ferras 1978: 182–3). Firstly, there is the possibility of moving into a central-area slum, basically open only to single men. In such inner-city areas a process of 'invasion and succession' may, in fact, be operative – Olives Puig (1969) has deliberately invoked such terminology – although it would appear that the migrant groups have historically replaced upper-class elements who have moved out rather than displaced them. Secondly, the migrant has had the option of moving into a squatter settlement or shanty-town, an option that was more attractive to the migrant accompanied by his family. Increasingly in recent years, purpose-built worker housing has been built to replace the shanty-towns (see Ch. 2, pp. 45–6), but access to such accommodation for southern migrants has often been via the remaining areas of illicit squatting (Ferras 1977b: 194). Shanty-towns have existed, at one time or another, in various parts of Barcelona, but the most enduring have lain on the Montjuich hill just to the south of the city-centre (Ferras 1977a: 255–6), along the coast north of the city, and in inland areas to the north where vacant land has been available in close proximity to industrial employment opportunities (Martinez-Marí 1966: 545–6). Of these shanty zones, that of Montjuich is the oldest and has housed a stable population originally of Murcian migrants but more recently consisting of the Barcelona-born descendants of the original movers. The other areas, still of active shanty growth in the 1960s, provided shelter for the first large waves

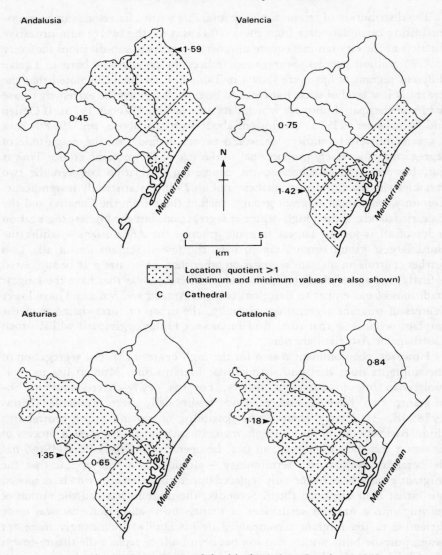

Fig. 4.3 Sub-populations defined by birthplace, Barcelona, 1970.
(*Data source*: Esteva Fabregat 1977)

of Andalusians. Proletarian housing in Barcelona, as elsewhere, is largely
peripheral housing, both in terms of the shanty-towns and the *grands ensembles*
that have replaced them. Only for single migrants have inner-city locations
been of major importance.

Figure 4.3 depicts the distributions of certain sub-populations, defined by
birthplace, within Barcelona, using location quotients such that values of
greater than one indicate over-representation of the relevant group. The age
of the migration stream and its social composition are of obvious importance.

Thus Valencians are concentrated in the older coastal areas of the city and in the central nucleus, reflecting their early arrival in Barcelona. The majority of more recent low-status migrants have gone to the two inland northern districts which in the mid-1960s were receiving 43 per cent of all the city's in-migrants (Sostres 1966: 622–3). The migrants who are over-represented in these northern districts are those from Andalusia, Murcia, Extremadura, and from the North African Spanish possessions of Ceuta and Melilla. The population of Catalan origin is most under-represented in these proletarian districts but it is also below par in the two districts of the city-centre where, over many years, migrants have been replacing the native population (Olives Puig 1969). The true Catalan heart of the city has now moved towards the more middle-class areas of the west, reflecting the fact that the large-scale introduction of an in-migrant southern labour force has permitted the upward social mobility of the native population viewed as a group. Migrants with a more urban background, or with the longest traditions of movement to Barcelona (such as the Asturians), are the groups with the greatest distributional similarities to the Catalans themselves.

Finally, as in the case of Turin, the peripheral settlements around the city are now gaining strongly through in-migration from other parts of the country, such that these surrounding municipalities are now undergoing proletarianization (Martinez-Marí 1966: 543). Municipalities near the coast north of Barcelona have seen in-migration of southerners at especially high levels, and within such municipalities the phenomena of peripheral shanty-towns and worker housing blocks have reproduced conditions in Barcelona (Naylon 1981: 245; Sola-Morales Rubió 1970: 178).

It may appear that the detailed examples given here of Turin and Barcelona are extreme because of the scale of domestic migration involved. However, similar phenomena have been identified in the post-war period throughout Southern Europe: domestic migration has been of similar importance everywhere.

For example, the increasing use of suburban areas or settlements beyond the city limits as stepping stones for migration into the city is attested in many cases. For Bologna, for example, Guidicini (1962: 369) has specifically invoked the concept of migrant succession but suggests that those who are 'succeeded' move towards the city proper rather than moving out from the centre. In the 1950s, Bologna was still a city where most migration was from local rural areas (Panieri 1962: 387), but although southerners were in a minority they were highly distinctive because of their strong masculinity and the dominance of single movers, whilst for more local migrants a rough sex balance and a stronger representation of families was the norm (Bellettini 1958: 531–7). In all the industrial cities of northern Italy, the post-war years of the economic 'miracle' saw a rapid increase in the importance of such southern migrants (Buzzi-Donato 1962: 331).

Gozalvez-Perez (1977: 91–4), in a study of in-migrants in Valencia in Spain, echoes several of the findings given above for Barcelona. The older the migration stream the better represented it is at the city-centre, so that more recent migrants, originating from outside the local area, tend to display the greatest dominance in the outer areas of the city. In addition, migrants from nearby provinces are less localized within the urban area whilst Andalusians in particular are concentrated in specific outer areas.

In Madrid the outer suburban areas with a high proportion of squatting and illegal housing show an over-representation of recent migrants. A 1973 survey of the illegal housing areas showed that 41 per cent of household heads came from Andalusia and a further 21 per cent from Extremadura: the whole population was basically agricultural in origin and also included large numbers of gypsies (Montes Mieza et al. 1976: 162–3). Salcedo (1977b: 532) has noted that southern migrants tend to concentrate on the southern edge of Madrid, a finding that interestingly accords with Ogden and Winchester's (1975) conclusions on the sectoral bias of migrant destinations within Paris in the nineteenth century.

Peripheral shanty-towns do not appear to be transitory places of residence for migrant families, but display a good deal of compositional stability. In Madrid, half the household heads in the illegal settlement areas in 1971 had been there for twelve or more years (Montes Mieza et al. 1976: 172). Ferras (1977a: 251–2, 263–4) reports on shanties in Barcelona where 19 per cent of the residents had been present for over twenty years: population stability had meant that many migrants who arrived in the shanty-towns as unskilled workers had improved their occupational status through time but maintained their same residence. A 1973 survey of 100 shanty-town families in Messina in Sicily showed that only five had arrived within the last five years (Ginatempo and Cammarota 1977: 119).

In many Southern European cities, traditional rural–urban migration patterns of young females for work in domestic service remain of importance. In the southern Spanish city of Murcia in 1965, 54 per cent of resident in-migrants were female, many of them 'living-in' in central city areas as servants and thus giving a stronger representation of migrants in the city-centre than in peripheral areas (Cano García 1971). Similar over-representation of female in-migrants occurs in the high-status central city districts of many southern cities (Capote 1976: 336–40). Movement into the city for employment in domestic service has also been important in the case of Athens where, in the 1960s, females exceeded males in the domestic migration stream (Carter, F. W. 1968: 103–5).

As Southern European cities modernize and industrialize, their migrant characteristics change. Female servants are replaced by male labour migrants. These changes can be seen in the recent example of Madrid. By the mid-1970s the dominant migration streams from the less developed rural areas of Spain were weakening in importance and increasing proportions of migrants were drawn from larger urban settlements and from developed areas such as Asturias, Valencia and Catalonia. Thus by 1973, technical and managerial workers constituted 25 per cent of Madrid's in-migrants (Ballesteros et al. 1977). It is not impossible to envisage a future scenario where further economic growth, not just in Madrid but in other major Southern European cities, results in the sort of substitution of foreigners for nationals in unskilled labour migration that the cities of Northern Europe have witnessed during the present century.

In sum, domestic migration to Southern European cities in the post-war period has displayed many of the features of Northern European nineteenth-century migration. The migrants are dominantly of rural backgrounds with poor education and no formal industrial or professional skills. Domestic service is an attraction for women whilst the men are required in the construction industry or in other low-paid sectors. The migrants often display some form of socio-cultural distinctiveness alongside the host populations. Migrant segregation in the city is common, being brought about partly by chain-migration processes and clustering but also being determined by the highly restricted housing opportunities available to the migrants, conditioning them to the poorest city-centre accommodation or to shanty-towns and cheaply-built mass housing at the periphery. Much migrant segregation can be interpreted as social class segregation. Structurally, the migrants have to a large extent filled the least desirable jobs, thus permitting the upward social and economic mobility of the locally-born, a phenomenon that in Northern Europe in recent years has been permitted by international rather than by domestic migration.

BELGIUM AND SWITZERLAND: DOMESTIC MIGRATION AND CULTURAL CLEAVAGE

The general model of domestic migration presented at the start of this chapter has now been validated for the cities of Northern Europe in the nine-teenth and for those of Southern Europe in the twentieth century. It has also been suggested that in Northern Europe the social impact of domestic migra-tion has been reduced as the migrants have ceased to be a distinctive group, identifiable by their rural backgrounds and occupational specialization within the city: the distinctive migrants are now of international origin.

This generalization might not be applicable in the cases of Belgium and Switzerland because of the particular multi-cultural identities of the nations concerned. For example, in Brussels in 1970, 16.1 per cent of the residential population had been born outside Belgium (Meeus 1975: 427) but the question of the linguistic region of origin of domestic migrants was still of some significance.

A major problem in the analysis of Belgium's linguistic divisions is the fact that these divisions are so sensitive that since 1947 language questions have been omitted from the census (Stephenson 1972: 505). Analysis of language in Brussels can be attempted via the examination of the provinces of birth of domestic migrants with, for the province of Brabant which is bisected by the Flemish–French language border, examination of the *arrondissement* or district of birth as well. From such a procedure it can be calculated that in 1947, 41.2 per cent of the domestic migrants living in Brussels were from French-speaking areas: by 1961 this proportion had risen to 43.5 per cent (Mols 1968: 244) and it remained at the same level in 1970 (Meeus 1975: 425–6).

Flemish-speaking migrants, or at least migrants from Flemish areas of Belgium, have been the majority in moves to Brussels, and that picture is equally true for the nineteenth century when Flemish migrants were even more dominant (Verniers 1958: 371–2). However, the remarkable fact is that, at a superficial level, Brussels has changed over the years from being a Flemish-speaking to a French-speaking city, despite the majority position of Flemish in-migrants. In 1842, out of a population of 113,000, 61 per cent were Flemish-speaking (Verniers 1958: 370). In 1866, 51 per cent of Brussels' residents claimed to be Flemish-speaking, 20 per cent French-speaking and 26 per cent bilingual: by 1947 the figures were 16 per cent Flemish, 34 per cent French and 41 per cent bilingual (Bogaert-Damin and Maréchal 1978: 117) – if the bilingual population is allocated according to the language 'mostly' used, the proportions were 24 per cent Flemish and 71 per cent French, despite the fact that an estimated three-quarters of the bilinguals were of Flemish mother-tongue (Nelde 1982: 38, 52). French has traditionally been perceived as the 'superior' tongue, for example it has been the language of administration and the professions, but despite the official parity of the two languages today there is massive circumstantial and survey evidence that large numbers of Flemish migrants adopt French or encourage their offspring to do so (Verniers 1958: 373; Nelde 1982: 42; Louckx 1978: 58–9).

Nevertheless, although from being the majority in six of the nineteen *communes* of Brussels in 1920, French came to majority status in them all by 1947 (Verniers 1958: 373), Brussels still contains the distinct traces of linguistic zones which are partly maintained through the patterns of domestic migration. Even in 1842, Flemish dominated the north-west of the city and the industrial areas whilst French was dominant in the 'upper' city of the south-east – 'upper' both topographically and socially (Verniers 1958: 370). This division has been maintained with migrants from Flanders and from Wallonia generally respecting this basic urban division, the continuation of which is demonstrated in Fig. 4.4 which shows that in 1961 Wallonian-born resident in-migrants were more strongly located in the south-east of the city and the Flanders-born in the north-west. The west of the city is traditionally more Flemish in composition and is anyway less favoured by domestic migrants from all regions – the population thus contains a higher proportion of the Brussels-born (Mols 1965: 322; 1968: 243–4).

If domestic migrants tend to go to areas of the city where there are already large numbers from similar origins, the proportions of Wallonian migrants would increase much more rapidly in *communes* with a heavy earlier representation of such in-migrants than in *communes* where Flemish in-migration had earlier been dominant. The method by which this can be examined is by the calculation of changes in the location quotients of Wallonian migrants between 1947 and 1961. In areas where the increase in the importance of the Wallonia-born has been greater than for the city as a whole, the result of dividing the 1961 location quotient by that for 1947 would be a value greater than one: in areas where the Wallonian increase was less than for the city as a whole, the result would be less than one. In fact (Fig. 4.4) there is no evidence that

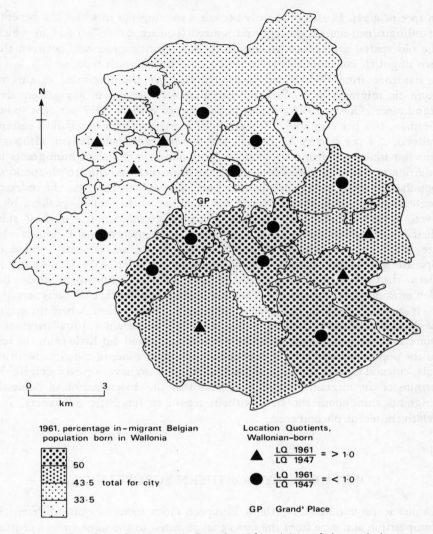

1961, percentage in-migrant Belgian
population born in Wallonia

50

43·5 total for city

33·5

Location Quotients,
Wallonian-born

▲ $\dfrac{LQ\ 1961}{LQ\ 1947}$ = > 1·0

● $\dfrac{LQ\ 1961}{LQ\ 1947}$ = < 1·0

GP Grand' Place

Fig. 4.4   Resident domestic migrants in Brussels, 1961: origins and changes in importance,
1947–61.
(*Data source*: Mols 1968)

migrants have, in the post-war period, continued to maintain community
separation in Brussels: indeed, the importance of Wallonian-born migrants has
increased, *vis-à-vis* the city as a whole, in several traditionally Flemish areas
of the north and north-west, while Wallonian migrants have not increased so
rapidly in dominance in some *communes* of the south-east. The conclusion must
therefore be that migration is now operating to reduce community segregation
within Brussels, as migration is increasingly distributing migrants, from
whichever region of origin, throughout the city instead of concentrating them

in specific areas. Brussels has truly become a melting-pot in which the benefits of bilingualism are increasingly recognized (Louckx 1978: 59) and in which the old spatial segregation (maintained by migration processes) between the two linguistic communities within the city is being much reduced.

Evidence from Switzerland also suggests that the linguistic origins of domestic migrants in a culturally-mixed country are not of any present-day significance. Of the 1971 resident population of Zürich, 82.7 per cent spoke German, 0.6 per cent spoke Romansch (the language of Switzerland's eastern valleys), 2.4 per cent spoke French, and 8.9 per cent spoke Italian, although this last figure unfortunately includes large numbers of Italian immigrants in addition to the Swiss from Ticino. Both the Romansch and the French-speaking populations are relatively evenly distributed throughout the city, the index of segregation of the Romansch being 8.6 and that of the French-speakers 14.5 over 34 administrative sub-districts: given the population size of these sub-districts, these are low levels of segregation. It is international migrants who are much more important in producing distinctive social areas – those of Spanish speech, for example, having a segregation index of 33.7. Similarly in Bern, data given by Gächter (1974) enable the observation to be made that domestic migrant segregation is far less important than that of foreigners.

It appears, therefore, that even in Belgium and Switzerland, where the origin of domestic migrants to the city can still carry important cultural overtones, homogenization is present such that the migrants stand out little from the rest of the population and are not confined to particular zones of the city. In Brussels, cultural change and 'frenchification' (*francisation*) have occurred despite the origins of the migrants, but it is notable that the dissemination of domestic migrants throughout the city, without regard to linguistic differences, is a relatively recent phenomenon.

CONTEMPORARY NORTHERN EUROPEAN CITIES

Domestic migration to Northern European cities today is quite different in composition and type from the flows that occurred to the same cities a century ago, or that have affected the cities of Southern Europe in the post-war years.

Pourcher (1964), for example, in his exhaustive survey of 3,130 provincial migrants living in Paris in 1961, found a slight predominance of females and noted that 55 per cent of his sample had been born in rural *communes*. However, they tended to be of above average educational background and had anyway proceeded to Paris by steps – on average the migrants had lived in 2.3 provincial places before their arrival in Paris, such that when their last place of residence was considered, most had come from urban areas and possessed urban skills and qualifications. After initial concentration in rented accommodation at the city-centre, these provincial migrants had moved outwards throughout the city such that their distribution mirrored that of the total population. Pourcher found no differences between migrants and Parisians in terms of family sizes or housing characteristics, and he concluded that the assimilation of provincial migrants seemed to be almost total (Pourcher 1964: 275).

In Vienna, Holzmann (1971: 118–19) similarly found a pattern of stepwise domestic migration to the city via medium-sized urban places. The actual migrants were young and single (Gisser and Kaufmann 1972: 246–7) and brought a continual rejuvenation of the urban population, but these domestic migrants took clerical and white-collar jobs so that international migrants were needed for employment as labourers – by 1973, 22 per cent of Vienna's manual workers were foreign migrants (Gehmacher 1974: 165).

Both Paris and Vienna are capital cities at the top of the urban hierarchies in their respective countries. At lower levels in the hierarchy, local rural migrants may still be of a certain, although diminishing, significance (Vince 1966: 536–7; Dyer 1969), and there may be a continuous net loss of migrants, particularly of tertiary sector employees, to the larger cities (Chatelain 1956). Other reasons for movement out of northern cities include retirement moves to rural areas (Cribier 1975). However, most common of all in producing the net migration losses referred to in Chapter 3 (pp. 59–62) are moves into the suburbs and surrounding commuter belts beyond the city boundaries.

For example, 92.3 per cent of the net loss of domestic migrants from Brussels relocated within the suburban ring, and a similar phenomenon occurs even in smaller Belgian cities such as Liège and Charleroi (Laurant and Declercq-Tijtgat 1978). Suburbanization dominantly involves families, so that whilst the numbers of single young people within city boundaries may increase through migration, the numbers living in family groups diminish. Amsterdam in 1969 experienced a net migration gain of 3,211 single people but a net loss of 20,254 members of family households: all social classes and skill levels were involved in this familial out-migration (Anon. 1970: 45–8; Cortie 1972a: 45). Similar results of domestic migration (the balance between in and out moves) have been noted in other cities such as Utrecht (Cortie 1972b: 318), Kiel (Killisch 1979: 114) and Ulm (Schaffer 1972: 149), the latter two in West Germany. There are signs of such suburbanizing moves beginning to increase in importance in Southern European cities as well, such as in Madrid where by the mid-1970s out-migration, dominantly to peripheral municipalities, was running at around 20,000 per annum (Ballesteros et al. 1977: 197).

The material pesented in this chapter has largely validated the first part of the general model of city-wards migration postulated at the outset. Nations undergoing urban industrial growth manifest large-scale rural–urban movement during the early phases and the migrants involved, being of possibly distinctive backgrounds and occupied in specific low-status urban employment sectors, are identifiable in several ways from those who are indigenous to the urban centres. That identification may be manifested in housing characteristics or in spatial segregation, as well as in the social segregation that results from the role the migrants are called on to fulfil. As modernizing socio-economic systems mature, as local rural migrant sources dry up, and as an increasing proportion of domestic migrants arriving in the cities are of urban origins and skills, the domestic migrant streams cease to have any intrinsic social significance for the detailed structure of the city, despite their undoubted demographic importance in reviving the flagging vitality of urban population structures. In Southern Europe, domestic migrants still hold a place of importance; in Northern Europe the spotlight has now shifted to international migrant flows.

CHAPTER FIVE

International Migration and the City

At the start of Chapter 4 a general model of the evolution of migration to growing industrial cities was put forward and the remainder of that chapter was devoted to an examination of the facts of domestic migration in an attempt to test the model. Throughout most of Northern Europe today, however, it is the question of international migration that is of greater significance, not just in the eyes of economists, administrators and social scientists, but in the minds of ordinary people as well. The presence of large numbers of *Maghrébins* (Moroccans, Algerians and Tunisians) in France became an issue in the Communist campaign for the 1981 presidential election. In Switzerland, repeated referenda have taken place on proposals for a reduction in international migrant flows or in the numbers of resident foreigners (Johnston and White 1977; Johnston 1980b).

Despite the great importance that must be accorded to international labour migration in the post-war European context, it is important to remember that not all international migration is of unskilled workers for the lowest status industrial and tertiary jobs. Indeed, it is only in the last fifty years or so that this type of international movement has come to prominence, and only since the Second World War that it has taken the dominant role throughout Northern Europe. Other types of international migrant flow have been, and still are, of some importance, notably migration by the high-level self-employed (merchants and major entrepreneurs), by the managerial employees of international organizations, and refugee flows.

THE EVOLUTION OF INTERNATIONAL MIGRATION

In a medieval Europe without the existence of major nation-states, anyone from outside the local area could be defined as a foreigner (Schenk 1975: 221). Nevertheless there were, from this period onwards, certain flows of population that could be called international migrations on the basis of present-day concepts of nations. Prime among these were the movements of merchants.

97

Origo (1963) has described the merchant and artisan colony of Italians and others in papal Avignon during the fourteenth century and shown how this expatriate colony of wealthy independent businessmen had its own consul and law-enforcement officers. All towns of any note had foreign trading-company representatives in this period of merchant activities. Braudel (1972: 134–5, 336–7) details medieval Greek colonies in Livorno and Venice, Cypriots in Cadiz and Italian merchant and banking communities in Lisbon, Seville, Lyon and Antwerp. The Jews generally had their own ghetto in all major cities. In Messina in Sicily each 'foreign' group had its own quarter of the town (Ioli Gigante 1980: 15). Foreign businessmen often encouraged the introduction of new manufacturing skills, and the diffusion of various branches of the all-important textile trade owed much to these entrepreneurial migrants (Braudel 1972: 416).

Ever since medieval times capital, and the entrepreneurs controlling it, has gone to wherever the investment opportunities were greatest. With the coming of real industrialization and urban growth in the nineteenth century, new waves of independent international migrants swept through Europe, for example with British industrialists heavily involved in Belgium. In Barcelona the French community of 5,000 in 1850 had doubled by 1900 as growing public works projects, textile companies, consumer goods industries, insurance and banking all drew in large-scale investment by French interests (Deffontaines 1966: 569–72). The present-day equivalents of these movements of the past lie in the employees of multinational companies and of international organizations – a group of generally highly-educated migrants working in high-status technical and professional occupations and comprising important population sub-groups in cities such as Geneva, Brussels and Strasbourg.

Easier transportation since the eighteenth century has also fostered other, less elitist, independent migrations by the smaller self-employed artisans and in commerce. Initially these were often seasonal migrants in petty trading, such as Italian ice-cream sellers or street entertainers (Gentileschi 1978: 333–4), but in time these activities have given way to more stable family enterprises in the manufacture of various consumer goods, in restaurant and hotel-keeping or, after the Second World War, in catering for the needs of large numbers of compatriot international migrants who had come not as independent workers but as labour migrants for economic growth.

Refugee settlement in European cities has an extremely diverse history. The Jews have always been among the greatest urban refugee settlers, from their expulsion from Spain in 1492 when many settled in Venice (Braudel 1972: p. 336) to those fleeing the nineteenth century *pogroms* in Russia who came west to Amsterdam, Paris and London. The Revocation of the Edict of Nantes in 1685, provoking the expulsion of the Huguenots from France, brought large-scale refugee movement to certain cities, such as Berlin, and had considerable economic effects wherever the migrants settled and set up their industrial, trading and commercial activities. However, it has been the last century that has produced the greatest refugee flows in Europe as a whole. The years immediately after the First World War saw the departure from Turkey of large numbers of expelled Greeks, many of whom settled in Athens where they continue to give a distinctive flavour to certain districts (Burgel 1972: 42–43). Athens also received a substantial section of the remains of the Armenian community, but most European capitals received at least some of this group, along with Russians fleeing the October Revolution of 1917.

After the Second World War there were more vast flows of refugee populations, especially of Germans, the *Volksdeutsche*, expelled from Eastern Europe possibly to the number of 13 million. Other post-war European refugee movements include that from Hungary after 1956 and from Czechoslovakia after 1968, Vienna being the chief initial recipient and redistribution centre in both cases. France absorbed an estimated 1.28 million *Français d'outre-mer* (overseas French) during the period from 1945 to 1968, over 900,000 returning from Algeria after that country's independence in 1962 (Guillon 1974: 644–5). The vast majority of refugee migrants in the twentieth century have taken up urban residence.

It is, however, the unskilled international labour migration of recent years that is of greatest overall significance for the social geography of the Western European city. In the medieval past, when most migrants to cities came from the surrounding countryside (Braudel 1972: 334–6), an element of 'international' labour flow was sometimes provided by slaves: for example in 1551, Lisbon had a population of 100,000 of whom one-tenth were slaves, brought in to replace native Portuguese labour which was draining away to the Indian trading ventures of the period (Atkinson 1960: 151). The use of slaves in Western Europe, however, died out by the seventeenth century.

Some short-distance rural–urban migration in the pre-industrial, and increasingly in the industrializing, period was across international boundaries where large cities stood near frontiers and drained a natural rural hinterland lying in two or more countries. Bordeaux, for example, has traditionally drawn some migrants from Northern Spain (Guillaume 1972: 72–3), whilst in Roubaix in Northern France, tucked against the Belgian border, continuous migration from Belgian Flanders meant that the town's population was 55 per cent of Belgian origin between 1866 and 1891 (Trenard et al. 1977: 360–1). The Ruhr drew many Dutch migrants throughout the later nineteenth century (Steinberg 1978: 80–2). International migration was relatively free of official controls in the years before the First World War, and in countries where urban economic growth, for one reason or another, was creating conditions of labour shortage, the numbers of resident foreigners began to grow. By 1900 there were 200,000 foreigners in Belgium; in 1907, Germany had 850,000 foreign workers, while France had reached the total of 1 million foreigners by 1881 (Böhning 1972). In 1911, 6.7 per cent of the population of Paris was foreign, the equivalent figures for London, Berlin and Vienna being 3, 2.6 and 2 per cent respectively (Ogden 1977: 12). The figure for Vienna must be treated with some circumspection since the Austrian Empire still enclosed vast non-Germanic territories at this date: when the Empire was split up in 1919,

340,000 foreign-language speakers left the city, suggesting that the pre-war contribution of 'foreigners' to the city's population may have been as high as 15 per cent (Bobek and Lichtenberger 1966: 129).

The early inter-war period saw an especially high demand for foreign labourers in France which had suffered devastating war losses (Armengaud 1973), and it was at this time that the first non-European labour migrants were brought in, France turning to her North African colonies for supply (El Gharbaoui 1969: 27–8). The depression of the 1930s curtailed new demand for labour and it was not until the 1950s that the present patterns of international labour migration finally started to emerge.

The framework and details of this post-war movement have been dealt with elsewhere (Böhning 1972; Castles and Kosack 1973; Paine 1974; King, R. l976; Rist 1978; Van Amersfoort 1982). The causes of labour shortage in Central and Northern Europe are well-known: the lack of further possibilities of large-scale local labour-shedding from agriculture; the effects of fertility decline and of small birth cohorts in the 1930s; the rapid rate of economic growth in the post-war period bringing economic expansion at a level undreamed of in the 1930s and creating large labour demands and full employment; the upward social mobility of indigenous populations leading to labour supply difficulties in jobs that were perceived as undesirable. As a result of the combination of these and other factors, the indigenous labour forces of Northern Europe were unable to fill all the jobs available. Only in Southern Europe, where fertility declines had started later and where movement out of agriculture had not progressed so far, could domestic rural–urban movement meet the demands of the urban labour market (as has been seen in Ch. 4, pp. 82–91), and, beyond that, supply export labour to Northern Europe.

The post-war evolution of international labour migration in Western Europe has therefore been in accord with the general model of migration outlined at the start of Chapter 4 (pp. 74–7). Although perceived as such by some countries (such as West Germany), this migration was not simply a solution to a short-term problem of labour supply; instead it became a rapidly evolving structural characteristic of the social and economic system of Western Europe. Foreign labour was seen as being 'cheap' labour which would accept low wages and poor working conditions, accepting also the de-skilling of jobs through more detailed divisions of labour and without recourse to unionization (Paine 1977; White and Woods 1983). However, whilst many foreign migrants were drawn into employment sectors that suffer boom and slump cycles (as was the case with domestic migrants in the nineteenth century – see Ch. 4, p. 80–1), others taking socially undesirable but essential jobs have become indispensable to the host countries. From time to time there is, in fact, evidence of lower levels of recession-induced unemployment among labour migrants than among indigenous workers – this occurred, for example, at the start of the West German recession of 1974 (Kreuzaler 1977: 140). In order to maintain the possibility of repatriating unwanted foreigners, labour migrants in some countries (most notably West Germany and Switzerland) have been kept in systems of constant short-term 'rotation', but by the early 1970s, as competition between countries to obtain migrants started to grow, and as the longer-term need for migrant labour was accepted, these systems were generally liberalized, allowing more permanent settlement and the movement of dependents to provide family reunification. As a result of these, and other, processes, labour migrants of foreign origins are now a permanent feature of Northern European societies and not even the depth of the recent recession has been capable of dislodging them and significantly reducing their numbers.

THE SIZE OF THE MIGRANT GROUPS

Data on the international migrant populations of individual European cities come from two sources. Firstly, there are census data which are available for almost all European countries, although the last full censuses available at the time of writing were generally taken in 1970 and 1971 (the exception being France). Secondly, data can also be obtained in some countries from the continuous population registers or from police records of foreigner registration. Tables 5.1 and 5.2 have been constructed on the basis of census information.

In Southern European cities it is birthplace, rather than nationality, that is the subject of census investigation and in Portugal no information is available on either topic. In the other three Mediterranean countries those born abroad but of Spanish, Italian or Greek citizenship respectively are indistinguishable from 'foreigners', a particularly important point in Athens where, in 1971, there were 13,616 Turkish-born residents, almost certainly all of them being of Greek nationality, the refugees of the 1920s (see above, p. 99): if these are excluded, the proportion of probable non-Greeks is reduced to 1.8 per cent.

Table 5.1 Foreign-born populations – selected Southern European cities, 1971

	Per cent of resident population born abroad
Spain – average for 9 largest cities*	1.7
Madrid*	2.1
Barcelona*	1.8
Valencia*	1.2
Cordoba*	0.4
Italy – average for 17 largest cities†	2.3
Rome	2.9
Milan	2.9
Turin	2.9
Florence	2.3
Naples	0.9
Messina	0.8
Greece: Athens	2.3

* 1970
†Excluding Trieste

Data sources: see Appendix

In Italy, Trieste has been omitted from the overall calculations because the 25 per cent of its population born abroad largely stems from international boundary changes in the local area since 1914.

By the early 1970s the cities of Southern Europe, as Table 5.1 demonstrates, were in receipt of few international migrants, although the capital cities and industrial centres such as Barcelona, Milan and Turin all had foreign-born populations of above-average representation. There have been suggestions in the later 1970s that Southern European cities are starting to experience the arrival of international labour migrants. At the start of the decade, female domestic servants from the Philippines, Somalia and Ethiopia started arriving in Rome and between 1975 and 1980 the growth of foreigners living in the city was by 45 per cent, more than half of these newcomers being from under-industrialized countries. Although in an embryo phase, the situation, both in Rome and Milan, is starting to replicate familiar stages in Northern Europe (Arena 1982). Further growth of international labour migration to Southern European cities is likely in the future, the most probable migrant sources lying in Africa.

The picture in the cities of Northern and Central Europe is a very different one although definitional problems still exist. Data here (Table 5.2) are for nationality rather than birthplace, but this creates its own difficulties – for example in the Netherlands the Surinamers have Dutch nationality (Van Amersfoort and Cortie 1973) whilst in France the residents of overseas *départements* (such as Guadeloupe or Réunion) are legally citizens of France (Ah-Peng 1976). In certain countries a significant number of foreign migrants have become legally naturalized or taken up citizenship of their host country. In France this amounts to an average of a further 3.6 per cent of the populations of the eighteen agglomerations reported in Table 5.2: in Greater Grenoble the population that has French citizenship 'by acquisition' amounts to 6.4 per cent of the total.

Despite these drawbacks to the data on which Table 5.2 is based, it is manifestly clear that in Northern and Central European cities the size of the international migrant community is almost everywhere larger than in Southern Europe. Out of the fifty-four cities constituting the data set for Table 5.2, only in nine cases was the proportion of foreigners less than that of the foreign-born in Rome, the Southern European city with the maximum proportion.

In the early 1970s variations from city to city within individual countries were quite marked (Fig. 5.1). Three reasons can be put forward for these variations. Firstly, those cities of Northern Europe with small foreigner presences are sometimes in areas where local rural migrants are still available: such is the case for Rennes and Nantes in France, both still able to tap Breton out-migrants. Secondly, cities that have been undergoing slow economic growth tend to have relatively low foreigner proportions in comparison with other cities in the same country: hence in West Germany the Rhine–Ruhr conurbation had fewer foreigners in 1970 (4.6 per cent) than the national urban average; in France the same applied to Lille and Nancy. Thirdly, certain cities of slow economic growth have foreigner populations that are larger than might be

Table 5.2 Resident foreign citizens – selected Northern European cities, 1970–5

	Year	Per cent foreign citizens
Austria – average for 3 largest cities	1971	3.4
Belgium – average for 3 largest cities	1970	13.6
Brussels	1970	16.1
Denmark: Copenhagen/Frederiksberg	1975	4.7
Finland – average for 3 largest cities	1970	3.4
France – average for 18 largest agglomerations	1975	9.9
Greater Grenoble	1975	12.8
Greater Paris	1975	11.9
Greater Lyon	1975	11.8
Greater Bordeaux	1975	5.1
Greater Nantes	1975	1.7
West Germany – average for 17 'largest agglomerations	1970	5.4
Greater Stuttgart	1970	11.5
Greater Frankfurt	1970	8.5
Greater Hanover	1970	4.3
Greater Kiel	1970	1.3
West Berlin	1970	6.1
Netherlands: Amsterdam	1975	5.4
Sweden – average for 3 largest cities	1970	7.0
Switzerland – average for 4 largest agglomerations	1970	20.6
Greater Geneva	1970	34.0

Data sources: see Appendix

expected, the reasons being historical. For example, the French northern coal-field agglomeration centred on Lens recorded 6.8 per cent of its population as foreign in 1975 (and a futher 5.7 per cent naturalized), these being largely the Poles who arrived between the wars to work in the mines and who still form the largest single foreign group.

Except in France, the Netherlands and Denmark, the data presented in Tables 5.1 and 5.2, and in Fig. 5.1, relate to 1970 or 1971. For those cities where continuous registration data exist, more recent estimates can be given for the position at the end of the 1970s (Table 5.3). The decade was an interesting one for international migration. The continuing economic advance of 1970–3 brought further massive immigration, especially in West Germany. Then, since the oil crisis of late 1973, the industrial economies of Western Europe have been subject to varying degrees of stagnation or decline with increases in unemployment levels everywhere. In such circumstances it might have been expected that large numbers of international labour migrants would be thrown out of work and be sent 'home'.However, the reality of the situation has been much more complex. Certainly there was a net outflow of foreigners from certain countries in the mid-1970s, especially where restrictions on new entries were tightened up. For example, West Germany saw a net migration loss of 433,000 foreigners during the years 1974–7, but this amounted to no more

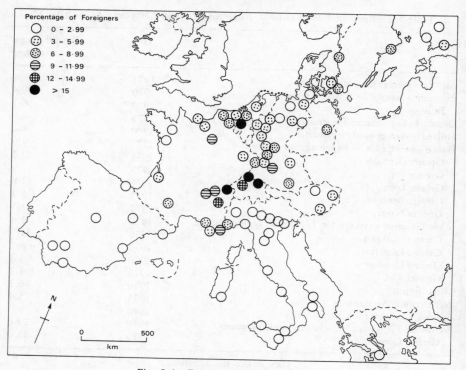

Fig. 5.1   Foreigners in cities, 1970–5.
(*Data sources*: see Appendix)

than 28 per cent of the net gain of 1.53 million during the previous four years from 1970 to 1973: by 1978 the foreigner population of West Germany had started to grow once again through migration (Rein 1982: 116). As a result of general policies liberalizing labour migrants' conditions in the late 1960s (applicable almost everywhere except in Switzerland), many migrants had obtained rights to unemployment pay and social welfare benefits, whilst, as argued above (pp. 100–1), others were employed in sectors little affected by recession. Where international migrants have returned 'home' in recent years they have often been more than balanced by new arrivals of the dependants of those staying on abroad.

The growth in the importance of the foreign population in all the cities listed in Table 5.3 occurred largely during the early 1970s. Absolute numbers of foreigners increased everywhere except in Zürich where there was a loss of 2,000 but where the Swiss population was falling much more rapidly so that the proportion of the total population made up of foreigners continued to increase. Evidence for other cities where only incomplete data are available confirm the continuing and increased importance of foreigners. In Greater Nuremberg the proportion of foreigners in the total population rose in just two years from 5.6 per cent in 1970 to 11.8 per cent in 1972 (Klamroth 1974: 141–2). In Frankfurt the proportion of foreigners rose from 10.2 per

Table 5.3   Evolution of foreigner populations, 1970–9 – selected cities

City	Country	1970 per cent foreign	Year	Per cent foreign	Per cent change in numbers of foreigners since 1970
Antwerp	Belgium	8.0	1978	11.8	+29.4
West Berlin		6.1	1979	11.1	+63.3
Gothenburg	Sweden	8.0	1976	9.0	+ 5.9
Munich	W. Germany	9.5	1979	16.7	+75.5
Stockholm	Sweden	6.3	1977	7.6	+ 6.5
Vienna	Austria	5.8	1979	8.9	+48.8
Zürich	Switzerland	16.7	1979	18.1	− 3.0

Data sources: see Appendix

cent in 1970 to 18.4 per cent in 1978; in Stuttgart the increase was from 12.2 per cent to 15.4 per cent, and in Bremen from 2.2 per cent to 4.8 per cent (O'Loughlin 1980: 258). In each case there had been rapid increases from 1970 to 1974 followed by relative stability thereafter.

The foreign migrant community in many cities is now achieving demographic maturity as the last ten years have seen family reunification and a consequent increase in rates of natural increase among the immigrants. Migration is beginning to lose its significance as the maintainer of the ethnic minority communities as they start to reproduce themselves within cities. It is now quite possible to envisage future growth of these communities even if all in-migration were terminated, the growth resulting from the low overall age-structure of the migrant communities and from their fertility levels that are commonly above those of the indigenous population. In Cologne the mid-year totals of foreigners rose by 12,529 between 1976 and 1979, but only 36 per cent of this absolute increase was attributable to net in-migration, the rest being due to natural growth of the foreign community. In Zürich the changes documented in Table 5.3 between 1970 and 1979 came about through a net migration loss of 11,300 foreigners balanced by a net natural gain of 9,300 resulting from the excess of births over deaths. As already pointed out in Chapter 3 (p. 62), births to foreign women now make up a substantial part of overall fertility in many cities. Hence by 1975 the German population of Stuttgart, for example, was declining by an excess of deaths over births, giving natural decline of 5.6 per thousand per annum (adding to net out-migration): the foreign population was experiencing natural growth of 18.3 per thousand per annum (Borris et al. 1977: 197).

Before concluding this section on the size of the migrant communities it is worth attempting to draw out certain general conclusions about the stages in the post-war evolution of international labour migration. Brief attention here will be given to the cases of Vienna in Austria, Stuttgart and West Berlin in Germany, Paris in France and Brussels in Belgium.

The post-war history of Vienna's non-Austrian population demonstrates very

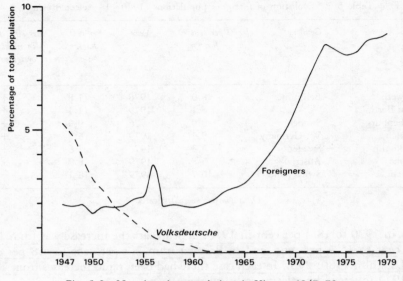

Fig. 5.2   Non-Austrian populations in Vienna, 1947–79.
(*Data sources*: *Statistisches Jahrbücher der Stadt Wien* 1948–79)

clearly the effects of refugee movements (Fig. 5.2). When the statistical series
begins in 1947 there were over 93,000 *Volksdeutsche* Germanic refugees from
Eastern Europe living in the city, but the accession to integration and Austrian
citizenship of this group, or their re-migration elsewhere, occurred relatively
rapidly. Nevertheless, even in the mid-1950s those still categorized as *Volksdeutsche* remained 1 per cent of the city's population and naturalized refugees
were of importance in the labour force. After 1953 the number of foreigners
came to exceed that of the *Volksdeutsche*. The effects of the 1956 Hungarian
Rising are obvious in the 20,000 refugees who fled to Vienna (these being
counted as foreign citizens): most were quickly provided with new opportunities
elsewhere and Hungarians as a group, who had leapt to the first rank of foreign
citizens in Vienna in 1956, fell to second place behind Germans in 1957, but
only moved down to third place in 1965 when they were overtaken by the
newly-arriving Yugoslavs. It was from 1960 onwards that Vienna started
witnessing large-scale labour migration and the increase continued until 1973
in which year foreign migrants constituted 12 per cent of all employed persons
and 22 per cent of the manual workers of the city (Gehmacher 1974: 165).
Although the post-1973 economic crisis has stopped this rapid growth, the
importance of foreigners has not, in practice, declined.

In West German cities, as in Vienna, there was no labour shortage in the
immediate post-war years because of the availability of refugees from the east.
In general it was not until the late 1950s and early 1960s that German
employers started to look abroad for large numbers of recruits. In Stuttgart the
foreign population was still only 2 per cent of the total in 1958, but from 1960
onwards growth was very rapid (Borris et al., 1977, p. 107; Gentileschi, 1977,

pp. 248–249). Those from Mediterranean countries increased most spectacularly, rising from 16 per cent of all foreigners in Stuttgart in 1955 to 67 per cent in 1961 and 84 per cent by 1976 (Borris et al. 1977: 13, 107).

In West Berlin the real demand for foreign migrants can be precisely dated to 1961 when the construction of the Berlin Wall deprived the western sectors of 10 per cent of their total work-force through the loss of 85,000 daily commuters from East Berlin and from East Germany beyond (Schulz 1975: 53). As in Stuttgart, the arrival of large numbers of foreign migrants has helped to compensate for the steady reduction in the numbers of resident Germans in the city.

In comparison with employers in the cities of West Germany, those in Paris and other French centres found themselves in need of the labour to be provided by international migrants very soon after the war, and the *Office National d'Immigration* was set up to regularize and supervise the flow (Ogden 1977: 8–9). From 1954 to 1975 the total number of foreigners living in Paris proper doubled whilst the total population was in decline: thus in 1975, foreigners composed 13.6 per cent of the population of the *Ville de Paris* whilst in the agglomeration as a whole their proportion was 11.9 per cent. One feature of French post-war history that may have depressed the need for migrants somewhat during the 1960s was the presence of those repatriated from Algeria of whom approximately 160,000 went to the Paris region during the years from 1962 to 1968. However, these repatriates went into employment sectors more representative of the native-born French themselves, and shunned the lower-status jobs for which foreign migrants were needed (Guillon 1974: 647, 660–2). It is a mark of the success of the French economy at that period that it was able to absorb so many new employees so successfully and so quickly.

Finally, in Brussels the proportion of foreign nationals actually declined between the censuses of 1947 and 1961 from 7.4 per cent to 6.7 per cent of the total population (De Lannoy 1975: 216–17). Belgium has had a relatively liberal policy on naturalizations, but the real cause of this stagnation of the foreigner population probably lies in the return to Belgium in the late 1950s, and especially in 1960, of large numbers of ex-colonists, of Belgian nationality, from the Congo (Mols 1968: 241–2). Foreign citizens constituted 80 per cent of the foreign-born in Brussels in 1947, but this proportion fell to 64 per cent in 1961 as a result of the increase in the number of foreign-born Belgians. Then between 1961 and 1970 the absolute number of foreign nationals in the city rose by just over 150 per cent, and by 1972 there were over 180,000 foreigners in the city (Meeus 1974: 677), constituting approximately 17 per cent of the total inhabitants. The case of foreign migrants in Brussels will be considered at greater length later in this chapter (pp. 126–8) because it illustrates the existence of both labour migrants and *élite* elements in international movements to a city.

The general conclusion from these six cities is that the early 1960s were the real take-off years of international labour migration in Western Europe. Differences between countries emerge in terms of the roles of refugees and repatriates, but the overall pattern is clear.

THE MIGRANTS: ORIGINS, CHARACTERISTICS AND OCCUPATIONS

The point has already been made that, whereas in the nineteenth century foreign migrants in Northern European cities had dominantly come from nearby countries, today the migrants originate from the Mediterranean basin and from the ex-colonies of the European powers. This can be illustrated by the case of Paris: in 1896 the dominant three migrant groups there were Belgians, Germans and Swiss, together constituting 52 per cent of the total foreigner population (Ogden 1977). By 1975, 82 per cent of foreigners in Paris came from the Mediterranean basin with the three dominant groups being from Portugal, Algeria and Spain.

This increase in Mediterranean migrants has been general throughout the cities of Northern and Central Europe, since it has been the countries around the Mediterranean basin that have generally retained higher population fertility rates longer, and which have had surplus manpower for export, especially from the agricultural sector. The only major Northern European countries offering similar possibilities of labour export have been Eire, with its migrants going to the United Kingdom, and Finland, which has been a supplier of labour to Sweden.

However, whilst the Mediterranean has been the chief post-war labour supply region there have been marked particularities in the distribution patterns of specific national groups between different destination countries and even between different cities within individual countries. Figure 5.3 shows, for thirty-four cities for which suitable data exist, the two first-ranking foreigner nationalities for the early 1970s, the exact years being those given in Table 5.2 for each country. Certain international contrasts are immediately obvious. In France the leading ranks are almost everywhere taken by Algerians, Spaniards, Italians or Portuguese: in Vienna and the limited number of West German cities for which comparable data are available, the greatest predominance tends to be of Turks and Yugoslavs. Amsterdam and the Belgian cities form an intermediate group with migrants from a variety of sources. Italians are dominant in Swiss cities, whilst in Gothenburg and Stockholm in Sweden, Finns are the dominant group.

These variations in migrant origins are brought out for a selection of cities in Table 5.4. The tabulation of such data involves great problems over the non-comparability of definitions, but the general patterns are relatively clear. Between one-fifth and one-quarter of foreign populations in North-Western European cities in the early 1970s generally consisted of migrants from countries at a similar stage of development – in other words from the rest of Northern and Central Europe (defined as the EC countries minus Italy and Greece, with the addition of Switzerland, Austria and Scandinavia). In Stockholm, 41 per cent of the 1970 foreigner population consisted of Finns – to some extent the equivalent of Mediterranean migrants in other cities. Except in this case, the foreigner populations drawn from Northern and Central Europe contain a relatively small proportion employed in low-status occupations.

108

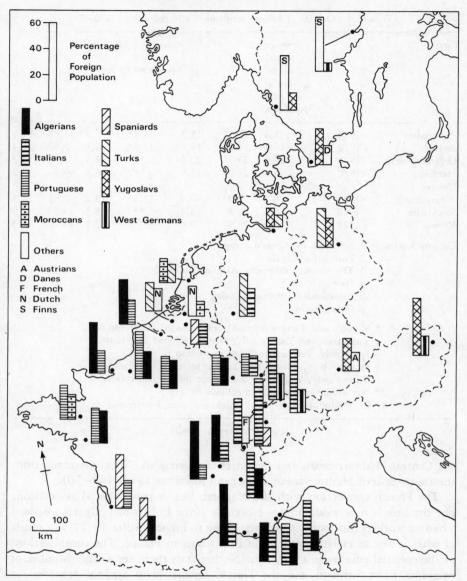

Fig. 5.3 Dominant foreigner nationalities, 1970–5.
(*Data sources*: see Appendix)

In the next four columns of Table 5.4 are detailed the origins of Mediterranean migrants. Whilst in France, Belgium and the Netherlands, North African migrants are of some importance, in the remaining countries they are not even identified in official figures. Directional biases appear, whereby France and the Low Countries obtain migrants from the south-western parts of the Mediterranean basin, Switzerland (represented here by Geneva) from Italy in

Table 5.4   Origins of foreign residents – selected cities, 1970–5

| City | Year | Foreign citizens as per cent of total population | Percentage of foreigners from | | | | | |
| | | | 1 | 2 | 3 | 4 | 5 | 6 |
					(see below for key)			
Amsterdam	1975	5.4	19.7	15.7	21.4*	7.3	21.8†	14.1
Brussels	1970	16.1	24.8	19.4‡	12.6¶	16.3	2.5‖	24.4
Greater Geneva	1970	34.0	29.2	20.5‡	**	38.3	1.8	10.2
Hamburg	1970	4.3	21.5	11.9	**	10.8	39.7	16.2
Greater Strasbourg	1975	8.5	9.2††	30.4	25.2	15.2	7.9†	12.1
Stockholm	1970	6.3	69.8	4.3	**	4.3	13.7	7.9
Vienna	1971	3.5	23.9	0.4‡	**	2.7	54.7	18.3

Column headings: 1 Northern and Central Europe
2 Portugal and Spain
3 The Maghreb (Morocco, Algeria, Tunisia)
4 Italy
5 Yugoslavia, Greece and Turkey
6 Other origins

* Morocco and Tunisia only, Algeria included in column 6
† Yugoslavia and Turkey only, Greece included in column 6
‡ Spain only, Portugal included in column 6
¶ Morocco only, Algeria and Tunisia included in column 6
‖ Turkey only, Yugoslavia and Greece included in column 6
** Not available, included in column 6
†† EC (excluding Greece and Italy) only, plus Switzerland

Data sources: see Appendix

the Central Mediterranean, and the cities of Austria and West Germany from the south-eastern Mediterranean countries (Johnston 1978: 149–50).

The French connection with the Maghreb lies in past colonial association, but the link is now weakening – especially since 1973 when Algeria imposed a ban on workers (but not dependants) going to France (Adler 1977), as a result of what it saw as racialist attacks on its citizens in France. The complications of the colonial past mean that in the Netherlands there are a large number of migrants from Surinam and the Dutch Antilles who are not regarded as foreigners. In Rotterdam in 1972, for example, there were 19,000 Mediterranean migrants, 7,000 of other nationalities (mostly from Northern Europe), plus 12,000 from the Dutch ex-colonies who can be disentangled from the Dutch population in statistical data only with difficulty if at all (Drewe at al. 1975: 204–5).

The patterns of migrant origin shown in Fig. 5.3 and Table 5.4 for the early 1970s are only a snapshot of an evolving situation. In the immediate post-war years, Italy provided the first migrant labour on any scale, particularly in Switzerland, but also in France. West Germany started taking in Italian workers in the late 1950s, but during the 1960s Italians (particularly from the south – the chief source area) were in increasing demand within their own country and consequently governments and employers in Switzerland and West Germany started to look elsewhere and to sign labour-supply agreements with more distant countries. Thus by the later 1960s, after the shortlived recession of 1967, Turks and Yugoslavs began to replace Italians as the chief migrant groups in the cities of Central Europe. In Stuttgart, for example, Italians were the dominant group until 1970 when they were overtaken by the Yugoslavs: by 1975 the rising number of Greeks in the city had pushed Italians into third place (Borris et al. 1977: 109). In Vienna, Yugoslavs were already the most important Mediterranean group by 1963, aided by proximity. The increase in the numbers of Turks and Yugoslavs in West German cities has been formidable. In West Berlin, Turks increased their representation in the foreigner population from 4 per cent in 1963 to 45 per cent ten years later.

In France the importance of Italians has also declined, with the 1960s in particular witnessing a rapid growth in migration from the Maghreb. This has also reduced the relative importance of the Spanish who, in the early post-war years, vied with the Italians for the role of leading migrant group in some French cities. By the early 1970s the Portuguese had become another migrant group of rapidly-growing importance in France (Ronzon 1979: 128–31). North Africans have also been absorbed into countries other than their traditional French destinations and, indeed, Belgian and Dutch cities saw their biggest migrant growth occurring from this area in the 1960s: the number of Moroccans in Brussels increased from 96 in 1961 to 21,852 in 1970 (De Lannoy 1975: 218).

In the early 1970s the net for migrants was spread wider still in the search for cheap sources of labour to maintain the supply into the lowest status but most essential jobs. By 1974, Paris had about 48,000 resident black Africans, dominantly from Mali, Mauretania and Senegal (Barou 1975: 363), many of whom enjoyed privileged rights of entry as a result of historic colonial links being replaced by neo-colonial paternalist ties. In West German cities there were small, but rapidly-growing, contingents from Iran, Jordan and Egypt by the end of the decade.

The age of a particular migration stream sometimes shows up in the local origins of the migrants, such that in the older streams (such as of Italians or Spaniards) it is the poorest rural areas that provide the migrants, but in the newer streams from Turkey or Yugoslavia the migrants originate in the most accessible and modernized regions, often from urban places (King, R. 1976; Clark 1977). However, there are many exceptions to these generalizations, and migrants most commonly come originally from rural areas, even if they have undertaken stage migration via the urban centres of their own countries. In Stuttgart in the mid-1970s, 70 per cent of Mediterranean migrants were born in villages, with the most rural contingents being from Yugoslavia, Greece and Italy: Turks appeared more commonly to come to Stuttgart via towns (Borris et al. 1977: 65–7). In France it has been observed that Paris receives a foreign migrant population that has a higher representation of those from urban backgrounds than is the case for the industrial cities, such as Lyon, where rural backgrounds predominate (Simon 1977: 260). Overall, however, rural origins predominate in contemporary international labour migration, just as they did in domestic migration to Northern European cities in the nineteenth century.

Newly-arriving migrant streams are overwhelmingly male and young (although not necessarily single – wives may be left at home initially): thus the sex ratios for new migrants are extremely unbalanced. In Stuttgart in 1974/5, for example, the overall sex ratio for all foreigners was 164 males to 100 females (Gentileschi 1977: 260) with the greatest imbalances occurring among the most recent migrants – 933 males per 100 females for North Africans, 400 for those from Black Africa and 326 for Turks (Borris et al. 1977: 27). Everywhere the older migrant groups, notably the Spanish and the Italians, have a better representation of females (Duchac et al. 1977: 10–11; Drewe et al. 1975: 208).

The age of the migration stream also shows up in the age-structure of the populations concerned. Newly-arriving migrants are almost exclusively in the young adult age-groups in new migration streams, as in Portuguese migration to the Lyon region in 1969 when a quarter of all migrants were in the single five-year age-group 25–9 (Poinard 1972: 39): similar results have been found in other detailed studies elsewhere (Geiger 1975: 64; Borde and Barrère 1978: 33). Newly-arriving migrants in older migration streams contain more prominent numbers of women and children as the innovative male migrants are joined by their families: indeed, such familial migration represents the most important migrant element at the present day in many cases.

Given the fact that large-scale migration is a feature only of the last twenty years or so, and that the initial migrants are always young males, it is inevitable that migrant communities should be dominantly composed of working adults and children, with an overall age-structure that emphasizes younger age-groups more than does that of the indigenous population. The more long-standing the migration stream the older is likely to be the age-structure: in Marseille in 1968, for example, 54 per cent of the resident Algerians were under 24 but only 20 per cent of the Spaniards fell in that age-group (Duchac et al. 1977: 10–11). In Nuremberg in 1972, 87 per cent of foreign men and 91 per cent of foreign women were under 45 years of age (Klamroth 1974: 143–4). In the *commune* of Brussels in 1970, 20 per cent of the population was foreign but 31 per cent of those aged 0–14 were of immigrant stock (Meeus 1974: 679; Mikkelsen et al. 1976: 67), a reflection both of the high proportion of foreigner families in the childrearing stages of the life-cycle and of migrant fertility that was above the local norm.

Very little is really known about the initial objectives of the labour migrants (White and Woods 1983), but the coventional wisdom is that the first wave of movers intended to stay abroad for only a short period, to save hard and to return home with as much money as possible (Böhning 1970: 23; Castles and Kosack 1973: 97). The temporary nature of their moves was often insisted upon by the host country through the system of short-term work permits and by categorizing many of them as seasonal workers. As these strict controls fell into reduced use in the early 1970s, and as the migrants achieved more permanent positions, they appear to have extended the time-scale of their stay abroad: arguably, some have done so as they have been socialized into the consumer aspirations of their host societies (Böhning 1972: 62–3), whilst another influence has been that many have found that they could not save as quickly as hoped perhaps because of their increased levels of expectations and desires. For these and other reasons concerned with acculturation, families are then sent for and, although the long-term intention to return 'home' may still be present, a lengthened stay in the migration destination becomes accepted. Whilst evidence of the continuation of the short-term migration intention in migrants at the time of movement continued to be produced during the 1970s (Gentileschi 1977: 266), a further body of survey results has started to accumulate suggesting that many migrants, for example from North Africa to France, have from the outset considered their moves as familial moves but with the dependants lagging behind the male household head and only joining him once accommodation had been secured suitable enough to satisfy the authorities into permitting family reunification, a process that may take five years or so (Duchac et al. 1977: 12; Rochefort et al. 1977: 180; Simon 1977: 255–7). Whatever the specific objectives of the migrants themselves, at an aggregate level it is generally found that the longer a particular migration stream has been in existence the greater will be the proportion of families within the migrant community and the higher will be the representation of the older age-groups (Gentileschi 1977: 260; Geiger 1975: 63).

Whilst these descriptions of migrant characteristics apply to the bulk of low-status labour migrants, somewhat different features pertain among high-status migrant groups and among refugees. Grimmeau and David-Valcke (1978) suggest that high-status, or middle-class, movement to Brussels is much more likely to involve nuclear families rather than just single male workers, and the same is doubtless true for other cities. Among refugees, taking the French *pieds-noirs* repatriates from Algeria in 1962 as an example, there is likely to be very little age-selectivity among the movers and also little sex-selectivity: this was a whole population on the move (Guillon 1974), as was also the case in the expulsion of the *Volksdeutsche* from Eastern Europe after the Second World War.

The established model of mass Mediterranean migration to Northern European cities is that the migrants are required for the lowest-status poorly-paid jobs; indeed, it is these jobs for which the migrants are most suited since they have poor educational backgrounds and have experienced limited opportunities for skill acquisition in their countries of origin. If, indeed, the migrants intend, at the outset, to stay only temporarily in the north, an extended period of training or apprenticeship is seen by them as both unnecessary and an impediment to their aim of amassing savings and returning home quickly. The general experience has therefore been that the mass of international migrants occupies the lowest rung in the Northern European occupational ladder (Schulz 1975: 56).

As for domestic migrants in Northern Europe in the last century and Southern European internal migrants today, so the building and construction industries are particularly dependent on migrant labour (Borde and Barrère

1978: 34): in addition, the widespread sub-contracting systems operating in these industries make them especially useful for those who are trying to evade official systems of registration and control. For example in the Lyon region of France in 1969, 77 per cent of the first jobs of illegal Portuguese migrants were on building sites (Poinard 1972: 39–42), a circumstance that was reminiscent of Southern Italians in Turin a decade earlier (see Chapter 4, pp. 82–3).

Apart from construction, the other key employment sector for foreign migrants is in manufacturing industry, almost always in unskilled or semi-skilled capacities. In Nuremberg in 1972, 50 per cent of foreign workers were employed in metallurgical industries, 15 per cent in general manufacturing and 16 per cent in construction (Klamroth 1974: 145–59). In Stuttgart in 1975, 67 per cent of working foreigners were employed in secondary activities – 40 per cent in manufacturing industry. A total of 92 per cent of the Mediterranean foreigners were categorized as manual workers against only 37 per cent of the German population of the city (Borris et al. 1977: 206–25). In the period 1966–8, 91 per cent of newly-arriving male foreign workers (*gastarbeiders*) in Amsterdam took employment in manual occupations (Anon. 1970: 48) and, at the end of that decade, 97.6 per cent of the new Mediterranean migrants could be categorized as being in the lowest two classes of a five-point categorization of background educational level (Cortie 1972a: 44–5).

Non-European migrants are particularly likely to be concentrated at the very bottom of the occupational hierarchy. In a study of migrants from the Maghreb in twelve industrial *communes* of the Paris suburbs, El Gharbaoui (1971) found that 86 per cent of the Algerian workers were classed as unskilled labourers and that this immigrant labour force was concentrated in larger firms where they formed a separate employment group outside normal management–employee relationships. El Gharbaoui also found that 88 per cent of North Africans living in the *commune* of Nanterre (with a North African population of 22,000) had no occupational qualifications whatsoever. Similarly in Lyon, North Africans are generally found in lower-status jobs than other foreigners (Dupré and Laferrère 1977: 301).

On the other hand, the migrants from the more long-standing migration streams (such as the Italians and Spanish), with their more balanced demographic composition, have also progressed further in the labour market and generally record lower proportions of unskilled workers. These nationalities are often found as site foremen or in other positions of greater responsibility, yet still dominantly within secondary activities or in public service employment (Poinard 1972: 42–3). Female international migrants, where they exist outside families, provide domestic service (Ogden 1977: 42, 44), the traditional role of female migrants in Western Europe. However, within families female employment rates tend to be low, further adding to the economic and social marginalization of the migrant groups (Borde and Barrère 1978: 35).

Whilst low-status migrants dominate in international flows, it is important to remember the other migrant groups. The numbers of low-status migrants from specific countries congregating in many cities has attracted independent migrants – shopkeepers, wholesalers, *restaurateurs* and various minor professions – to serve the needs of their fellow-countrymen by replicating the tertiary sector of the source areas. A significant proportion of this self-employed sector may, in fact, have 'risen' from the ranks of the labour migrants (Gentileschi 1978).

Refugees form a very complex group in terms of occupations. The *pieds-noirs* repatriated to France in 1962 integrated quickly within Paris and replicated the occupational patterns of French domestic migrants rather than those of other 'foreign' movers (Guillon 1974: 655–62). Eastern European refugees in West Germany after the Second World War showed more willingness to take industrial employment, albeit at a skilled level, and did much to keep down West Germany's need for Mediterranean migrants until the late 1950s (Elkins 1968: 154–5). The refugee flows from Hungary after 1956 and Czechoslovakia after 1968 were composed largely of intellectuals, but recent flows from the Horn of Africa to Italy have been absorbed only as highly marginal reserve workers in the lowest occupational classes (Arena 1982).

In total, despite the existence of *élite* migrant flows for employment concentrated in quaternary activities, the dominant picture of post-war international migration into Western European cities is of unskilled labour migrants with the exact characteristics of each migrant stream from source to destination being largely a function of the length of time that migration stream has been in existence. Migrant streams have generally approached maturity in the 1970s, so that the earlier dominance of the male single worker has been replaced by the moves of families, creating true ethnic minority communities in the destination cities rather than simply transitory groups of individuals.

MIGRANTS IN THE HOUSING MARKET

Research experience in Britain, by those looking at minority communities from the outside, has suggested that low-status foreign labour migrants may suffer relative disadvantage in the housing market from three causes (Johnston 1971). Although these influences may not all be of direct immediate concern to the migrants themselves, particularly where the migrant group holds strongly to the 'myth of return' to their original country at a future date, it is worthwhile considering in some detail the three factors that have been isolated.

The first is that, given the low wage-levels of the occupational sectors in which the migrants are concentrated (and their possible reluctance to pay much for housing anyway as this would reduce the level of their savings), the cards are stacked against them when they compete for housing in the open market where economic pricing operates. As has been seen in Chapter 2, rent controls have often kept prices down in the privately-rented sector in the past, but these controls have been reduced in many countries in recent years and, in addition, controls have rarely applied to sub-tenancies: hence international labour migrants may face economic difficulties in securing satisfactory accommodation on the open market in Northern European cities today, just as domestic migrants in the past became the victims of the poorest housing (see Ch. 4, pp. 80–1).

The second position of disadvantage of labour migrants today concerns the publicly-supported housing sector where allocation policies very often act to keep recent migrants out of contention for housing. Indeed, a 'Catch-22' situation has developed in some instances where single migrants are ineligible for public sector housing but where family members cannot be granted entry documents until satisfactory accommodation has been secured. The issuing of residence permits to dependants is commonly conditional upon the head of household having obtained accommodation that satisfies certain specified norms (Poinard 1972: 49–50; Mik and Verkoren-Hemelaar 1976: 276).

The third cause of disadvantage for migrants in the housing market may lie in prejudices against migrants, especially given the fact that recent migrants are often ethnically highly differentiated from indigenous populations. As a result of these three causes of disadvantage it might be expected that labour migrants will be very much concentrated into limited sectors of the housing market (White and Woods 1983).

The first places of residence of new migrants in many cities have been provided by employers; indeed, in West Germany and Switzerland, employers have generally had to guarantee lodging for the workers they wish to recruit before being permitted to sign them up (O'Loughlin 1980: 256). The chronic housing shortage in West Germany after the Second World War prompted large companies to build hostels and dormitories in order to secure their work-force, much as they had earlier done in the last years of the nineteenth century (see Ch. 1, p. 17). In the 1950s the occupants of these hostels were the refugees and *Volksdeutsche* from the east, but during the 1960s the Mediterranean migrants took over both the industrial roles of, and the accommodation that had been provided for, the refugees (Clark 1977: 26). Company accommodation (known as *Wohnheime* in German) has been most often provided by the largest employers who have been the most active direct recruiters of labour from abroad. The *Wohnheime* are built next to the factories, indeed often on the same sites, providing a strong element of potential segregation of the new single migrants. It is only after a year or two in such accommodation that migrants start to move, changing employers and making local migrations into private accommodation (Clark 1977: 17). Inevitably, therefore, the most recent migration streams involve higher proportions of migrants living in company housing, with more long-standing migration streams having witnessed the diffusion of their individual migrants into other forms of accommodation. In general in West Germany, the Yugoslavs are particularly over-represented in company housing (Rist 1978: 163–4): in Stuttgart in 1975, 29.9 per cent of all Mediterranean foreigners lived in company housing, but the rate stood at 50 per cent for Turks and 40 per cent for Portuguese, two of the most recently-arrived migrant groups. A total of 40 per cent of those housed in company accommodation worked in building and construction (Borris et al. 1977: 130–5).

Company housing has been less commonly provided in other countries, but in France it has been of some importance, especially in the building industry where workers have been housed in huts, caravans and prefabricated dwellings on the construction sites (Poinard 1972: 47–8). In France there is a further type of accommodation for single workers in which employers have played a role: these are the *foyers-hôtels* usually organized by 'mixed' companies involving both public and private finance (but sometimes built for a consortium of large employers) and often run by the police authorities. Workers must apply through their employers for a room (El Gharbaoui 1969: 46) but the rents are generally relatively high and consequently the *foyers-hôtels* have not always proved very popular, especially as there is an uneasy aspect of regimentation about them (Poinard 1972: 48). In Marseille, for example, only 15 to 20 per cent of Algerian single males have chosen to live in these *foyers-hôtels*: more prefer to stay in the remaining shanty-towns (*bidonvilles*) which offer greater collective psychological security (Kinsey 1979: 341). In West Germany, certain equivalents to the *foyers-hôtels* exist, for example the dormitories run by the *Jugend Sozialwerk* ('Social Work for Youth'), again with some employer involvement in the capital financing of construction (Clark 1977: 41): in Stuttgart in 1975, 3 per cent of Mediterranean migrants lived in such accommodation (Borris et al. 1977: 130).

New migrants who do not find accommodation waiting for them at the hands of their employers commonly go straight into the private rented housing sector as tenants or, more commonly, sub-tenants. Indeed, in the cities of Belgium and the Netherlands where employer-provided accommodation has been very rare, this has been the almost universal housing type for new migrants: in Amsterdam in the late 1960s, 90 per cent of new foreign migrants were being first housed as lodgers (Cortie 1972a: 48). Of course, the private rented sector does not just house new single migrants; it is generally the commonest housing sector for families as well and thus in West Germany, where company housing for new migrants is common, the proportions living in privately-rented property increase for older migration streams as single migrants move out of company property and are joined by their families (Clark 1977: 55; Rist 1978: 166). The privately-rented sector is a fluid one in which migrants move from sub-tenancy to sub-tenancy with great frequency, seeking to improve what are often their very poor housing standards; hence intra-urban migration rates for migrants in this sector are often very high (Rist 1978: 166; Borris et al. 1977: 172; see also Ch. 6, p. 136).

Recently-arrived single migrants often live together collectively in rented property or inhabit lodgings housing several individuals. In Paris in the early 1970s it was estimated that over 60 per cent of the black African workers lived in rented collective households with chain-migration processes leading to the clustering in each dwelling of males from one source village (Bergues 1973): such collective dwellings are generally known as *garnis* or *meublés* in France, distinguished from the *foyers-hôtels* by being privately owned and, unlike the *foyers-hôtels* which are sometimes purpose-built, generally located in older property. Chain-migration has been indicated as the cause of distinctive migrant groupings in other cities (Mik and Verkoren-Hemelaar 1976: 276; Geiger 1975: 66).

The actual properties rented by foreign labour migrants are overwhelmingly concentrated at the end of the market characterized by the poorest housing conditions, sometimes exacerbated in sub-tenancies where circumstances may be particularly scandalous with the owners of the properties (at least in France) being dubbed 'sleep merchants' (*marchands de sommeil*) because all they are providing is a bed, often used on a shift basis (Borde and Barrère 1978: 42). In Brussels in 1970, only 7 per cent of Moroccan migrants and 11 per cent of the Turks had the use of a bath or shower within their dwellings (De Lannoy 1975: 231–3). Similarly in Utrecht it was these two nationalities who lived in the poorest conditions whilst the older migrant groups such as the Spaniards and Italians (who were more likely to have their families with them) lived in better housing (De Smidt 1979: 24–5). In Frankfurt in 1974, only 42 per cent of the foreign migrants living in private flats had the use of a toilet within their own dwelling (Rist 1978: 164). In many of these respects the housing conditions of international migrants in Northern European cities today echo those of domestic migrants in Southern Europe, as exemplified by the case of Turin (see Ch. 4, pp. 84–85).

Whilst the private rented sector has been the major housing sector available for families of migrants, alternatives have been available. In France, large numbers of migrants have been housed in shanty-towns (*bidonvilles*), right up until the early 1970s. Other countries have managed, by and large, to avoid the creation of this housing class for migrants. The growth of *bidonvilles* around major French cities was a feature of the 1950s and, more especially, of the massive influx of North African labour in the 1960s. Although a law was passed in 1964 aiming at the resorption of the *bidonville* populations into 'normal' housing, progress was slow and still incomplete in the mid-1970s, especially in Marseille. Whilst single males have been an element in *bidonville* populations, a far larger contribution has generally been made by families: the *bidonville* has not been the first residence in the city of the head of the family, although his wife and children have often moved directly to such accommodation. El Gharbaoui (1971) provides a detailed study of the *bidonvilles* of the western Paris suburbs in the late 1960s. At that time the *commune* of Nanterre had 13 *bidonvilles* housing 8,180 people (32 per cent of the total resident immigrants and 9 per cent of the total population): 59 per cent of the *bidonville* residents were in family groups. By the later 1970s the *bidonvilles* around French cities had been much reduced in extent – those around Lyon had been eliminated by 1970 (Poinard 1972), whilst around Bordeaux they had all been cleared except for one housing 3,000 Spanish gypsies (Borde and Barrère 1978: 48). However, in 1973 in Marseille the *bidonville* population remained at 15,000 (Duchac et al. 1977: 19).

The movement of migrant families into public housing has been very slow almost everywhere except in Sweden where the government, at least until 1976, fostered deliberate integration of the migrants. Generally there have been problems over residence qualifications or the length of time to be spent on waiting lists. In West Berlin, where the city council has had specific policies to encourage the provision of housing for immigrants, only 1 per cent of migrants were in public housing in the mid-1970s (Rist 1978: 175). Nevertheless in Stuttgart in 1975, 7.3 per cent of Mediterranean foreigners were living in publicly-financed housing, with a further 4.3 per cent in housing association property (Borris et al. 1977: 130). Where migrant groups have started to arrive in areas of public housing, this has sometimes been seen as an indication of the lengthening time-horizon of 'temporary' migration, as the migrants take on certain of the attitudes to accommodation and way of life that dominate in the host society (Poinard 1972: 54).

However, one of the major reasons for the movement of migrant populations into public housing has lain in slum-clearance schemes destroying the poor inner-city rented property they had previously lived in. In France the clearance of the *bidonvilles* has similarly brought about rehousing in public sector accommodation, an intended half-way stage being the *cité de transit* in which it was the belief that the shanty-town population could be socialized to the norms of behaviour expected in 'normal' housing. For ex-*bidonville* residents, the length of stay in the minimal standard *cité de transit* was never supposed to exceed three years, but a study of such accommodation in the *commune* of Gennevilliers in the western suburbs of Paris in the mid-1970s showed that some families had lived in *cités de transit* since 1961 and that they were becoming a dumping place for immigrant families rather than providing the bridge to 'normal' public sector housing (Gokalp and Lamy 1977: 377, 391, 399–400). In Marseille, *cités de transit* have also been used, very few North African families passing into public housing without going through them (Duchac et al. 1977: 63)

Finally, it must be added that there is very little evidence indeed of international labour migrants moving into the owner-occupied sector. Certainly some of the landlords of poor-quality rented accommodation are themselves migrants but they form a very small group. Once again it is the age of the migration stream that is of importance: it is only the earliest migrant groups who have achieved any degree of owner-occupation (Borde and Barrère 1978: 39).

The housing of high-status international migrants can be quickly dealt with. Such migrants are sometimes offered 'tied' accommodation (for example by their multinational company employers) but most often they compete in the normal market for rented property – few move into either the owner-occupier or the publicly-financed sectors because of the usually temporary nature of their stay in any one city.

The *pieds-noirs* repatriates to France of 1962 were put in a special position *vis-à-vis* public housing: 30 per cent of all vacant places in such accommodation were reserved for repatriates for the next two years and certain new housing projects were started specifically for them. The overall result has been to concentrate the repatriate population into areas of housing completion during the period 1962–4 (Guillon 1974: 663).

The general conclusion on the housing of the foreign migrant population is that accommodation type varies according to the age of the migration stream with a change-over sometimes occurring once single workers are joined by their families. Certain housing types exist solely to cater for the migrant worker (for example the German *Wohnheime* and the French *foyers-hôtels* and *cités de transit*) but a large proportion of migrants find themselves competing in the open market for privately-rented property, where they invariably find themselves able to secure accommodation only at the lowest standards of amenity.

SEGREGATION

Social and spatial segregation of minority migrant groups in cities has given rise to a vast literature in the Anglo-Saxon world (Peach 1975). In general, three major influences on the integration of migrant groups have been identified (Johnston 1971: O'Loughlin 1980: 268–9). Firstly, there is possible discrimination by the majority population. Secondly, there is the control influenced by the socio-economic status of the minority group, this being particularly important in determining the position of the migrants in relation to the housing market. Thirdly, there is the question of the degree of self-identity and ethnic affiliation demonstrated by the migrants themselves. These three controls are not, however, completely independent: for example, migrants faced by prejudice may increase their own internal cohesiveness as a group, and thus there may be a time sequence in the operation of the three influences.

In the Anglo-American world, great stress has often been put on the first of these factors (Rex and Moore 1967), and prejudice and discrimination certainly exist in Western Europe, being almost institutionalized in the handling of migrant families by public housing authorities in France. Nevertheless there are generally fewer mechanisms available for converting prejudice into spatially observable discriminatory practices than exist in the USA, so that prejudice, where it does exist, may not be so apparent in spatial patterns. However, an example of the effect of prejudice is considered later in this chapter in the case of St Etienne in France (p. 130).

The second factor, that of socio-economic status, is likely to be of great importance in Western Europe, given the migrants' *raisons d'être* in the city. If apparent segregation of migrant groups exists, it is therefore useful to ask whether this might not simply arise from social class and whether, if social class is controlled, the segregation is still discernible. These questions have been similarly asked in North America (Darroch and Marston 1971) where the general answer has been that ethnicity (or migrant status) is more important than social class.

It is arguable that the third factor, of migrant self-identity, has been of greatest importance in Western Europe. If the real intention of many migrants has been to save money as fast as possible and then return home, it is possible that there might be a collective migrant mentality that is uninterested in any form of social or cultural integration or assimilation to the host society. A result of this might be the concentration of migrants, brought together by chain-migration, in specific parts of the city to replicate the life-style of their origins.

Earlier sections of the present chapter have indicated the significance of the age and date of the migration stream, whereby those streams with a longer history contain more family groups and display a tendency to greater permanency of composition within the host areas. This is related to differences in housing between older and newer migrant groups and may thus be associated with differentiated spatial patterns of residence, these perhaps also being observable between earlier and more recent migrants in specific migration streams.

In considering the importance of migrant self-identity it is necessary to point out the great difficulty of getting the authentic voice of the migrants. Large numbers of surveys have been carried out, often using members of the migrants' own communities as interviewers and interpreters, but the fact remains that most published literature is written from the outside looking in. The material that gets nearest to the migrant viewpoint is that produced by members of the minority communities, such as Dahya's work among Pakistanis in England (Dahya 1973) and that by El Gharbaoui (1969; 1971) and Ben Sassi (1968) amongst North Africans in France: the last of these is particularly interesting for it quotes extracts from unstructured interviews with over 140 Tunisians working in the Paris area.

El Gharbaoui's work (1971: 47) suggests that the general outline of migrant objectives given earlier in the present chapter (pp. 112–13) is broadly correct. Migrants quickly found that their initial objective of a speedy return home was impossible because the high cost of living in France meant that they could not save very quickly: consequently their objective quickly changed to that of working in France for as long as possible before family or other commitments took them home. If those commitments could be transferred to France (for example, if the family could be brought over) then the period of residence in France could be further extended. A similar attitudinal change has been noted by Poinard (1972: 44–6) amongst Portuguese migrants in Lyon. Here it took around two years for the single male migrants to accept that a quick fortune was impossible, and to take steps to bring the family in. In both of these reported cases, however, the long-term intention was still to return 'home', and the migrants' practice of living with others from the same origin reinforced the 'home' culture and retarded the possibility of assimilation to the host society.

The long-term prospect of 'return' becomes, of course, much more complex for the second generation of the migrant community, many of whom have been born in the cities of North-West Europe. Migrant community children who have grown up and attended school in France or West Germany, whilst often facing considerable educational difficulties over language acquisition and use (Gentileschi 1977; El Gharbaoui 1971: 50), nevertheless become socialized in some respects to the host society's norms and expectations. This may result in stress within migrant families (Schnapper 1976: 487) and to the desire amongst the children for a greater degree of integration. These questions lead on to wider issues of the long-term role of the ethnic minority communities as suppliers of labour exclusively to limited sectors of the economy.

One important factor fostering the self-identity of certain migrant groups is religion, the Islamic populations of North and West Africa and from Turkey perhaps grouping within their own communities for psychological security against the surrounding Christian society (Clark 1977). Barou (1975) has contrasted the black Africans in Paris – dominantly Islamic from Mali, Mauretania and Senegal – with those in Lyon who are from the Christianized south coast of West Africa. In Paris there is clustering into collective dwellings where the migrants attempt to reconstruct the life of their home villages; in Lyon they play a more participative role in urban society, less isolated from the world outside their lodgings.

As a general conclusion it may be suggested that the dominant pattern of labour migrant community involvement in Northern European cities is to a large extent controlled by the considerable degree of self-identity within the migrant groups. Surveys sometimes show that the migrants wish to have more contact with the indigenous population: for example in Rotterdam in the early 1970s, 53 per cent of Spaniards, Italians and Turks interviewed said they wanted more contact with the Dutch (Drewe et al. 1975: 211). But this desire for contact is based only on a strong pattern of migrant community solidarity – it is not actually integration that is sought, as indeed is unlikely in a situation where 62 per cent of the surveyed migrants arrived in the city through chain-migration processes (Drewe et al. 1975: 212).

In some cases, extreme social segregation occurs (as with the Islamic West Africans in Paris), but even where a high degree of social contact exists between migrants and hosts, the migrants are distinguished by their obvious and self-perceived membership of a separate community (Geiger 1975: 69), additionally set apart by the long-term wishes of a substantial proportion of its members to return to their native lands. This applies not only to the labour migrants *en masse* but also to the middle-class and professional migrants in such cities as Strasbourg, Amsterdam, Geneva and Brussels (Grimmeau and David-Valcke 1978).

Among the few migrant groups with a positive desire for assimilation are those who have little chance of returning (such as refugees) or those of higher educational background from societies which can offer no future to them. An example of the former are the *pieds-noirs* from Algeria who have assimilated well into the Parisian social and occupational structure (Guillon 1974). An example of the latter is the small community from the Indian Ocean island of Réunion now living in Toulouse: this community is dominantly of the technically skilled and eschews the use of creole with the intention of turning their children into true French (Ah-Peng 1976). These, however, are exceptions to the general pattern.

When consideration is given to the spatial distribution of migrants within the city, the spotlight turns to the socio-economic status of the migrants. Just as the indigenous population has shunned certain jobs and has been replaced by the labour migrants, so it might be expected that a similar transformation should occur in housing, with the migrants replacing the native population in the poorest accommodation. The migrants should then be concentrated in areas of the cheapest rented housing where they should display relatively little segregation from the native-born classes nearest to them in the status hierarchy. However, this association in the Western European case is likely to be disturbed by the existence of specific housing for migrants which may be scattered throughout the city. For example, the important sector of company housing in West Germany tends to be relatively peripheral in location, being tied to the large industrial plants which often lie in suburban areas. Thus O'Loughlin (1980: 269) found that when he correlated the distribution of migrants in Düsseldorf in West Germany with that of Germans at similar status levels the result showed only a relatively weak association. The explanation must lie largely in the presence of foreigners in company housing in some areas where similar-status Germans were only weakly represented and the absence of foreigners from many areas of public housing.

In fact the apparent suburbanization of foreign migrants is a feature that is present in many cities. In the Lyon region in 1975 the city itself had a population consisting of 9.9 per cent foreigners, while in the rest of the agglomeration 13.1 per cent were foreign: in Zürich in 1970 the proportions of foreigners were 17.5 per cent in the city and 21.1 per cent in its surroundings. Similar phenomena exist in other cities such as Grenoble, Lille and Geneva. In general, however, the normal pattern is for greater concentrations of foreign migrants to occur towards city-centres, although the existence of migrants in villages at the urban fringe is far from rare, just as contemporary domestic migrants in Southern Europe have often taken up residence in peripheral settlements around the urban centres (see Ch. 4, p. 84). In Geiger's (1975) study of Tamm, a village to the north of Stuttgart and within easy commuting distance of the city, he found 13.2 per cent of the resident population in 1972 to be foreign labour migrants: in the centre of the village, built before 1880, there were 145 *Gastarbeiter* to 144 Germans, whilst in the post-war areas of the settlement foreigners were almost entirely absent. Spatial concentration of the migrant population can therefore occur at a variety of scales. In general, O'Loughlin's conclusion (O'Loughlin 1980: 259) that:

the spatial distributions of foreigners in German cities display two consistencies – concentration near the city centre and near industrial areas

can be accepted as being applicable elsewhere as well.

The concentration of foreign migrants is immediately apparent in Fig. 5.4 where the distribution of foreigners is mapped for five cities varying in size from Antwerp (population 197,000 in 1978) to the central area of Paris (1968 population of 2.5 million). A great drawback to the production of such comparisons is the varying size of the administrative units in each city. Antwerp in particular includes large semi-rural areas within the city boundary to the north along the estuary of the River Scheldt. In the case of Paris the map relates only to the twenty *arrondissements* of the city proper and ignores the surrounding suburban *communes*.

One feature that is immediately apparent from Fig. 5.4 is that there are few districts in any of these cities where foreign migrants are virtually absent in relation to the city as a whole. The area of under-representation in Antwerp is the semi-rural belt. In Brussels, West Berlin and Zürich there is under-representation in the most affluent parts of the city, although in Brussels the

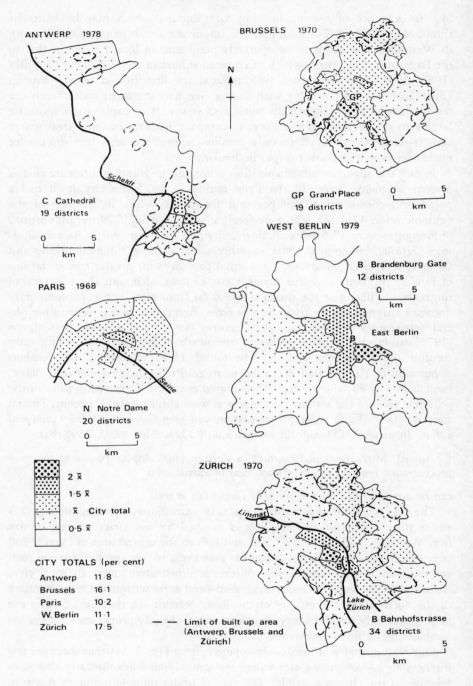

Fig. 5.4   Foreign migrants in Antwerp, Brussels, Paris, West Berlin and Zürich.
(*Data sources*: see Appendix; Meeus 1974; Ogden 1977)

traditionally Flemish areas of the north-west are also shunned – the migrants being often French-speaking from North Africa (Nelde 1982: 44). Of the twenty *arrondissements* in central Paris, none had a representation of foreigners that was less than half that of the overall city in 1968. However, the relative ubiquity of foreigners in this and other cities to some extent masks the fact that high-status and labour migrant elements tend to be distributed very differently, each concentrating in a separate area. This point will be further examined below (pp. 126–8) for the case of Brussels.

Figure 5.4 also indicates that there is a general concentration at or near the city-centre, the densest concentrations in fact often lying just outside the centre in the oldest areas that are still dominantly residential: this is the case in Brussels and also in Paris and Zürich where the heaviest migrant over-representation is just to the north of the central business districts. It is worth examining certain case studies of migrant distributions in greater detail before further general conclusions can be put forward.

For Paris, Ogden's (1977) work is a useful starting point as it provides an historical perspective to present-day distributions. Using principal components analysis of the distribution of 21 nationalities through the 20 *arrondissements* of Paris in 1896, Ogden found his first component to link a series of high-status migrant groups with the domestic servants employed by them, the two divisions being, respectively, the British, Americans and Scandinavians, and the Portuguese and Spanish. Within the city they were concentrated in the more affluent western areas towards the Bois de Boulogne and the Champs Elysées and there was almost total avoidance of the more industrial east of the city. The second component for 1896 grouped the Germans, Hungarians, Belgians, Austrians and Swiss – all major providers of commercial and industrial labour to the Parisian economy and the contemporary equivalents of labour migrants: these were dominantly located in the central and north-eastern parts of the city. The relevance of these groupings shown by the two components has a history going back at least to the first third of the nineteenth century (De Bertier de Sauvigny 1977: 177).

Ogden repeated his analysis for 1968, this time for 14 nationalities. Once again a high-status component scoring positively in the affluent west emerged, with avoidance of the industrial north-east. The nationalities involved were Belgians, British, Dutch, Germans, Swiss and Spanish, the Spaniards continuing to fill the role of domestic servants (Ranger 1977: 816). It is notable that the Belgians, Germans and Swiss had changed from being labour suppliers in the late nineteenth century to being high-status migrants today; their position in the second component, once again with highest scores in the centre and north-east, had been taken by the North Africans, Yugoslavs and Poles.

Between 1896 and 1968, therefore, the two foreign migrant districts of Paris (the prosperous west and the commercial–industrial centre and north-east) have remained stable in location and status but with the composition of the migrant groups evolving as all Northern European migrants have progressively moved into the high-status category, being replaced as labour migrants by Mediterraneans.

Nevertheless there are dangers in seeing a too-simple dichotomy between the migrant areas of Paris, especially if the suburban *communes* are added to the picture. The pattern of industry surrounding the city (Fig. 9.1) and the complexities of housing provision distort the simple east—west split. Beyond the Bois de Boulogne to the west lie *communes* such as Nanterre in which high concentrations of North Africans occur in areas that once accommodated Paris's biggest *bidonvilles*. Apart from the Algerian quarter in the 18th *arrondissement* to the north of the city-centre, already well established by 1960 (Cobb 1980a), there are few neighbourhoods dominated by immigrants, although extreme concentration does occur at the level of the street-block, particularly where migrants are housed by building speculators as a means of publicizing the unhealthiness of property that they wish to demolish and redevelop (Ceaux et al. 1979: 106). The sysem of *garnis* or lodgings used by migrants creates a localized pattern of labour migrant distribution with 'islands' of such migrants scattered throughout the old artisan areas both of the inner-city and of the inner industrial suburbs (Barou 1975: 369–70).

The distinction between high- and low-status migrant areas made in Paris is much clearer in the case of Brussels where the selection of the city as the headquarters of NATO, of the European Community and of many multi-national companies in the period since 1946 has brought in large numbers of foreign personnel *de haut standing*, alongside the labour migrants from the Mediterranean basin. The occupational separation between the two groups is acute: in 1970 only 15.4 per cent of the British in Brussels were classed as manual workers, 11.4 per cent of the Germans and 2.7 per cent of the Americans (Grimmeau and David-Valcke 1978: 33–4): amongst the Turks, by comparison, 86.2 per cent were in this category (De Lannoy 1975: 233). The general spread of foreigners throughout Brussels, apparent in Fig. 5.4, is thus composed of two specific sub-groups of very different social status.

From the information published in the 1970 census it is, in fact, possible to calculate the indices of dissimilarity between different groups of migrants in Brussels. This has been done to produce the linkage tree shown in Fig. 5.5. When the indices of dissimilarity between individual groups are examined, the French and Dutch are the most alike in spatial distribution through the city's nineteen *communes*. When the indices are recalculated with the French/Dutch as one amalgamated group, the lowest index is between that amalgamation and the British. This procedure was repeated through nine steps until all the migrant groups had been brought in. The result of this clustering procedure is to distinguish very clearly between high-status and low-status migrants on the basis of spatial dissimilarity. Somewhat surprising, perhaps, is the extreme isolation of the Turks who, in 1970, constituted only 2.4 per cent of the total foreigner population and were highly concentrated in a single zone of the city near the North station (De Lannoy 1975: 227): this appears to be a clear case of segregation brought about by chain-migration among the most recent migrant group.

De Lannoy has, in fact, calculated indices of segregation for the most important migrant groups for 1970 on the basis of a division of Brussels into

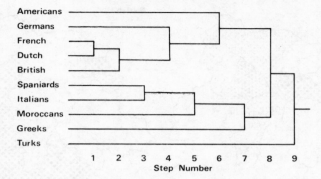

Fig. 5.5   Foreigner clusters on the basis of indices of dissimilarity, Brussels, 1970.
(*Data sources*: see Appendix; Meeus 1974; De Lannoy 1975)

567 census tracts (Table 5.5). The smallest groups, such as the Turks and Americans, display a high degree of segregation but certain large low-status migrant groups, such as the Spaniards and the Moroccans, are more spatially concentrated than smaller higher-status groups such as the Germans and British. The most recently-arrived groups tend to display greater segregation than older groups of similar size (De Lannoy 1975: 235).

The spatial zonation of the city is relatively straightforward with the Mediterranean migrants concentrated around the centre and along the industrial belt from north-east to south-west along the line of the canal: in this area the migrants are partly replacing the Belgian population who are leaving for the city periphery (Mikkelsen et al. 1976: 66), but areas of young foreign migrants also tend to have over-representations of older Belgians so that the foreigners also bring rejuvenation (De Lannoy 1978: 19). The high-status migrant areas are especially on the plateau to the south-east of the city-centre in the suburbs beyond the European Community headquarters. Figure 5.6 illustrates the contrast in distributions between two representative groups, the Moroccans and the British. It is immediately apparent that the two maps are

Table 5.5   Segregation indices for foreign nationalities, Brussels, 1970

Nationality	Per cent of total foreigners	Index of segregation
Spaniards	19.4	50.6
Italians	16.4	34.9
French	13.4	21.7
Moroccans	12.6	58.1
Greeks	5.5	63.4
Dutch	4.0	26.4
Germans	3.1	45.1
British	3.0	38.6
Turks	2.4	68.3
Americans	2.4	61.3

Data sources: Meeus 1974; De Lannoy 1975

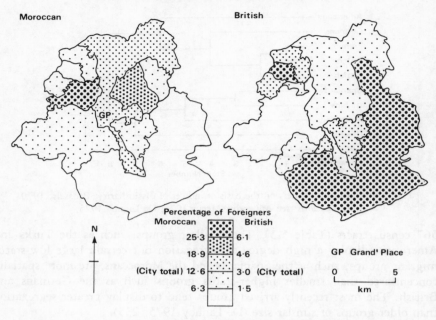

Fig. 5.6   Distributions of Moroccans and British in Brussels, 1970.
(*Data source*: Meeus 1974)

almost mirror images of each other, with areas of Moroccan concentration having very few British and vice versa.

Even within the two broad zones of the city, however, there are different detailed patterns of distribution for different nationalities (Mols 1968: 248). Even the high-status migrants display the tendency for those from a common nationality to group together in a particular district (Grimmeau and David-Valcke 1978: 41), perhaps a reflection of limitations of information flow, a feature which goes against the established notion that high-status migrants are unlikely to create distinct clusters but will spread throughout the social areas to which they are most suited by their socio-economic levels (Boal 1978: 75).

In relation to Fig. 5.4, it is useful to make a final comment about West Berlin where *Gastarbeiter* have helped to fill the labour vacuum caused by the ageing of the indigenous population, the loss of East German commuters after the building of the Wall, and the continuous emigration of young Berliners to the Federal Republic. By the mid-1970s, approximately 30 per cent of annual births in the city were to foreign women. Realizing the long-term importance of foreigners to the city, the authorities in West Berlin have done more than many elsewhere to create housing for foreign workers, with generous subsidies for company housing and improved access to public sector accommodation. However, West Berlin arguably has the greatest degree of migrant segregation of the cities illustrated in Fig. 5.4, with a strong over-representation in the three central-city districts which, in 1979, held 36 per cent of the city's migrants against only 18 per cent of its total population: in one of these districts, Kreuzberg, foreigners formed 26.9 per cent of the resident population. Since 1975 the authorities have refused entry permits for new immigrants who intended to take up residence in any of these three inner-city districts (Rist 1978: 157, 169) although that has no influence on intra-urban migration. Internal migration of foreigners within West Berlin displays a feature common to other German cities – that new migrants are less segregated than others and that the first intra-urban move by a new migrant generally takes him to a more segregated neighbourhood: this is a reversal of the normal simple model of decreased segregation through time (Lieberson 1963). Because of the great importance of company housing for new migrants, they are scattered throughout the city, but as they stay longer and move into privately-rented housing successive moves tend to group specific migrant nationalities together and increase segregation (Rist 1978: 169). It is only as a result of later intra-urban moves, perhaps accompanying the arrival in the city of the worker's dependants and taking the family group out to peripheral public sector housing, that a reduction of measurable segregation occurs. Because of this latter process the overall distributions of foreigners in West Berlin have fanned out in recent years. The overall segregation of individual foreign groups, as measured by segregation indices, has generally fallen during the 1970s; for example, the index for Turks fell from 49.4 in 1973 to 38.0 in 1979 whilst that for Yugoslavs fell from 29.6 to 23.4 over the same period.

In many other cities throughout Western Europe these patterns of migrant distributions seen in Paris, Brussels and West Berlin are, to some extent, replicated. Even the embryonic growth of foreign migrant communities in Southern European cities displays the familiar features of concentration in poor-quality rented accommodation close to the major railway stations of Milan or Rome (Arena 1982).

The division between high-status and low-status foreign migrants is observable in Bordeaux in the nineteenth century where the British and German merchant classes were spread throughout the better-off parts of the city, whilst the Spanish were concentrated in an inner-city area just south of the centre where they still form a distinctive feature, although now joined by North Africans and others (Guillaume 1972: 72–80; Barrère and Cassou-Mounat 1980: 10). In both Bordeaux and Lyon it is the oldest residential areas that are the habitat for the newest migrants, France not having as much company-provided housing as West Germany: the newest migrants tend to replace older migrant groups in the poorest housing, often scheduled for demolition (Borde and Barrère 1978; Barou 1975: 371; Poinard 1972: 52–3). Within Marseille, immigrants are concentrated in the poorest inner-city *arrondissements* and in industrial and port areas to the west, with a strong tendency for the grouping of migrants from common origins (Duchac et al. 1977: 13–16).

However, throughout France increasing numbers of migrants are being moved into the peripheral *grands ensembles*, as a result of city-centre slum-clearance, the removal of the *bidonvilles*, or by residence qualification for public housing: however, such peripheral housing, with its lack of easy access, is not popular with the migrants (Duchac et al. 1977: 50). There is a continuing pattern of single migrants in city-centres and families on the outskirts, only the families now live in public-sector housing instead of in shanty-towns.

France also provides examples of the effect of prejudice being translated into behaviour creating segregation. In a study of forty *communes* of greater St Etienne, Ronzon (1979) found that where school catchment areas were not formally demarcated and parental choice of school was free, the schools were strongly segregated but residential neighbourhoods could be mixed. Where school district boundaries were rigidly enforced, French families moved out of the 'migrant' districts thus increasing segregation. The flight of the French appeared to occur once migrant schoolchildren amounted to about 30 per cent of school rolls, this being the level perceived as significant by both teachers and parents alike (Ronzon 1979: 154–6).

Larger French provincial cities such as Lyon also demonstrate spatial separation between Northern European and Mediterranean migrants, as in Paris and Brussels. In Lyon the North Africans live in the centre and east of the city and the Northern Europeans in the middle-class west, although their absolute numbers are relatively small (Rochefort 1977: 329). In the Swiss city of Bern, the labour migrants live in the centre and the high-status migrants live in the rural fringes to the south-east of the city (Gächter 1978).

In the Netherlands, as pointed out earlier (p. 102), the examination of labour migration is made more complex by the presence of Surinamers of Dutch citizenship. In both Amsterdam and Rotterdam, new labour migrants at the start of the 1970s were being drawn to turn-of-the-century areas close to the city-centre, in the absence of peripheral employer-provided housing: in particular there were concentrations in areas of large property that could be sub-divided (Drewe et al. 1975; Van Amersfoort and Cortie 1973: 289). Utrecht similarly displayed central-city foreign migrant concentration, with foreigners congregating at the centre to a far greater extent than was the case for Dutch migrants of similar status (Cortie 1972b: 325). Ethnic identity was also felt to be of greater importance than social class in leading to clustering within Amsterdam (Cortie 1972a: 52), although it is difficult to give too much credence to this conclusion since the ethnic groups do not contain a reasonable cross-section of social classes. In Utrecht, as in Brussels (p. 126), different nationalities within the labour migrants showed different spatial distributions and the calculation of indices of dissimilarity suggested that the newest migrant groups (such as the Turks and Moroccans) were most localized, with older groups (such as the Spaniards, Greeks and Italians), who were more likely to have their families with them, having a spatial distribution that was more akin to that of the Dutch themselves (De Smidt 1979: 23–5), possibly therefore reflecting decreasing segregation through time (Lieberson 1963).

In West German cities there are everywhere marked migrant concentrations in older districts: for example by 1973, foreigners already constituted over 30 per cent of the population of the central district of Frankfurt (Rist 1978: 161–3). Almost everywhere foreigners act to compensate the declines of the German population in city-centres as the Germans leave for more periph-eral locations (Gentileschi 1977: 253; Schenk 1975: 230): the same has occurred to increase the importance of foreigners in industrial areas (Sprengel 1978: 145; Borris et al. 1977: 116–21). In Hanover, as in West Berlin, the 1970s saw large-scale movement from the peripheral *Wohnheime* into more centrally-placed private accommodation as migrants were joined by their families, but certain peripheral areas also saw increases in foreigners as a result of housing allocation policies by public housing agencies (Sprengel 1978: 141–4). In considering the distributions of migrants of different nationalities, even within the general group of labour migrants, studies in West German cities have once again shown the varied patterns that emerge. In Düsseldorf, O'Loughlin and Glebe (1981) found that different independent environmental variables had the greatest explanatory power for the distributions of different nationalities – the distribution of Turks, for example, was best explained by the proximity to industrial areas, whilst the distribution of Greeks was most closely correlated with poor housing standards. In general, however, throughout West German cities the low-status foreigner populations are less segregated from each other than from the Germans, with the oldest migrant groups, such as the Italians, being the least segregated. To talk of segregation is, however, to use the term with a much less extreme meaning attached than would be the case in US cities – here, as elsewhere in Western Europe, segregation is only complete, if at all, at the level of the apartment block; at street-block scale it exists in a watered-down fashion whilst at census district scale it is strictly only true to speak of degrees of over- or under-representation (O'Loughlin 1980: 266–8).

CONCLUSIONS

Chapter 4 and the present chapter have together presented a specific historical evolutionary scenario of migration to Western European cities. That overall scenario is, in many of its broad respects, unique to the European continent and this means that the features of migrant settlement in the cities are not necessarily directly comparable with events and patterns elsewhere.

In particular, the process by which domestic rural–urban migration has been replaced by international labour flows does not have a counterpart in developed countries in other parts of the world. In the countries of the 'new' developed world (North America and Australasia), rural–urban migration within the countries concerned could never be of major significance, except in the case of the United States: national patterns of population distribution were, from an early date, dominated by urban areas and the cities largely grew by international migration from Western Europe. In the United States, large-scale domestic rural–urban migration, when it did occur during and after the First World War, was of blacks from the southern states to the northern cities with a timing that was the reverse of the European experience: domestic migration occurred only after the halting of large-scale international migration. In another country of the developed world – Japan – urban–industrial growth has been a post-war phenomenon in which local rural areas have been able to supply sufficient labour, at least until recent years when the phenomenon of *Kaso* (severe depopulation) has become a problem.

A very important aspect of post-war international labour flows in Western Europe has been that many of those involved, both the public authorities and the migrants themselves (for different reasons), have perceived migrants' stays in their places of destination to be temporary. Even now, when families have joined the earlier single male migrants, the long-term intention of 'return' is a significant attitudinal feature of the migrant communities, although arguably weakening in importance as the number of second- or even third-generation migrants begins to increase and as the minority communities move over from being based on migration in common to a basis of ethnicity in common. This perceived self-identity, or separateness, of the migrant group is both generated by, and reinforces, the 'myth' of return and appears to be of considerable importance in producing clustering amongst individuals and families from a common origin.

However, clustering is not solely a result of the desire of migrants to stay apart; it is also very strongly influenced by the socio-economic status of the labour migrants and by the life-cycle characteristics of the migration streams. As migration streams have aged, migrant communities have normally become dominated by family groups whereas in the earlier stages of migration single males formed the vast majority of the movers. Accordingly, in all cities there are differences of demography, occupation and distribution between resident foreigners of different nationalities so that it is more accurate to speak of a variety of migrant groups rather than of labour migrants as a single unitary entity in any one city. Recently-arrived single migrants are concentrated in inner-city areas, just as other single people (such as students and the old) are similarly concentrated. Family groups are more noticeable in more peripheral housing areas, just as is the case for the indigenous populations, although it would also be true to say that the speed of movement out from central areas has been relatively slow. This is because foreign migrants are under-represented in areas of public sector housing so that they are confined, to a great extent, to the cheapest levels of the privately-rented sector and such property is most concentrated in and around older inner-city areas. In terms of occupation and status level, therefore, foreign migrants share certain inner-city areas with indigenous workers at a similar place in the hierarchy but are severely under-represented in the peripheral post-war *grands ensembles* that make up the other major belt of worker housing.

Since the pattern of distribution of foreign labour migrants within Western European cities to some extent replicates the overall distributional characteristics of the indigenous population of similar socio-economic and life-cycle status, it is perhaps unsurprising that segregation levels of the migrant communities are relatively low. Migrant segregation commonly occurs on a house-by-house level, less frequently on a block-by-block basis, and never at the scale of a district as a whole. Low-status migrants are distributed to individual houses and apartment blocks throughout the low-status areas of the city and there are no signs of the development of minority ghettos (to use an Italian word that has been subject to redefinition elsewhere). The closest approximation to exclusive migrant communities existed in the *bidonvilles* around various French cities and in their replacement in the *foyers* and *cités de transit* (Rochefort 1977: 331). The West German *Wohnheime* company lodgings have similarly been occupied exclusively by migrants, but their lengths of stay have been relatively short as they have filtered into 'normal' housing within a few years of arrival to be replaced by the next cohort of migrants.

Prejudice among the majority community certainly exists, being reflected in violence against Algerians in Marseille, and in the riots in Rotterdam in 1972 (Drewe et al. 1975: 213–15), and it can also be seen at the root of the slow but steady pace of out-migration of native populations from areas of growing migrant concentration, but the formalizing and institutionalizing of prejudice into administrative structures is largely absent. There is little evidence of the real existence of an invasion-succession process in inner-city areas (O'Loughlin 1980: 271), and in suburban areas increases in the numbers of foreigner families gaining public sector housing, albeit at a slow pace, will create more mixed neighbourhoods without the likelihood of stronger segregation. For these reasons European commentators have spoken against attempts to transplant into the European context American models of ethnic minority development in the city: these have been condemned as both irrelevant and unhelpful (Pahl 1970b: 5; De Lannoy 1975: 234; Van Amersfoort and Cortie 1973: 285).

It is possible that the evolutionary model of migration to Western European cities developed in the last two chapters may now be played out. With zero economic growth over large parts of the Continent, international labour migration has largely stopped, although the movement of dependants continues to produce more balanced migrant communities with, as pointed out earlier, the potential for self-replacement rather than the need for constant replenishment by fresh waves of migration. In Southern Europe the rural labour reservoir is now starting to empty in certain regions, but it is possible that economic growth will be too slow to require new international labour flows. Everywhere, however, it is feasible to see further increases in the importance of high-status migrants, employed by international organizations and multinational enterprises, who contribute their own distinct patterns to the social geography of many Western European cities.

Post-war international migration in Western Europe has occurred on a massive scale and has transformed the economic and social geography of the region as a whole. Within the cities it has brought new complexities of population composition, new social structures and created new subtleties to the social organization of urban space. In many cities, foreigners constitute a significant proportion of the total population and everywhere they have played a major role in the evolution of the macro-scale structural organization of the host societies and economies.

CHAPTER SIX

Intra-urban Migration

Chapters 4 and 5 have painted the picture of domestic and international migration to the cities of Western Europe, both in the past and at the present, and have demonstrated the vital effect of such external migration in maintaining overall population stability or growth and in determining the course of social evolution within cities. However, migration has other roles to play at the level of the individual urban area, for intra-urban migration is the most important direct determinant of the stability or transformation of the demographic and social composition of urban neighbourhoods. Intra-urban migration may act to introduce new elements into an area (in the style of the invasion-succession model) thus acting in a transformational manner; or it may remove old elements from a neighbourhood (such as those who have passed beyond the dominant life-cycle characteristic of a district) and act as a stabilizing force. In short, intra-urban migration may act, alongside external migration, either to perpetuate or to revolutionize social area characteristics.

The major reason for distinguishing intra-urban moves from those to and from the city as a whole is that the motives are commonly believed to differ between these two types of migration. Migration to or from the city is 'total displacement' migration, using the terminology of Roseman (1971), in which economic opportunities or job availability play the dominant role with the change of actual residence following from that. Moves within the city are more directly explained by questions of housing, life-cycle change and social evolution − they are generally 'partial displacement' moves in which the migrant changes residence but retains many of the same termini for his daily movements (to work or for shopping, for example) as he had before (White and Woods 1980: 3–4). Inevitably, of course, complications arise in making an arbitrary distinction between moves external to the city and those classed as intra-urban moves, and correlating these with total displacement and partial displacement migrations respectively: a significant body of moves out of the city is, in fact, usually made up of moves into suburban locations (see Ch. 3, p. 59).

In several European countries the study of intra-urban mobility is facilitated by the existence of continuous registers of population in which all changes of residence are recorded, with summary tables computed annually, and published as matrices of inter-district (and, often intra-district) flows. It is on such sources that much of the work reported in this chapter has been based.

THE VOLUME OF MOVEMENT

Table 6.1 provides information on the total numbers, and rates, of intra-urban migration in eight major Western European cities in recent years. The rate of intra-urban movement varies between just over 5 per cent of the population per annum in Stockholm and almost 12 per cent in Amsterdam. In total, the rates are relatively high, especially when compared with normal estimates of total annual mobility for all types of residential movement of 10 per cent in Britain and 20 per cent in the United States (Robson 1975: 30; Simmons 1968: 622). Table 6.1 only presents the rates for intra-urban mobility: when total migration rates for these cities are calculated for the relevant years (including migration to and from the city as well) the figure for Amsterdam is 216 moves per thousand residents per annum, that for Zürich is 280 and even that for Stockholm reaches 148 moves per thousand. Inevitably, however, there will be an element of double-counting in these estimates since some people will move twice in a year: in Greater Brussels it has been found that almost 15 per cent of entrants to the conurbation made a further move across an internal administrative boundary of the city within a year of arrival, adjusting their housing in the light of further information gained about local opportunities (Meeus 1975: 429).

Intra-urban mobility rates have declined drastically since the late nineteenth century, but there is some evidence of increases occurring in recent years. Large-scale migration to, and from, the growing industrial cities of the nineteenth century (Ch. 4, p. 81) was accompanied by great pressure on housing and this led to very high intra-urban mobility levels as lodgers moved between households with monotonous regularity. In 1900 the rate of intra-urban movers

Table 6.1 Intra-urban migration – selected cities

City	Country	Date	Resident mid-year population in thousands	Intra-urban migrants	
				Absolute numbers in thousands	Rate per thousand population
Amsterdam	Netherlands	1977	733.6	87.6	119.5
Cologne	W. Germany	1978	980.3	87.7	89.4
Copenhagen	Denmark	1977	613.0	70.1	114.3
Rome	Italy	1964	2151.3	152.6	70.9
Stockholm	Sweden	1978	656.2	33.9	51.6
Vienna	Austria	1978	1581.0	85.2	53.9
West Berlin		1978	1918.3	225.9	117.8
Zürich	Switzerland	1978	378.0	39.2	103.9

Data sources: see Appendix

per thousand population stood at 416 in Cologne, 413 in Essen, 389 in Berlin and 226 in Duisburg (Niethammer and Bruggemeier 1978: 119; Jackson 1982: 249–50). Taking fourteen of the largest cities of West Germany as the data base, Schaffer (1972: 129) found that between 1908 and 1969 there was a decline in the intra-urban mobility rate from 312 per thousand population to 92: similar declines have occurred elsewhere in Western Europe as housing tenure has become more stable and the practice of lodging has declined.

However, in recent years the growth of the international migrant population has tended to raise intra-urban mobility levels once again, this group being in a not dissimilar position in the privately-rented housing market to that of the domestic migrants in nineteenth-century Northern European cities. Thus in Stuttgart in 1976, foreigners had an intra-urban mobility rate of 181 per thousand, compared to 59 for the indigenous population, so that foreigners made up 35.9 per cent of all internal movers in the city (Borris et al. 1977: 172). Similar patterns have been found in other Western European cities (Borde and Barrère 1978: 39; O'Loughlin 1980: 277), and in the German city of Ulm, Schaffer (1972) found the intra-urban mobility rate of foreign workers in 1969 to be as high as 700 per thousand.

The basic controls on intra-urban migration levels lie in housing opportunities and constraints. Where publicly-rented accommodation is a significant element in the housing market, it might be expected that local mobility will be reduced by the relative inflexibility of this housing class as regards changes of residence: that has certainly been the experience in the United Kingdom (Bird 1976). However, in Western Europe, public sector housing has often been managed in ways which allow greater possibilities of interchanging tenancies (Bléry 1975: 62), although turnover is still below the levels found in privately-rented properties. Nevertheless, variations in the existence of public sector housing are not the sole explanation of variations in local mobility – if it were then Amsterdam and Vienna, with almost identical levels of public housing (Table 2.3), should have similar rates of intra-urban migration which is most definitely not the case (Table 6.1). The existence of rent controls in the private sector is a second vital factor, for the effect of such controls has generally been to reduce local mobility severely: tenants hold on to their low-rent properties because moving involves the acceptance of higher-cost accommodation in a property where the rent will have been permitted to rise on vacancy. The institution of rent-control legislation in Vienna cut the rate at which dwellings changed hands in the 1920s to around 2 per cent per annum from its earlier levels of 30 per cent (Bobek and Lichtenberger 1966: 134). Although rent-control legislation had generally been weakened or eliminated in most countries by the mid-1970s, its legacies may perhaps be seen in the relatively low local mobility rates in Vienna and Stockholm, two cities where controls were of the greatest overall significance.

Other influences on levels of local migration include the expansion or contraction of housing supply. Short-term increases in mobility commonly accompany periods of new construction within the city boundaries as the overall residential structure adjusts to the moves of established residents taking up the new accommodation (Sick 1979: 258; Mols 1965: 312). Slum-clearance and urban-renewal schemes are also likely to increase local moves (Angenot 1965; Ballesteros et al. 1977: 219): this may be of importance in producing higher intra-urban migration rates in Amsterdam and West Berlin in Table 6.1.

The connections of intra-urban migration with questions of housing opportunities are therefore highly complex and, beyond citing the importance of housing variables, it is difficult to produce precise explanations of the marked variations in intra-urban migration rates between cities as seen in Table 6.1. Everywhere, however, intra-urban movement makes a significant contribution to patterns of change in the population composition of city districts; hence questions of the characteristics of the migrants and of the spatial patterning of flows are of considerable importance.

THE MOVERS AND THEIR MOTIVES

An increasing number of surveys have been conducted in recent years in the attempt to elucidate the motivations of those involved in intra-urban migration in Western European cities, and the results can be broadly summarized as validating Anglo-American theories on the importance of social and housing factors in determining who migrates (Brown and Moore 1970; Short 1978).

Certain investigations have been concerned with respondents' attitudes to their present residences and their intentions for the future. In the West German city of Kiel, Killisch (1979) found a relationship to exist between a person's age, his length of residence in his present dwelling and satisfaction with that dwelling: the inter-relationships between the three variables were all positive. However, in the two inner-city areas studied, 37 per cent of families with children had dominantly negative views of their housing although only 7 per cent disliked the neighbourhood. In inner Utrecht, in the Netherlands, there were also positive views of the neighbourhood and 57 per cent of respondents did not expect to move from the inner-city, but a substantial number wished to move locally, the reasons most commonly being related to the dwelling itself (Den Draak 1967: 220–2). In a study of the reasons people gave for requesting a publicly-rented property in Rouen, Putz and Prié (1975: 53) found overcrowding at the present residence to be the dominant factor.

Studies of actual movers have confirmed the importance of housing questions in motivations. Sick (1979), looking at Freiburg im Breisgau in south-west Germany, found that 43 per cent of his sample of movers gave personal reasons for moving, such as setting up a new household, for example at marriage. A further 17 per cent indicated the need for more spacious accommodation to house a growing family whilst 35 per cent had moved for reasons concerned with the neighbourhood and its amenities. In his study of Ulm, Schaffer (1972: 145) used broader categories of motives, finding that 50 per cent of intra-urban moves were responses to housing or neighbourhood conditions, 40 per cent to family conditions, whilst only 10 per cent of moves were brought about by occupational reasons. In Kiel, 41 per cent of actual movers gave reasons relating to dwelling size, changes in family conditions or marriage (Killisch 1979: 127), these reasons being closely related to phases in the life-cycle. In Rome, Rossi (1959: 36) estimated that 10 per cent of internal migration was due to marriage.

Researchers concentrating on intra-urban moves to specific housing areas have again emphasized housing and social motivations. Rochefort et al. (1977: 203) looked at North African movement to a peripheral public housing scheme near Lyon and found that 37 per cent of moves came about because previous accommodation had been too small for a growing family, 19 per cent because of the slum nature of the previous residence, 16 per cent through moves from a *cité de transit* (see Ch. 5, p. 119), and 9 per cent through eviction from the previous dwelling: in total, 87 per cent of the reasons concerned housing. At the other end of the status scale, the dominance of housing considerations is also present: in a study of movement to new owner-occupied housing in the Bordeaux suburbs, Cheung (1980) found housing questions to dominate in 74 per cent of the cases examined.

The dominance of housing and family reasons for intra-urban migration shows up in the selectivity of the movers. Two particular groups are especially involved: firstly, young single adults who move from flat to flat in a relatively transient manner; secondly, young families moving to attempt to match their housing with their growing family requirements. Foreign migrants predominantly belong to the first of these groups although with increasing representation in the second.

In Freiburg, 36 per cent of the movers were in the age-group 18–24, which comprised only 15 per cent of the total population, whilst 37 per cent were aged 25–44 (29 per cent of the total population). In total, 65 per cent of the movers were single, a proportion influenced by the large numbers of students in the city (Sick 1979: 258–60). In Ulm, 60 per cent of the movers were under 35 years of age (Schaffer 1972: 141).

When migrant characteristics are examined, not at the level of the city as a whole but for individual city districts, the role of intra-urban migration in perpetuating or transforming social area characteristics becomes apparent. Intra-urban migration wholly within the inner-city is inevitably characterized by the single people, including large numbers of young adults, who are over-represented in the population composition of such areas. Those making intra-urban moves into the centre are rarely family groups; those moving in the opposite direction are generally families.

These last two assertions have been examined by Putz and Prié (1975) looking at an inner-city and a peripheral public housing estate in Rouen in France. Moves to the peripheral estate were dominated by those in the child-rearing stages of the life-cycle, often of those obtaining their first dwelling after lodging with parents. Moves to the city-centre estate involved a much older population sub-group without children, seeking the advantages of inner-city access. These contrasts obviously reflect the different demands made of their housing and neighbourhood by different groups of people. Working solely with a group of students in order to restrict the effect of several other variables, Petersen found that two broad groups of respondents emerged when asked to rank preferred residential districts in Aarhus in Denmark (Petersen 1976): those who were single held a different set of preferences from those who were engaged or married and who were thus moving into the next stage of the life-cycle.

The patterning of destinations of intra-urban migrants both reflects and determines the characteristic demographic patterns of cities outlined in Chapter 3. Inner-city areas retain young single migrants and gain the old whilst outer areas witness a net influx of those aged 25–45 with their young children. Those who leave peripheral areas tend to be older than the average residents and a significant proportion move to areas nearer to the city-centre (Bléry 1975). Those leaving the centre to move towards the periphery are younger than the average age of inner-city residents because very few old people are involved (Costa et al. 1980: 404).

Intra-urban migration also involves selective moves by different social-status groups. Such migration in Paris is reducing the absolute numbers of all status groups at the city-centre but there is a more rapid net loss at the 'lower' end of the hierarchy such that inner Paris is, as a result of this pattern of intra-urban migration, seeing a raising of its overall social-status level (Freyssenet et al. 1971: 11). Similar features and results of intra-urban migration have been occurring in other cities such as Venice and Bordeaux (Costa et al. 1980: 404; Pailhé 1978). Further attention to such social change will be given in the next three chapters.

The Western European experience of the motivations for intra-urban migration and the characteristics of the migrants themselves is similar to that elsewhere. Intra-urban moves, being partial displacement migrations, are not conditioned by changes of occupation but by stresses introduced into the relationship between the individual or family and the dwelling or neighbourhood. Such stresses are very often associated with movement between different stages in the life-cycle and result in characteristic selectivity of the migrants involved.

PATTERNS OF MOVEMENT

One of the general foundations of much urban theory rooted in the ecological tradition is the assumption that new migrants to the city congregate at or near the city-centre and that as these migrant populations become integrated into the surrounding urban society they will fan out to be replaced by other later migrants. It has already been seen that the dominant intra-urban movement out of inner-city areas is of young families, whilst in Chapters 4 and 5 evidence was presented that the inner-city is indeed an important residential location for recent migrants to the city although peripheral areas are much more significant as migrant receivers than might be expected from pure urban ecological tradition. In such circumstances there might well be a form of complementarity between moves to the city from outside and intra-urban moves, with intra-urban migration acting in some respects to redistribute long-distance migrants once they arrive in the city. The alternative view to complementarity, however, might be of migrants to the city being drawn in necessarily to replace those departing from undesirable occupations and undesirable locations within the urban structure.

Some sort of complementarity certainly appears to be the case in Zürich (Fig. 6.1). Here in 1978, population gain through migration to the city dominated throughout the inner-city and around the lakeshore, but it was almost exactly the same set of areas that was losing population through net loss of intra-urban migrants. Peripheral areas of the city gained from intra-urban moves but lost through external migration across the city boundaries, dominantly through suburbanizing moves (see Ch. 3, p. 60).

Given the evidence presented in Chapter 5 that recent international migrants to Western European cities do not display intense segregation at the district level, it is likely to be inaccurate to consider the sort of pattern displayed in Fig. 6.1 in terms of an invasion and succession model. As migrant groups have increased their familial characteristics there has been a process of infiltration into the housing of peripheral areas but by no means a process of 'invasion'. Certainly some studies have looked at the connections between external and internal migration in Western European cities using the approach of the invasion—succession model, but although the tendencies of low-status migrant arrival and higher-status intra-urban migrant departures at city-centres are present, the movements of recently-arrived populations out towards the periphery are everywhere overwhelmed by the accompanying similar moves made by the native population (Cortie 1972a; 1972b).

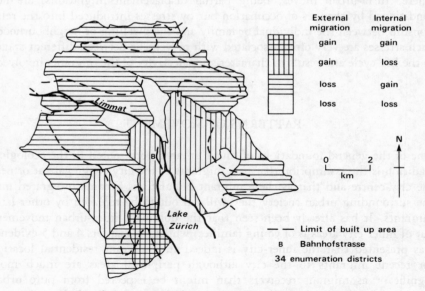

Fig. 6.1 External and internal migration in Zürich, 1978.
(*Data source*: *Statistisches Jahrbuch der Stadt Zürich*, 1978)

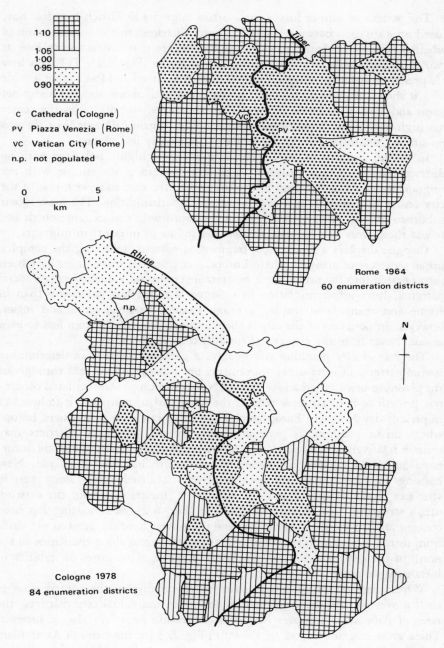

Fig. 6.2   Net intra-urban migration, Rome 1964, Cologne 1978.
(*Data sources*: see Appendix)

The pattern of gain or loss of intra-urban migrants in Zürich is a clear one, based on a division between inner and outer districts. In the consideration of whether similar concentric patterns exist elsewhere it is instructive to look at two further examples, those of Cologne and Rome (Fig. 6.2). The data here are presented as ratios between internal migrants gained and lost so that a value of 1.0 shows overall net balance, whilst areas with ratios above 1 show net gains and areas with ratios below 1 have net losses. In both cities the centre has high net loss with peripheral areas tending to gain migrants, but there is no simple concentric pattern recognizable, especially in Cologne.

In Rome, patterns of intra-urban migration are highly polarized with no districts in approximate balance. A sectoral pattern is discernible with net migrant losses occurring even in the suburbs to the east and south-east of the city-centre in areas of relatively old pre-war suburbanization. The most recent suburban growth in 1964 had been in the south-west and extreme north and it was these areas that had the greatest net inflow of intra-urban migrants.

Cologne displays a much more fragmented pattern, reflecting the complex urban structure of many Northern European cities where old villages have been incorporated into the urban fabric but retain certain individual effects on social patterns. Intra-urban migration in Cologne is much less polarizing than in Rome and many areas display a rough balance between gains and losses: however, in no sector of the city is there a steady progression from loss to gain as one moves from the city-centre towards the periphery.

The role of city planning is arguably of great importance in determining spatial patterns of intra-urban movement, not just in Cologne but throughout the planning-oriented urban societies of Northern Europe. Unregulated concentric growth of housing areas around the whole urban periphery is unheard of in present-day Northern European cities and it is rare even in Southern Europe where urban planning is generally less effective. Peripheral districts may contain relatively old housing (as in south-east Rome), both through the incorporation of old villages and because later growth has been restricted. New housing in most cities has been relatively localized, both along certain stretches of the periphery and also filling the interstices within the existing urban structure. In Cologne, for example (Fig. 6.2), new housing has been concentrated to the south of the city and these areas have the greatest net gains from intra-urban movement, whilst the industrial areas along the Rhine to the north of the city, where little new housing exists, show losses or stability in intra-urban moves.

Whilst patterns of net intra-urban migration display the contribution of such moves to population growth or decline in individual city districts, the rates of population turnover (the gross migration rates) are also of interest. These gross migration rates are shown in Fig. 6.3 for the cities of Amsterdam and Stockholm, the total intra-urban migration rate for each city being given an index value of 100 with other rates indexed accordingly. The overall rate of movement in Amsterdam is twice that of Stockholm, but in both cities the inner-urban core stands out as an area of high population turnover with peripheral areas having lower levels of mobility. In central Amsterdam the peak rate

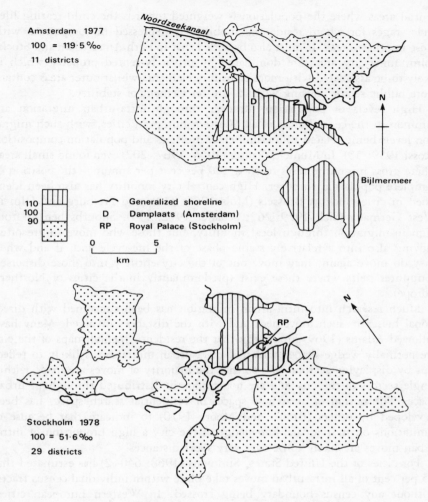

Fig. 6.3   Gross intra-urban migration rates, Amsterdam 1977, Stockholm 1978.
(*Data sources*: see Appendix)

reached 334 movers per thousand population: the high mobility zone covers all those parts of the city that had been built up by 1900 – districts now inhabited by a mixed population of the highly transitory unmarried young alongside the stable elderly. The highest gross mobility rate in Amsterdam as a whole in 1977, however, occurred in the separated district of Bijlmermeer, the site of a major new housing development which grew in population total in 1977 alone by 6,315 individuals (a rate of 15 per cent growth), of whom 6,203 were intra-urban migrants. The role of new housing in generating intra-urban moves is thus eloquently demonstrated in this case.

In Stockholm the high mobility area is broadly the city as it stood in 1930, with areas of lower gross internal mobility being inter-war or post-war residential areas where the population is weighted towards the child-rearing life-cycle stages for whom residential mobility is depressed in comparison with those in other stages. It must also be added that in both Amsterdam and Stockholm, inner-city areas are dominated by privately-rented property which is likely to be associated with more transitory elements whilst outer areas contain more public sector housing with its greater element of stability.

High levels of population turnover through intra-urban migration are common to the central areas of all Western European cities, with such migration levels being related to housing characteristics and population composition (Rossi 1959: 55). In Munich, Ganser (1966; 1967: 202) even found small areas where gross migration rates reached 100 per cent per annum – the position of complete population turnover. High central-city mobility has also been identified in cities such as Brussels (Mols 1965: 312), and Freiburg and Ulm in West Germany (Sick 1979: 262; Schaffer 1972: 155). Suburbs benefit from high in-migration through local mobility, but those who move in are often moving also into a relatively stable phase of the life-cycle and, if and when they do move again, may move out of the city entirely into more dispersed commuter belts where these exist (predominantly in the cities of Northern Europe).

Much research into intra-urban migration has been concerned with directional biases in such movement and with the distances involved. Many have followed Adams (1969) in arguing that the residents' mental maps of the city are normally wedge-shaped and that intra-urban migration is likely to reflect this by displaying sectoral bias so that the majority of moves are made within single sectors of the city and are not randomly distributed throughout urban space. The notion of awareness space, or residential search space, has been developed by others (Brown and Moore 1970) to indicate that because of limitations on individuals' knowledge of the city a high proportion of intra-urban moves are likely to be over very short distances.

For cities of the United States, Simmons (1968: 640–2) has estimated that 25 per cent of all intra-urban moves take place within individual census tracts, without any census boundary being crossed. In Western European cities,

Table 6.2 Migration within urban administrative sub-units

City	Date	Number of sub-units	Average sub-unit population	Migration within sub-units as per cent of all intra-urban moves
Amsterdam	1977	12	60,728	30.4
Copenhagen	1977	20	26,458	31.3
Rome	1964	60	36,342	28.8
Stockholm	1978	29	22,549	47.9
Vienna	1978	23	68,739	37.2
Zürich	1978	34	11,072	27.3

Date sources: see Appendix

similar conclusions emerge, although the size of the smallest administrative units is variable between cities (Table 6.2): short-distance moves again predominate. The percentages given in Table 6.2 are, of course, totals for the whole city but the proportions of intra-unit moves tend to be much lower in the city-centres than in outer areas of the city (Gans 1979: 107; Sick 1979: 261). Part of the reason for these variations undoubtedly lies in the much larger extents of suburban administrative sub-units, but distances of movement are generally greater for those leaving city-centres and taking up suburban residence than for those already living in the suburbs who are more likely to move simply to change the size or type of dwelling but staying in the same neighbourhood.

Intra-urban migration thus obeys the normal laws of distance decay with more movers travelling short than long distances. An illustration of this is provided by Fig. 6.4 which shows the percentage of movers by 500 m bands in the West German federal capital of Bonn in the early 1970s. This analysis shows that while distance decay applies to all types of movers, it acts differently in different cases: thus a high proportion of moves made by those in the child-rearing phase of the life-cycle are extremely local within the neighbourhood whilst old people tend not to make so many highly local moves and young single adults are more prepared to change district. It has been suggested, for example by Boyce (1969), that higher social-status groups may move further in intra-urban moves, reflecting the more spatially-limited availability of top-

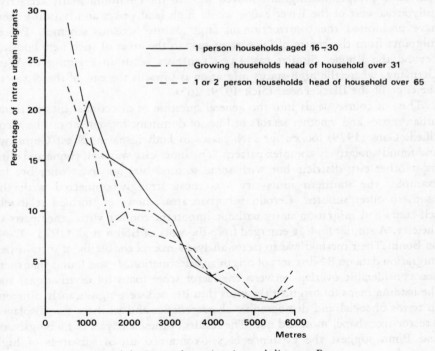

Fig. 6.4 Intra-urban migration and distance, Bonn.
(*Source*: redrawn from Böhm et al. 1975)

145

class housing opportunity, but no evidence of such class differentiation by distance was found in Bonn: indeed, if high-status areas were to be sectorally arranged there is no reason why high-status migrants should move over greater distances.

However, there is somewhat conflicting evidence, on the one hand, that the friction of distance is weakening through time and, on the other hand, that the arrival in western European cities of international labour migrants has brought in a group with high intra-urban mobility but tightly constrained distances of movement. Clark and Avery (1978: 155) have shown that in Amsterdam in 1960, 17 out of 89 registration districts recorded 15 per cent or more of their intra-urban migrants as remaining in the district: by 1970 this number had fallen to only 3 districts.

The very short migration distances of foreign workers, reflecting both restricted mental maps of the city and limited housing opportunities, are attested in several West German cities (O'Loughlin 1980: 270). In Stuttgart, for example, 42 per cent of foreigner intra-urban moves in 1976 did not cross any sub-district boundary (Borris et al. 1977: 176).

Apart from the existence of sub-populations whose migration distance distributions differ, it is also certain that different status groups and other identifiable classes move in different directions. Bonneville (1974: 121–6) studied all electors moving out of the central *arrondissements* of Lyon and found that more prosperous migrants moved west to the environmentally attractive hilly areas west of the River Saône where high land prices and building costs have prohibited the construction of large public housing schemes. Poorer migrants from the centre of Lyon went east to the areas of such new housing beyond the Rhône. Similar east–west contrasts occur in Freiburg in West Germany, where the high-status migration is towards the east of the city – to the edge of the Black Forest (Sick 1979: 265).

This, of course, leads into the general question of directional bias in intra-urban moves and whether sectors or lines of dominant movement can be identified. Gans (1979) looked for such biases in Ludwigshafen, West Germany, and found a relatively complex pattern. The inner-city was well connected with most other city districts but with some sectoral bias apparent whereby, for example, the southern inner-city was most strongly connected with the southern outer suburbs. Certain suburban areas, however, formed relatively self-contained migration units without important contact with other parts of the city. A similar finding emerged from the work of Böhm et al. (1975: 92–4) on Bonn. Their method was to factor analyse a matrix consisting of intra-urban migration data on 84 districts of origin and destination. It was found that there was considerable overlap between the factor score maps (of destinations) and the loading maps (of origins): the areas thus defined were significantly different in terms of social and demographic characteristics and whilst a few displayed a sector-like shape, most did not. The results of these analyses of Ludwigshafen and Bonn suggest the existence of self-contained urban sub-areas of high migration connectivity reflecting not a simple sectoral pattern of awareness space but the complexities of social space within the city.

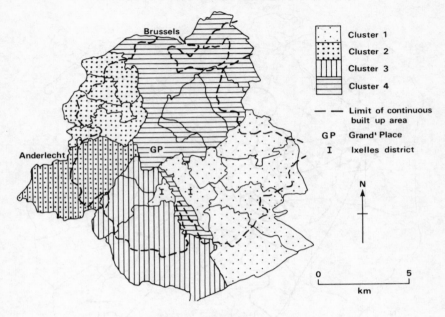

Fig. 6.5   Intra-urban migration districts in Brussels.
(*Source*: redrawn from Meeus 1975)

These conclusions from work in West Germany differ in certain respects from the results of a study of migration between the nineteen *communes* of Brussels, although similarities also occur (Meeus 1975). As in Bonn, a factor analysis was performed, and Meeus produced four areal 'clusters' of overlapping origins and destinations (Fig. 6.5) by a subjective appraisal of the statistical results. The *commune* of Brussels itself is an extremely unusual and unwieldy shape, driving a wedge between the two halves of the *commune* of Ixelles, but the overall pattern of migration districts is very simple with only Anderlecht belonging to two 'clusters'. Unlike the districts in Bonn, those in Brussels were relatively heterogeneous and did not coincide with the social areas of the city (although this may in part be a result of the relatively coarse spatial units of the analysis). Within each 'cluster', the dominant movement trend was towards the periphery.

A useful technique for investigating an intra-urban migration matrix for sectoral biases is that of nodal flow analysis (Bell 1980). In this technique, subdistricts are ranked according to their total of migrants received. The moves out from each district are then examined and the greatest outflow is labelled the 'first-order flow' as long as it is to a district ranked higher in the list of destinations: second-order flows can be similarly determined. Districts from which the largest flow is to a district ranking lower in the list of destinations are termed 'independent' districts.

Figure 6.6 presents the results of the analysis of first-order flows in Rome in 1964 from a flow matrix with a dimension of 60 × 60 cells. Several impor-

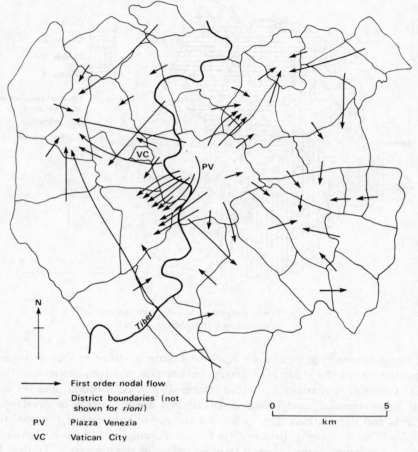

Fig. 6.6 Nodal flows in intra-urban migration – Rome, 1964.
(*Data source: Annuario Statistico della Città di Roma* 1964)

tant features can be observed. Firstly, all but one of the *rioni*, the central districts of the city, send their largest migrant flow out of the city-centre: only one *rione* receives a nodal flow and that is from another central district. Secondly, there is a distinct sectoral bias to nodal flows out of the centre with flow-lines rarely crossing each other: the sectoral pattern is particularly strong in the north-east and south-west of the city. Thirdly, sectors are far less noticeable in suburban areas where there are cases of several flows from all directions focusing on specific districts. This is, in fact, a result of the localized nature of new housing developments and gives rise to areas of migration connectivity, just as in Ludwigshafen, Bonn and Brussels. Fourthly, the nodal flows display a dominance of short-distance moves with only one notable exception (and that is to one of the new housing areas). In total, intra-urban migration out of central Rome is relatively simple in structure, but movements within the suburbs are more complex: this is far from being a straightforward continuous

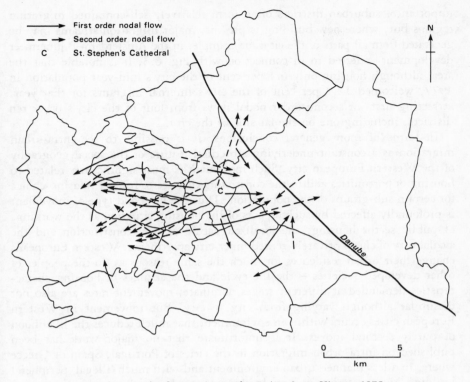

First order nodal flow
Second order nodal flow
C   St. Stephen's Cathedral

N

Danube

0   5
km

Fig. 6.7   Nodal flows in intra-urban migration – Vienna, 1978.
(*Data source*: *Statistisches Jahrbuch der Stadt Wien* 1978)

wave of sectorally outward-bound migration like the ripples from a stone dropped into a pond.

The conclusions from an analysis of nodal flows in Vienna (including second-order flows) are not dissimilar (Fig. 6.7). Nodal flows are dominantly outwards, particularly from the city-centre and inner suburbs, but in the outer suburban areas there is less of a sectoral pattern with more 'lateral' interchanges between proximate suburban districts irrespective of sectors. There is, however, a very clear division between the eastern and western halves of the city. The concentration of nodal flow destinations in three city districts of recent housing is especially noticeable: 28 out of the 36 flows shown are to these three districts.

From the evidence presented in these and other analyses it is possible to state three broad generalizations about the patterning of moves within the Western European city. Firstly, intra-urban migration out of inner-city districts is predominantly towards suburban areas on the same side of the city-centre: moves across the centre are relatively rare (Van Hulten 1968: 112–15). Secondly, a high proportion of intra-urban moves are extremely local in character, with the movers taking up new residences very close to their old ones. Thirdly, moves within suburban areas are often spatially very complex and do not display simple sectoral tendencies. The location of new housing is of importance: suburban districts often form relatively self-contained migration regions but, where new building is present, major migration streams may be generated from all parts of the city: for example, in the Amsterdam–Bijlmermeer development, referred to in connection with Fig. 6.3, it is notable that the area, although housing only 6.1 per cent of the city's mid-year population in 1977, welcomed 12.7 per cent of the city's internal migrants for that year, attracting first- or second-order nodal flows from four of the city's other ten districts, including one on the far side of the city.

In terms of more general conclusions, it is possible to see intra-urban migration as a constant underlying structural feature of the social geography of the Western European city. Such movement is most significantly related to housing opportunities and to the constraints that act to restrict housing choice for certain sub-groups of the population. Thus the level and type of movement is profoundly affected by such aspects of the housing situation as the workings of public sector housing, the localized nature of new construction and the availability of cheap privately-rented inner-city apartments. Western Europeans change their urban residences for much the same reasons as do the peoples of other developed societies – the life-cycle and the changes of housing characteristics demanded at different stages dominate; movement rates are also not dissimilar although varying from city to city. But movement in Western European cities occurs within an environment that much reduces the likelihood of purely sectoral moves. It is unfortunate that no major work has been published on intra-urban migration in the cities of Portugal, Spain or Greece where, in a less planned urban environment and with much 'illegal' peripheral building, the constraints on new development are less so that cities appear more prone to grow in a concentric fashion likely to generate more coherent intra-urban migration patterns.

Everywhere intra-urban migration operates to perpetuate spatial social differentiation in the urban system. Rates of movement are highest in city-centres, which are net losers by this process, and lowest in the suburbs, where there is greatest gain. But intra-urban movement is, in this respect, partly complementary to external moves affecting the city since it is the city-centres that usually experience net gain from movements to the urban area from elsewhere. In terms of the composition of the migrant streams, intra-urban movement operates to maintain the segregation, demonstrated in Chapter 3, between family-builders in peripheral areas and other life-cycle groups towards the centre. The differential migration of various sub-populations therefore plays a vital role in the social patterning of the city.

CHAPTER SEVEN

LESLIE DIENES
Department of Geography

The Residential Kaleidoscope

In earlier chapters some of the key building-blocks of social geography have been examined. The role of the past has been indicated, the housing structure of the city has been summarized and the facts of demography and especially migration have been emphasized as the forces dictating population evolution and compositional change. Running through much of this material have been underlying themes of economic development, labour supply and political activity (the last of these being of particular importance in housing).

The culmination of any work of urban social geography must, however, lie in discussion of how people live within the city, how urban space is used by different groups within society, and how the residential pattern of the city may be described and interpreted. It is the intention of the present chapter to consider these questions at the level of the Western European city as a whole, with the following two chapters focusing on specific areas within the city – the centre and the suburbs.

A variety of approaches has been adopted by European geographers investigating residential structures and this is not the place to review such approaches in depth. Empiricist studies of individual neighbourhoods or, more recently, of data sets for whole cities using factorial methods are common in the literature. The latter studies have shaded into more positivist investigations seeking to explain urban patterns by means of normative theories of economic or social behaviour. Behaviouralist studies have not been lacking, nor have humanistic approaches, both drawing inspiration from the pioneering work of Chombart de Lauwe et al. (1952). Structuralist and Marxist interpretations of urban social space have become prominent in recent years and the works of Castells and Godard (1974) on Dunkirk and, more recently, Ferras (1977a) on Barcelona stand out. The present chapter adopts an eclectic approach to these various philosophies and methodologies but places emphasis on certain structural features of Western European urban societies and cultures.

SOCIAL STRUCTURES

Analyses of urban residential structure generally rely heavily on some concept of differentiating social class or status as a major explanatory factor (Johnston, 1980a: 149). In practice, the words 'class' and 'status' have been accorded many different meanings, and the problems of definition are compounded when recourse must be made, in pursuing comparative studies, to data sources derived from censuses which themselves adopt definitions that differ from country to country. Among the various methods used in Western European censuses to indicate social hierarchies can be found such distinctions as income levels; relationship to the means of production ('class' in the strict sense); occupation according to industrial/tertiary sector; occupation according to skill or education level needed; and combinations of two or more of these. In 'class' terms the work-force can be divided into those who control others, those who control themselves, and the controlled: of these, in the Western European context (as will shortly be shown), the class of self-employed, controlling their own labour power, is of considerable importance.

More generally useful in the pragmatic analysis of socio-spatial structure in the city, however, is a division of occupational groups largely on the basis of status or prestige (Halsey 1978), even though such groups may then be designated, on the basis of common usage, by terms such as 'middle class', 'working class' and so on. Halsey (1978: 24) uses three broad classes in his analysis of British society. His 'middle class' is made up of professional, managerial and administrative employees along with the professionally self-employed. The 'lower middle class' consists of a rather heterogeneous mixture of non-manual employees, self-employed artisans and supervisors of manual workers. His 'working class' is made up of all manual workers of whatever skill level.

It is possible to extend the use of these broad classes from the British context to that of the rest of Europe and to match them against the categories that can be derived from most censuses. It is, however, necessary to remember that these are coarsely-defined classes and that their meaning may vary from society to society. For example, the 'middle class' in Portugal or Greece is generally formed of a group with a traditional measure of prestige derived from a 'good' family background. Such a group customarily also includes a substantial number of the controllers of large amounts of capital, particularly in property – a true urban *rentier* sector, for whom the economic concept of class is relevant. In Northern European urban societies, on the other hand, the middle class is more nearly a group of high educational status engaged in the liberal professions and in the administration of major organizations.

It is necessary to add two further groups to this basic tripartite division of society in order to increase its applicability as a basis for the discussion of residential areas in the Western European city: these two further groups are those of the small self-employed businessman and those working in what may broadly be termed 'personal services'.

Contemporary urban life in most Western European societies displays a far greater dependence on the small self-employed artisan or shopkeeper than is the case in the British Isles or North America. Particularly in Southern Europe, the bulk of urban retailing is in the hands of small family-owned and-run businesses – department stores and national retailing chains have only appeared within the last two decades in Italy, for example – and the same applies to a whole range of urban services. Much manufacturing activity is also on a very small scale, especially in Portugal, in many ways being a continuation of pre-industrial urban craft organization (see Ch. 1, p. 7). Northern Europe is rather more like the British case, especially in manufacturing: although many small urban retailers do still exist, there are increasing numbers of co-operative buying arrangements between small shops and there is also a higher representation of national or regional companies operating urban services such as petrol stations or restaurants, but it is only in Finland that the distributive trades are as concentrated in multiple chains as in Britain (Williams, S. 1981: 119). The contrast between the English public house with its brewery-appointed manager and the family-run Italian bar is the contrast between an urban society of employees and one with a high representation of the small self-employed. France and Belgium stand somewhere between the Northern and Southern European extremes, with their rapid postwar growth of peri-urban shopping centres and hypermarkets and of national chains occurring alongside the continuation of *le petit commerce*.

Throughout Western Europe the small self-employed class is undergoing a reduction in both number and importance as more 'modern' retailing and service sectors are taking over or where urban redevelopment is destroying the habitat of the old craft industry workshops (Pailhé 1978: 14–15). In Paris this class fell from being 9.8 per cent of the population in 1954 to 5.7 per cent in 1975 (Ranger 1977: 813). Elsewhere their representation is higher: 9 per cent of the population in Vienna in 1971 (Lichtenberger 1977: 285); in Venice proper in 1971, 16.2 per cent of the working population was in this class and even 11.4 per cent in the industrial mainland sub-city of Mestre where the size of this class can owe little to local survivals (Zanetto and Lando 1980: 219). On the other hand, in Stuttgart in West Germany only 5.6 per cent of the work-force was self-employed in the mid-1970s (Borris et al. 1977: 232).

The other occupational class that it is useful to distinguish in the Western European context is that of workers in personal service. This category is distinguished in most censuses although the detailed definition varies widely, generally including receptionists, *concierges* and domestic servants along with other activities such as hairdressing and other specialized tertiary activities: all these activities generally have a heavy over-representation of female labour (Joly 1978: 390–1): as mentioned in earlier chapters, domestic service has traditionally been a vital recruiter of female migrants and the importance of this sector of urban employment used to be considerable – in 1879, 25 per cent of the employed population in Athens were servants of one sort or another (Burgel 1978: 187). Today, the proportions working in 'personal service' are everywhere in retreat, although this sector retains some importance in Southern Europe.

Table 7.1 gives an estimated crude break-down of the social class compo-

Table 7.1   Social composition of four Western European cities

| | Percentages of working population | | | |
	Bordeaux 1975	Brussels 1970	Naples* 1971	Paris 1975
Middle class	12	17	11	17
Lower middle class	38	38	23	41
Working class	31	32	42	22
Self-employed	8	8	12	6
Personal service	8	4	11	11
Others	3	1	1	3

* Percentages of working heads of households

Data sources: Pailhé 1978; De Lannoy 1977; Bastano 1976; Ranger 1977

sition of the working population for four cities of Western Europe. As much as possible the class categories have been made equivalent across the four examples, but the results are only rather rough and ready comparisons: in particular, it is unfortunate that the figures cannot here be broken down according to sex composition. In the case of Naples, the data relate only to occupied heads of households, thus depressing the proportions of employment in the lower middle-class group where females are generally over-represented.

Variations in social composition obviously occur from city to city (Pumain 1976). In Table 7.1 the two capital cities (Brussels and Paris) display the greatest importance of the middle classes: a similar phenomenon occurs in capitals elsewhere in Europe (Giannoni 1976). In Athens in 1971, for example, 12 per cent of the working population could be categorized as middle class (Burgel 1978: 187–8), a higher proportion than in other urban settlements in Greece. These social composition patterns are not, however, constant but are evolving through time. Certain general features of changes in composition stand out.

The middle-class group is generally increasing in importance in all cities as economies become more tertiary-oriented. In the Paris region as a whole the importance of this class grew by 50 per cent between 1954 and 1968 (Freyssenet et al. 1971: 20), whilst in Paris proper the rate of growth was much more rapid, aided by differential migration rates affecting different social groups (Ranger 1977: 813). The importance of the lower middle classes is also growing everywhere, although often more slowly than the growth of the middle class itself. Such changes in social composition obviously occur at the expense of the working class and, to an extent, the self-employed and personal service sectors (Joly 1978: 390–2; Roncayolo 1972: 13). As Northern European societies move into the post-industrial phase, there is a tendency towards decreases in both the numbers and proportions of manual workers and increases in the white-collar sectors (Guibourdenche and Joly 1979: 262–3). Even in Southern European cities, where post-war industrial growth has been rapid, there is more rapid growth of white-collar employment at the present time (Burgel 1978: 188–9). In Northern Europe the diminution of the importance of the working-class sector has been accompanied by the increase in the use of foreign labour, so that migrant workers now constitute a substantial proportion of those employed in working-class occupations in many cities (Pailhé 1978: 15–17).

The five social classes identified in Table 7.1 are, of course, extremely broad and coarse categories that hide a great deal of variation both within classes and between different urban societies. Nevertheless, these broad groups each tend to play a separate and distinctive role in the sub-division of urban residential space.

RESIDENTIAL SEGREGATION AND HOUSING VARIABLES

It is commonly accepted that social groups in modern cities display some degree of spatial separation one from another so that social distance between groups is converted into spatial distance (Carter, H. 1981). In addition, Duncan and Duncan (1955), and others since, have found that residential segregation tends to be greatest for groups at opposite ends of the social hierarchy and least for those in the middle. Before the examination of the question of residential segregation by neighbourhood in the Western European city can be undertaken, however, it is first necessary to consider two other types of segregation that may be of significance.

Firstly, there is the problem of vertical segregation. In Chapter 1 it was seen that an aspect of the pre-industrial mercantile city was the co-existence, within single houses, of individuals and families at different positions in the class hierarchy, and that these residential patterns continued to be of significance with the development of large apartment blocks in the nineteenth century, although by this time the inhabitants of the blocks no longer held a functional relationship to each other in the way that they had in the mercantile city. Some authors (Berry 1973: 126–7; Johnston 1980a: 159–60) have argued that vertical segregation was acceptable as long as class boundaries were rigid, but that as greater fluidity develops in society then social groups distance themselves from each other in order to demonstrate their status through their addresses, and to provide group protection for their own interests.

However, vertical segregation does appear to retain some significance in many Western European cities, although statistical information on the topic is difficult to obtain because of the absence of suitable census data. Laquerbe (1967: 5–6) took a 20 per cent sample of buildings in central Montpellier, France. He found that in buildings that were entirely in residential use, almost all ground-floor flats were occupied by what he rather unspecifically termed the 'proletarian' class; these formed only 70 per cent of the households on the first and second floors but 85 per cent on higher floors. Vertical segregation was strongest in the old city-centre where there was the greatest representation of a *bourgeois* population: here only 58 per cent of first-floor households were proletarian, 55 per cent on the second floor, 80 per cent on the third and 81 per cent on the fourth.

Vertical stratification has been less present in the cities of Northern than of Southern Europe: in the north, nineteenth-century industrial growth led to the creation of worker housing or tenements and 'normal' spatial segregation quickly developed. In some of the largest cities, such as Vienna or Paris, vertical divisions persisted, but often the gradations were subtle involving sub-strata within classes rather than vastly different social groups. In Southern Europe, vertical stratification still has significance today: for example, throughout central Naples, except in entirely slum areas or modern housing districts, the middle classes and the working classes still live together in vertically segregated apartment blocks, the middle classes living on the first and second floors (Döpp 1968: 238). Such stratification is, however, being reduced as older apartment blocks designed for this type of class co-residence begin to decay and are taken over by immigrants and as new housing, throughout Western Europe, has ceased to create the variety of dwelling-sizes within blocks that would maintain the conditions necessary for such a class admixture.

The second alternative to neighbourhood segregation is segregation between the front and back of residential buildings. Much nineteenth-century apartment building produced blocks with large, light, airy and desirable dwellings over-looking the street, and small, dark and airless flats at the back overlooking interior courts (Bobek and Lichtenberger 1966: 72–89). Obvious social differ-entiation thus occurred in such blocks with the poorest at the back and the richest at the front. Where apartment blocks with interior courts still exist, such differentiation may persist today: Deneux (1981: 55) found this to be the case in the twentieth-century apartment blocks he investigated in Paris. Unfortunately, of course, as with verical stratification, these questions of micro-scale spatial segregation are difficult to examine with normal census materials.

In Chapter 1 it was argued that various degrees of spatial segregation of classes may have existed almost from the outset of urban history in Western Europe. The modern evolution of segregation is a function of housing although, as will shortly be discussed, the direct links between housing classes and social classes are not as obvious in the Western European city as might be supposed.

The specific provision and development of housing built for the working class from the middle of the nineteenth century onwards has been a very important generator of spatial separation between classes. Already by 1880, 72 per cent of Bochum's miners lived in just four of the city's twelve wards, the result of the localized provision of company housing for these workers (Crew 1979: 191–2). Elsewhere it was the building of housing specifically for the middle classes that brought increased segregation as in Brussels (Verniers 1958: 20). In Helsinki, separation between middle class and working class owes its origins to town-planning schemes and building regulations of the years 1812–17 (Åström 1979: 60). At the other end of the continent, rebuilding in Messina after the 1908 earthquake and the 1943 bombing provided *bourgeois* dwellings in the centre with shanty-towns (*baracche*) and, later, worker housing at the edge (Ioli Gigante 1980: 154). The spatial separation of different social

Table 7.2   Segregation of social classes, Brussels, 1970

	Indices of dissimilarity					Index of segregation
	1	2	3	4	5	
1 Middle class	—	22.5	46.5	32.1	30.9	31.7
2 Lower middle class		—	30.8	21.7	18.9	18.0
3 Working class			—	23.0	23.3	30.5
4 Self-employed, commerce				—	15.8	14.1
5 Self-employed, industry					—	14.0

Source: De Lannoy 1977: 207

classes therefore has a considerable history in Western European cities, but what is the extent and nature of this separation?

De Lannoy (1977) calculated indices of dissimilarity and segregation between five social groups in Brussels for 1970 using 494 administrative sub-areas of the city. The indices of segregation demonstrate the customary high degree of spatial exclusivity of the middle class (1) and the working class (3) at either end of the status hierarchy. The lowest segregation indices are for the two self-employed groups who, in status terms, should be placed in the centre of the hierarchy: segregation thus demonstrates a U-shaped pattern, familiar in other parts of the developed world, with the least segregation occurring at the centre of the hierarchy. De Lannoy (1977: 201) points out that the self-employed, whilst concentrated in the old city-centre of Brussels, are also widely dispersed elsewhere, particularly in the commercial centres of the older suburbs: they are a relatively ubiquitous class – a conclusion that applies throughout Western Europe, given the significance of this class in the day-to-day commercial activities of cities.

Similar U-shaped patterns of class segregation have been identified in other cities. In Bonn, Böhm et al. (1975: 115–17) found this to be the case with social groups identified partly on the basis of educational qualifications: the topmost group was more strongly segregated than the lowest. The same was also found to be the case in Vienna (Gisser and Kaufmann 1972: 271) and for the other five largest urban centres in Austria (Kaufmann et al. 1978: 71). In Bordeaux, Pailhé (1978: 23), using less satisfactory methods of analysis, observed the highest segregation amongst the middle class and working class and least for the lower middle group, and also found that the degree of segregation appeared to have increased between 1968 and 1975. In Amsterdam, the most localized social groups were those at the top and bottom of a six-point hierarchy (Gastelaars et al. 1971: 412). In Southern Europe, data produced by Bastano (1976) also show the great segregation of the professional classes in Naples, although here there is also a high concentration of the small self-employed in the city-centre – the small traders and workshops making up the *economia del vicolo* (the alley economy). It is possible that this greater segregation of the small self-employed also exists in other Southern European cities, with their customarily uni-centric form and lack of old suburban commercial centres.

In total, therefore, residential segregation within Western European cities appears to follow the pattern of other developed countries, of greatest separation of the topmost and bottom-most social classes. However, the highest class is generally the most segregated, a feature not commonly found elsewhere where this position normally goes to the working class.

The argument, quoted earlier, that social class is the primary determinant of residential area characteristics is strongly based on the idea of a particular and dominant set of correlations between social classes and housing classes. If a true hierarchy of housing classes exists in terms of perceived desirability and access, then this will be translated into price which will permit the most wealthy to have the first choice of housing with increasing constraints applying for successive classes in the social hierarchy.

However, as argued in Chapter 2, the identification of a perceived hierarchy of housing classes in Western European cities is far from easy. In particular, the lack of a substantial owner-occupation sector and the presence of an extremely broad private renting sector in many countries leads to difficulty with any housing class hierarchy based largely on tenure status. Relationships between social classes and housing are more likely to emerge on the basis of considerations of housing amenities, size or age.

For Brussels, De Lannoy (1977: 209) performed a series of correlations between social class representation and housing characteristics across the sub-districts of the city. It was notable that social class was poorly correlated with single-family housing, demonstrating that apartment life is a general feature of the city and not specific to certain classes. However, in other respects, certain housing correlates of social class did emerge: the middle class were concentrated in city districts of owner-occupied dwellings with high levels of housing space per person and good levels of housing amenities. The working class were over-represented in areas of the opposite characteristics and, to some extent, in areas of older property, although the correlations between social class and housing age were generally not high: only the lower middle class showed any real relationship with housing age, tending to live in areas of more modern housing.

In Vienna, Sauberer and Cserjan's (1972) work on the 1961 census results showed strong positive relationships between dwelling size, housing space and both the self-employed group and the middle class, whilst housing amenities were positively correlated with the lower middle class: it might have been expected that housing age might underlie these relationships but this was not, in fact, the case.

In Le Havre in France, Damais (1974), surveying areas needing housing renovation, noted that whilst those occupying such housing generally tended to be of low social status, in some parts of the city two-thirds of the property of poor standard was in fact in owner-occupation with the owners drawn from all social classes.

Correlation analyses and factorial ecologies of many Western European cities provide local evidence on social status and housing, although caution has to be exerted over the possibility of the ecological fallacy – the mistaken interpretation that because a particular social group and a specific housing type are both over-represented in a specific district there is a direct link between them. In Copenhagen, Matthiessen (1972: 9–10) found social class and amenity levels to be related, but such measures as dwelling size and persons per room bore no simple relationship with social status. On the other hand, in the analysis of three Danish provincial cities – Aarhus, Odense and Aalborg – it was housing space that had the strongest apparent relationships to social class (Pedersen and Rasmussen 1973).

In Amsterdam, analysis showed that the most significant housing variable connected to social class was household amenity level: as in Brussels, housing age was of little importance, but upper income groups had larger dwellings (Gastelaars and Beek 1972: 69–72; Gastelaars et al. 1971: 415). In Rotterdam, Herzog et al. (1977) found analagous results in that low social rank appeared to be strongly related to the distribution of defective housing. Further south in the Swiss city of Bern, social status was found to relate to size of dwellings but not to housing age, ownership characteristics or housing type (apartments or houses): indeed, single-family owner-occupied dwellings were a feature only of older areas of inter-war worker housing (Gächter 1978: 7–8).

In Southern Europe, equally complex patterns emerge. In her detailed analysis of two districts in Barcelona, Lowder (1980: 29–30) could find no meaningful relationships between home ownership and occupation. Finally, in Venice a series of detailed analyses has produced some interesting results. For Venice proper, high status was related to good levels of housing amenities and larger dwellings: status was not correlated with housing age, nor with type of tenure – renting occurred equally in high- and low-status areas (Lando 1978; Costa et al. 1980: 400–1). When attention was shifted to Venice's industrial satellite of Mestre it was found that the relationship of the middle class with good-quality dwellings held true but that this class preferred to rent property in the centre rather than own on the periphery so that there was a distinct relationship with tenure (Zanetto and Lando 1980: 246).

It is therefore by no means easy to produce even tentative overall conclusions on the relationships between social status and housing variables in Western European cities. It is possible, however, to state that there is an obvious and expected relationship of social status with housing quality in its broadest sense, involving both amenities and dwelling space. Conversely, housing age and housing tenure have little general validity as explanations of social area differentiation and nor does housing type play any major role. These, however, are extremely generalized conclusions and within individual cities these variables may be of some importance. In general it is possible to state that the Western European city contains a housing stock in which social classes of different levels in the hierarchy live in housing of varying tenure characteristics, age and type with only housing quality being a differentiating characteristic between social strata.

SOCIAL CLASS AND LOCATION

Since housing quality is the only major housing variable almost universally correlating with social status, and as it is quite possible for housing quality to be independent of location in the city, it is likely that the pattern of residential areas in the Western European city will be relatively complex spatially, with both high- and low-status areas occurring in various parts of the city with little formal relationship with distance from the centre. Distance from the centre would, of course, normally be closely related to housing age, which has been shown to be of little significance in determining the social composition of neighbourhoods. The most useful approach to the elucidation of the pattern of social class distributions through residential space is through an empirical examination of the evidence coupled with the consideration of various possible explanatory theories. Attention here will be concentrated on the middle class and working class with more limited consideration given to the other three groups identified in Table 7.1.

The middle class

One of the most observable or distinctive residential features of Western European cities is the existence of important high-status residential districts either in or very close to the city-centre, a feature most clearly found in Southern Europe but also of significance in most Northern European cities where this high-status district often spreads into a high-status sector radiating out from the centre. The antecedents of such city-centre high-status concentration have been discussed in Chapter 1, but its continuation in the twentieth century requires more explanation.

Various American authors such as Sjoberg (1960) and Schnore (1965), observing the patterns of city-centre high-status neighbourhoods in both nineteenth-century US cities and those of Latin America at the present time, have put forward evolutionary models for the development of city structures. As a result of modernization processes accompanying industrial and economic growth these models envisage the loss of the dominant high-status character of the city-centre with a gradual reversal of the pre-industrial pattern such that the centre is left to the lowest classes with the social *élite* at the periphery. The simplified general explanations put forward for this evolutionary process concern increases in the possibility of personal mobility which permit the more wealthy classes to have a greater choice of residential location, allowing them to obtain more housing space and a pleasanter environment at the city edge, albeit at the cost of an increased length of journey-to-work, but which allows them to distance themselves from the more stressful environment of the city-centre and from less wealthy classes who cannot afford such high daily commuting costs and must live nearer their places of employment. These evolutionary models assume that all urban societies are similar and evolve in the same way (Bassett and Short 1980: 16–17).

In practice, these models do not apply to the Western European city, for a variety of reasons. Whilst in Northern Europe there has been some tendency for high-status populations to move out to peripheral locations, inner-area high-status districts are still in evidence, whilst in Southern Europe even the centre–periphery moves have been less marked. Everywhere, as will be seen in the following chapter, city-centres are undergoing gentrification through urban renewal processes. It will be useful briefly to examine the European evidence on high-status areas before suggesting explanations for the emergent patterns.

In Athens, the higher socio-economic classes are over-represented in the city-centre and in three narrow sectors of similar over-representation stretching out from it. Lower-status populations are concentrated in more peripheral areas of the city, particularly in those areas of recent urban expansion (Burgel 1972). McElrath (1962: 389–90) put forward very similar findings from his work in Rome, using an index of social rank composed of occupational and educational data. He found that social rank was highest in the old centre of the city, declining slightly to the early twentieth-century suburbs and with markedly lower status being characteristic of the more recently developed peripheral areas. Present-day upper-income housing in central Rome dates from the late nineteenth century with the replacement of aristocratic villas by middle-class apartments after Rome's elevation to capital-city status (Ghirardo 1980: 227).

In Turin, the high-status central city district still exists, although perhaps shrunken in size from that evocatively described by Susanna Agnelli, the grand-daughter of the founder of Fiat, in the inter-war years (Agnelli 1975); but Turin also has a peripheral high-status district on the hills to the east of the city (see below, pp. 164–5). Venice's middle-class population lives in the centre of the city and the social status of these central districts is increasing rapidly owing to the differential out-migration of the lower middle and working classes, thus reinforcing the initial characteristic of the centre (Costa et al. 1980: 404).

In Barcelona, the highest-status areas are just to the north of the crowded city-centre, in the areas of the earliest nineteenth-century suburban expansion of the *Ensanche* (see Ch. 1, p. 24). In Madrid, high status is characteristic of the central areas of the city and the inner nineteenth-century suburbs and this is reflected in the housing values (Abrahamson and Johnson 1974: 526–7; Gago Llorente 1979).

In each of these large Southern European cities, therefore, the pattern of high-status residential areas is similar to that which would be described by evolutionary models of city structure as 'pre-industrial'. High status is concentrated in the city-centres in both old and newly rebuilt or upgraded property (Ballesteros et al. 1977: 207) with peripheral areas having a noticeable under-representation of middle-class elements, yet it would obviously be far-fetched to describe Barcelona or Turin as pre-industrial cities, even though there may be some limited degree of justification in applying the epithet to Athens or Rome. The evidence from Northern Europe is less clear-cut but displays some similar tendencies.

For example, Vienna is a city which, at least in 1961, partially displayed what might be termed a 'Southern European' pattern of status. The city-centre had the greatest over-representation of the middle class with a ring of lesser over-representation around it: the high-status central area included the Ringstrasse district, built up as a wealthy district after the removal of the fortifications in the middle of the nineteenth century (Ch. 1, pp. 24–5). Two higher-status sectors stretched out from the city-centre towards the north-west and west – towards the evironmentally-desirable area fringed by the Vienna Woods (Gisser and Kaufmann 1972: 271). However, there were also a higher number of peripheral middle-class areas than customarily found in Southern European cities, these middle-class districts being distributed in an arc around the city (Sauberer and Cserjan 1972: 300–1). In the small Swiss city of Bern the high-status central district is absent, but there is a distinct middle-class sector stretching out from the centre towards the south-east (Gächter 1978: 7, 10).

Riquet (1978) has reviewed the evidence of social zoning in 68 city-regions of West Germany and found that in general the ratio of non-manual to manual workers drops consistently from central city to suburbs, to urbanized zone and to rural fringe; the same is true for the representation of the university-educated which is greatest in the central cities. However, Riquet (1978: 17–19) also noted that there were differences between cities of different sizes: in the smaller cities, high-status indicators were concentrated at the centre, in larger cities there was greater representation of the middle-class element in city suburbs. High-status sectors are a common feature of larger West German cities, although certain city-centre districts may also have an over-representation of the middle class, so that the pattern of high-status areas is relatively complex (Kreth 1977: 145–7; Niemeier 1969: 206).

The location of high-status areas in French cities may be considered in relation to the cases of Paris and Bordeaux. For Paris, Chauviré and Noin (1980) factor analysed the 1975 census information on the distribution of 9 socio-professional classes across 124 administrative units of the Paris region as a whole. They used the resultant factor scores in a grouping procedure to produce eight classes of social area on the basis solely of occupation. In the first class, the typical area had over a third of its working population in the middle class with personal service also over-represented (and obviously reliant on the first group). Only five spatial units were of this class and these were the four western *arrondissements* of central Paris and the contiguous inner-suburban *commune* of Neuilly, forming the obvious high-status areas around the Champs Elysées and the Bois de Boulogne. Two other statistical classes showed an over-representation of the middle classes and the areas making up these classes also lay to the west of the city; in total, therefore, Paris has a western high-status sector with the greatest concentration of the middle class at the hub of that sector closest to the city-centre.

In Bordeaux there is over-representation of the middle class in certain inner-city districts, and this over-representation is growing as city-centre depopulation removes disproportionately large numbers of the working class to more peripheral locations. However, the central concentrations of higher-status populations are matched by rapid increases in the representation of these groups in certain of the peripheral *communes* of the agglomeration (Pailhé 1978). Similar changes are also occurring in Grenoble (Joly 1978: 1979). In Lille, nine of the twenty-six city districts have an over-representation of the middle classes, these being above all in the city-centre and adjacent renovated areas (Dang 1978).

It is in Belgium, the Netherlands and Scandinavia that there is least manifestation of high-status central areas in cities. In Brussels, the middle class are under-represented within the historic centre, living instead in peripheral areas, particularly to the south-east (De Lannoy 1977). Similarly in Amsterdam, it is a high-status sector (to the south) that stands out rather than a central middle-class concentration, although this is a city where evolutionary theories appear to have some validity since the city-centre was the location of high-status groups until about 1860 (Gastelaars and Beek 1972: 69–72, 77; Gastelaars et al. 1971: 416–18). In Copenhagen there is a high-status sector stretching out to the north of the city-centre (Matthiessen 1972; 1973), whilst in other Danish cities the middle-class populations tend to live in peripheral locations although weakly-developed sectors also exist (Pedersen and Rasmussen 1973: 53).

In general, therefore, summarizing this wealth of empirical material, it is possible to state that the cities of Southern Europe retain their high-status central areas in a relatively pure form whilst in Northern Europe more complex patterns emerge involving a variety of class areas scattered through different parts of the city. It is only a minority of cities that do not display a high-status central district and even there a high-status sector is the common pattern. Most Northern European cities retain some central high-status area even if it may be only a 'relict' feature (Ganser 1966: 111).

What factors can be suggested as creating these patterns of middle-class residence? A variety of partial explanations can be put forward.

The first explanation relates to the fact that in certain European cultures a much greater value is placed upon access to city-centre amenities than on access to open space or the countryside. Economic models of cities stress the high prices of land at the city-centre and Anglo-American models see the effect of this on residential structure as occurring via the crowding together of working-class populations into small dwellings at high density at the centre with the middle classes taking cheaper peripheral land for their more expansive single-family houses with large gardens. The mainland European view is rather different: because land prices are high at the centre, only the richest can afford to live there and the poorer must go to cheaper land in the suburbs – the richest can, of course, afford large city-centre apartments even given high prevailing rents (Claval 1981: 138). This interpretation of the translation of land values into residential patterns is obviously completely at variance with the Anglo-American view.

The difference occurs because English culture has, on the whole, a negative view of the city and a positive view of the countryside (Williams, R. 1973) whilst in Europe rather the reverse situation prevails. In England, rural life and the natural environment are desirable features to be emulated, where possible, in middle-class low-density suburban or commuter village developments. In Western (and most especially Southern) Europe the countryside has in the past been seen as being inhabited by ignorant peasants (Weber 1977) and the city represents the desirable entity, progress and civilized cultured life: maximizing access to the centre is thus the objective rather than fleeing to the periphery. The reasons for these contrasts probably lie in the agricultural and social histories of the countries concerned: in the ex-peasant farming societies of Southern Europe the negative image of the countryside is strongest and the centralizing force greatest, whilst in the historically more commercial (or, at least, less dependent) farming societies of Northern Europe the centralizing force, although still present, is usually weaker.

This cultural interpretation of high-status city-centre living is not, however, a complete explanation: various other controls are of some significance. After the cultural explanation, a second factor is the extent of second-home access. Particularly in Northern Europe, the wealthier elements in society can often combine access to city-centre amenities with access to the countryside via the renting of an urban apartment and ownership of a rural second home. The prevalence of renting among middle-class urban dwellers is an obvious correlate with the ownership of a rural property. Although figures are difficult to obtain, it would appear that in most Northern European countries (the United Kingdom being the outstanding exception) between 8 and 20 per cent of urban residents have access to a rural second home (Coppock 1977).

The particular environmental circumstances of individual cities constitute a third explanatory factor. Rome, for example, set in the midst of the treeless, featureless and arid Campagna, provides few peripheral environmental attractions to encourage social groups with real residential choice to move out of the accessible central areas. On the other hand Turin, with the attractive hill-country to the east of the Po lying on the city's doorstep, has an important peripheral middle-class district there as well as the central high-status area (Adamo 1969: 41). The sectoral arrangement of certain high-status areas in many cities, such as Brussels, Copenhagen and Vienna, owes much to the location of environmental attractions.

A fourth, and very important, control on the spatial patterning of residential areas in the Western European city (and not just on the distribution of the middle class) lies in the location of industry within cities, a factor that has been of some importance elsewhere as well (Warnes 1973). As has been demonstrated in Chapter 1, many Western European cities grew to a considerable size even before the onset of industrialization. When larger-scale factory-production techniques became the norm during the nineteenth century, the new industries were set up in greenfield sites around the urban periphery, creating cordons of industrialization around the city-centres. The twentieth century has seen the continuation of these developments: the results for a single city (Turin) are seen in Fig. 7.1. In Turin, two industrial belts are discernible: the first, at about 2 kilometres from the city-centre (Piazza San Carlo), is of nineteenth-century origin reflecting the built-up area as it stood then; the second belt, at 5

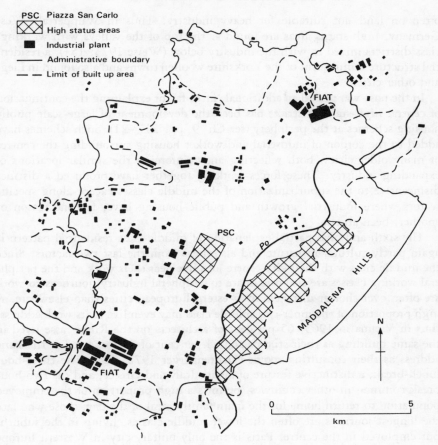

PSC Piazza San Carlo

High status areas

Industrial plant

Administrative boundary

Limit of built up area

Fig. 7.1   Industry and high-status areas, Turin.

kilometres from the centre, is dominated by the twentieth-century complexes of the Fiat enterprises near the present edge of continuous physical urbanization. Peripheral industrial growth, throughout the older cities of Western Europe, has been accompanied by the growth of peripheral housing for industrial workers and technicians, and this pattern is still continuing (Guibourdenche and Joly 1979). As in Turin, therefore, the professional classes, administrators and public employees remain in their traditional locations close to the city-centres and to their places of employment, whilst the working class becomes increasingly suburbanized, this being an explanation of the increasing status levels of some city-centre populations as discussed earlier in this chapter.

In Northern Europe there was a greater degree of creation of new industrial cities in the nineteenth century and in such cases, as in the cities of Yorkshire and Lancashire in England, the link between worker housing and factory was close but with the embryonic middle classes, instead of being 'walled in' in city-centres, taking to more attractive peripheral areas or non-industrial sectors, often on land not suitable for heavy industry. Thus in Wuppertal, West Germany, high-status areas are found at the top of the valleys with working-class districts mixed in with the industry below (Weise 1973: 151), a residential structure reminiscent of the Yorkshire woollen towns and also found in Liège and other cities.

5.) In the post-war period an additional, fifth, factor explaining the continuation of central high-status districts has been the development of large-scale public housing schemes at the periphery (see Ch. 9, pp. 217–21). Such schemes have added to the cordon of industrial and worker housing surrounding the centres of many older cities, both reflecting and reinforcing the similar locations of expanding industry. These forces working together have produced a distinct disincentive to the suburbanization of the middle classes except along specific sectors where industrial growth and public housing have, for one reason or another, been absent.

6.) The sixth and final partial explanation of middle-class residential pattern is again partly cultural in nature and also flows from the last two factors. Since the middle class with their city-centre jobs live near their work and the peripheral working classes are also proximate to peripheral industry, journeys-to-work are often over shorter distances in Western European cities than elsewhere. A high proportion of the inner-city middle class may even live at its work address: thus in Vienna in 1963, 65 per cent of architects on the Ringstrasse lived in the same building as their studios and 51 per cent of doctors lived at the same address as their consulting rooms (Lichtenberger 1972: 223). The three-hour lunch-break, a distinctive feature of Spain, Italy and Greece, and the two-hour break common in other countries, permits a high proportion of the employed population to return home for the main family meal of the day: those who face the longest journeys are often the lower middle classes, living in the suburbs but employed in the centre. Paris is the only unitary city in Western Europe large enough to prohibit a homeward lunch visit for a substantial proportion of the employed population. Proximity of residence and workplace, or at least speedy access from one to the other, is seen as desirable, thus again reinforcing the value of a city-centre residential location for the middle-class groups who work there. Change in the pattern of working hours is strongly opposed, as was seen in the mid-1970s when various governments tried to concentrate the working day in the wake of the energy crisis.

In total, therefore, a variety of explanations can be advanced for the continued significance of high-status central districts in many Western European cities, these explanations being rooted in cultural values and in the spatial repercussions of the historical evolution of urban morphology, such forces operating to invalidate simplistic uni-dimensional models of the evolution of urban form based solely on American experience. But whilst the inner-city high-status district is a distinctive feature of many cities in Western Europe, 7.) it should not be forgotten that it is by no means absent in cities of the English-speaking world: London in particular has several such *élite* districts and has even seen the recent creation of a new purpose-built development in the Barbican with its privately-rented apartments commanding minimum rents of £5,000 per annum in 1982. The fact is, however, that in other British cities similar inner-city high-status areas, although of importance in the past, have now disappeared, whilst even in London the proportion of the *élite* living at the centre is lower than in Paris or other Western European cities.

The working class

The fact of the existence of high-status inner-city neighbourhoods in most cities does not preclude the parallel existence of significant working-class districts close by within the inner-city: indeed, a notable historic feature has been the close proximity of upper- and lower-class neighbourhoods within many cities, a proximity that is only now being broken by trends towards greater segregation.

Such increasing segregation is largely fostered by the post-war provision of public housing schemes in peripheral areas in which the working class are over-represented, alongside considerable proportions of the lower middle class (Clerc 1967: 156–61, 166). A feature of many Western European cities in recent years, especially in Southern Europe and France, has been differential intra-urban migration taking the working classes out of the city-centres and leading them to the peripheral *grands ensembles*, but city-centre worker concentrations are still of importance.

In practice, therefore, working-class populations exist in all types of urban location, in both old and new property, in both city-centre and periphery (Niemeier 1969: 202), but with a general tendency towards increasing concentration in the periphery. The only general relationships with housing variables that can be stated are the negative ones with levels of housing quality (dwelling size and amenity provision) and, less universally, the negative relationship with owner-occupation – in the inner-city the working class rent from private landlords, in the periphery they rent from a public housing authority. Two 'polar' types of working-class neighbourhood therefore exist (Dang 1978): the old stable city-centre working-class district and the new periphery areas of recent development. Between these two extremes a variety of other working-class neighbourhoods emerge, whilst in certain Southern European cities an accentuated 'polar' type is found in the peripheral shanty-town (see Ch. 2, pp. 45–7).

The city-centre or inner industrial suburban working-class district is exemplified by neighbourhoods such as Belleville in the 19th *arrondissement* of Paris (see Ch. 8, p. 194), the Marolles district of Brussels, the area around the Via Roma in Naples, Trastevere in Rome or Sant Cugat del Rec in Barcelona. In such areas live the descendants of the nineteenth-century urban artisan population working in small, almost pre-industrial, enterprises along with those employed in the earliest of the larger factory plant brought by the Industrial Revolution. In a sense, judged strictly on class-composition criteria, such neighbourhoods are mixed rather than purely working class because of the presence of significant proportions of the small self-employed, both in industry and commerce. In Paris, for example, the 'purest' working-class areas lie in the *communes* of the nineteenth-century industrial suburban belt rather than in the

areas of eastern inner Paris that are generally perceived to be those most dominated by the traditional urban proletariat (Chauviré and Noin 1980: 59–61;
Bentham and Moseley 1980: 61).

Nevertheless, it is the inner-city working-class areas throughout Western
Europe that are under the greatest threat from urban renewal programmes and
from creeping gentrification (Ferras 1977b: 193–194). The result has been the
proliferation of urban social protest movements which have achieved much in
terms of sound and fury (often with non-local, non-working-class leadership)
but little in real terms other than the slowing down of the destruction of such
communities. Alternatively, the traditional inner-city working-class inhabitants find themselves 'threatened' by the arrival of foreign labour migrants to
compete in the shrinking market of central cheap-rent working-class housing
(Drewe et al. 1975: 213–15).

Peripheral housing estates may be called the 'new' working-class districts
although large numbers of the lower middle classes often inhabit such areas.
In practice, although there may appear to be some mixing at the aggregate
level, when individual apartment blocks are considered there is often segregation between the social classes (Maurice and Deloménie 1976: 33). Post-war
peripheral working-class concentrations are found in almost all Western
European cities, even in those, such as Brussels, where there is still strong
working-class over-representation near the centre.

The peripheral provision of public housing has been dictated by the scale
of developments envisaged and the consequent need for extensive areas of cheap
land which could only be secured in peripheral locations. The similar locations
developed by recent industry have helped to create a range of local employment
opportunities although women, more likely to be employed in unskilled non-
manual work, are disadvantaged by the lack of local work for them. In many
cities, certain peripheral districts have been earmarked for the receipt of both
public housing and industry, as in Cannes where such activities have been
shunted off to a peripheral district of the 'de luxe' city (Jardel 1967). Nevertheless, there are many cases of public housing being built with no consideration of
access to employment, and generalized problems of accessibility have loomed
large in many developments (see Ch. 9, p. 220). These problems, coupled with
the low construction standards often applied, and with the low level of amenity
provision, have made some new working-class districts fertile areas for politiciza-
tion (Logan 1978).

The general pattern of evolution throughout Western Europe is towards the
continued expansion of the working-class dimension in selected areas (often
sectors) of the city suburbs rather than in city-centres: middle-class expansion
is similarly occurring in other outer sectors, at least in Northern Europe
although it is largely absent further south. The continued overall dilution of
the working-class presence in most city-centres appears to be likely to continue.
Thus, rather than inner-city areas moving down in social class, as suggested
by classical theories of filtering processes, the reverse is often the case (Pailhé
1978; Joly 1979): in many cities the tendency is for the growing ranks of the
middle classes to replace the workers rather than the other way round

(Roncayolo 1972: 13; Arnauné-Clamens 1977). Such a process is facilitated by the growth of the non-manual population as Western European economies move towards the post-industrial phase.

Only in some of the cities of Northern Europe, such as in Amsterdam, Rotterdam and Utrecht, are there substantial elements of higher-status populations involved in the flight from the city-centres and these classes may even predominate in such movement such that the pauperization of the centre results rather than its *embourgeoisement* as is the case elsewhere (Boyer 1978; Den Draak 1966). Even here there are important working-class areas in newer public housing at the city edge with segregation between social classes in the suburban belt.

Other social classes

The location within the city of the other three social classes identified at the start of this chapter can be briefly dealt with: these are the lower middle class, the small self-employed and those working in personal service.

This last group is the easiest to deal with since it is generally dependent upon the middle class for employment and residence and thus is found living in the same areas, indeed in the same buildings, as the high-status populations. In Paris, for example, those employed in personal service are highly correlated in location with the distribution of the liberal professions and administrative classes, congregating in the same city districts (Chauviré and Noin 1980: 54, 59). However, in peripheral middle-class districts throughout Western Europe the personal-service class tends to be absent: the keeping of domestic servants and the *concierges* of apartment blocks are features of traditional *bourgeois* life in city-centres but have not been translated to the more recent suburban middle-class belts.

As indicated earlier (p. 157), the small self-employed sector is relatively ubiquitous in the Western European city, although with specific concentrations in city-centres and the older suburbs. It is largely absent from newer peripheral areas and this absence contributes to the deficiencies of such districts in terms of the amenities expected for everyday life. Consequently, whilst inner-city working-class districts have a strong representation of the self-employed, suburban working-class areas do not. In Southern Europe, where a higher proportion of urban commerce and industry is in the hands of the traditional small self-employed class, this group tends to display a higher degree of segregation within the city-centre than is the case elsewhere (Costa et al. 1980).

Finally, there are those in the lower middle classes whose spatial distributions are, according to measures of segregation, spread relatively evenly through most cities. This group is found throughout urban space but especially in middle-aged suburban areas dating from the first half of this century. As indicated earlier (p. 168), there is also a significant representation of the lower middle class in the post-war public housing developments.

The lower middle class really began to grow in size and importance, at least in Northern Europe, only with the industrialization and modernization of society in the later nineteenth century. As a small but growing interest, members of this class often secured the better apartments in the working-class apartment blocks built at that period or even formed a substantial enough market for specific apartment construction to occur to match their pockets. However, in the early twentieth century, with the creation of the first public housing agencies for worker housing, the lower middle classes began to encounter housing difficulties throughout much of Northern Europe where their numbers were growing rapidly. The common solution was recourse to some form of self-help construction. In Scandinavia this took the form of housing co-operative and housing association schemes building single-family or two-family housing in suburban locations. Elsewhere there was less formal organization. Perhaps the most extreme case of chaos came around Paris where suburban land was quickly bought up by speculators who divided it into small plots and sold it to individuals for the construction of single-family housing. Often the purchasers could not afford to employ a builder and so built their houses themselves. No public services were laid on and there were no building or planning controls: the result was the creation of a suburban slum inhabited by the lowest of the lower middle class along with some elements of the upper working class (Evenson 1979: 226–31). Many other cities saw similar waves of self-help construction (although not on such a disastrous scale) during the inter-war years. In the post-war period the normal housing market has come to provide apartment blocks and houses at a price acceptable to lower middle-class populations, sometimes aided by state housing support (Ch. 2). The result has been that this class is generally spread throughout the city although with under-representation in city-centres and with a general concentration in suburban areas, often those that are of middling distance from the city-centres rather than being at the very edge.

SOCIAL DIMENSIONS AND SPATIAL PATTERNS

The discussion in this chapter so far has been almost wholly concerned with social class and the relationships between class, housing and location in the Western European city. However, the character of residential areas is not solely determined by social class variables. Earlier chapters have examined the existence of demographic space (Ch. 3) and certain dimensions of migration space concerning domestic, international and intra-urban migration (Ch. 4, 5 and 6). These, and other features, coalesce to produce the subtleties of residential and social space that distinguish one neighbourhood from another or often, in the older city districts, one street from another. In this section the recognition of residential areas will be considered via the media of ecological analyses whilst in the following section a more behavioural approach will be discussed.

Considerable use has been made in Western Europe in recent years of investigative techniques such as social area analysis and factorial ecology, the latter having been used by researchers working on many different cities.

Social area analysis, based on the approach of Shevky and Bell (1955), assumes that economic status, family status and ethnicity are the three basic underlying structures determining the characteristics of all urban societies. As a North American technique, some of the actual variables used in scoring these dimensions are of doubtful validity in Western Europe, notably the emphasis on single-family dwellings in the determination of family status (McElrath 1962: 379–80), whilst the ethnicity dimension, if present at all, is likely to work in a much more complex manner than in the United States (Ch. 5). Nevertheless, American researchers have used social area analytical methods in Western European cities, sometimes without regard to their cultural relevance. Thus Abrahamson and Johnson (1974: 522) lamented that they could not obtain ethnicity data in Madrid without questioning whether ethnicity was likely to be of any relevance. McElrath (1962), in his study of Rome, also appears unaware of the cultural differences between Italian urban society and that of the United States. European authors have been more ready to adapt the expected ethnicity dimension into one concerned with the importance of migration and population turnover (Pedersen and Rasmussen 1973: 504; Burgel 1972): this was, indeed, accepted by McElrath (1965) after he had completed his work on Rome.

McElrath's (1962) analysis of the city is nevertheless of some interest. He analysed 354 census sub-areas for 1951 using a social status (or economic status) index composed of occupational and literacy data and a family status index of fertility and working women. The results showed that 38 per cent of Rome's sub-areas had both low social rank and high family status (few working women and/or high fertility). Following the principles of social area analysis, high family status was referred to as a low score on 'urbanization'. These areas of low rank and low urbanization were spread round the outer suburbs of the city (Fig. 7.2) with the only significant areas of this type in the inner-city being the old working-class district of Trastevere and its extension to the east of the Tiber. At the opposite end of the scale, 34 per cent of the census sub-areas were of high social rank and low family status (high urbanization), with older, smaller families living in the inner-city and in the north-eastern suburbs beyond the gardens of the Villa Borghese (*borghese* coincidentally means middle class or *bourgeois*). Only a minority of sub-areas were of intermediate characteristics, and because of the positive correlation between scores on the dimensions of social rank and urbanization it could be argued that these are not truly separate components of overall societal structure.

Athens has also been subjected to social area analysis (Burgel 1972). The collection of data proved to be a great problem, and because of the inadequacy of the 1961 census a sample survey of 3,000 individuals was undertaken, spatially stratified on a grid-square basis in order to get representation of all city districts. Burgel's indices concerned the proportion of management and administrative personnel (representing social rank), the proportion of simple conjugal households (representing family status or urbanization), and the proportion of non-Athenian born, replacing the ethnicity dimension. As mentioned earlier (p. 161), social rank was highest in the city-centre and in three sectors stretching out from it. The familial variable produced a concentric

171

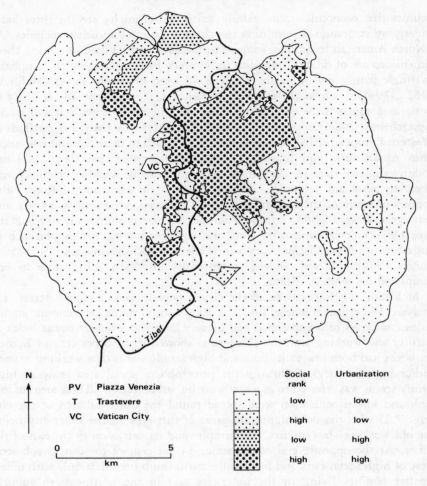

Fig. 7.2 Social areas in Rome, 1951.
(*Source*: redrawn from McElrath 1962)

pattern with low proportions of conjugal families in the centres of Athens and Piraeus and values rising with increased distance from these centres. The distribution of migrants was less simple, consisting of nodes throughout the urban fabric. The distribution of the three defined dimensions thus accorded quite well with Murdie's (1969) statement of social area analysis in terms of social status sectors, concentric familial zones and ethnic (migrant) clustering: however, the redefinition of ethnicity is of importance, as is the central-city high-status district.

Given the apparent relationships between social rank and family status (high rank, low familism) in both Rome and Athens, the question may be raised as to whether these are indeed the most important dimensions for the description and analysis of social areas in Southern European cities. It is, of course, the case that in Northern Europe the correlation of social rank and family status may not, indeed, exist. In their social area analyses of twelve Flemish towns, Pattyn and Van Eeckhoutte (1977: 73) found very weak correlations between their life-cycle and social status constructs. In the light of these points, and of the complexities of the relationships between social classes and housing variables referred to above (pp. 155–9), it is instructive to pay some attention to the studies that have been conducted on Western European cities using factorial ecological methods: such studies are likely to produce evidence on the significant social dimensions of the city and on the spatial patterns that both create and reflect these dimensions.

A large number of factorial ecological studies has now been carried out on Western European cities, but the comparison of results between one study and another is fraught with dangers. Firstly, there are difficulties over the size of the administrative units used as data bases: where large units are used there are problems over spatial averaging such that the variability between units is likely to be reduced. Analyses in Western Europe have used units of a variety of scales: in Amsterdam, Gastelaars and Beek (1972) used 65 districts whilst in Copenhagen, a city of similar size at just under three-quarters of a million population, Matthiessen (1972) used 242 districts. At the other end of the scale, Abrahamson and Johnson (1974) used only 12 sub-areas in Madrid with its population of over 3 million.

A second, and major, problem lies in the variables used in each study since the coverage and variety of the variables is a vital determinant of the components and factors that are extracted. Emphasis in the following discussion is placed on a set of studies that utilize similar ranges of variables but detailed problems of comparability nevertheless exist. Where a study omits consideration of variables on, say, migrants, then no migrant dimension to social structure can emerge.

A third comparative problem arises from the lack of detailed information in many studies on the exact analyses performed. Insufficient distinction is sometimes made between factor analysis and principal components analysis, and the use of various rotational solutions is sometimes left unexplained. It is because of the different techniques used, the varying sizes of unit areas, and the different numbers and details of variables introduced that no variance explanation figures are quoted in Table 7.3 for individual components, although the components are quoted in descending order of explanatory power and an overall explanation percentage is given. In certain cases in Table 7.3, component names have been adjusted from the originals in order to facilitate comparisons between studies.

Before proceeding to a comparison of the ten analyses in Table 7.3, it is necessary to make one or two brief comments about some of the studies and their objectives. The studies with the greatest diversity of original variables (not just in number but in type) are those by Gächter (1978) of Bern and Kesteloot (1980) of Brussels. Several of the analyses include either none or only one variable dealing with foreigners or migrants, whilst at the other end of the scale the analysis of Lyon by Jones (1982) is largely concerned with elucidating

Table 7.3 Social dimensions derived from multivariate analyses – selected cities

City	Country	Sub-areas	Variables	Date of variables	Source of results	Explanation level (dimensions)	Dimension I	Dimension II	Dimension III	Dimension IV	Dimension V
Amsterdam	Netherlands	65	31	1960–5	Gastelaars and Beek 1972	73.7 per cent (I–IV)	Social rank	Urbanization*	Familism	Religion	n.n.
Barcelona	Spain	128	15	1969–70	Ferras 1977a	73.8 per cent (I–V)	Social rank	Housing and demographic age	n.n.	n.n.	n.n.
Bern	Switzerland	165	65	1970	Gächter 1978	64.2 per cent (I–V)	Social rank	Foreigners	Recency	Household size	Housing type and tenure
Brussels	Belgium	512	48	1970	Kesteloot 1980	65.2 per cent (I–V)	Social rank	Inner-city	Housing*	Self-employment	Age and feminization
Copenhagen	Denmark	242	20	1965	Matthiessen 1972	71.0 per cent (I–V)	Social rank	Non-familism	Housing	Activity rates	Youth
Helsinki	Finland	70	42	1960–1	Sweetser 1965b	92.4 per cent (I–V)	Social rank	Progeniture	Residentialism	Established familism	Postgeniture
Lyon	France	173	23	1975	Jones 1982	71.5 per cent (I–V)	Economic and ethnic status	Life-style	Ethnicity and life-style	Housing	Quality of life
Mainz	West Germany	100	50	1970–5	Kreth 1977	36.7 per cent (I–II)	Employment status	Age and household structure	n.n.	n.n.	n.n.
Venice	Italy	134	38	1971	Lando 1978	64.0 per cent (I–V)	Social rank	Self-employment*	Demographic vitality	Housing tenure	Recency
Vienna	Austria	212	35	1959–67	Sauberer and Cserjan 1972	77.0 per cent (I–V)	Social rank I	Physical and demographic age	Social rank II	Suburbanization	Non-residential uses

* Name changed from that of the original source

n.n. Dimension not named or described in the original source

174

the position of migrants within the urban ecological structure so that migrant variables are several and play a significant role in the dimensions identified. All the studies dealt with in Table 7.3 include variables on social class or occupation, on demographic structures (age and sex) and on housing (generally age of property, housing density and amenities; less often type of tenure). The inclusion of other variables differs from case to case: for example, in Amsterdam religion could be of some significance and was included in the analysis but in Venice this cultural factor is an irrelevance on which no data are available.

It is a notable feature of the results reported in Table 7.3 that social status in some form is the first-ranking dimension in every case, thus adding to the similar conclusions reached by analyses of cities in the English-speaking world. The composition of the variables making up the first component varies from city to city, but several general features stand out. As mentioned earlier (p. 159), housing amenity levels are closely associated with social status. This was the case in Amsterdam (Gastelaars and Beek 1972: 69–72), Bern (Gächter 1978: 7), Brussels (Kesteloot 1980: 26), Copenhagen (Matthiessen 1972: 9), Lyon (Jones 1982: 210), Venice (Lando 1978: 130) and Vienna (Sauberer and Cserjan 1972: 294). In certain of the analyses the high-status end of the social rank dimension was strongly negatively correlated with the presence of migrant workers: in Barcelona, for example, low status was associated with the presence of high proportions of the Southern-born, of industrial workers and of dominantly masculine populations (Ferras 1977a: 449) – much as would be expected from the discussion in Chapter 4 (pp. 85–9). In Lyon, low status was similarly associated with migrants although in this case they were international movers (Jones 1982: 210). On the other hand, in Brussels (Kesteloot 1980: 26) high status was linked to the presence of those foreign groups who were themselves of middle-class occupation (see Ch. 5, pp. 126–8). In all the cities where educational variables were included in the analysis, this first social rank dimension produced significant loadings on educational level attained. In total there is a remarkable degree of similarity across the ten cities in terms of the composition of the first social dimension from these analyses.

However, social rank in some different form emerges as of further importance in certain of the analyses reported in Table 7.3. In Brussels (Kesteloot 1980: 67) and in Venice (Lando 1978: 133–4, 136) the ecological situation of the self-employed class within urban space is such that an important urban dimension is largely characterized by their presence. The same is to some extent true in Vienna (Sauberer and Cserjan 1972: 294–8) where the two emergent social rank dimensions are differentiated by the middle classes being the highest-scoring element on one dimension and the self-employed on the other. The significance of the continued existence of the self-employed economic class, referred to earlier (pp. 152–3), is thus demonstrated in these three cities.

According to the tenets of social area analysis, a second important dimension, after social rank, should be some index of family status or of the degree of urbanization as measured through female activity rates or fertility. Indeed, dimensions broadly of this type do emerge in most of the ten analyses reported in Table 7.3, but the results are complex and the composition of the dimensions varies from city to city.

In Amsterdam the second dimension held positive loadings on variables such as the proportion of unmarried residents, the proportion of working women, migration turnover levels and the proportion of older dwellings, whilst there was a negative score for distance from the city-centre (Gastelaars and Beek 1972: 73–4). This is clearly an urbanization dimension analagous to that of classical social area analysis. A very similar dimension emerged at the second rank in Brussels (Kesteloot 1980: 45–7), whilst in Vienna the same occurred although with a straightforward reversal of the signs on the loadings so that Sauberer and Cserjan (1972: 299) labelled it 'suburbanization' but pointed out its similarity to the 'urbanization' dimension of Shevky and Bell (1955).

Elsewhere the index of family status tends to be much fragmented into dimensions dealing with different life-cycle stages, this being most clearly the case in Helsinki where Sweetser (1965b) identified three such dimensions, labelled 'progeniture' (the family-building phase), 'establised familism' with older children, and 'postgeniture' with high proportions of the retired: each of these dimensions tended to measure presence or absence rather than producing a true scale.

In Amsterdam, a familism dimension was separately identified yielding high loadings on demographic variables indicating the presence of young families, with some connection with recent house-building (Gastelaars and Beek 1972: 74–5). In Bern a similar dimension emerged, determined by the presence of young children in recently-built housing, the dimension being labelled 'recency' (Gächter 1978: 8). On the other hand, in Venice young families are not associated with new building so that 'demographic vitality' and 'recency' stand out as separate dimensions (Lando 1978: 136). In Copenhagen, rather as in Helsinki, three life-cycle stage dimensions are apparent: 'youth' – a dimension especially associated with student districts of the city; 'activity rates' in which the absence of working women can be taken to indicate the family-rearing stage; and 'non-familism' which is characterized by the over-representation of the old (Matthiessen 1972: 10–11).

The emergence of a distinctive urban ecological dimension concerned with the situation of old people occurs not just in Helsinki and Copenhagen but in several of the other studies as well. The association of older people with older, often rented, property gives its character to the second dimension in Barcelona (Ferras 1977a: 449), the fifth in Brussels (Kesteloot 1980: 71), the second in Lyon (Jones 1982: 216), the second in Mainz where the dimension forms a continuous scale from old to young households (Kreth 1977: 144), and the second in Vienna (Sauberer and Cserjan 1972: 298–9).

It is clear that family structures are important aspects of spatial differentiation within the cities studied here, but there is no simple universal description possible of what those family structures might be. In general, as demonstrated in Chapter 3 (pp. 70–1), life-cycle groups tend to be somewhat segregated in the Western European city so that dimensions emerge that are determined by the representation of specific age and family groups, often related to housing age.

The third major structure of classical social area analysis after social rank and family status is ethnicity. As reported earlier (p. 175), the presence or absence of migrant groups showed up in some cities on the first dimension of social rank. Only in Bern did a true dimension of migrant worker representation emerge, determined on the basis of mother tongue, activity rate, religion and employment status as well as on the proportion of foreigners (Gächter 1978: 7–8): this is a city with a high concentration of low-status migrants at the centre whilst the equivalent indigenous population lives elsewhere. In Brussels, foreign migrants are associated positively with the 'inner-city' component but do not create an urban dimension of their own (Kesteloot 1980): in Lyon, Jones' (1982) third component is one of foreign migrants with a youthful population but this is far from being exclusively an ethnic dimension. Kreth (1977) found that in Mainz no foreign migrant dimension emerged because of the intermingling of foreign populations with Germans of similar status level: ethnicity was subsumed within social class.

In Amsterdam a religious dimension differentiating areas on the basis of the proportion of Catholics did emerge (Gastelaars and Beek 1972: 75) and in the German federal capital of Bonn, Böhm et al. (1975: 37) have indicated that a similar religious dimension may be important, Bonn being a Catholic city which has received a large number of Protestant migrants in the post-war years: if such segregation exists, however, it reflects the localization of recent house-construction rather than any major cultural divide. In Helsinki, Sweetser (1965a: 216–17) searched his results for evidence of an ethnic dimension involving the Swedish-speaking population of the city but could find nothing.

Finally, it has been the case in many factorial ecologies of British cities (Robson 1969; Davies and Lewis 1973) that housing variables have emerged as producing a distinct dimension. This is far from being universally the case in Western Europe. In Bern, two housing dimensions did emerge (Gächter 1978), the first dealing with household size and density and the second bringing together the variables of single-family dwellings and owner-occupation. It is, of course, notable that these latter variables were not associated with high-status groups: indeed, they tended to be over-represented in older working-class areas whilst the overall levels of both single-family housing and owner-occupation were anyway very low for the city, as throughout Swiss urban areas (see Ch. 2). In Brussels, Kesteloot (1980: 57–9) identified a dimension linking several housing variables but in no causal or easily interpretable fashion. More easily understood is Matthiessen's (1972) housing dimension in Copenhagen which is a measure of the quality of housing analogous to Robson's (1969) component of housing conditions in Sunderland. A similar dimension occurs in Lyon (Jones 1982: 220), whilst in Venice housing tenure is of significance but has no relationship with social class (Lando 1978: 136). The emergence of components entitled 'residentialism' in Helsinki and 'non-residential uses' in Vienna is a reflection of the inclusion of land-use data in the studies of those two cities (Sweetser 1965b; Sauberer and Cserjan 1972).

In conclusion to this discussion of the ten studies summarized in Table 7.3, it is clear that social status is a dominant indicator of social area characteristics in Western European cities, with the importance of self-employment emerging as an interesting secondary finding. Life-cycle characteristics are also of considerable importance, various stages in the life-cycle being associated, in a complex manner, with the existence of social areas of different types. Ethnicity is not, in general, an independent determinant of social areas, migrant groups being more commonly associated with indigenous populations of similar status, at least at the aggregative levels of analysis reported here. Housing is of some local importance as an independent dimension of urban structure but, given the great complexity of the housing situation throughout Western Europe (Ch. 2), it is unsurprising that the only consistent finding on housing is the association of amenities with social class: other housing variables often appear to vary in an autonomous and independent manner.

It is useful to add briefly the conclusions of certain other factorial studies that have been undertaken in Western European cities. Pedersen and Rasmussen (1973) incorporated data for the three Danish cities of Aarhus, Odense and Aalborg into a single analysis from which they identified family status and social status as the two most important components with the third component differentiating between the cities rather than within them. Zanetto and Lando (1980) analysed the Venetian mainland sub-city of Mestre, identifying two social rank components followed by one of housing and one dealing with familism. In an analysis of certain suburban municipalities near Barcelona, Sola-Morales Rubió (1970) identified a complex first dimension bringing together certain demographic as well as occupational variables, suggesting, once again, the correlations between family status and social status constructs in some Southern European societies. In Northern Europe, Grönholm (1960), in an advanced early use of factorial techniques, studied ecological differentiation as an explanation for the distribution of certain symptoms of social disorganization in Helsinki: he found these symptoms to be clearly related to ecological variables in two factors, the first being one of urbanization or stress and the second a factor of socio-economic status. Similar overall conclusions emerged from a study of Rotterdam by Herzog et al. (1977) looking at similar topics.

Geographers have traditionally placed much emphasis on the spatial patterns that emerge in the score maps from factorial ecological analyses. However, the studies reported in Table 7.3 add relatively little extra detail to the patterns of social class representation identified earlier in this chapter and to the spatial distributions of housing and demographic variables discussed in Chapters 2 and 3 and migrant space considered in Chapter 4 and 5. However, by the use of cluster analysis techniques on the score data from ecological analysis it is possible to produce composite maps of the apparent residential structure of whole cities. Attention will be paid here to two such studies.

Sauberer and Cserjan (1972: 300–1) produced a classification of the census

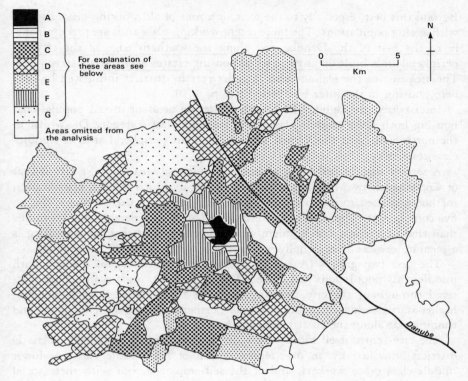

Key: A Business city, high percentage of middle-class
     B Administrative city
     C Working-class areas, predominantly older dwellings but some recent development
     D Lower middle-class districts with some workers
     E Working-class low-density suburbs
     F Inner-suburban lower middle-class districts
     G Peripheral middle-class districts

Fig. 7.3   Residential districts in Vienna, 1961.
(*Source*: redrawn from Sauberer and Cserjan 1972)

districts of Vienna in 1961 on the basis of the scores on seven components derived from their principal components analysis of the city (Fig. 7.3). Certain districts were omitted because of small population totals or uniqueness.

The old city core of Vienna stands out, divided into two residential areas. The 'business city' has an over-representation of the middle class, especially in the liberal professions, but is a relatively heterogeneous area with the presence of the self-employed and other class groups. The 'administrative city' is more homogeneous, with the absence of the self-employed and the greatest over-representation of managerial staff.

Surrounding the city-centre is the area of good-quality nineteenth-century apartments occupied by what might be termed the 'upper' end of the lower middle class: here, notably, there is a relatively aged population structure.

179

Beyond this belt, especially to the west, is a zone of old working-class districts with ageing populations. The more recent working-class areas are predominantly to the east of the Danube and along the southern edge of the city, in peripheral areas built up as large social housing estates over the last sixty years. The area east of the Danube also includes certain districts influenced by self-help housing in the inter-war period (see p. 170).

Interspersed throughout the urban fabric are areas of mixed populations, housing both lower middle classes and working class (category D), whilst in the north-west, near the Vienna Woods, there are peripheral areas of middle-class residences.

A second analysis providing a detailed residential area map of a city is that of Copenhagen by Matthiessen (1972; 1973), in which Ward's classification method was used to produce nine groups of districts on the basis of scores on five components. The ensuing pattern (Fig. 7.4) is considerably more complex than that of Vienna, one problem arising from the fact that Frederiksberg is a separate *kommun* lying wholly within the outer boundary of Copenhagen.

The first two groups (A and B) consist of a mixed bag of districts with middle-class populations and balanced age-structures. Such districts are scattered throughout the city, but it is possible to recognize a weak sector of higher-status residence pivoting in the northern part of the city-centre and running out along the coast to the north.

The city-centre itself forms a very distinct element in the pattern (class D districts), marked by an over-representation of the middle class, of lower middle-class office workers, and of the self-employed, but with these social groups inhabiting relatively small housing units.

Around the city-centre are three rather fragmented belts of distinct residential neighbourhoods identified in large part by housing characteristics. The most interesting of these belts is that made up of districts with features similar to the classical 'zone in transition' (category H): low social status, poor housing, an over-representation of the old coupled with a large number of young people (often students) and a lack of conjugal families. Such districts are concentrated in the inner suburban ring of the city, most typically immediately to the north-west of the city-centre in areas built up in the late nineteenth century as speculative tenement developments: however, certain peripheral areas, often those shared by industry (as in the south-west), also display these social and housing characteristics. The other two of those fragmented inner belts concern housing association properties (categories E and G) dating from the early years of the century, the categories being differentiated not by social class (both are of lower middle-class dominance) but by the high numbers of old people in areas of category G.

The three remaining categories (C, F and I) all tend towards peripheral locations. Cateogory C districts are areas of inter-war housing with both single-family dwellings and apartment houses: the occupants are predominantly of the lower middle class with some middle-class representation. In category F districts the housing is of good-quality villas and single-family residences but the population structure is an ageing one. Finally, category I districts are

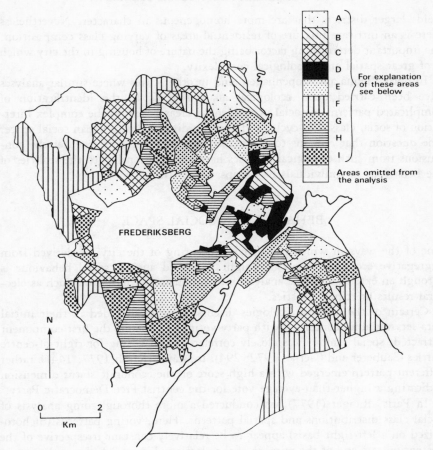

For explanation
of these areas
see below

Areas omitted from
the analysis

FREDERIKSBERG

N

0   2
Km

Key: A Heterogeneous areas, dominantly middle-class
     B Middle-class areas, late nineteenth-century housing
     C Inter-war lower middle-class and middle-class areas
     D Central-city districts
     E Lower middle-class areas, housing association property
     F Peripheral villa areas, ageing middle- and lower middle-class population
     G Old housing association areas
     H 'Zone in transition' characteristics
     I Working-class areas

Fig. 7.4   Residential districts in Copenhagen, 1965.
(*Source*: redrawn from Matthiessen 1973)

marked by high-standard apartment blocks of fairly recent construction, built
by the public authorities and housing the modern working-class population.

In total, the emergent patterns in Copenhagen are complex, particularly in
the inner parts of the urban core where there is great fragmentation of residential areas: towards the periphery, twentieth-century estate development

yields larger districts that are more homogeneous in character. Nevertheless there is an intricate mixture of residential areas of varying class composition, one important determining factor being the nature of housing in the city which is of great spatial and typological complexity.

In both Vienna and Copenhagen (and in other cities where similar analyses have been carried out), ecological analysis leads to the identification of complicated patterns of social or residential areas based on the complex interaction of social class, life-cycle, and housing dimensions to urban social space. The question that remains to be investigated, of course, is whether the conclusions from such ecological analyses have any relationship to the realities of the behaviour of individuals or groups within the city.

BEHAVIOUR IN SOCIAL SPACE

One of the ways in which the social structuring of the city, as derived from aggregative ecological analysis, might be tested against social behaviour is through an extension of the analysis into various social indicators such as electoral results or crime statistics.

Certain of the factorial ecologies discussed earlier included in their initial data sets variables concerned with party voting. In Vienna the first component extracted, social rank I, was closely correlated with voting for right-of-centre parties (Sauberer and Cserjan 1972: 294). In Mainz (Kreth 1977: 144) a rather different pattern emerged with a high score on the economic status dimension indicating a higher-than-average vote for the centrist Free Democratic Party.

In Paris, Ranger (1977) has conducted a more thoroughgoing analysis of social class distributions and spatial patterns. Here, voting patterns (dichotomized on a left/right basis) appear to be relatively constant irrespective of the abstention rate and of the purpose of the election. Figure 7.5 shows the extent of this consistency for eleven of the ballots in the city during the period 1965–77 and compares the electoral map with one showing the dominant social class in each city *quartier* in 1968. The correspondences are obvious, with 'right' voting in the old *bourgeois* western *quartiers* and 'left' voting in the working-class east. The zone of intermediate populations, including significant representations of small artisans and self-employed shopkeepers, of the northern part of the inner-city to a large extent forms a buffer between the two extremes, both socially and in electoral behaviour.

Paris has given a majority vote to right-of-centre parties in almost all elections since the war, a reflection of the continued high level of representation of middle-class elements in the city. In contrast, the *communes* surrounding Paris, outside the old fortification lines (see Ch. 1, pp. 25–6), have been known as the 'Red Belt' as a result of their left-wing political persuasions deriving from their predominantly working-class populations. It is only in the post-war years, as a result of more middle-class housing developments on the outer edge of this belt, that control of some *communes* has been wrested away from the communists and socialists (Moreau 1968).

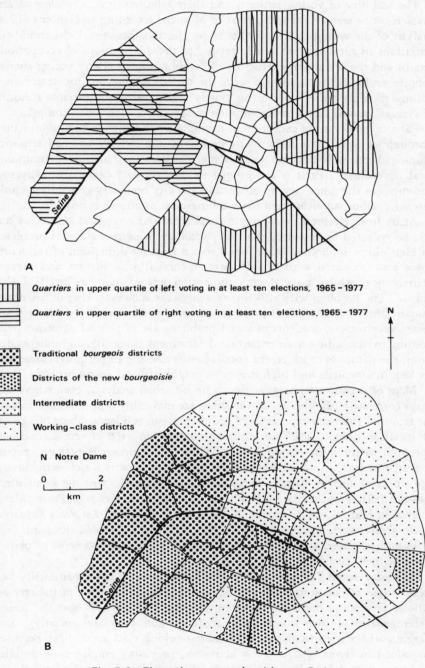

Fig. 7.5 Electoral patterns and social areas, Paris.
A: Voting patterns in eleven elections, 1965–77.
B: Social class dominance, 1968.
(*Source*: redrawn from Ranger 1977)

The stability of voting patterns and their relationships to residential area characteristics seen in Paris also exist in Munich, according to Ganser's (1966) analysis of the voting district results of six elections between 1956 and 1962. Variations in turnout were closely related to the distributions of occupational groups and the sex and age-structure of neighbourhoods. Party voting showed definite ecological relationships with the overall socio-economic structure of polling districts rather than being closely related to single-variable measures of average income or the representation of specific occupational groups.

Paris is, however, an exception in having a right-wing electoral dominance. Throughout Western Europe many cities, by the late 1970s, had left-wing municipal control sometimes, as in Bologna, with a long history of communist local government. Paris is exceptional in that the city boundary really only encompasses the inner-city: in other cases the city boundary generally includes extensive suburban areas with the working-class estates thus brought in.

Apart from electoral data, urban social areas and ecological structures may also be reflected in measures of social pathology or perceived social problems. In Helsinki, Grönholm (1960) found that a housing dimension of residential space was associated with suicide rates, mental illness, divorce and juvenile delinquency, whilst a social rank dimension related more to levels of alcoholism. The problem with this sort of analysis is, however, that of discerning causality: do certain types of social area cause divorce or do they attract divorcees? Nevertheless, students of social problems are in general agreement that housing overcrowding is an important determinant alongside, and independent from, the nature of much recent *grand ensemble* housing in peripheral areas with its lack of amenities and high degree of neighbourhood anonymity.

Maps of urban social areas as drawn up by urban analysts, even where such maps correlate with other social variables, are inevitably high-level abstractions far removed from the experience of ordinary urban residents. Short of a period of social anthropological 'participatory observation', the closest second-hand approach to the everyday existence of the *vie des quartiers* is perhaps through the urban novel, in which recent French literature boasts a rich vein through the works of authors such as Maxence van der Meersch, writing about life in the northern French city of Roubaix, Raymond Queneau in Paris, Marcel Pagnol in Marseille and Christiane Rochefort in her novel *Les Petits Enfants du Siècle* about working-class life in a Parisian *grand ensemble*. Richard Cobb (1980b) has played a major role in conveying the flavour and sense of place of some of these authors to the English reader.

Everyday social life in the Western European city has traditionally been experienced at two scales: that of the neighbourhood and that of the city as a whole. Given the dense urban fabric of older city districts and the relative heterogeneity of their composition (both economically and socially), many neighbourhoods, particularly in the more working-class areas, have been self-contained in terms of day-to-day activities, providing employment, retailing and recreational functions for their inhabitants. At the level of social ceremonial, however, another scale has been important – that of the whole city focused on the centre. Thus, in Southern European cities especially, the tradition of the evening or Sunday promenade (in Italian the *passeggiata*) along a fixed itinerary is of great importance, especially for the more elevated ranks of society. There is no Anglo-Saxon equivalent to these social and cultural manifestations of the importance of urbanism which can fill city-centres with a perambulating population on Sunday afternoons at a time when, in England, the streets are deserted.

Recent years have seen a reduction in the overall importance of these two elements of social space, more especially of the neighbourhood. The steady imposition of planning, in all its various forms, in the twentieth century has brought greater functional segregation to the use of space within cities (Georgulas and Markopoulou 1977: 73), particularly through the creation of estate housing in which not only social class segregation but also homogeneity of life-cycle groups is brought about (Bontinck 1978: 566–9), whilst access to non-residential urban functions is much diminished. Consequently, an increasing proportion of the urban population lives in districts that are far from being self-contained and in which the social importance of 'neighbourhood' is unlikely to develop. In some countries, such as Sweden (see Ch. 9, pp. 229–30), determined attempts have been made to create neighbourhoods in the suburbs via insistence on housing and functional diversity in suburban planning, but it is noticeable that in Southern Europe, where the ethos of urbanism and the unitary city is stronger, such initiatives (with a few exceptions such as EUR in Rome) have been conspicuous by their absence.

It is possible to approach an understanding of the traditional importance of the neighbourhood or *quartier* through the published work of several researchers, most notably through the research team under Paul Chombart de Lauwe working in Paris (Chombart de Lauwe et al. 1952). Looking in greatest detail at the working-class inner-city districts, they found that the true neighbourhood or action space of individuals generally contained no more than 2,000 people and was often very tightly geographically limited by a barrier such as a wide busy street. The activity space of urban inhabitants was thus much smaller than even the smallest census tracts normally available for aggregate analysis. Only for the *bourgeois* households sampled were social spaces and contact patterns more extended, with complex patterns of inter-household relationships and visiting.

More recently, Metton and Bertrand (1974), also studying the Paris region, have reiterated these conclusions. They again found the tendency for activity spaces (*espaces vécus*) to be bounded by major roads or railways, with radial routes often producing narrow 'squeezed' neighbourhoods in the interstices between them. Most significantly, it was found that different types of housing area were associated with different characteristics of activity space. In areas of single-family dwellings north of Paris, the concepts of the neighbourhood scarcely had any relevance since all local service points, the nodes around which an individual's activity space is constructed, lay too far away from most residents. The European housewife's traditional preference for daily shopping has been facilitated by the ubiquity of small retailers in inner-city areas: the acceptance of the weekly visit to the out-of-town hypermarket has been rendered essential, in contrast, for the new suburban housewife.

The second level of social space, of the whole city focused on the centre, has also come under investigation and the conclusions generally affirm that the city-centre is of great importance for the social activities of the middle classes but that working-class populations, more likely anyway to be more isolated by distance from the centre, are far less involved in the use of the centre and have a poorly-developed mental image of the city as a whole. For example, Bianchi and Perussia (1978) discovered that working-class respondents to their survey in Milan visited the centre much less frequently than middle-class respondents, and that the latter group expressed a much greater degree of satisfaction with the social opportunities provided at the centre. Similarly in Paris, Lamy (1967) found that whilst middle-class suburbanites made many trips to the city-centre for entertainment, shopping and other activities, working and lower middle-class suburban families were much more strongly tied to their residences and went into the centre relatively little.

The most important determinants of the mental image of the city-centre appear to be occupation or social status followed by age: sex is of little importance, but the location of the respondent's present residence has been found to be important in some studies (Wehling 1981). In Liège, Belgium, occupation and age were significant in explaining strong disagreements between respondents over which of two locations was the centre of the city (Mérenne-Schoumaker 1979: 17–24). In a study of map designs of the centres of Milan and Rome, Francescato and Mebane (1973) found that middle-class respondents' maps showed many more locational elements than those of lower-class respondents, with respondents who were under thirty also showing more elements than older residents. Rome was a city rather like Liège in that there was no single focal point agreed on by a majority of respondents, but the citizens' image of Milan was strongly centred on the cathedral and its square (Francescato and Mebane 1973: 135; Bianchi and Perussia 1978: 84). Amsterdam and Mulhouse (France) are other cities in which residents disagreed on the location of the central focus (Heinemeyer 1968: 38–9; Woessner and Bailly 1979: 1045).

The conclusion must be, therefore, that the notion of the Western European city as a unitary social space is important only for middle-class populations, a feature that both reinforces and reflects the continuing importance of the city-centre as an area for high-status residence. Working-class groups are more dominated by their own neighbourhoods whilst those who inhabit the new suburban estates and *grands ensembles* may live in a social vacuum, devoid of any real participation in a local community.

One further important point concerns the social space of immigrant populations. Single male labour migrants appear to make considerable use of city-centres as places of attraction for entertainment or just for meeting other migrants, often at stations. The importance of the centre is particularly enhanced for those living in peripheral employer-provided accommodation, as in many West German cities (Ch. 5, p. 116). Such single migrants have very little knowledge of their own residential neighbourhood but the city-centre is enlarged in their perceptions (Clark 1977: 81–98, 143–6). On the other hand, migrant families, particularly those living in peripheral estates, become encapsulated in urban space with the unifying force of the family and the absence of local cultural, political or religious centres yielding a very attenuated local awareness space whilst, for them, the distant city-centre scarcely exists (Schnapper 1976: 496–7).

Actual social space in the Western European city therefore differs markedly from individual to individual according to social class or status. The traditional working-class *vie des quartiers* still exists in many inner-city areas where socially functional neighbourhoods are intensively used and limited in extent: such neighbourhoods are often, however, under threat from processes such as slum clearance. The peripheral *grands ensembles* and other forms of suburban living have reduced feelings of neighbourhood and community for those transferred there from inner-city districts. Inner-city neighbourhoods, where they continue to be of importance, are rooted in the traditional multi-functional heterogeneity of the inner-city urban fabric and in the commonplace amenities of everyday life rather than on planned or monumental spaces: for example, in the 7th *arrondissement* of Paris, local residents' mental maps, when drawn out, rarely mentioned the Eiffel Tower lying within the district although most indicated the local recreational space around it (Metton and Bertrand 1974: 145). In contrast with the working class and its traditional neighbourhood spaces, the urban middle classes have tended to use the city more as a unit with particular emphasis placed on the centre, this being true even for the middle-class groups who reside in peripheral or suburban locations. Different social classes not only live in spatially-separated parts of cities, they also make different uses of urban space.

The identification of behavioural, as opposed to ecologically-derived, urban spatial constructs suggests that the aggregative approaches, whilst highlighting important social dimensions to the city, operate spatially at scales which are not of universal applicability. The traditional city neighbourhood is a far smaller and more subtle building block of urban space than are the census tracts, whilst for certain groups the city as a whole forms behavioural space. Thus whilst ecological analyses operate at a meso-scale, both the micro-scale and the macro-scale are also of relevance in considerations of how urban people structure their lives within the city. Various research approaches can thus contribute in their own ways to the elucidation of urban social relationships in space.

CONCLUSIONS

Figure 7.6 presents an extremely general model of the spatial social structure of the Western European city, incorporating all the more commonly-found general features discussed in the present chapter along with some elements

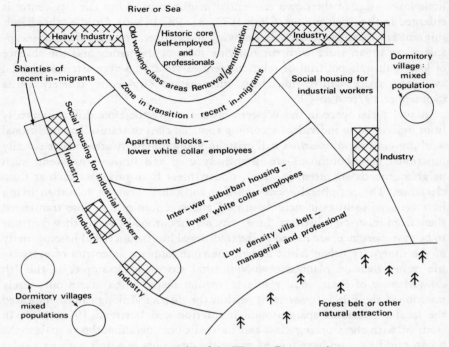

Fig. 7.6 A model of the Western European city.

(such as shanty-towns and dormitory villages) discussed elsewhere in the book. The model is loosely based on a variety of cities and is not tied to one specific case as was the case in Lichtenberger's model based on Vienna (Lichtenberger 1970). It must thus be stressed from the outset that the model is a composite amalgamating features found in cities in different parts of the region. No single city displays all the features of the model although all cities display some of the features, generally in a blend that is unique to each city, given the diversity of social patterns that emerges from city to city, despite the existence of certain underlying common elements. The pre-existing physical features in the model consist of the sea or a navigable river and an area of environmental attraction such as a forest or hill-land lying away from the waterfront.

The historic core of the city provides residential space for the middle class and the self-employed and also for the older working-class artisan populations who are increasingly threatened by gentrification and urban renewal (see Ch. 8). This belt may well be bounded by the line of the old city fortifications such that the next zone, that of transitional characteristics and industry, is the physical legacy of nineteenth-century urban industrial growth. The urban core, in contrast, has a long pre-industrial past.

The zone in transition consists of sub-standard nineteenth-century property occupied by a relatively transient population of students and recently-arrived migrants, often living in close company with more aged indigenous working-class elements. Along the waterfront lie industrial areas with associated older housing, but newer industry is in peripheral locations, beyond the intermediate zones of lower middle-class housing which date from the years between 1900 and the Second World War. New peripheral industry is closely associated with social housing (generally publicly rented but occasionally with some housing association or employer interest) for industrial workers. Shanty-towns housing immigrants are located close to industrial employment: in reality, of course, this housing type is limited to a small number of cases in Southern Europe and is the least general feature of the model.

Only in the area closest to the peripheral environmental attractions is peripheral industry totally absent, land here having been developed for middle-class housing, providing a sectoral characteristic to high-status distributions. Beyond the urban limit lie dormitory villages in which the population composition may be mixed, including older indigenous elements as well as middle-class commuters or even recent working-class migrants.

Several general conclusions can be distilled from the material and discussion presented in this chapter. The first point relates to the class structure: the self-employed artisan, shopkeeper or businessman plays a far more important role in the societies of mainland Europe than in those of the English-speaking world. Napoleon is purported to have sneered that England was a nation of shopkeepers, but the jibe could be more appropriately directed at most Western European countries, particularly those of Southern Europe. The presence of this self-employed class in most city areas (except the new peripheral estates) and its concentration in older districts are vital elements of the European urban scene, traditionally colouring much of day-to-day life within the city.

A second conclusion is that social segregation in Western European cities conforms to the pattern found elsewhere of greatest segregation of those at opposite ends of the status hierarchy. However, it is often the case that the high degree of segregation of the middle classes is a reflection of their almost total absence from many intermediate and peripheral city districts rather than resulting from their overwhelming and exclusive dominance of a limited set of areas. Middle-class areas of cities often include inner-city districts where there is some degree of heterogeneity of status composition. This is in part an historical legacy of earlier patterns of segregation within apartment blocks on a floor-by-floor basis, but important cultural reasons persist in maintaining, and reinforcing, the desirability of the city-centre as a location for middle-class residence. Certainly as the ranks of the middle class grow, increasing proportions of this status group are found in peripheral locations, but over-representation of the middle classes near to city-centres is still a notable feature.

Thirdly, the residential map of the Western European city is a complex one as a result of the lack of direct connections between social status and housing variables, except with regard to housing amenities. In particular, the syphoning off of the working classes towards new peripheral housing in the post-war period precludes the existence of simple social relationships with housing age, whilst the complexities of the housing market and the general importance of privately-rented property reduce connections between social class and housing class.

Nevertheless, the fourth conclusion is that at the meso-scale of analysis, social class is the primary characteristic of social area distinctiveness, just as in modern urban societies elsewhere in the world. On the other hand, the role played in social area differentiation by life-cycle stage characteristics is a complex one in which demographic features come to play a significant part in shaping social areas whilst intra-urban migration (Ch. 6) acts to stabilize the system. Ethnicity does not emerge in any meaningful way as a vital dimension of social area distinctiveness, since ethnic variables are most commonly linked to social class and occupational variables, and anyway, as shown in Chapter 5, ethnic community concentrations more often occur on a house-by-house or block-by-block basis rather than at the level of neighbourhood.

Finally, behavioural studies produce a picture of urban social life at a variety of scales, the significance of which varies according to social class. Working-class urban life has traditionally been centred on the immediate neighbourhood whilst the middle classes operate throughout urban space but with especial focus on the centre. The working-class quarter is, however, being ruptured as a result of change in the old city districts and the progressive suburbanization of the population.

The remaining two chapters of this volume consider some of these conclusions, and those from earlier chapters, by broadly dividing cities into central districts and suburbs: the emphasis in these chapters is then placed on paths of contemporary evolution rather than on static description.

CHAPTER EIGHT

Change in the Inner-City

In the majority of Western European cities the modern urban core bears a close relationship to the location of the historic limits of the pre-industrial or even medieval city. The importance of the legacy of old fortification belts has been discussed in Chapter 1 (pp. 22–7), one of their most significant effects on contemporary cities being the clarity with which the city core can be recognized at ground level. Within this traditional *intra-muros* space, the city core has always been characterized by the multiplicity and spatial intermixture of functions, often with what might be termed 'multiple land use', whereby a variety of industrial, commercial and residential functions were combined under one roof.

The coming of the Industrial Revolution, of new forms of economic activity, of new social trends and of urban planning since the nineteenth century have brought a series of changes to this historic pattern. In particular, the rapid growth of 'higher-order' economic functions has resulted in the diminution of residential space and population decline in inner-city areas. But historical continuity is still manifest in such phenomena as the continued existence of high-status neighbourhoods within the urban core, as discussed in the previous chapter.

The present chapter considers three aspects of the inner-city in some detail: social composition, the question of depopulation, and the processes of urban renewal and renovation, these topics being of particular importance in the contemporary evolution of the social geography of city-centres.

DEMOGRAPHIC AND SOCIAL COMPOSITION

Earlier chapters have produced some general evidence on the composition of inner-city populations. Demographically the inner-city tends to have an excess of females and to be characterized by an over-representation of both the older age-groups (thus giving an appearance of demographic ageing) and of young single adults (see Ch. 3): there is a dearth of young families.

Socially, Chapter 7 has demonstrated that inner-city areas often contain a rather heterogeneous population with both middle-class and working-class populations living in close spatial proximity. In Chapter 7 these classes, and their locations, were dealt with separately. It will be useful here to identify the mixture of populations present in certain individual city-centres.

The large Southern European city can be represented here by Lisbon (Gaspar 1976). The components of the population of the inner-city here involve, firstly, the middle classes, including some of the most elevated sections of Portuguese society. Secondly, there are large numbers of older single-person households in the oldest and most degraded property. Thirdly, central Lisbon houses single young adults and couples without children living in small apartments. Finally, there are working-class and lower middle-class families in privately-rented furnished accommodation. Thus the city-centre is marked by vastly different social classes living in close proximity to one another but with distinct patterns of local segregation isolating the different classes into different sub-districts of the centre: the current tendency is for an increase in the proportion of the middle classes (Gaspar 1976: 131–5).

In smaller cities the diversity of city-centre residents is often less, and more overt polarization occurs. In St Etienne in France, for example, the centre is almost equally divided between *bourgeois* and proletarian districts (Vant 1973). The working-class sub-districts were largely homogeneous in the social status of the residents, although there was also a substantial proportion of foreigners (18 per cent plus 9 per cent who held French citizenship through naturalization). On the other hand, the *bourgeois* districts were more mixed in composition: as in Lisbon, growth in the proportion of the middle class was evident.

The West German city of Augsburg can be taken as a third example. Here, three specific groups are over-represented in the inner-city. Firstly, there are the young unmarried who form a dynamic and mobile group with a high turnover rate and great instability of composition. In contrast are the second group, consisting of older working-class households, often with connections to the district going back several generations. Thirdly, there are middle-class families (Poschwatta 1978).

A social class of considerable importance in inner-cities throughout Western Europe is that of the self-employed (Wolcke 1968: 163–6; Den Draak 1967: 215–16), as discussed in Chapter 7. This class tends to be relatively ubiquitous throughout the centre, although with under-representation in middle-class areas and over-representation in working-class districts.

Spatial segregation within the inner-city may be very strong indeed, with the marked existence of neighbourhoods of opposing social class composition. As an example, the Museo *barrio* in central Madrid housed a population of 6,177 in 1965 of whom 62 per cent were female, a reflection of the fact that 35 per cent of the resident employed population were living-in domestic servants – cases of four or five servants per household were not exceptional and half of all females in the 15–19 age-group were servants. Outside domestic service, virtually the whole of the rest of the work-force was engaged in the liberal professions or in top-level administrative posts. Interestingly, over three-quar-

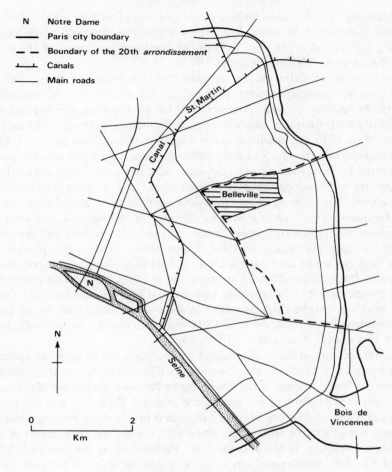

N Notre Dame
—— Paris city boundary
– – – Boundary of the 20th *arrondissement*
⊥⊢⊥ Canals
—— Main roads

Fig. 8.1 The location of Belleville, Paris.

ters of dwellings were rented flats (Capote 1976). Other Mayfair-like high-status neighbourhoods can be found around the Corso Stati Uniti in Turin, in the 16th *arrondissement* in Paris or around the Ringstrasse in Vienna, although in Northern Europe domestic servants do not feature as such a vital component of household population structure.

At the other end of the social scale are the working-class inner-city districts (Ch. 7, pp. 167–8), often built during the early years of nineteenth-century urban–industrial growth explicitly as working-class housing and thus displaying great historical continuity broken only in recent years by such processes as redevelopment or downgrading to the status of immigrant-receiving slum quarters. In many of these traditional working-class districts, housing filtering processes have occurred only marginally – the present housing occupants are the heirs in social role of those who first lived in such districts, even if the traditional stability of the population composition has weakened,

193

thus reducing the old characteristic *vie des quartiers* (Prouvost 1966: 55–6). It is worth considering in some detail the evolution of one such working-class district, that of Belleville (Fig. 8.1) in the north-eastern corner of the city of Paris (Ceaux et al. 1979; Jacquemet 1975).

The *commune* of Belleville lay outside the city limits of Paris until the administrative boundaries were changed in the middle of the nineteenth century. Population growth, however, had been rapid from the beginning of the century with the total number of residents increasing from 1,684 in 1801 to 57,699 in 1856 and reaching nearly a quarter of a million by 1936. Much of the increase was the result of intra-urban migration from the old city-centre, exacerbated by Haussmann's redevelopment schemes there: the construction of the new city fortifications in the 1840s also stimulated the growth of Belleville. Until about 1860, almost all new building resulted from speculative ventures by individuals, often building both for themselves and for rent, but after that year private and public companies became increasingly involved and these were almost the only builders after 1900. Construction utilized the poorest materials, and the small land parcels used resulted in a very chaotic arrangement of the new-built environment. The tenants were incapable of paying high rents so the cheapest style of construction was essential and this also involved a much lower building height than elsewhere in Paris: thus whilst the modal height in the wealthy 8th *arrondissement* in 1891 was seven storeys, in Belleville it was merely two storeys (Ceaux et al. 1979: 93).

The inhabitants of Belleville earned a reputation for proletarian solidarity in the uprising of 1848 and the *Commune* of 1871 and took over the reputation 'enjoyed' by the residents of the Faubourg St Antoine during the Revolution. In the last twenty years of the nineteenth century, Belleville was the poorest district of Paris; it had the highest proportion of labourers and the lowest of domestic servants in the whole city, along with the highest proportions of over-populated dwellings. It was also the most 'Parisian' of all districts with 52 per cent of its 1891 population born in the city against only 36 per cent for the city as a whole: foreigners were markedly under-represented. Only after 1900, with the effective cessation of movement into Belleville from the old centre of Paris, did the proportion of the district's population born in Paris begin to fall, but it was not until the 1950s that foreigners began to arrive in significant numbers (although some Armenian refugees had settled there in the 1920s). The real transformation of traditional Belleville did not start until 1960 when, with the expectation of urban renewal, property speculators moved in, bringing degradation through planning blight and leading to a rapid increase in the immigrant population. By 1968, foreigners totalled 15 per cent of the district's population, reaching over 50 per cent within certain house-blocks. Thus in less than half a century the most Parisian quarter of the capital became one of its most cosmopolitan, whilst retaining its proletarian status.

In many other Northern European industrial cities, quarters similar to Belleville exist, although the building arrangements often display greater regularity where housing was built by employers or where large private property companies were involved from the outset. In the triple city of Lille – Roubaix –

Tourcoing in Northern France, for example, the dominant inner-city working-class housing has been that of the long monotonous row of one- or two-storey brick houses built around interior courts. In Roubaix, these courtyard houses date back to 1839 and as late as the early 1960s, 25 per cent of the town's housing stock was still of this type, involving poor and unhealthy living conditions, recently witnessing influxes of foreign workers (Prouvost 1966).

Such courtyard housing is still very common throughout Northern Europe (Shaw et al 1970: 26–7; Achilles 1969: 121–2; Kouvelis 1979: 113–14), a high proportion of such housing being originally built specifically for worker use by large employers rather than originating in the speculative market. Successive years often saw the original courtyards reduced in size or built over completely to produce very high ratios of built-up land: in Hanover on the eve of the Second World War, 92 per cent of the land in some building blocks was covered (Grötzbach 1978: 187–8), whilst in Paris a figure of 90 per cent was reached in some areas, more often where a free speculative market operated (Lemay 1970: 56). Such nineteenth-century housing is now subject to urban renewal or rehabilitation schemes throughout Western Europe.

Despite the long traditional continuity of many inner-city districts in terms of their overall status, high or low, it would be erroneous to suggest that filtering processes and compositional changes do not occur in the population of individual areas. Filtering processes are normally believed to be created by the wealthier members of society moving to new property so that the existing housing stock progressively changes hands down the social hierarchy. Allied to this is the concept of the zone in transition which results from the reduced residential desirability of central districts because of their proximity to expanding commercial land-users: hence those who can opt to leave such areas do so and those with no choice congregate there, these including the poor, recent immigrants and students.

There are, however, three reasons why the features of filtering and of zones in transition, although of relevance, may be weaker in operation in Western European cities than in North America where they were first conceived. Firstly, there is no necessary social *cachet* in Western Europe attached to the occupation of new property, indeed a case could be made out that the reverse is sometimes the case as long as the old property has been provided with modern amenities. The middle classes thus do not display an overwhelming urge to seek new housing, generally at the city edge, although a significant proportion may follow this trend, particularly in Northern Europe. Instead, in some cities the emergent new middle class seek to demonstrate their new-found status by moving to older city-centre properties (Gaspar 1976; Abrahamson and Johnson 1974).

Secondly, as has been demonstrated in Chapter 7, the Western European middle-class citizen does not shun the city-centre as a residential location because of its proximity to non-residential functions, indeed the reverse may apply (Den Draak 1967: 220–2). Even the encroachment of commercial activities does not inevitably diminish the desirability of city-centre residence, as is evidenced by the success of the construction of luxury apartments over shops and offices in many recent urban redevelopment schemes (see pp. 206–8).

Thirdly, commercial expansion in the Western European city has, itself, been subject to various degrees of planning constraint in most countries, the exceptions lying in Southern Europe. Whilst central business districts throughout the Continent have undeniably undergone rapid growth during the recent past, often leading to urban redevelopment (as in Brussels, for example), the spatial expansion of the CBD has not occurred purely under free-market forces. Instead, there have been regulated extensions to commercial districts (as happened during the planned post-war reconstruction of many West German cities after Allied wartime bombing), whilst in certain cases there have been specific schemes for the creation of sub-CBDs away from the old core of the city. This has occurred in Stockholm (George 1967: 290–1) where 'central' functions for the population of the city have been decentralized, and on a rather different scale in the Défense development in Paris and the Part-Dieu development pole in Lyon (Tuppen 1977).

These, then, are reasons why filtering processes and the emergence of zones in transition may be somewhat weaker in Western European cities than elsewhere. Nevertheless these concepts are still of relevance even if the time-scales over which the processes operate are rather extended. For example, it took eight hundred years for the riverside district of Paris immediately north of the Ile de la Cité to progress from being the location of aristocratic residences through to housing the lowest social classes who came to dominate the district of the central market (*Les Halles*) in its last days before demolition (Mallet 1967).

Elsewhere in Paris it is possible to identify processes of neighbourhood change operating at a rather more rapid rate: the southern part of the 9th *arrondissement*, lying along the *grands boulevards*, is such an area. This was a district of large apartment-block construction for the middle classes following Haussmann's activities (see Ch. 1, p. 28). Richard Cobb (1980b) has eloquently described the life-style here of the remnants of this well-to-do class in the years immediately before the Second World War. By then, however, most of the better-off had moved west into the 8th and 16th *arrondissements* bordering the Champs Elysées and the Bois de Boulogne. Their immediate replacements in the early years of the present century were immigrant Sephardic Jews from Southern Europe and the Mediterranean, but these gave way to Muslim North Africans in the 1950s as the earlier Jewish communities themselves moved out into districts further removed from the centre of the city (Baillet 1976). These changes in population composition accompanied the progressive degradation of the housing stock thorough the sub-division of the original apartments. The first locations of the new populations were generally vertically rather than spatially distinguished – in other words the taking-over of the top floors of six- or seven-storey properties often presaged more rapid later changes.

Filtering processes have been recorded in other Western European cities. In Turin the central high-status district has been reduced by property sub-division and the arrival of southern immigrants (Adamo 1969), although more recently gentrification is leading to the reversion of the area to its old status (Lusso 1978: 50). In Nice, Toesca and Trojani (1977) have described how the northern quarter of the city-centre has changed over the last fifty years from being populated by wealthy foreigners to housing North African migrant workers. In West Berlin, filtering and neighbourhood change have occurred as a result of abnormal processes – districts along the Berlin Wall, often truncated in character by the Wall, have seen their better-off populations move away, the replacements increasingly being foreign migrant workers (Kouvelis 1979: 113–14).

However, a notable feature in many cities has been the conversion of high-status housing directly into commercial uses without the neighbourhoods undergoing a 'transition' stage. This has occurred in Amsterdam (Heinemeyer and Gastelaars 1971: 212) and it is also developing within the high-status Museo district of Madrid (Capote 1976: 346–8). It is a general feature of many other cities.

A further aspect of change in the population composition of inner-city districts in recent years has been the rapid increase in the representation of students within certain residential districts of cheaper privately-rented property as a result of university expansion (Shaw et al. 1970: 26–7). This, of course, is part of the trend, especially apparent in Northern Europe, for the city-centre to become the residence of sizeable numbers of single people (Ganser 1967: 211). The question of adequate accommodation provision for young adults has assumed crisis proportions in many cities, leading to rioting in Amsterdam, West Berlin and Zürich. Students have accompanied immigrants in taking over old inner-city working-class housing. Multi-occupation, sub-letting and squatting have been 'acceptable' to the young people as 'solutions' to their housing problems, but such 'solutions' are generally viewed unfavourably by city administrations.

Finally it is important to point out that neighbourhood change in the inner-city does not necessarily operate through the downgrading of the status level of the residents. As will be demonstrated later in this chapter, gentrification is a common feature of many cities either through the rehabilitation of existing older property or through the actions of urban renewal schemes.

As a general conclusion it can be stated that inner-cities have traditionally been characterized by a very mixed population but that at the present time there is a tendency towards polarization with an accentuation of the representation of both the topmost and the lowest groups in the social hierarchy. Only in some of the larger Northern European cities, such as Amsterdam (Heinemeyer and Gastelaars 1971: 212), is there an under-representation of the highest social classes in the city-centre as a whole. The neighbourhood characteristics of inner-city areas in Western Europe have been, perhaps, rather more stable than elsewhere, both as a result of the purpose-built nature of working-class housing and through the continued desirability of inner-city residence amongst the middle classes. Nevertheless, changes are occurring and one of the correlates of change is population decline.

CITY-CENTRE DEPOPULATION

The overall reduction of the residential population of the inner-city is a general feature throughout Western Europe. Chapter 3 has demonstrated the characteristics of contemporary population evolution at the level of cities as units and it has been seen there that the total populations of many cities are declining; at the level of the inner-city, decline is almost ubiquitous.

In demographic terms, city-centre depopulation generally results from both natural decline and net migrant loss. Natural decline is unsurprising in view of the elevated proportions of older people found in city-centres and the fact that, whilst young adults are over-represented, there are few young families. In terms of migration, city-centres are almost universally net receivers in terms of migration exchanges with places beyond the city boundary but overall net losers of migrants because of the scale of intra-urban migration, redistributing population away from the centre towards more peripheral areas within the city (Ch. 6). By the nature of their selectivity, the intra-urban migration flows originating in the city-centre compound the picture of natural decline by removing the younger family-building elements. It is therefore legitimate to view migration as the basic cause of inner-city population decline.

The depopulation of Western European inner-cities has a long history. The date of the inner-area population maximum in several of the larger older cities lay in the middle of the nineteenth century (Kaufmann et al. 1978: 17; Van Hulten 1968: 69). By 1900, population decline was endemic in at least some inner-city districts of all larger Northern European cities, and as the present century has progressed the smaller Northern cities have joined this trend along with many in Southern Europe.

In Brussels, the city-centre population (within the 'pentagon' traced by the old fortifications) reached its maximum in 1890 and decline during the next thirty years alone reduced the population by 25 per cent (Verniers 1958: 18). In Amsterdam, the 1889 population of the city-centre was 310,000 and this had fallen to 121,401 by 1961, a decline of 61 per cent (Angenot 1965: 47–9): decline started at the very centre of the city and had spread, by the late 1940s, into all those city districts that had been built up by the end of the previous century (Van Hulten 1968: 69–72).

In the Norwegian city of Bergen, city-centre population decline started in 1910 and continued at a rate of 0.6 per cent per annum in the years before the start of the Second World War, with decline fastest in the central business district (Helvig 1976: 140–2). The historic centre of Bordeaux witnessed a population decline of 45 per cent between 1900 and 1975 (Barrère and Cassou-Mounat 1980: 10–11) presaging population decline in the city as a whole after 1954 (Pailhé 1978: 11–12). In St Etienne, also in France, the population of the centre fell by 22 per cent between 1901 and 1968 such that by the latter year the centre housed only 7 per cent of the city's population of over 200,000 (Vant 1973: 29–30).

In Southern Europe, the population living in the historic core of Milan fell from 113,000 in 1901 to 35,000 in 1971, a decline of 69 per cent (Dalmasso

Table 8.1   Inner-city population declines – selected cities

City	Country	Period	Inner-city population at end of period	Per cent annual rate of inner-city population decline
Rome	Italy	1963–71	194,916	−3.8
Amsterdam	Netherlands	1970–77	54,828	−3.7
Antwerp	Belgium	1970–78	121,046	−2.6
Zürich	Switzerland	1977–78	7,194	−1.3
Cologne	W. Germany	1977–78	117,557	−0.6

Data sources: see Appendix

1978: 172). Population decline in the city-centre of Rome has been occurring since 1931 (Rossi 1959: 27–9).

Table 8.1 provides evidence on the rate of recent inner-city population decline in five cities, in each case the inner-city being defined on the basis of the urban core within the old line of fortifications. It is notable that within such core areas rates of population loss often vary markedly between sub-areas. This can be clearly seen in the case of Bergen (Fig. 8.2). Here the overall rate of population decline in the centre was 3.3 per cent per annum between 1960 and 1975, but in what Helvig (1976) calls the 'hard core centre' the rate of loss was 4.4 per cent per annum, reducing to 3.4 per cent in the rest of the central business district and 3.1 per cent in those areas of the centre that still had predominantly residential characteristics.

Population decline is thus today general in the inner areas of almost all cities. The city of Paris saw a population loss of 300,000 between 1968 and 1975 whilst the inner suburbs were also in decline (Bentham and Moseley 1980: 58). Between 1951 and 1971 the historic centre of Venice witnessed a net loss of 59,000 migrants, resulting in rapid overall population loss (Piasentin et al. 1978: 582). In Bern in Switzerland, all the older parts of the city were in decline during the years 1960–75 (Gächter 1978: 3), whilst in Karlsruhe the years 1961–70 saw a population decrease of 12,340 in the inner-city during a period when the outer areas increased by 32,744 inhabitants (Traband 1978: 42).

The causes of city-centre depopulation are complex and rooted in the institutional, social, demographic and economic structures of Western European cities. In the study of these causes it is useful, first of all, to highlight the case of a single city; Amsterdam provides a useful example (Angenot 1965; Van Hulten 1968) which illustrates the factors at work.

The historic core of Amsterdam is bounded by the Singelgracht canal, around which used to stand the city's ramparts. In 1889, over 75 per cent of the city's population lived within this core area (Fig. 8.3). At the end of the nineteenth century, a municipal campaign against unhealthy basement dwellings led to the removal of 20,000 inhabitants from the city-centre. It is also from this period that pressure from the expansion of commercial and administrative activities started to bring the replacement of residential land uses by

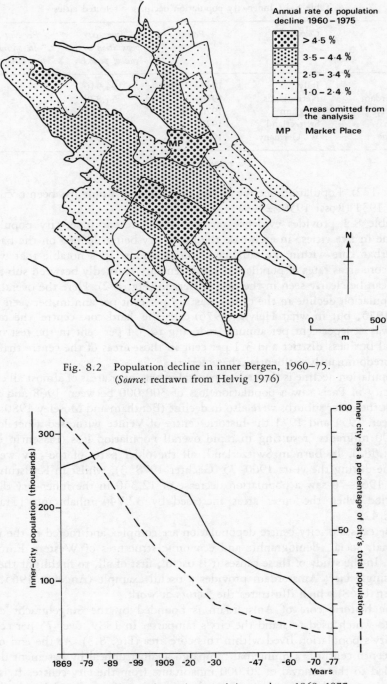

Fig. 8.2 Population decline in inner Bergen, 1960–75.
(*Source*: redrawn from Helvig 1976)

Fig. 8.3 Population change in central Amsterdam, 1869–1977.
(*Data sources*: Van Hulten 1968; see Appendix)

other functions, often within the existing building fabric. As a result of these two long-term processes of slum clearance and conversions of property use, the number of dwellings in central Amsterdam declined by 29 per cent between 1919 and 1961. However. the population decline over the same period was much greater, at 53 per cent, as a result of the operation of a third process – that of the decline in average household sizes resulting from both the national reduction in family sizes and the steady replacement in the central area of 'normal' family households by a population weighted towards young adults and the old living at lower average densities of persons per dwelling (3.04 in 1961) than for the city as a whole (3.28). Over half the population decline between 1920 and 1960 can be attributed to changes in household size (Van Hulten 1968: 77).

Three reasons thus lie behind central-city population decline in Amsterdam – firstly, slum clearance and the reduction of overall population density through such schemes; secondly, the conversion of residential land uses to other activities; and thirdly, changes in household sizes, this latter process also being associated with changes in population composition, especially in terms of age-structure. These three causal factors are of general relevance throughout Western Europe.

Clearance of poor-quality housing has occurred in recent years in almost all cities, largely as a result of municipal pressures and initiatives. Reductions in overall population densities are generally seen as being a desirable adjunct to such clearance and renewal operations, whilst housing rehabilitation in delapi-dated areas similarly often results in a reduction of overcrowding and in population decline with 'surplus' numbers being rehoused in more peripheral locations (Barrère and Cassou-Mounat 1980; Bonneville 1974: 105–6). The desirability of population decline through these processes is well illustrated by the case of Naples. Here the first clearance and redevelopment programme was put forward in 1884 as a result of a serious cholera epidemic (Döpp 1968). By 1931, however, there were still 41,000 one-room dwellings (bassi) in the city-centre, housing 212,000 people. Reference has been made in Chapter 2 (p. 53) to the exceptionally high peak population density of 825 persons per hectare in Naples in 1951, the overall inner-city density in that year being 467 per hectare. By 1971 the net out-migration from the centre of 140,000 individuals had reduced the population total to 482,000 and the density to 295 per hectare, but there was still a feeling that further population reduction was desirable to reduce overcrowding still more, reductions of up to 40 per cent in some districts being felt to be necessary (Bastano 1976; Döpp 1968: 341–4).

Slum clearance and urban renewal do not, however, necessarily bring population decline. In many cities the removal of small overcrowded dwellings has permitted their replacement by taller apartment blocks housing a larger population although at reduced ratios of persons per room and per dwelling. In the Croulebarbe district of south-eastern Paris, for example, population density rose from 405 per hectare in 1954 to 450 per hectare in 1965 as a result of this sort of process (Lemay 1970): similar density increases are not uncommon elsewhere (Rapoport 1966).

In many cases, slum clearance has been an accompaniment to major public works projects with the areas of poorest housing being affected in a manner that enables municipal authorities to attain several objectives at once. Such was the case in the late nineteenth century with the razing of several thousand hovels to permit the building of the *Palais de Justice* in Brussels or, most notably, in Haussmann's works in Paris (see Ch. 1, pp. 27–8). In the twentieth century, major housing clearance and depopulation in conjunction with public works have occurred in Rome (Rossi 1959: 27–9), and with the establishment of new urban transport networks in several cities.

In some respects, slum clearance in association with public works could be regarded as part of the second process leading to inner-city depopulation, that of land-use conversion. However, land-use conversion *per se* operates solely according to economic criteria with considerations of housing policy bearing no weight. Activities such as industry, retailing, governmental acitivities and, above all, commerce offer higher bid-rents than do many residential uses. Nevertheless, the provision of high-quality high-status housing still presents possibilities of investment profits so that, given the continuing level of demand for such housing possibilities in the inner-city from the middle class (see Ch. 7, pp. 160–7), residential uses have not given way entirely to other functions although even in high-status areas some changes of property use have occurred (Capote 1976: 346–8).

Throughout Western Europe, commercial growth has encroached on residential inner-city areas in a process that may be traced back at least a century. In Hanover the inner-city, by the mid-1970s, contained only 911 dwellings where in 1939 there were 2,549, the reduction resulting from the expansion of the business district (Grötzbach 1978). Residential functions have been similarly reduced in central Karlsruhe (Traband 1978: 42). In Bergen, Helvig (1976) found that commercial area growth, and the consequent reduction in numbers of dwellings, provided the most significant explanation of inner-city population decline. Office growth has brought a loss of housing in cities such as Rome and Paris (Rossi 1959: 29; Bentham and Moseley 1980: 58), whilst in Utrecht the number of housing units fell, through this cause alone, by 7.5 per cent in the five years from 1956 to 1960 (Den Draak 1966: 180).

Reductions in household size have also been universal as causes of inner-city population decline. Schinz (1968: 11) noted that in certain districts of inner West Berlin the proportion of one-person households rose from 8.6 per cent in 1910 to 43.0 per cent in 1961, and similar changes in household structure (although rarely so extreme) have occurred elsewhere in Western Europe. The inter-related processes of reductions in family size and increases in the proportions of small non-family households have been put forward as explanations of city-centre population decline in many cities (Den Draak 1966; 1967; Taubmann 1969; Coppolani 1977; Van Hulten 1968).

Central-city population densities, which generally rose in the earlier part of the nineteenth century throughout Western Europe, are now falling, and peak densities now often occur not in the centre but in the inner suburban ring

(Wolcke 1968: 163–4). Population decline is now starting to occur in this belt as a result of the three processes outlined above.

Three further general points must be made about depopulation in the Western European city. Firstly it is necessary to realize that there is not, as yet, any overall trend towards a decline in employment opportunities within the inner-city. Certainly cases do exist of stagnation in total inner-urban employment (Taubmann 1969: 337) but they are matched by many other cases of employment growth, often as a result of urban redevelopment and the creation of new office complexes. Herein lies a problem, however, since the universal trend is for the tertiarization of inner-city employment leading to a potential imbalance between the size of the working-class resident group in the inner-city and the jobs available for them. In practice, the transfer of the working-class towards the suburbs has generally progressed in a manner that has, without specific planning or design, maintained a rough and ready balance between labour force and jobs. Hence Bentham and Moseley (1980: 69) conclude that

manual workers in Paris appear to have moved to the suburbs to a much greater extent than have their British counterparts,

so that Paris has rather less of an inner-city problem of working-class unemployment than is the case in British cities such as Liverpool or London.

A second, and related, general point concerns the question of social class and depopulation. It was suggested earlier in this chapter that increasing class polarization is the norm in many Western European inner-cities. Increases in the representation of the middle class in inner areas come about partly through gentrification following urban renewal (see below, pp. 206–9), but also through differential net out-migration from the city-centre by those from different classes. The effect of this can be seen in Venice where, over the years from 1967 to 1976, only 56 per cent of the lower middle class leaving the city-centre were replaced by similar in-migrants; for the working class the replacement rate was 73 per cent whilst for the managerial and administrative sub-group of the middle classes it was 111 per cent (Costa et al. 1980: 404). Whilst such extreme selectivity of movement may not be matched in many other cities, similar processes do exist elsewhere. City-centre depopulation does not affect all social classes equally and hence it contributes to patterns of social change in the inner-city.

Finally, it is necessary to put the existence of inner-city population decline into proportion. Although decline is general throughout Western Europe, it is important to note that inner-cities retain an important residential function in most cities (Verbanck 1975: 324), certainly in comparison with the City of London or with other cities in the English-speaking world. This is partly a reflection of the economic possibilities occasioned by high-status interest in inner-city living so that residential uses, of a limited kind, can compete with other land uses. In addition, the tradition of admixture of residential, commercial and small-scale industrial uses within individual districts or even

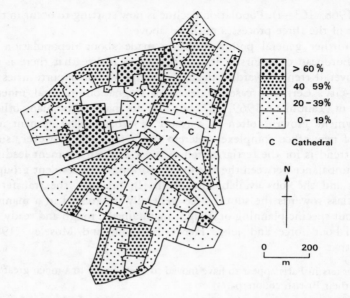

Fig. 8.4   Proportion of total floor space in residential use – central Aarhus, 1963.
(*Source*: redrawn from Taubmann 1969)

individual buildings continues to be of importance. In big West German cities
such as Düsseldorf, Stuttgart and Essen, over 23 per cent of inner-urban floor
space was still in residential use in the 1960s (Taubmann 1969: 341). Figure
8.4 illustrates the proportion of residential uses in the inner area of the Danish
city of Aarhus, demonstrating that a mixture of functions including housing is
the norm: residential uses dominate on the upper floors whilst the lower floors
have commercial or artisan uses – a legacy of historic styles of urban living
(Taubmann 1969). Even in bigger cities, then, significant residential functions
occur in city-centres so that central business districts are never exclusively
commercial in nature (Matthiessen 1976).

RENEWAL AND REDEVELOPMENT; RESTORATION AND
REHABILITATION

The volume and character of the housing stock is never fixed and immutable.
Throughout history, cities have undergone a constant process involving the
demolition of buildings which are nearing the end of their useful life or which
have become inconvenient for changed styles of living, the replacements often
being of housing of a different type. Other property has been subjected to
alteration, extension, partial demolition or remodelling. Thus renewal and
restoration are ages-old urban processes. What is different now is the scale at
which these phenomena are occurring. Urban renewal at the level seen in the
1960s and 1970s is without general precedent.

The words renewal, redevelopment, restoration and rehabilitation have often been used in a vague and interchangeable manner. 'Renewal' and 'redevelopment' are here defined as denoting the destruction of the existing fabric followed by reconstruction, such a process operating at a variety of scales from that of the individual building to the total razing of a whole district (in French *renouvellement à bulldozer*). Restoration and rehabilitation, by contrast, consist of the improvement of existing property, sometimes involving partial re-modelling and the demolition of accretions such as extra storeys added after the building was finished. Restoration has often come to have a conservational meaning, but in certain schemes other considerations have been paramount.

The dominant social theories of urban renewal originate in France and especially from the works of Castells (Castells and Godard 1974; Castells 1973; 1977; 1978). The basic tenet of these theories (Castells 1973) is the interpretation of urban renewal in terms of renovation and deportation whereby old working-class districts are redeveloped as new office areas and *de luxe* apartments whilst the original residents are removed to other parts of the city, dominantly the periphery. This serves the interests of property companies and big business, firstly through the large-scale new inner-city developments and secondly through the demand for new suburban housing (Accame 1973: 17). Municipal planning decisions to encourage the suburban building of public sector housing can be seen as a permissive precursor for such renewal since they set the chain in action whereby accommodation is provided for those displaced from the centre (Huet et al. 1975: 4), this then allowing the 'reconquest' of the centre by middle-class interests.

Castells' *rénovation-déportation* thesis is, in practice, too simple to match reality in many parts of Western Europe, and too specific to the French case with its complexities of interlocking planning and development agencies (Burtenshaw et al. 1981: 61). It is possibly only directly applicable in cities where power is largely in the hands of the controllers of a limited number of large-scale companies, as was the case in Dunkirk, the city that formed the empirical test of the thesis (Castells and Godard 1974). In cities without a controlling monopolistic structure, such as those where power lies with the traditional small-scale *bourgeoisie*, entrepreneurial interests in renewal are likely to be more diffuse with objectives being more piecemeal in nature (Ledrut 1977; Blanc 1979). Indeed, the new *bourgeoisie* may be more interested in restoration, particularly if this can open the way for gentrification in desirable inner-city property.

One further criticism of explanations of renewal couched in terms of monolithic power structures is that landownership in many Western European cities is extremely fragmented, the only major exceptions being in some of the industrial cities that grew in the nineteenth century with individual companies taking control of substantial areas of residential land as well as of land needed for their own expansion. Initial urban development very often occurred on land that had been sold off in small lots, this being especially the case in areas destined for working-class housing (Vant 1973: 11–13). This fragmented pattern of landownership presents problems for large-scale renewal schemes which inevitably affect the interests of a variety of landowners (Aust 1980). In Hanover, for example, land was overwhelmingly in private hands as late as 1945 and, even in 1974, 72 per cent of city-centre land was owned by small private companies or even individuals (Grötzbach 1978: 191–3). In Naples, the rebuilding of the harbour areas destroyed in the Second World War took over twenty years, largely as a result of difficulties over the multifarious titles to landownership (Döpp 1968: 223–224). The importance of the fragmentation of ownership stands out in any analysis of renewal schemes, militating against general overall city-wide strategies on the part of the parties concerned.

Modern large-scale urban renewal really started in the late 1950s (except in cities that had been badly affected by the war), and throughout the period up to 1973 many cities started on major, and expensive, renewal projects. Costs were not, in fact, accurately predicted in many schemes and it quickly became apparent that rehousing the original working-class populations in the rebuilt areas would be much more expensive than building peripheral estates for them on green-field sites (Russac 1968). During the 1970s the emphasis has progressively shifted from renewal to restoration, largely as a result of municipal belt-tightening exercises in an era of rising inflation rates and also, arguably, in response to the controversies aroused by some of the earlier renewal schemes. In France the government, in fact, took steps in 1977 to discourage further large-scale renewal projects. It is worth, however, paying some attention to the scope of some of the large-scale renewal schemes of the earlier period.

Renewal of the St Georges quarter of Toulouse was first proposed in 1939 but only agreed in 1956. The plan was to raze 7 hectares in which 3,700 people lived at a density of 550 per hectare in accommodation with very poor amenity levels (Beringuier 1966). The first intention was to build 1,200 new dwellings in the area to house the original population, but it quickly became obvious that a high proportion of this working-class population would be unable to afford the rents even of subsidized-cost public housing and that such housing would not be viable: although construction costs could be subsidized, rents could not (see Ch. 2, p. 44). Consquently, provision was made to rehouse the original residents in peripheral estates even though many expressed a strong desire to stay in St Georges. Until 1960 the municipality used a policy of negotiation to fix compensation levels with the old private landlords but after that year expropriation powers were used and arbitrated compensation levels began to rise rapidly. By 1966 the costs of renewal had risen such that only private property companies could expect to get a return from investment, and then only by changing the orientation of reconstruction towards the provision of shops and offices with luxury apartments above (Arnauné-Clamens 1977). Although the first rebuilt sector (completed in 1967) provided some housing for the original residents, all following housing blocks completed contained only *résidences de grand standing* constructed privately (Saint-Raymond 1979).

Although St Georges was a small renewal scheme in comparison with those in many other cities, it demonstrates several important points. As costs rose, private capital was substituted for public, largely as a result of delays and costs over property acquisition. The result was that, with the operation of market forces, lower-income residents were squeezed out but not by a simple coherent policy of *rénovation-déportation* as Castells envisaged. Toulouse is a city, typical of many others throughout Europe, in which the old urban *bourgeoisie* have traditionally invested in property rather than in industry or commerce: monolithic interests were absent from the St Georges redevelopment at the outset, control over property being vested in a *rentier* class (see Ch. 7, p. 152).

Brussels is a city that has seen many large-scale renewal projects over the last thirty years, accompanying the city's rise to eminence as the headquarters of the European Community and as an important business centre for multi-national companies. In the largest schemes, both public and private investment have been involved, for example in the Manhattan scheme on the northern edge of the city-centre (Huet et al. 1975: 20). Here the intention was to redevelop a whole *quartier* at once, involving the relocation of 20,000 inhabitants. These were moved out by 1973, but the spiralling cost of the project resulted in its abandonment, affected also by a growing urban protest movement. The first success of such protest in the city had earlier come with the modification of an initial government plan to demolish and totally rebuild the working-class district of the Marolles in the southern part of the city-centre. Such rebuilding would, in fact, have replaced an out-dated housing structure by local public housing, but it met strong opposition and a plan for the rehabilitation of the existing property was substituted with guarantees of public authority involve-ment at all stages to prevent private speculative interests moving in (Fontaine 1977).

The case of rehabilitation is most strikingly demonstrated in Bologna where the communist municipal authority has resolutely set its face against large-scale renewal and urban expansion via speculative and unpopular suburban devel-opment (Accame 1973; Huet et al. 1975). In Bologna there has been a political desire to retain an important working-class population in the centre, to prevent gentrification and thus to keep a 'left' political orientation there as well as in the working-class suburbs. The working class should be housed in improved accommodation, according to these desires, alongside other less profitable urban space users (such as traditional self-employed artisans), the means being a strictly-controlled rent structure. Old properties have been improved intern-ally and have been restored to their original appearances, a common feature of rehabilitation throughout Western Europe (Kain 1981: 212), A variety of powers has been used by the municipal authorities, but a large number of the small proprietors have been willing to co-operate in agreements whereby funds have been made available to them for restoration purposes, sometimes from the compulsory contributions made by employers to provide working-class housing. In return the municipality has taken the power to control rent levels for periods of up to twenty-five years, and has also obtained control over the granting of new tenancies, using this power to rehouse in the centre those displaced by restoration and also to balance the age-groups of new tenants. This Bolognese initiative is thus at variance with the general operation of more free market forces in renewal and rehabilitation elsewhere in Western Europe, and flows naturally from the political viewpoint of the city's government. It is not an entirely unique policy as aspects of it (for example, nomination of tenants for privately-rented property) have been used in renewal areas of central Stockholm (Sidenbladh 1975: 37–8).

A general feature of both urban redevelopment and of restoration schemes throughout Western Europe has, however, been gentrification. This was just as much the case in the past, for example, through Haussmann's schemes in Paris which resulted, in many cases, in the replacement of workers' hovels by middle-class apartments. As conservation planning has become more important, greater emphasis has been put on rehabilitation, the dominant concerns being architectural rather than social (Huet et al. 1975: 70). The promulgation of the *Loi Malraux* in France in 1962 provided for the designation of conservation areas for housing rehabilitation in inner-cities, and by 1979 sixty such areas had been demarcated (Barrère and Cassou-Mounat 1980: 9): however, the objectives in the creation of these 'safeguarded sectors' were aesthetic and the results of rehabilitation have inevitably been increased housing rents and gentrification. The most famous of these *secteurs sauvegardés* is the Marais district of Paris, in which the familiar features of increased speculative investment, inflated rents and rising levels of middle-class representation have occurred (Kain 1981). Piecemeal urban renewal on the level of individual blocks of houses has, throughout much of Western Europe, also led to gentrification via the construction of *de luxe* property to replace the old (Lemay 1970), but even where large-scale schemes involving public money have constructed housing for the publicly-rented sector the social class of the affected neighbourhoods has generally risen as a result of the inevitably higher rent levels in the new property (Branchereau 1980).

One way of attempting to offset the high costs of urban renewal has been to seek to produce multi-functional development involving higher-order commercial and retailing functions as well as housing. In Lyon, the initial intention in the Part-Dieu district was to provide housing through redevelopment, but as planning and costing progressed other functions were added and a complete revision of the plan in 1973 resulted in the district being designated as a new CBD for the city, retaining provision of only four apartment blocks offering a thousand relatively expensive dwellings (Tuppen 1977). In Paris, housing redevelopment in the Plaisance district of the south-western part of the city-centre was broadened to include a variety of public service activities as a way of helping to cover costs (Bilet et al. 1970). Even in Bologna there is a planned increase in commercial activities on the ground floors of the renovated properties, thus increasing the likely economic return.

In West Germany, post-war renewal has followed its own particular course as a result of inner-city destruction brought about by the Second World War which gave the chance to wipe the slate clean – a chance that was not universally accepted for reasons discussed in Chapter 1 (pp. 30–1). In general, inner-city slum clearance and urban renewal have played a significant role only in smaller German cities in the last twenty years, although in cities of the older industrial north it is the inner suburban belts of nineteenth-century workmen's terraces and tenements that are in greatest need of attention (Achilles 1969). An exception was, of course, the case of West Berlin. At the end of the Second World War, 34 per cent of Berlin's housing stock had been destroyed and 54 per cent damaged; only 12 per cent remained completely intact (Trebbi 1978: 16). The early post-war emphasis inevitably went on repair and on the construction of new housing and it was not until the 1960s that attention was really given to the need for urban renewal (Trebbi 1978: 178–80). The first renewal plans were put forward in 1963 and these involved a mixture of redevelopment and rehabilitation schemes focusing on inner-city districts such as Kreuzberg, Neukölln and Wedding (Kouvelis 1979; Sijbrandij 1974; Aust 1980). The extent of the designated areas in West Berlin (449 hectares in 1963) and their total population (140,000 in 1961) are such that large-scale gentrification in renewed districts was not conceivable. Although the public authorities have made considerable use of compulsory purchase powers in affected areas, the major changes in landownership have nevertheless seen land move from ownership by private individuals (*rentiers*) to the big property companies. However, a considerable amount of publicly-rented housing has, in fact, been constructed in the renewed inner-city districts over the last twenty years, aided by generous financial provision. West Berlin, therefore, stands somewhat apart from other Western European cities in both the scale and results of its recent urban renewal and rehabilitation programme.

The general post-war pattern in Western Europe has been for urban intervention to move from large-scale renewal to smaller-scale rehabilitation. The years of the later 1950s and the 1960s, when Western European economies were in relative boom, saw the drawing up of large-scale plans for the redesign of whole neighbourhoods. Both public and private funds were generally involved, but a general feature was the upgrading of the affected areas' social status as a result of the effect of market forces on housing costs. Hence renewal has brought an increase of middle-class representation in inner-city areas (Lichtenberger 1976: 99). Even where publicly-rented property has been successfully built, the occupants are customarily of a higher rank than the initial residents before renewal because subsidization of rents is rarely practised in Western Europe. Often it appears that the original residents wanted property restoration and improvement and the elimination of slums, but instead they saw their whole neighbourhoods eliminated (Beringuier 1966: 213): and where there was no public finance involved in such renewal schemes, planned rehousing elsewhere was far from being automatic (Lowder 1980: 8).

Small-scale renewal (at a house-by-house level) and rehabilitation have come into greater prominence since the early 1970s, but the effects in terms of gentrification have been similar or, in some cases, even more extreme. The costs of sensitive property restoration are high, sometimes even higher than the costs of total renewal, and it is only in rare instances, such as that of Bologna, that these costs have not been passed on to the residents. Restoration of old city-centre property has been even more prone to create gentrification than has large-scale renewal, because of the great attractions to the middle class of life in a picturesque city-centre location behind an attractive architectural facade but with all modern housing amenities (Lichtenberger 1977: 260). In some cities, however, there are now growing signs of an over-provision of high-quality, high-cost apartments, both in Northern and Southern Europe (Bentham and Moseley 1980: 58; Ginatempo and Cammarota 1977: 116), contrasted with the growing shortages of low-rent housing for the young and single, shortages which have led to sporadic civil unrest, most notably in Amsterdam in 1980. Urban social protest movements have generated a good deal of attention in many cities, but their real achievements have been few. Whilst a greater degree of consultation has been progressively built into the urban planning process (Kouvelis 1979; Whysall and Benyon 1980: 82), it is arguable that the reduction in scale of renewal schemes during the 1970s was more a response to changed economic realities in the property market than to local popular pressure. Although Castells' interpretation of urban renewal assumes too unified a structure to urban power, his emphasis on the dominance of the free market is essentially correct and it is market forces that explain the course, processes and effects of recent changes in the inner-urban built environment.

As a general conclusion to this chapter, it is therefore possible to point to the overall picture of the inner-city in most Western European countries as being an area of steady population decline but of rising social status. However, social polarization has generally been occurring, with the increase of those at opposite ends of the status hierarchy and the decrease of those at the middle. Amongst the lower-status groups are found transitory populations of students and young single adults, immigrant labourers and the very poor along with more permanent communities of older, traditional working-class origin. The first three of these groups often come to inhabit areas that are under the threat of future change, such as through renewal, thus forming the last groups of housing occupants before such changes occur and being those most affected by them. Certainly in the 1950s and 1960s, many renewal schemes struck at organic working-class neighbourhoods, but that is much less the case in more recent years. In fact the period of housing marginalization in Western European cities has come to occupy a steadily reducing length of time. Given the scale of the growing middle class and its demands for city-centre residence in many cities (excluding some of those in Northern Europe – see Ch. 7, pp. 161–3), and the pace of post-war economic growth leading to pressures for commercial and administrative area expansion, the economic motives for renewal and rehabilitation have been very strong, often reinforced by social motives concerned with the prestige of city-centre locations. At the same time, single young adults retain a desire for city-centre living but they do not have the purchasing power to generate new purpose-built housing and the supply of cheap rented property is diminishing. Whilst the 1981 riots in English cities were a manifestation of frustrations arising from economic and employment problems, the same causes are not apparent in urban unrest in the rest of Western Europe. There, such unrest stems from the imbalance between the decreasing supply of marginalized inner-city housing and the demand which is, if anything, increasing from students, immigrant workers and socially marginal groups (the *provotariaat* in the Netherlands; in West Germany those 'outside society' – the *asoziale*).

It is, however, necessary to put these urban struggles in perspective. Whilst attention has been focused here on certain dynamic elements of the social geography of the Western European inner-city, it is necessary to reiterate that the inner-city retains considerable importance as a residential location, certainly more so than in many other cities of the developed world. The conversion of residential areas to other uses, accompanied in many cities by social processes of gentrification in the remaining residential areas, may be apparent at the scale of the inner-city as a whole, but it is still possible to find many neighbourhoods within the inner areas of most cities where social changes are scarcely apparent and where traditional styles of urban living, whether *bourgeois* or working class, remain relatively unchanged.

CHAPTER NINE

The Suburbs and Beyond

Earlier chapters have introduced discussion of certain aspects of the suburbs as part of the consideration of broader city-wide social patterns. Thus in Chapter 7 it was seen that suburban areas contain a relatively heterogeneous mixture of social groups with segregation between those groups being clearly marked. Chapters 3 and 6 demonstrated that it is the peripheral areas of cities that are still experiencing population growth, both through natural increases characteristic of populations with a high proportion of those in the childbearing and childrearing phases of the life-cycle, and also through net gains of intra-urban migrants. These features of population growth in peripheral districts accord with the phenomenon, observable throughout the developed world, of a secular decline in urban population density gradients as measured from the inner-city areas of peak density (Berry et al. 1963). This is accentuated, as Chapter 8 showed, by city-centre depopulation.

The present chapter is intended to provide a fuller discussion of the various types of suburb observable around Western European cities, along with consideration of the journey-to-work. The word 'suburb' is interpreted in a broad sense as including all residential developments outside the old urban cores, but particular emphasis will be put on present-day patterns of evolution, including discussion of the settlement of urban populations in villages beyond the built-up limits to cities.

THE HISTORY OF SUBURBAN GROWTH

Unlike the position in Britain or North America, the suburb has not played a major role in the collective European consciousness of the city. Where European city planners have adopted a specific viewpoint on the growth of suburbs or suburban settlement, they have generally adopted English models, often derived in part from the Garden City movement or from ideas on the planning of neighbourhood units put forward by planning theorists such as Abercrombie (Sidenbladh 1975: 31). A major reason for this lack of interest in the suburbs has undoubtedly lain in the more dominant urban culture of mainland Western Europe (Ch. 7, pp. 163–4) which has meant that, except in some northern countries, the suburb has not been an area of positive residential choice by its inhabitants who have, instead, been 'sent' there by the exigencies of the housing market, especially in the publicly-rented sector in recent years. In addition, housing types in Western European suburbs often differ much less from those of the inner-city than is the case in Britain or North America. The overall suburban belts of most larger European cities demonstrate much higher population densities than are found in suburbs in the English-speaking world (Thorns 1973: 70– 1), and multi-family housing is much more common than the single-family dwellings found in Britain or North America. Much of the recent housing, in Britain as well as in the rest of Western Europe, has been provided or controlled by public authorities, a feature which again contrasts greatly with the North American picture (Vance 1978: 114–18).

The earliest suburbs of European cities were those settlements that grew outside the city walls but which were functionally dependent on the city itself. These settlements were generally inhabited by newcomers to the city and by the more marginal elements in society: their populations were often outside the control and protection of the medieval guild system and were certainly outside the physical security afforded by residence within the defences of the city. These historical suburbs, populated by the lowest social classes, play a key role in Sjoberg's model of the evolution of urban spatial structure (Sjoberg 1960; see also Ch. 1, pp. 5–6).

The major growth of the suburbs, however, did not come until the nine-teenth century, brought about by the development of industrialization and population growth and leading, in turn, to the dismantling of old city forti-fications (Ch. 1, pp. 22–7). The creation of new industries and of the factory system brought the generation of larger industrial units which could only be established outside the existing limits of the older cities and which brought increased separation between residence and workplace for significant sectors of the population although, as will be seen later in this chapter (pp. 215–7), industrial and residential expansion in the new suburbs generally went hand-in-hand. The separation of secondary from tertiary activities inherent in the decline of the importance of artisanal industry, and the social stratification thus emerging, produced conditions favouring the development of a more spatially-zoned structure to cities than had been the case with the earlier intense inte-gration of all city functions and activities. Economic growth brought popu-lation growth and urban expansion through suburbanization.

Conventional geographical wisdom has it that large-scale suburban growth was impossible without a cheap and efficient means of transportation. Thus, as Caralp (1965: 111) states:

the railway can be considered as the creator of suburban living from the second half of the nineteenth century.

After the railway came the tram, either horse-drawn or steam-powered at first but later run by electricity. The turn of the century saw the first metro lines in cities such as Paris and Berlin, whilst the inter-war period saw the growth of bus services as major transport means in suburban areas. In the post-war years, personal means of transport have become dominant as incomes have risen: the car may be the pinnacle of personal transport but the bicycle and the motorbike (or often the motorized bicycle) remain important means of journey-to-work in many smaller cities.

However, the view that suburban growth was universally facilitated by a uniform evolution of transport possibilities would be erroneous. Many nineteenth century developments of industrial suburbs, for example, did not require mass transportation of the work-force since housing sprang up in close proximity to the industry. It would also be very easy to overestimate the importance of the railway system in suburban development in many cities. Of the larger European cities today, only Paris has a suburban railway network that remotely resembles that of London in its scope, Berlin's extensive and important network having been severely reduced in its efficacy by the partitioning of the city. Many large cities such as Amsterdam, Rome and Madrid have never had a suburban rail network, and even in Paris, suburban areas provided with good rail links since the middle of the nineteenth century often did not witness rapid population growth until well into the twentieth century. In general in mainland Western Europe, large-scale middle-class interest in suburban living was lacking during the period of railway development so there was no guarantee that the provision of new suburban lines would generate housing development and railway profits as happened around London in the late nineteenth century.

In many cities the provision of tramways, buses and metro lines came under municipal control from an early date so that networks often terminated at city boundaries and left peripheral areas badly served. In Paris, for example, none of the metro lines went beyond the old walled boundary of the administrative city before 1930 and even after that date the extensions were only into the nearest long-established suburbs (Evenson 1979). The inner-city bus service in Paris still runs only to the old city gates from where a separate network takes over for suburban transport. Only with the construction of the new RER rail-lines (the *Réseau Express Régional*) has Paris acquired a mass-transit commuter network capable of stimulating further suburban growth. Where cities in recent years have modernized their public transport systems, sometimes building new metro networks as in Lyon, Brussels or Milan, the driving force has often been the desire to reduce city-centre congestion as much as to facilitate transport from the suburbs.

Much suburban growth has thus taken place in advance of adequate transportation provision, and that has been particularly true of post-war public sector housing provision in peripheral districts. Access problems thus loom large in the complaints of suburban residents, especially the working class who are unable to afford the means of personal transport except for the humble bicycle. Higher suburban population densities in Western Europe may not be simply a reflection of the acceptance of apartment living (Ch. 2); they may also be a response to poorer transport facilities whereby housing developments cluster to maximize access to those rail-lines and bus routes that do exist.

214

TYPES OF SUBURB

In the consideration of the diversity of social classes and life-styles in the suburbs of Western European cities, it will be instructive to highlight certain types of suburb. Four will be discussed here: the industrial suburb; the modern working-class public housing project; the middle-class suburb; and finally the detached suburb or dormitory village beyond the city limits.

The industrial suburb

As an example of the history of an industrial suburb, that of Villeurbanne, in the eastern part of Lyon, provides some useful discussion points (Bonneville 1978). Villeurbanne developed on a large scale from about 1880 as Lyon industrialists adopted factory-oriented production processes and moved out of the crowded old city to new peripheral sites. By 1914, Villeurbanne had a population of 44,000, many living in *cités-ouvrières* specifically built by firms to house their own workers so that each factory was surrounded by housing. This phenomenon first developed in France in Mulhouse earlier in the century (Meyer 1968: 95–6). By 1939 the population of Villeurbanne had risen to 83,000 and 80 per cent of the working population were manual workers, although stratification occurred within this group on the basis of skill levels. The office functions of the industrial firms had been left behind in the city-centre, only the production processes moving out, so that segregation was created between manual and non-manual workers in terms of place of employment and in terms of residence. The inter-war years saw the construction of low-standard single-family dwellings in Villeurbanne along with public housing blocks, while the post-war period brought large-scale *grand ensemble* construction by public funds. Not until the 1960s did the industrial dominance in Villeurbanne start to decline and lower middle-class residents to increase, but in 1968 the suburb still remained much more industrial than the city of Lyon as a whole, 66 per cent being employed in industry in Villeurbanne against 47 per cent for the whole of the Lyon agglomeration.

Many of the older cities of Western Europe have developed their own equivalents of Villeurbanne during the last century or so. The impossibility of inserting large factories into restricted city-centre sites brought the creation of suburban industrial belts with their attendant working populations. The adoption of the factory system came very late in some cities, especially in Southern Europe where industry has remained craft-based until well into the present century. On the other hand it is possible to point to the cities of the Ruhr or of the northern coalfield in France as cases where large-scale industrial development created cities around industrial plant, but these are exceptions: in most Western European cities, industry today is peripheral rather than central in its location in urban space. This point is clearly made in Fig. 9.1 which shows the present industrial ring around Paris, a pattern that is by no means unique (see also Fig. 7.1 of the case of Turin).

Paris retained its fiscal barriers (the *octroi*) until the end of the nineteenth

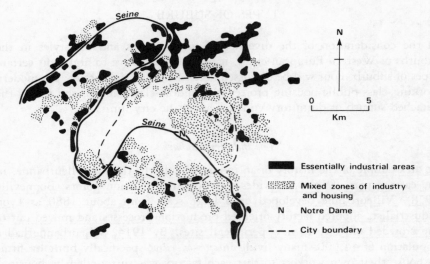

Fig. 9.1 Industrial areas in Paris
(*Source*: redrawn from Bastié 1975)

century (see Ch. 1, p. 26), and this meant that a suburban location for industry offered financial advantages as well as permitting easier transportation for raw materials and finished products via the railway yards that were established in suburban sites. One of the chief areas benefiting from industrial growth was that immediately to the north of the city where industrialization dates back to the start of the nineteenth century, first concerning industries such as chemicals and tanning which were not welcome in Paris itself because of their pollution-creating nature (Brunet 1970). As early as 1830 there were *bourgeois* fears about the localized proletariat concentrations being created in such suburbs: the Prefect Chabrol wrote to Louis-Philippe that

your prefects of police are allowing the capital to be blockaded by a belt of factories. Sir, these will be the rope which will strangle her one day (quoted in Brunet, 1970: 232).

Despite such protests, the new industrial ring around Paris was completed by the end of the century, and the proletarian character of these inner suburbs was later increased by the demolition of the city walls and their partial replacement by working-class housing (Vance 1978: 111; see also Ch. 1, p. 26).

In many cities a complete circle of industrial suburbs has not developed because of local factors of physical relief or access to transport routes, so that such suburbs are limited to specific sectors of the city rather than taking a concentric form. This is, of course, most common in ports, such as Marseille (Maurice and Deloménie 1976), but industrial desires for flat land and communications (the two often going together) have limited the industrial suburbs of cities such as Brussels or Stuttgart to a sectoral form. In the special case of Venice, the landward settlements of Mestre and Porto Marghera can be regarded as industrial suburbs to the old lagoon city.

The characteristic industrial suburb, tracing its origins back to the late nineteenth century, displays a mixture of housing with old industrial cottages, terraces or courtyard dwellings rubbing shoulders with more recent publicly-financed apartment blocks. Such suburbs have traditionally had a pattern of only short distances separating homes from workplaces. In recent years, however, commuting has generally increased from such suburbs as older industries have declined and as those allocated to public housing have not necessarily been locally employed: self-sufficiency in employment is thus weakened and problems have become apparent through the lack of easy access of such suburbs to the city-centre, especially important in restricting opportunities for the employment of females in tertiary activities (Leroy 1971; Maurice and Deloménie 1976: 91). In the industrial suburb of Fontaine in the Grenoble agglomeration in 1968, 68 per cent of the resident working population travelled daily to work elsewhere in the city (David 1971: 146–7). In the industrial suburbs to the east of Paris in the same year, commuting across *commune* boundaries affected between 51 and 71 per cent of the employed population (Leroy 1971: 65–6). The older industrial suburbs are thus losing their internal cohesion and progressively becoming working-class dormitory areas.

Other general features of these older suburbs are also of note. The populations are now often ageing somewhat with demographic structures that demonstrate an under-representation of young families (Maurice and Deloménie 1976: 30–1). This is accompanied throughout Northern Europe by substantial increases in the presence of foreign workers, whilst in Paris the industrial suburbs to the west of the city-centre have been the location of the main North African squatter settlements (see Ch. 5, p. 118). In Chapter 4 (p. 87), the link between industry and shanty-towns populated by migrant workers has also been demonstrated in Barcelona.

The industrial suburb has evolved from its nineteenth century origins but it is now, in general, seeing a transformation of its composition as de-industrialization occurs and as social marginalization results. Such suburbs are now no longer the chief areas of working-class population, that role having passed to the newer peripheral estates.

The new working-class suburb

Although publicly-financed suburban housing predates the Second World War in most Western European countries (see Ch. 2), it has been the post-war years that have seen the real explosive growth of public housing provision in peripheral locations for the working-class and lower middle-class populations. The reasons for this have been demonstrated elsewhere in the present volume: wartime destruction, urban renewal, continued population growth through in-migration and city-centre depopulation have all conspired to increase housing demand, and the most economic means of satisfying that demand has been through the use of large parcels of cheap peripheral land on which systems-building techniques could be used. In addition, a certain vogue in architectural and social design, derived largely from Le Corbusier's concept of 'towers in a park', brought enthusiasm for the construction of *grands ensembles*, even if such enthusiasm was not necessarily shared by the man-in-the-street.

In many countries, specific legislation was enacted to facilitate rapid estate development in peripheral areas. In France such areas could be designated as priority urbanization zones (*ZUP*), whilst in Italy the expropriation of land at the city periphery could take place at agricultural, rather than development potential, prices (Huet et al. 1975: 49). It is important to note, however, that the resulting developments have not solely concerned publicly-financed housing. Especially in Southern Europe, private building has also occurred and some of the public authority housing has been built for sale (see Ch. 2).

Four features of these post-war suburban housing developments for lower-income households are deserving of discussion here: these are size, population composition, amenity provision and access.

In order to achieve maximum economy in the provision of housing units, the scale of peripheral housing developments has generally been very large. Often a small number of monolithic multi-storey apartment blocks houses upwards of 20,000 people on a limited site. In France, the first *grands ensembles* around Paris provided dwellings for 40,000 inhabitants, with a maximum of 80,000 in one of the earliest developments at Sarcelles to the north of the city (Evenson 1979: 245–9): later schemes were often somewhat smaller at around 15–20,000 inhabitants (Josse 1968: 260–1), but multi-storey living continued to dominate – in Clerc's (1967) survey of the residents of *grands ensembles* throughout France, he found that 35 per cent of households were in apartment blocks of five or more storeys. In France, gross population densities in the earlier developments averaged about 560 persons per hectare, well over twenty times the level in nearby single-family housing (Rapoport 1969: 342–3; Josse 1968: 258–9). The French experience has been repeated elsewhere. In West Berlin, the new Markisches Viertel was planned from the outset for a population of 50,000 in high-rise blocks (Trebbi 1978: 116–22). In Barcelona, all new peripheral housing constructed after 1960 by the public housing authority contains a minimum of 1,500 dwellings, chiefly in tower blocks (Lowder 1980: 7), although here the development of true suburban estates of such property has not occurred, as a result of the general lack of central planning. Around Italian cities, new public housing is customarily in blocks with an average of six or seven storeys (Sarracco 1972: 200–2). The Bijlmermeer scheme in Amsterdam (see Ch. 6, p. 143), involving the residential development of an old marshy polder beyond the city boundary, is planned eventually to house 110,000 people in tower blocks of nine to sixteen storeys: 90 per cent of the housing will be in public ownership (McClintock and Fox 1971). It is therefore clear that the types of dwelling construction utilized in these peripheral developments in mainland Western Europe are more akin to the tower-block schemes that accompanied inner-city urban renewal in British cities, rather than the lower-density, often single-family, dwellings that have characterized much peripheral public housing provision in Britain.

One of the prime determinants of the social and population composition of the new low-income suburbs is the 'target' population at whom the development was aimed, whether the displaced traditional working class from urban renewal areas, recently-arrived provincial migrants, foreign immigrant workers and their families or some other group. In publicly-financed schemes, housing allocation policies play a major role alongside the willingness of various subgroups to live in such accommodation, or their need to do so in the absence of alternatives. The general result of the interaction of these controls has been that the new low-income suburbs contain high proportions of large families, of young couples in the childrearing stages of the life-cycle and of children, whilst the social class composition is almost completely dominated by manual workers and those in the lower white-collar occupations requiring lowest skill levels. In Clerc's (1967) survey of French *grands ensembles*, he found that 42 per cent of their populations were aged 0–14 and only 1 per cent were over 65; 85 per cent of the household heads could be classified as working class or lower middle class. These general features are attested in a large number of individual studies of new suburbs throughout Western Europe (Coppolani 1977; Doré 1972; Trebbi 1978: 120). In total, an important characteristic of the new peripheral working-class suburbs is their relatively high degree of internal homogeneity of population and social composition. The exception occurs with foreign migrant families, although even here there is similarity in terms of age-structures and social class. The representation of foreign workers in peripheral housing developments, however, varies according to local conditions and policies. In France, some housing schemes have been specifically designed as *cités de transit* housing exclusively migrant families (Ch. 5, p. 119). Similarly in Southern European cities, peripheral estates have been built specifically to rehouse migrant squatters (Regni and Sennato 1973: 923). In Northern Europe there are often policies restricting the concentration of foreign migrants in peripheral estates. For example, in one suburban area of the Lyon agglomeration, 18 per cent of tenants in a certain *grand ensemble* were foreigners in 1975, but the proportion could have been much higher if vacant dwellings were let to foreigners, an option that was prohibited by an agreement between the public housing agency and the *commune* on whose land the housing lay. Here the peripheral estate was unattractive to the French who could, in fact, often elect for tenancies in other estates: it was also unattractive to the foreigners but it represented their only chance of a modern dwelling (Chazalette 1980).

The third general feature of the new peripheral working-class suburbs is their overall lack of amenities. In the earliest developments, the need was for the speedy provision of housing units to reduce a serious crisis and little attention was paid to housing externalities. It is also arguable that the general existence of quasi-autonomous public housing agencies not directly connected to local municipal administrations tended to preclude a more integrated and planned view of the totality of needs of the new developments. The provision of shops, health care, schools, parking facilities and, above all, safe play areas for children has often been sadly lacking. This is the case whether we are considering the *barrios proletarios* around Madrid (García 1977: 291), the *grands ensembles* of France or early post-war housing in West Germany built largely for refugees and with amenities provided only by church organizations rather than by the municipal authorities (Riquet 1960: 129–30). One of the results of the large scale of developments ought to have been to raise population totals to viable threshold levels (Rochefort 1970: 209), but inadequate space was generally made available for private retailing and commercial activities whilst investment in public amenities has customarily lagged far behind investment in housing. Often the independent suburban *communes* on whose land the new developments lay did not have the funds available to provide suitable infrastructure until the local tax income grew once people had moved in; in other cases the rapidity of population growth has simply been too great (Martinez-Marí 1966: 544). Even in the years since the early 1960s as the need for more integrated planning of new estates has become generally accepted, complaints about the low level of service provision in such developments continue to be voiced, and the vandalism and delinquency that have become features of many *grands ensembles* have often been attributed to the boredom of youngsters and to the lack of pride in their environment shown by adults in areas where a true feeling of neighbourhood has not evolved because of the absence of the normal daily foci to life (Bontinck 1978; Chazalette 1980; see also Ch. 7, pp. 186–7). These generalized feelings of discontent are more reminiscent of decaying inner-city areas in other urban societies.

The final feature of interest in the new peripheral districts is their state of overall accessibility within the urban system. The recency of such housing developments means that they are dependent on road transport rather than on railways since land alongside railways was generally used up earlier for other forms of suburban growth. The absence of industrial development in close proximity to new housing has also increased the need for transport, whilst adequate bus services have been difficult to provide in such large estates so that residents have been forced to resort to private transport (Josse 1968: 259). Given the dormitory nature of the new areas, good access is vital: only 1 per cent of the early residents of the Markisches Viertel in West Berlin held local employment (Trebbi 1978: 120), and in his Dijon study-area, Doré (1972: 211) found that only 2 per cent were locally employed within their peripheral estate. Apart from its generally poor availability, public transport is also generally deficient in providing routes tangential to the city-centre that would be important in transporting workers to other peripheral industrial areas. The outlying nature of the new estates also increases journey-to-work times markedly: for example, only 15 per cent of male *grand ensemble* residents around Paris in 1960 were able to get home for lunch, against a total of 28 per cent for the suburbs as a whole and 40 per cent for those living in Paris proper (Clerc 1967: 308–9). Complaints about the poor accessibility of the new peripheral estates are common throughout Western Europe.

The new working-class suburbs of Western European cities have played a major role in helping to reduce the post-war housing crisis, and many of their residents appear to give basic approval to them on pragmatic grounds (Clerc 1967: 389). However, whilst the internal standards of the housing are generally satisfactory, the externalities are often poor. The provision of amenities to serve the barrack-like apartment blocks is often deficient and the residents have feelings of being cut off from urban life and of anonymity, the peripheral locations and their problems of accessiblity being a major contributory factor. These new suburbs were conceived without any overall plan for the future of urban structure: the planned alternatives of mixed neighbourhood units and new towns will be considered at the end of the chapter.

The middle-class suburb

In Chapter 7 it has been argued that there is an important Western European cultural tradition emphasizing the city-centre as a desirable area for middle-class residence. It was, however, noted that suburban middle-class districts also occurred and that in the cities of Northern Europe, where the high-status city-centre districts were less marked, middle-class suburbs were of considerable importance.

It was certainly the railways that permitted the growth of middle-class interest in residence at the city fringes, as in the English-speaking world, and some of the more wealthy sought to obtain greater living space at the periphery at the expense of greater travel costs. The first growth of middle-class villas along the edge of the Vienna Woods south of the Austrian capital coincided with the construction of the railway from 1848 onwards (Seger 1972: 316), and led also to the expansion of the older rural settlements along the line of the railway. Similar developments occurred along the railway lines leading out of Paris (Josse 1968) but, as mentioned earlier in this chapter (p. 214), population growth was far from being spectacular. By and large it was not until well into the twentieth century that the real expansion of middle-class suburbs started around most mainland Western European cities, and when this expansion occurred it was partly based on road transport instead of on the railways but, more importantly, it was preceded by the 'opening-up of the suburbs' by the lower middle classes.

Three reasons can be tentatively suggested for the slowness of growth of middle-class suburban interests in much of Western Europe. Firstly, there is the perceived cultural desirability of the city-centre residence, as discussed in Chapter 7 (pp. 163–4). Secondly, during the late nineteenth century, Hauss-mannization and other public works schemes in the city-centre (Ch. 1, pp. 27–9) were increasing the supply of middle-class residences roughly in line with the growth in demand. Thirdly, there were the features of the housing market whereby large-scale availability of mortgage funds for the construction and purchase of property for owner-occupation was absent: hence the invest-ment potential of high-status suburban housing was low. Certainly in Central and Northern Europe (particularly in Switzerland, Austria and Germany) suburban villas for rent were built, but the bulk of the middle classes elsewhere continued to prefer to rent in accessible central districts rather than in in-accessible peripheral locations.

The inter-war years were important in creating lower middle-class interests in suburban housing at a time when the embryonic publicly-rented sector was providing property chiefly for the working class (Ch. 7, pp. 169–70). At this time the only types of owner-occupier housing that could viably be built in suburban areas, given the lack of demand from the wealthiest, were on a very modest scale, often with an effective system of self-help by those involved. This is clearly seen in France where district after district around many cities was rapidly built up with *pavillons* – small owner-occupied single-family dwellings often built to very poor standards and with a low level of general amenity provision (Josse 1968; Moreau 1967; Rochefort 1970: 202–3). Such developments generally now stand in need of public intervention to bring both housing and infrastructure levels up to modern standards (Damais 1974).

In post-war France, as housing finance for owner-occupation has become steadily easier to obtain, and as the size of the middle-class housing demand has grown, the more wealthy classes have begun to take to *pavillon* life in suburban areas, albeit in housing of a vastly improved standard (Rochefort 1970: 203). The dormitory character of such estates (and their pre-war forebears) is overwhelming, as also are the sizes of the estates as landowners on the rural fringe have divided their holdings up into extensive *lotissements*, portioned out to building companies using standard methods to produce monotonous tracts of uniform housing.

Whilst this evolution from lower middle-class to middle-class suburban housing interests was most characteristic of France, it also occurred in Belgium, the Netherlands and Germany. In these other countries, however, the wealthiest groups in urban society took some interest in suburban living relatively early on, and this was especially the case in Scandinavia. These were the societies where the cultural dominance of urbanism was less and where many cities were industrial creations with less tradition of inner-city high-status neighbourhoods. Around Stockholm the well-to-do started moving out of the central city from about 1870 with the creation of the first commuter railways (Popenoe 1977). From 1905 to 1930, several middle-class garden suburbs were created under the influence of English models, and these became prized low-density districts providing single-family housing much demanded by the wealthy. Elsewhere in Northern Europe the garden suburb was more often a continuation of the older paternalistic housing for workers provided by employers (Bollerey and Hartmann 1980: 149–52) or, increasingly, by the new public housing authorities (De Lannoy 1978: 42). In Southern Europe, Rome started building her first middle-class garden suburb in 1920 (Regni and Sennato 1973: 922), but this was not an example generally followed elsewhere in the Mediterranean world.

In the early post-war years most governments sought to alleviate the general housing crisis through subsidized housing but increasingly, as the scale of the crisis has reduced, the importance of private building for sale or rent has grown, the preferred house-type generally being the single-family dwelling although small apartment blocks have been important in some countries such as Switzerland. There is generally a very marked spatial segregation between the new middle-class dwellings and the publicly-financed housing. Even where new developments have attempted to integrate all classes within one suburb, the difference between rented and owner-occupied blocks picks out the class boundaries – a new feature of social geography in Western European cities where social class and housing class have not normally been very strongly linked. Thus the experimental class integration in the residential use of the Olympic village at Grenoble has not been the success that was desired (Joly 1979: 11–14).

Most Western European cities do contain real middle-class suburbs within their otherwise working-class or lower middle-class peripheral areas. Southeastern Brussels, western Amsterdam, the suburb of Tapiola to the west of Helsinki, the lakeshore areas of Zürich, the villa area of Florence stretching out towards Fiesole, the Posillipo district along the coast west of Naples, the St Cloud district west of Paris – all these are suburban areas of relatively high status, in some cases (such as in Zürich, Brussels and Amsterdam where no inner-city high-status area exists) containing the *élite* of the city's society. Where the middle-class suburbs of Western Europe, taken as a whole, differ from those elsewhere is that they form a smaller proportion of the total suburban realm.

The commuter village

In mainland Western Europe, as in Britain (Pahl 1965), the 'exurban' suburb or commuter village often contains a considerable mixture of social groups – working-class natives as well as middle-class newcomers. In Northern Europe, population growth in these commuter settlements today derives from the in-migration of the well-to-do middle classes. In Southern Europe, middle-class commuting from semi-rural to urban areas is much rarer and instead population growth in detached settlements around the city is more often a reflection of the arrival of recent working-class migrants.

Given the weakness of development control planning in some Western European countries, at least until recent years, a number of exurban suburbs of the past have been absorbed within the urban structure of many expanding cities, so that the outer urban fringes contain the remains of old village cores with the accompanying complexities of their remnant social structures. As pointed out in Chapter 3, throughout Western Europe cities are growing much less quickly than their surrounding cordons of semi-rural and suburban parishes and municipalities, this phenomenon being the case in Southern Europe just as much as further north (Adamo 1969; Coppolani 1977: 16).

The case of Brussels is a useful one to examine as a background for discussion of commuter village growth. The greatest rates of population expansion around the city have recently occurred to the south-east, that being the area of preferential urban growth for over a century as a result of the ease with which the larger land-holdings in that direction could be carved up for development (Deplancke and Vandermotten 1978: 43–4). In addition, Brussels has the added complication of the Flemish–French linguistic frontier to the south which results in the elevation of population growth rates in *communes* just inside the French-speaking area but within easy access of the city (Laurant and Declercq-Tijtgat 1978: 125). Nevertheless, all the 62 *communes* surrounding

Brussels grew in population during the 1960s and in all but one the net migration balance was positive. Not uncommonly, over 40 per cent of the in-migrants originated in Brussels with a sectoral pattern of movement from the city to its surroundings being evident (André et al. 1970). Some of the peripheral *communes*, in fact, consist of higher proportions of the Brussels-born than is the case in some of the inner suburbs of the city itself (Mols 1965: 327–31). What is most noticeable, however, is the fact that this exurban growth around Brussels is dominated by the selective migration to this area of those with middle-class occupations, particularly in the liberal professions (Bruyère and Damas 1977: 31).

The extent of the peripheral growth ring varies from city to city: around Brussels it stretches out to about 19 km, around Liège to 28 km, but around the smaller Belgian city of Namur there is no appreciable exurban growth at all (Laurant and Declercq-Tijtgat 1978: 108–18). Around Amsterdam, the area of fringe growth is narrow on the north but wider on the south, on the side of the city facing the 'Green Heart' of Randstad. Two parishes adjoining the city on its southern edge were the chief beneficiaries of exurban growth between 1951 and 1969, and the fact that migrants from the city arriving here were dominantly in the family-building life-cycle stage and from higher-status occupational groups shows that the development of commuter settlement in this case was simply an extension of the processes of intra-urban migration in the city (see Ch. 6). Exurban growth around Amsterdam has consistently involved the selective out-migration from the city itself of those with higher occupational skill levels (Anon., 1970; Gastelaars and Cortie 1973). The dominance of the middle classes in the growth of commuter villages has been shown elsewhere in Northern Europe, for example in Bordeaux (Cheung 1980: 73).

However, this development of commuter villages is a relatively recent phenomenon. Van Ginkel (1979) has made an exhaustive study of recent exurban expansion in the Green Heart of Randstad Holland and has found that real growth did not become of significance until after 1960, but that by the mid-1970s the central area was absorbing 21 per cent of all those moving out of the four edge (*rand*) cities of Amsterdam, Utrecht, Rotterdam and The Hague. In the newly-built developments of this central area, 72 per cent of housing was in single-family units and 43 per cent was owner-occupied, both these figures being well above the levels typical of the nearby cities and reflecting the well-to-do nature of the arriving populations. It was also notable that in some of the affected areas the new commuter population had effectively swamped the small pre-existing communites.

Where the growth of commuter settlements has occurred more slowly, complex patterns of population composition can emerge, involving spatial segregation within settlements. In the 'village' of Mödling, beyond the city boundary of Vienna, successive waves of population growth have occurred, each affecting a different part of the settlement and resulting in the village now being almost joined in physical urbanization to the city (Seger 1972). Within Mödling the middle class (the first commuters) live in villas along the edge of the Vienna Woods, the lower middle class live in the old village centre and its extensions, whilst in the post-war period a new area of lower-income commuters has been established further east providing a clearly-zoned structure to the settlement. In a similar study of a growing commuter village near Freiburg im Breisgau in West Germany, Mohr and Plattner (1978) also found spatial segregation, although here it was not between different commuter groups but between natives and newcomers. Although some of the newcomers had moved into the old village-centre, none of the native residents had penetrated into the newly-built areas where the population tended to be exclusively of family-forming white-collar workers.

The development of high-status commuter village populations has not yet taken place in Southern Europe, nor is it likely to occur on any major scale in the near future. Faccioli (1978: 24–5) has, however, recently discussed interesting examples of the establishment of ultra-modern, ultra-equipped self-contained residential condominia for the wealthiest classes along the road to the coast south-west of Rome. It is too early to say whether this American-style experiment will catch on or be repeated elsewhere.

It should not, however, be generally assumed that in exurban settlements 'newcomer' equals 'commuter', nor that 'native' is equated with the locally-employed. Continued agricultural labour-shedding, coupled with increased urban employment opportunities, have conspired to encourage long-standing residents of peri-urban settlements to take urban employment, sometimes on a basis of a 'worker-peasantry' retaining a small holding as a part-time activity (Piasentin et al. 1978: 594; Lichtenberger 1976: 87). In an investigation of commuting into the Finnish city of Turku from 52 surrounding parishes, Saviranta (1970) found that approximately half of all the commuters had lived in their present residences before commencing commuting to Turku and that this group tended to commute over longer distances than did those who had moved into the exurban belt as commuters from the start. Because of the size of this commuter group from a rural background, there was an over-representation of industrial employment and construction work amongst commuters and an under-representation of much white-collar employment, an interesting contradiction of the generalization from the English-speaking world that white-collar workers tend to travel furthest to work (Herbert 1972: 241). Similar relationships between agricultural decline and the growth of commuting were apparent in the Oslo region (Rasmussen 1966). In Southern Europe, relatively long-distance commuting by a basically agricultural population is sometimes the only major type of commuter movement, although around the industrial cities recently-arrived migrant worker populations have swelled existing settlements.

In total, then, the development of commuter villages has been a recent and accelerating phenomenon in much of Northern Europe, with growth being dominated by private housing for more affluent social groups. However, these developments have been almost totally absent in Southern Europe. The phenomenon of commuting itself, however, requires more explicit consideration.

THE JOURNEY-TO-WORK

Systematic information on journey-to-work patterns in Western European cities is sadly lacking. Whilst census information is sometimes collected on mode of transport used, distances travelled and numbers moving, important social questions such as the timing of journeys and the proportions returning home for lunch are not tackled. From the materials that are available it appears that there are profound differences between commuting patterns in Northern and Southern European cities. However, before these differences are considered it is also necessary to point out that significant proportions of the population in many cities actually live in the same building as their place of employment. This is the case for a majority of the small self-employed artisans and retailers who have been identified in Chapter 7 (pp. 152–3) as an important class in the Western European urban context. Add to these the large numbers of those in the liberal professions who have their offices, studios or consulting rooms at their residences (Ch. 7, p. 166) and the total living and working in the same place can be substantial. Urban renewal and its accompanying gentrification reduce the numbers of the small self-employed, but this may be compensated by growth in the presence of those in the major professions working from home (Lichtenberger 1977: 260). Adding together those of all social classes who resided at the address of their employment, Mols found that in Brussels in 1961 these totalled 20 per cent of the working population (Mols 1966). This figure would certainly be as high, if not higher, in many Southern European cities.

In Southern Europe, with the middle classes living near their offices in the centre and the working class at the edge near the factories, the need for large-scale daily population movements is reduced. In Athens, a questionnaire survey carried out in 1963 found that the average journey-to-work was only 3.7 km, a very short distance in comparison with figures for United States cities of similar size (Pappas and Virirakis 1972). Given the general lack of commuter village development around Southern European cities, long-distance daily movement is also much reduced. Although there are exceptional individuals, the maximum journey-to-work distance to Messina in Sicily is 5 km from the south and 15 km from the north of the city (Ioli Gigante 1980: 156); around the much larger city of Barcelona, the normal maximum distance is 20 km (Ferras 1977a: 213). Only in some of the largest Italian cities such as Turin and Milan does it appear that these distances are exceeded.

One particular Southern European problem with the journey-to-work pattern is that of the existence of four 'rush hours' as a result of the extended lunch-break, with large numbers of workers returning home for a meal. This phenomenon is shared by France but is only present to a lesser extent in Northern Europe although it is still of some significance even there. The pattern is at its most acute in cities such as Athens or Madrid with their 3- or 4-hour breaks when virtually the whole working population returns home. Surveys in France in the early 1960s showed that in Marseille the median lunch-break lasted 2 hours and 3 minutes. Paris had the shortest French lunch-break with a median of 1 hour 19 minutes (Vaudour 1966: 37), no doubt a function of the size of the city and the distances many people travelled to work such that even a 2-hour break would have been insufficient for many people to return home. In 1960, those living in Paris itself who went home for lunch undertook an average one-way journey of 29 minutes (Clerc 1967: 309) and the pattern remained unchanged ten years later so that the average Parisian spent 2 hours a day in 1970 travelling to and from work (Evenson 1979: 119). The introduction of shorter lunch-breaks has been generally resisted throughout Western Europe.

In Northern Europe, journey-to-work patterns involve much greater distances than further south, a reflection of greater social area complexity resulting in smaller proportions of the population living close to their employment, and also reflecting the more widespread development of suburban settlements and commuter villages. Nevertheless, there are still the tendencies for workers to live nearer industry and for office workers to live nearer the business districts (Gastelaars et al. 1971: 416). The scale of population movement is, however, completely different from that in Southern Europe. In the Paris agglomeration in 1971, for example, taking into account only those moves across some administrative boundary, 850,000 commuted daily into Paris from its suburbs while 200,000 went the reverse direction; 900,000 moved between suburban areas whilst 700,000 moved within Paris itself – a grand total of 2.65 million daily movers (Evenson 1979: 116). Mols (1966) calculated figures on a similar basis for Brussels in 1961: he found that 189,000 commuted into the city from beyond its boundaries, these providing 33 per cent of the city's labour force; a further 210,000 travelled between the constituent *communes* of the city itself, whilst 93,000 worked in the same administrative division of the city as their residence but at a different address. In Rouen in France in 1962, the city had a daytime working population that was 40 per cent greater than the resident work-force with daily commuter arrivals totalling 26,000 (Allain 1971). Commuter movements in Rouen had increased rapidly in the early post-war years as a result of the establishment of new suburban housing, and the commuters included high proportions of females working in tertiary sectors in the city-centre whilst their husbands obtained more local industrial employment.

Journey-to-work movements have thus become more significant in Northern Europe over recent years. In the case of Oslo (Rasmussen 1966), the city was already receiving 30,000 daily commuters from surrounding parishes in 1950; by 1960 this had risen to 40,000 of whom 25,000 went to the inner-city. The distances involved were also rising: in 1930, 79 per cent of the commuters came from within 15 km of the city but by 1960 only 53 per cent came from within this range, whilst the proportion commuting from over 35 km had risen from zero to 11 per cent over the same period. However, between 1950 and 1960 there were no new areas brought into the commuter field – it was just that movement within the existing commuter belt became more intense. In general, it would be true to say that the larger the city the wider the commuter field is likely to be. These figures for Oslo can be compared to those from the

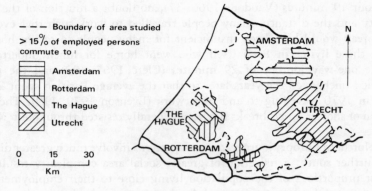

Fig. 9.2 Commuting in the Green Heart of the Randstad.
(*Source*: redrawn from Van Ginkel 1979)

much smaller Finnish city of Turku where, in 1960, 59 per cent of the 10,000 commuters into the city came from within 5 km of the city's administrative border (Saviranta 1970).

The normal phenomenon of distance decay in journey-to-work patterns is shown in Fig. 9.2 which maps the general commuter pattern of the 'Green Heart' of Randstad Holland. In no case does the effective commuter limit (defined here as 15 per cent of the employed population working in the city) exceed 15 km. Harts (1978) has made a detailed study of commuting into Utrecht, looking at the relationships between travel time from the city and three other variables – the percentage of newly-arrived migrants who came from Utrecht; the proportion of newly-arrived migrants commuting to Utrecht; and the proportion of long-standing residents commuting to Utrecht. In each case travel time was highly significant in explaining variations in the other three features. In particular, it was noted that 50 per cent of recent arrivals from Utrecht had moved into areas within 15 minutes' journey of the city-centre and commuting was very rarely beyond half an hour's journeying. Harts' work, and that by Rasmussen (1966), confirm a phenomenon suggested earlier in this chapter (p. 225), that patterns of journey-to-work from outside city boundaries involve two population sub-groups: those who work in the city and move out to live in the fringe, and those who live in the fringe and then take work in the city. The first group rarely migrate far from the city, the second group form those who undertake daily moves over longer distances.

Despite the larger scale of the journey-to-work phenomenon in Northern Europe than in the south, and especially the greater presence of longer-distance moves, it is clear that commuter patterns in the mainland Western European city are less marked than in Britain or North America and that the phenomenon of the dispersed city is less apparent, except in certain special cases such as that of Paris. Certainly, patterns of rapid suburban growth in the post-war years coupled with the start of commuter village development in some areas are increasing the volume and distances of movement. However, particularly in smaller cities, a high proportion of the total population still lives in relatively close proximity to their places of employment, and more traditional patterns of daily movement, although under threat by the growth of separation between residence and workplace, are still of considerable significance.

ALTERNATIVES TO SUBURBAN GROWTH

The continual expansion of the urbanized population of metropolitan regions through the growth of dormitory suburbs is not the only avenue for urban development. In certain cities, decisions have been made to seek alternative models and it will be instructive in this final section of the volume to look at how these alternatives have evolved in two rather different situations – the cases of Stockholm and Paris – followed by a more general consideration of developments elsewhere in Western Europe. In all cases there has been a considerable input from British schools of planning thought – from Ebenezer Howard and the Garden City movement, from the ideas of Radburn and Abercrombie on neighbourhoods, and from the post-war English new towns.

In Stockholm, suburban growth in the early years of the twentieth century followed the experience of many other Northern European cities, providing middle-class garden suburbs influenced in layout by Howard's English examples in Letchworth and Welwyn but without the employment self-sufficiency desired by Howard (1902). Alongside the garden suburbs, low-rise workers' flats were also built in suburban locations, such workers' areas being typically under-provided with transport and public amenities (Popenoe 1977: 34–5). Then in the 1940s came a complete re-orientation of Stockholm's housing development programme. An important backdrop to this change was the fact that the municipal government had, since the start of the century, steadily been purchasing land, initially with the intention of aiding the growth of garden suburbs (Davies 1973: 246). By the 1930s the authorities were acquiring almost all the land coming on to the market within the city boundaries outside the old urban core, and by 1967 the municipality owned 80 per cent of the city's suburban land and was now purchasing land in surrounding parishes (Davies 1973; 1976; Sidenbladh 1975: 29–30).

During the 1940s the decision was taken to build a series of detached suburbs clustered along a new underground railway network, each suburb being planned to have a relatively high degree of self-sufficiency in commerce and employment. These new suburbs were to be of high-density housing including tower-blocks near the commercial centres with low-rise apartment blocks near the edge. They were conceived as neighbourhood units with sizes varying from 10,000 to 50,000 according to their rank in the urban hierarchy, although the latter figure was quickly found to be the most viable for service provision. High-density apartment blocks were chosen as the housing-type in order to maximize accessibility to the new railway stations and also to minimize building costs. The planners and architects were enthusiastic advocates of apartment blocks whilst the Social Democratic government of Sweden (and Stockholm) was against the provision of single-family houses on the grounds that areas of such property tended to become stratified according to class and life-cycle stage, thus weakening the possibility of the creation of an egalitarian society (Popenoe 1977: 224–5). Apartment housing was therefore designed to provide a variety of dwelling sizes within individual blocks so as to produce an age mix of tenants. There is some evidence of consumer desires for single-family suburban dwellings, but since the municipal authorities controlled land access they were in a position to dictate what was, in fact, provided (Popenoe 1977: 41–3).

The first of these new suburbs (Vällingby – 12 km to the north-west of the city-centre) was completed in 1954, and between then and 1970, when development started to slow down, 27 units were completed around Stockholm. In practice, these detached suburbs have not been as independent of the old city as was originally intended and commuter movements have been at a relatively high level along the new railways. The objective of a social mix appears to have been achieved: Popenoe (1977: 62–3) found that in Vällingby the social class composition was almost the same as for the city as a whole, but in general the upper middle classes are under-represented in these suburban developments and remain in the central city.

The utopian zeal of the early 1950s in Stockholm seems to have dissipated somewhat and the most recently-planned suburbs are rather different from their ancestors. Planned population totals are larger, there is greater homogeneity of housing provision without the variety of dwelling-sizes that marked earlier developments, and the proportion of lower-income residents is growing, often including substantial proportions of foreign migrants. In the biggest planned development of the 1970s, an exurban scheme beyond the city boundary, the concept of neighbourhood units has been dropped (Sidenbladh 1975; Popenoe 1977). Thus Stockholm is now producing more 'normal' suburban growth after the experimentation of the early post-war period, and the years of right-wing government (rare in Sweden) from 1976 to 1982 were years of new emphasis on the provision of single-family housing.

The original Stockholm post-war suburban plan can be seen as an attempt to create the spirit of the Garden City but with a very different architectural composition and in a location where subservience to the old city was inevitable. Although the degree of this dependence has been greater than intended, the general verdict is that the satellite suburban units have been successful in providing a full range of amenities within the suburbs and in preventing sprawl.

The new towns planned around Paris are a rather different phenomenon (Goursolas 1980; Tuppen 1979). The initial incentive for their construction came from expansionist forecasts of rapid economic and population growth in the Paris region: there was a desire to avoid further concentric suburban expansion around the city with the likely accompanying problems of poorly-equipped dormitory areas and the growth of commuting and pressure on transport facilities. The original plan was for the creation of eight new towns approximately 30 km from the centre of Paris on agricultural land expropriated at current agricultural values. In 1969 the plan was revised to produce only five new towns, each with a target population of between 300,000 and 1 million, of whom 80 per cent were to be locally employed.

By the time of the 1975 census, the populations of the five new town areas totalled 326,000 but only 80,000 lived in newly-built districts, the rest inhabiting older settlements. During the early 1970s the new towns, intended to take the lion's share of population growth in the Paris region, accounted for only 15.7 per cent of new housing in the whole metropolitan area. Private property companies preferred to invest elsewhere to avoid the complex controls exercised by the new town authorities (these authorities themselves being some-what Byzantine in complexity), so new housing in the new towns was domi-nated by the state-aided sector. In 1975, only 30.6 per cent of housing was of single-family dwellings, but since 1977 official encouragement has been given to the creation of this type of accommodation and private developers have been enticed in. Tower-block provision has generally been avoided, but the resultant low-density development and architectural diversity have raised infrastructure and construction costs. Only in the centre of the new town of Evry, south-east of Paris, has a real urban core been created (Evenson 1979: 349–51).

Employment growth in the new towns has been slower than desired and in 1975 no more than half of their residents worked locally. The real problem with the new towns around Paris is that they were conceived, planned and built too late. As a reaction to the suburban sprawl of the 1950s, and to the problems of the *grands ensembles*, they are a success, but as decentralized growth-points for the Paris of the future their timing has been unfortunate because economic growth in the Paris region has slowed drastically since the onset of recession in the Western world. In such conditions, decentralization has become a difficult policy no longer finding high political favour, and the long-term plans for the new towns are in danger of being scaled down out of all recognition.

The planned developments discussed here around both Stockholm and Paris can be interpreted as attempts to create integrated settlements combining residences, services and employment in a manner that has not generally occurred in post-war suburban expansion with its tendency to produce spatial segregation between urban functions. In other cities there have been less radical experiments, but there have been definite trends, throughout Northern Europe, towards the adoption of neighbourhood planning strategies in attempts to create more integrated urban growth. West Berlin is an obvious case where Stockholm's experiments with mixed suburban neighbourhoods have been reproduced in a more urban context (Trebbi 1978: 106–11). Many smaller French cities, such as Orléans and Tours, have planned for, and in some cases achieved, detached suburbs with a relatively high degree of self-sufficiency. Lille is in the process of creating a new town at Villeneuve d'Ascq based largely on employment in quaternary economic activities (Ralite 1969; Trenard et al. 1977: 480–1).

But all these developments, including the new towns around Paris, are much more subservient to the centralizing attractions of the old city than is the case with the British new towns – they are satellites rather than separate urban systems (Lichtenberger 1976: 97). In Southern Europe, even such satellites and neighbourhood units are rare. In Rome, rapid urban growth in the inter-war years led to the foundation of the planned southern suburb of EUR, complete with its own range of employment, but EUR, completed in 1955, is not an unqualified success and has not been emulated elsewhere (Faccioli 1978: 18–19). In general in Southern Europe, cultural traditions favour the idea of the unitary city rather than a fragmented urban space, and centralizing forces have maintained an inward-looking view of urbanism rather than the outward-looking view that predominates in much of the English-speaking world. In looking at post-war suburban growth in Western European cities, and at future possibilities of further expansion, it is hard to banish the feeling that rapid suburban growth has in the past generally been viewed as a necessary evil, the only viable cure for the housing shortage of the early post-war years. Today there are increasing numbers of people who make a free-will choice of suburban living, at least in Northern Europe, but the suburbs of mainland Western European cities as a whole are still distinct and different from those of the English-speaking world. Suburban growth has brought new features to the urban social geography of Western Europe, for example in the generation of mono-functional residential areas and in increased links between social class and housing class, but beneath these symptoms of change the underlying traditional urban ethic of society has remained of considerable importance, stronger in the Mediterranean world, weaker in Scandinavia, but everywhere present and playing a major role in the way social space and daily activities are organized within the city.

LONGMAN INC.

1560 BROADWAY   NEW YORK, N.Y. 10036

EE DESK OR EXAMINATION COPY FOR

PROF L DIENES UNIV OF KANSAS	117382 CC734 92-04 PUB DATE 84-05

NUMBER   AUTHOR   AND   TITLE

300479 WHITE WEST EUROPEAN CITY

; THERE AN ASSOCIATE OF YOURS WHO SHOULD EXAMINE A
JPY OF THIS TITLE. IF SO, PLEASE FILL IN THE NAME
ND ADDRESS IN THE SPACE PROVIDED BELOW.

ME AND TITLE

MPANY OR INSTITUTION

ISION OR DEPARTMENT

CAL ADDRESS

Y STATE ZIP CODE

E HOPE YOU WILL FIND TIME TO USE THE SPACE BELOW TO
IVE US YOUR OPINION OF THIS TITLE AND LET US KNOW
BOUT YOUR PLANS FOR ITS USE IN YOUR COURSES.
AY WE QUOTE YOU   YES//OR NO//

FOLD, TAPE, AND MAIL

BUSINESS REPLY MAIL

FIRST CLASS PERMIT NO. 50745, NEW YORK, N.Y.

FIRST CLASS POSTAGE WILL BE PAID BY

LONGMAN INC.
1560 BROADWAY
NEW YORK, N. Y. 10036

COLLEGE DEPARTMENT

Appendix – Data sources for figures and tables

Many of the figures and tables in this volume have made use of statistical information originating in various census volumes, vital registration summaries, city statistical yearbooks and other official publications. The sources used are itemized here as a consolidated list: the chapters in which the data are used are indicated in brackets ( ).

Austria. *Ergebnisse der Volkszählung vom 12. Mai 1971* (5). *Statistisches Jahrbuch für die Republik Österreich 1973* (2). *Statistisches Jahrbuch der Stadt Wien 1974* (2); *1978* (3, 6); *1979* (5).

Belgium. *Recensement de la Population, 31 Décembre 1970, Tome 2B* (2); *Tome 4* (5). *Statistiques Démographiques, 1980, No. 1: Mouvement de la Population des Communes en 1979* (3). *Statistisch Jaarboek 1978, Stad Antwerpen* (5, 8).

Denmark. *Folke- og Boligtaellingen, 9 November 1970* (2). *Befolkningens Bevaegelser 1975* (5); *1978* (3). *Statistisk Årbog for København og Frederiksberg, 1979* (6).

Finland. *Väestölaskenta 1970, Osa I* (5); *Osa XIV* (2). *Väestönmuutokset, 1975* (3).

France. *Recensement Général de la Population de 1975: Résultats du Sondage au 1/5ᵉ* (2, 5).

West Germany. *Volkszäblung vom 27. Mai 1970: Heft 4* (5). *Wirtschaft und Statistik, 1969, Heft 9* (2). *Zeitschrift des Bayerischen Statistischen Landesamts, 1979* (3). *Berliner Statistik, Sonderheft 169, Februar 1971* (2). *Statistisches Jahrbuch Berlin 1971* (5); *1979* (6); *1980* (5). *Statistisches Jahrbuch 1970/71, Hamburg* (5). *Statistisches Jahrbuch der Stadt Köln 1969* (2); *1971* (5); *1978* (6, 8). *Statistisches Taschenbuch 1980, München und seine Stadtbezirke* (3). *Statistisches Jahrbuch München 1971* (5); *1979/80* (5).

Greece. *Results of the Population and Housing Census of 14 March 1971 (Sample Elaboration), Vol. I* (2, 5).

Italy. *11° Censimento Generale della Popolazione, 1971, Vol. VIII, Abitazioni, Tomo I* (2); *Vol. IX, Risultati degli Spogli Campionari, Tomo I* (5). *Popolazione e Movimento Anagrafico dei Comuni 1979* (3). *I Censimenti del 1971 del Comune di Roma: Fascicolo Primo* (8). *Annuario Statistico della Città di Roma, 1964* (6, 8).

The Netherlands. *14e Algemene Volkstelling, Annex Woningtelling, 28 Februari*

1971 (2). Jaarboek 1976, Bureau van Statistiek, Amsterdam (5); 1978 (6, 8); 1979 (3).

Norway. *Folke- og Bolig-telling 1970: Hefte IV (2). Statistisk Årbok for Oslo 1977* (3).

Portugal. *1° Recenseamento da Habitação 1970, Estimativa a 20% (2).*

Spain. *Censo de la Población, de la Vivienda y de los Edificios en España, 1970, Tomo 1 (2); Tomo 2 (5).*

Sweden. *Folk- och Bostadsräkningen 1970. Del 3 (5); Del 6 (2). Folkmängd 31 dec. 1979, Del 1 (3). Befolkningsförändringar 1979, Del 1 (3). Statistisk Årsbok Göteborg 1977 (5). Statistisk Årsbok för Stockholm 1979 (5, 6).*

Switzerland. *Eidgenössisches Volkszählung 1970, Band 7 (5); Band 9 (2). Statistisches Jahrbuch der Stadt Zürich 1978 (3, 6, 8); 1979 (5).*

Notes on further reading

There are three possible approaches to the recommendation of further reading on Western European cities: the approach by topics, the linguistic approach and the city-by-city approach. The student who wishes to follow up a particular topic is advised to read the relevant section of the present volume for an indication of which works the present author has found to be of greatest use.

Undoubtedly a major constraint for the vast majority of those wishing to extend their reading will be linguistic competence. Brief consideration will be given here to materials in French, German, Italian and Spanish as well as English. For those confined to English, several important items are nevertheless available. Burtenshaw et al. (1981) stress the role of planning and management whilst Berry (1973) and Elkins (1973) are shorter and more general accounts. A most important paper is that by Lichtenberger (1970) on the distinctiveness of the Western European city. Several of Castells' works have been translated into English and are thus accessible introductions to Marxist analysis of European urban structures (Castells 1977; 1978).

Historical developments may be investigated further via Crew (1979) and Jackson (1982), both on the Ruhr; or via Sutcliffe (1970) and Evenson (1979), which together provide an excellent discussion of changes in Paris over the last century. The broader sweep of historical evolution is dealt with in Vance (1977) and Braudel (1981).

The question of migrants in cities in recent years has generated a useful literature in English of which the following may be recommended: Clark (1977), De Lannoy (1975), Drewe et al. (1975), Ogden (1977), O'Loughlin (1980), Rist (1978) and Van Amersfoort (1982). In the consideration of social space and residential structures in the city, Lowder's paper (1980) on two neighbourhoods in Barcelona is of interest, as also is Bentham and Moseley's (1980) analysis of the Paris agglomeration and Popenoe's (1977) discussion of suburban growth around Stockholm.

Those who can read French will find a vast but somewhat uneven literature open to them. An excellent overall text on urban geography displaying a French viewpoint is that by Claval (1981). Historical works of some importance are those by Chevalier (1950) and Guillaume (1972) dealing with Paris and

Bordeaux respectively. The formation of the urban population is dealt with by Pourcher (1964) for Paris and by Mols (1968) for Brussels, whilst Clerc's (1967) volume on the population of the *grands ensembles* remains unequalled. Students of behaviouralist approaches should read the influential work by Chombart de Lauwe et al. (1952) on Paris and the more recent work by Metton and Bertrand (1974) on the same city. De Lannoy's (1978) atlas of the spatial social structure of Brussels merits perusal. Two major recent works in French have concerned cities elsewhere in Europe: the discussion by Borris et al. (1977) of foreign migrants in Stuttgart, and the masterly analysis of Barcelona by Ferras (1977a).

Much of the German-language material is to be found in the irregular serials issued by the German universities. Among the most generally useful of these are the works by Böhm et al. (1975) on Bonn, by Döpp (1968) on Naples, and by Steinberg (1978) on population development in the Ruhr. Other interesting papers in German are those by Sick (1979) and by Gans (1979) on intra-urban migration. Austrian geographers, notably Lichtenberger, have been influential in urban geography: the most useful of their works are by Bobek and Lichtenberger (1966), Lichtenberger (1977), and Gisser and Kaufmann (1972), all dealing with aspects of Vienna. An excellent brief paper analysing the spatial social structure of the Swiss city of Bern is that by Gächter (1978).

The reader of Italian will find much of interest in Rossi's (1959) discussion of population growth in Rome. Bastano's (1976) consideration of recent population change in Naples is also worthy of note. More recently, excellent work has been done on Venice, analysing social areas in the city (Costa et al. 1980; Zanetto and Lando 1980). Trebbi's (1978) book in Italian on the post-war reconstruction of West Berlin merits consideration.

Spanish writers have produced interesting analyses of aspects of the social geography of Barcelona and Madrid, and two discussions of individual neighbourhoods may be recommended (Olives Puig 1969; Capote 1976). Salcedo's (1977a) excellent book on Madrid came to the present author's attention too late for consideration in the present volume.

The student wishing to make a more thorough investigation of a single city would be advised to choose from Amsterdam, Barcelona, West Berlin, Brussels, Madrid, Paris, Rome, Stockholm or Vienna. On each of these there is a useful variety of material available in the major languages. For Amsterdam, Angenot (1965), Gastelaars and Cortie (1973), and Cortie (1972a) may be recommended, whilst Gastelaars and Beek (1972) and Van Hulten (1968) are important works in Dutch. The starting-point for work on Barcelona must be the book by Ferras (1977a), other useful items being by Picheral (1969), Olives Puig (1969), Lowder (1980) and Naylon (1981).

On West Berlin, important works are by Liang (1970), Schinz (1968), Schulz (1975) and Trebbi (1978). Brussels is subjected to historical study by Verniers (1958) and other useful works are by Mols (1965; 1968), Grimmeau and David-Valcke (1978), and De Lannoy (1975; 1978). Important works in Flemish include those by Meeus (1974; 1975) and by Kesteloot (1980). The major spatial analysis of Madrid is by Salcedo (1977a), whilst other works on the city that can be recommended are those by Ballesteros et al. (1977), Capote

(1976), De Terán (1961) and Soubeyroux (1978), the last of these being a major historical study of social conditions in the city in the eighteenth century.

There is a vast bibliography on Paris. Historical questions may be referred to in Chevalier (1950), Ogden and Winchester (1975), Evenson (1979) and Sutcliffe (1970). A starting-point for contemporary study might be the analysis by Chauviré and Noin (1980) of social class distributions in the agglomeration. Chombart de Lauwe et al. (1952) and Metton and Bertrand (1974) have produced important considerations of behaviour in the city. Other items worth perusal include Pourcher (1964), Ogden (1977), Ceaux et al. (1979) and Bentham and Moseley (1980).

Work on Rome might start with Rossi's (1959) book, followed by Giannoni (1976), Federici (1964), McElrath (1962) and Arena (1982). Stockholm has been discussed, in English, by Sidenbladh (1975), Råberg (1979) and Hammarström (1979), all from an historical perspective; and by Popenoe (1977), whose work deals with the new suburban satellites. Vienna is admirably dealt with by Bobek and Lichtenberger (1966), Lichtenberger (1977), Gisser and Kaufmann (1972) and Sauberer and Cserjan (1972).

Finally, those wishing to pursue work on Western European cities would be advised to make full use of the *Bibliographie Géographique Internationale* which has by far the best coverage of the Continent, on a country-by-country basis (albeit with over-representation of material on France).

References

References are listed in strict alphabetical order ignoring spaces in surnames: for example, De Lannoy appears before Deneux.

Abele, G. and Leidlmair, A. (1968) 'Die Karlsruhe Innenstadt', *Berichte zur Deutschen Landeskunde*, 41, 217–30.

Abellan Garcia, A. (1976) 'Estructura por sexo y edad de los distritos de Madrid', *Estudios Geograficos*, 37, 303–17.

Abrahamson, M. and Johnson, P. (1974) 'The social ecology of Madrid: stratification in comparative perspective', *Demography*, 11, 521–32.

Accame, G. M. (1973) 'Il diritto alla città: Bologna centro storico', *Casabella*, 37, 17–27.

Achilles, F-W. (1969) 'Typen sanierungsbedürftiger städtischer Wohnviertel im Ruhrgebiet', *Geographische Rundschau*, 21, 121–7.

Adamo, F. (1969) 'Recenti variazioni demografiche e loro riflessi nell' agglomerazione torinese', *Cronache Economiche*, 4, 37–44.

Adams, J. S. (1969) 'Directional bias in intra-urban migration', *Economic Geography*, 45, 302–23.

Adler, S. (1977) *International Migration and Dependence* (Farnborough: Saxon House).

Agnelli, S. (1975) *We Always Wore Sailor Suits* (London: Weidenfeld and Nicolson).

Ah-Peng, Y. (1976) 'Les Réunionnais à Toulouse', *Revue Géographique des Pyrénées et du Sud-Ouest*, 47, 399–403.

Allain, F. (1971) *Migrations Quotidiennes et Transports dans l'Agglomération Rouennaise* (Rouen: Institut de Géographie, Université de Rouen).

André, R., Reybroeck-Quenon, J. and Ruelens, E. (1970) 'Les migrations dans la banlieue bruxelloise', *Revue, l'Institut de Sociologie*, 4, 781–94.

Anfossi, A. (1962) 'Differenze socio-culturali tra gruppi piemontesi e meridionali a Torino', in Centro di Ricerche Industriali e Sociali di Torino, *Immigrazione e Industria*, 243–66 (Milan: Edizioni di Comunità).

Angenot, L. H. J. (1965) 'Le phénomène de dépopulation du centre d'Amsterdam', *Tijdschrift, Koninklijk Nederlandsch Aardrijkskundig Genootschap*, 82, 47–55.

Anon. (1970) 'Migratie vanuit en naar Amsterdam', *Op Grond van Cijfers*, 6, 43–52.

Arena, G. (1982) 'Lavoratori stranieri in Italia e a Roma', *Bollettino, Società Geografica Italiana*, 11, 57–93.

Armengaud, A. (1973) *La Population Française au XXe Siècle* (4th edn), (Paris: Presses Universitaires de France).

Arnaud, J-L. and Masini, A. (1973) 'La population tuberculeuse dans l'agglomération marseillaise: étude de géographie médicale urbaine', *Méditerranée*, 12, 3–27.

Arnauné-Clamens, A-M. (1977) 'L'opération de rénovation urbaine du quartier Saint-Georges à Toulouse', *Revue Géographique des Pyrénées et du Sud-Ouest*, 48, 89–101.

Åström, S-E. (1979) 'Town planning in imperial Helsingfors 1810–1910', in Hammarström, I. and Hall, T. (eds), *Growth and Transformation of the Modern City*, pp. 59–67. (Stockholm: Swedish Council for Building Research).

Atkinson, W. C. (1960) *A History of Spain and Portugal* (Harmondsworth: Penguin).

Aubenque, M. (1968) 'Quelques données sur la mortalité et sur les causes de décès à Paris suivant les arrondissements: note documentaire', *Etudes et Conjoncture*, 12, 97–120.

Aust, B. (1980) 'Die Veränderung der Eigentumsverhältnisse bei Stadterneuerungsverfahren an ausgewählten Beispielen aus der Bundersrepublik Deutschland', *Erdkunde*, 34, 29–36.

Baillet, P. (1976) 'Le bouleversement commercial et social du faubourg Montmartre', *Economie et Humanisme*, 229, 49–62.

Ballesteros, A. G. (1977) 'Notes sobre el crecimiento natural y real de los distritos de Madrid', *Revista Internacional de Sociologia*, 23, 429–40.

Ballesteros, A. G., Brandis, D. and Del Río, I. (1977) 'Los movimientos migratorios de la población de Madrid', *Revista Internacional de Sociologia*, 22, 193–224.

Barou, J. (1975) 'La répartition géographique des travailleurs immigrés d'Afrique Noire à Paris et à Lyon', *Cahiers d'Outre-Mer*, 28, 362–75.

Barrère, P. and Cassou-Mounat, M. (1980) 'L'évolution récente du secteur sauvegardé de Bordeaux', *Revue Géographique des Pyrénées et du Sud-Ouest*, 51, 9–18.

Bassett, K. and Short, J. R. (1980) *Housing and Residential Structure: Alternative Approaches* (London: Routledge and Kegan Paul).

Bastano, I. (1976) 'Napoli: radiografia demografica', *Nord e Sud*, 23, 53–77.

Bastide, H., Girard, A. and Roussel, A. (1982) 'Une enquête d'opinion sur la conjoncture démographique (janvier 1982)', *Population*, 37, 867–904.

Bastié, J. (1975) 'Paris: Baroque elegance and agglomeration', in Eldredge, H. W. (ed.), *World Capitals: Towards Guided Urbanization*, pp. 55–89 (Garden City, N.Y.: Anchor/Doubleday).

Beijer, G. (1963) *Rural Migrants in Urban Setting* (The Hague: Martinus Nijhoff).

Bell, M. (1980) 'Past mobility and spatial preferences for migration in East Africa', in White, P. E. and Woods, R. I. (eds), *The Geographical Impact of Migration*, pp. 84–107 (London: Longman).

Bellettini, A. (1958) 'La provenienza degli immigrati e la destinazione degli emigrati nel comune di Bologna', *Statistica*, 18, 529–42.

Bellettini, A. (1966) 'Le relazioni fra i fenomeni della natalità e della mortalità ed i caratteri economico-sociali di una popolazione urbana', *Statistica*, 26, 3–71.

Bellettini, A. (1969) 'L'analisi della struttura e della dinamica della popolazione urbana attraverso la gestione automatizzata dell'anagrafe comunale', *Statistica*, 29, 535–62.

Ben Sassi, T. (1968) *Les Travailleurs Tunisiens dans la Région Parisienne*, Hommes et Migrations, Cahier No. 109.

Bentham, G. and Moseley, M. J. (1980) 'Socio-economic change and disparities within the Paris agglomeration: does Paris have an "inner-city problem"?', *Regional Studies*, 14, 55–70.

Bergues, H. (1973) 'L'immigration de travailleurs Africains noirs en France et particulièrement dans la Région Parisienne', *Population*, 28, 59–79.

Beringuier, C. (1966) 'La rénovation d'un quartier ancien: Saint-Georges à Toulouse', *Revue Géographique des Pyrénées et du Sud-Ouest*, 37, 205–17.

Bernhardt, E. M. (1972) 'Fertility and economic status – some recent findings on differentials in Sweden', *Population Studies*, 26, 175–84.

Berry, B. J. L. (1973) *The Human Consequences of Urbanisation* (London: Macmillan).

Berry, B. J. L., Simmons, J. W. and Tennant, R. J. (1963) 'Urban population densities: structure and change', *Geographical Review*, 53, 389–405.

Bianchi, E. and Perussia, F. (1978) *Il Centro di Milano: Percezione e Realtá* (Milan: Unicolpi).

Bilet, F. et al. (1970) 'Rénovation du secteur Plaisance: un exemple de reconquête urbaine', *Urbanisme*, 117, 19–25.

Bird, H. (1976) 'Residential mobility and preference patterns in the public sector of the housing market', *Transactions, Institute of British Geographers*, 1, 20–33.

Blanc, M. (1979) 'De la rénovation urbaine à la restauration', *Espaces et Sociétés*, 30–1, 5–14.

Bléry, J. P. (1975) 'La mobilité résidentielle dans la Z.U.P. de Grand-Quévilly', *Cahiers Géographiques de Rouen*, 3, 62–80.

Boal, F. W. (1978) 'Ethnic residential segregation', in Herbert, D. T. and Johnston, R. J. (eds), *Social Areas in Cities: Processes, Patterns and Problems*, pp. 57–95 (Chichester: John Wiley).

Bobek, H. and Lichtenberger, E. (1966) *Wien: Bauliche Gestalt und Entwicklung seit der Mitte des 19. Jahrhunderts* (Graz: Hermann Böhlaus).

Bogaert-Damin, A-M. and Maréchal, L. (1978) *Bruxelles: Développement de l'Ensemble Urbain, 1846–1961. Analyse Historique et Statistique des Recensements* (Namur: Presses Universitaires de Namur).

Böhm, H. et al. (1975) *Studien über Wanderungsvorgänge im Innerstädtischen Bereich am Beispiel von Bonn*, Arbieten zur Rheinischen Landeskunde No. 39 (Bonn: F. Dümmlers Verlag).

Böhning, W. R. (1970) 'Foreign workers in post-war Germany', *New Atlantis*, 2, 12–38.

Böhning, W. R. (1972) *The Migration of Workers in the United Kingdom and the European Community* (London: Oxford University Press).

Boleat, M. J. (1980) 'Competition between banks and building societies', *Quarterly Review, National Westminster Bank*, November, 43–57.

Bollerey, F. and Hartmann, K. (1980) 'A patriarchal utopia: the garden city and housing reform in Germany at the turn of the century', in Sutcliffe, A. (ed.), *The Rise of Modern Urban Planning, 1800–1914*, pp. 135–64 (London: Mansell).

Bolos y Capdevila, M. D. (1959) 'La inmigración en Barcelona en los dos últimos decenios', *Estudios Geográficos*, 20, 209–49.

Bonneville, M. (1974) 'Les migrations résidentielles de la presqu'île lyonnaise', *Revue de Géographie de Lyon*, 49, 99–137.

Bonneville, M. (1978) *Naissance et Métamorphose d'une Banlieue Ouvrière: Villeurbanne: Processus et Formes d'Urbanisation* (Lyon: Presses Universitaires de Lyon).

Bontinck, I. (1978) 'Cultural dimensions of architecture and town planning in Europe', *International Social Science Journal*, 30, 560–90.

Borde, J. and Barrère, P. (1978) 'Les travailleurs migrants dans la communauté urbaine de Bordeaux', *Revue Géographique des Pyrénées et du Sud-Ouest*, 49, 29–50.

Borris, M. et al. (1977) *Les Etrangers à Stuttgart* (Paris: Editions du C.N.R.S.).

Boyce, R. R. (1969) 'Residential mobility and its implications for urban spatial change', *Proceedings, Association of American Geographers*, 1, 22–6.

Boyer, J-C. (1978) 'Exode urbain et occupation sociale dans la Randstad Holland', *Bulletin, l'Association de Géographes Français*, 449, 23–8.

Branchereau, J-P. (1980) 'Les mutations d'un quartier pauvre à Angers: le quartier Saint-Nicolas dans la Doutre', *Norois*, 27, 387–403.

Braudel, F. (1972) *The Mediterranean and the Mediterranean World in the Age of Philip II*, Vol. I, trans. S. Reynolds (London: Collins).

Braudel, F. (1981) *Civilization and Capitalism, 15th–18th Century*. Volme I. *The Structures of Everyday Life: The Limits of the Possible*, trans. S. Reynolds (London: Collins).

Breitling, P. (1980) 'The role of the competition in the genesis of urban planning: Germany and Austria in the nineteenth century', in Sutcliffe, A. (ed.), *The Rise of Modern Urban Planning, 1800–1914*, pp. 31–54 (London: Mansell).

Brown, L. A. and Moore, E. G. (1970) 'The intra-urban migration process: a perspective', *Geografiska Annaler*, 52B, 1–13.

Brunet, J-P. (1970) 'L'industrialization de la région de Saint-Denis: histoire du développement d'une banlieue', *Acta Geographica*, 4, 223–60.

Bruyère, J. and Damas, H. (1977) 'Migrations entre Bruxelles et la Wallonie. Etude de la structure par âge des migrants et de leur répartition socio-professionnelle', *Population et Famille*, 41, 1–57.

Burgel, G. (1972) 'Utilisation d'un échantillon de population à l'étude de la division sociale de l'espace urbain', *Bulletin, l'Association de Géographes Français*, 395, 37–47.

Burgel, G. (1978) 'Les couches moyennes dans la production et la division de l'espace urbain athénien', *Villes en Parallèle*, 2, 187–92.

Burtenshaw, D., Bateman, M. and Ashworth, G. J. (1981) *The City in West Europe* (Chichester: John Wiley).

Buzzi-Donato, A. (1962) 'Alcuni risultati di relevazioni statistiche relative alla popolazione immigrate nel comune di Milano', in Centro di Ricerche Industriali e Sociali di Torino, *Immigrazione e Industria*, pp. 323–33 (Milan: Edizioni di Comunità).

Calabi, D. (1980) 'The genesis and special characteristics of town-planning instruments in Italy, 1880–1914', in Sutcliffe, A. (ed.), *The Rise of Modern Urban Planning, 1800–1914*, pp. 55–69 (London: Mansell).

Cano García, G. M. (1971) 'Población inmigrada en el municipio de Murcia', *Estudios Geográficos*, 32, 23–74.

Capote, C. (1976) 'El barrio del Museo en Madrid', *Estudios Geográficos*, 37, 319–50.

Caralp, R. (1965) 'L'évolution des transports de banlieue dans la région parisienne', *Information Géographique*, 29, 111–18.

Carlsson, G. (1966) 'The decline of fertility: innovation or adjustment process', *Population Studies*, 20, 149–74.

Carter, F. W. (1968) 'Population migration to greater Athens', *Tijdschrift voor Economische en Sociale Geografie*, 59, 100–5.

Carter, H. (1981) *The Study of Urban Geography* (3rd edn) (London: Edward Arnold).

Castells, M. (1973) *Luttes Urbaines et Pouvoir Politique* (Paris: Maspero).

Castells, M. (1977) *The Urban Question: A Marxist Approach*, trans. A. Sheridan (London: Edward Arnold).

Castells, M. (1978) *City, Class and Power*, trans. E. Lebas (London: Macmillan).

Castells, M. and Godard, F. (1974) *Monopolville: L'Entreprise, l'Etat, l'Urbain* (Paris: Mouton).

Castles, S. and Kosack, G. (1973) *Immigrant Workers and Class Structures in Western Europe* (Oxford: Oxford University Press).

Ceaux, J., Mazet, P. and Ngo Hong, T. (1979) 'Images et réalités d'un quartier populaire: le cas de Belleville', *Espaces et Sociétés*, 30–1, 71–107.

Charles, G. (1969) 'Besançon: données démographiques, économiques et sociologiques: situation et perspectives', *Revue Géographique de l'Est*, 9, 215–28.

Chatelain, A. (1956) 'La formation de la population lyonnaise. Les courants de migrations au milieu du XXᵉ siècle d'après le fichier électoral', *Revue de Géographie de Lyon*, 31, 199–208.

Chatelain, A. (1969) 'La vie des migrants maçons limousins dans le Vᵉ arrondissement de Paris au début du XXe siècle', *Etudes de la Région Parisienne*, 23, 32–45.

Chatelain, A. (1970) 'Complexité des migrations temporaires et définitives à Paris et dans le Bassin Parisien (XVIIIᵉ–XXᵉ siècles)', *Etudes de la Région Parisienne*, 25, 1–10.

Chatelain, A. (1971) 'L'attraction des trois plus grandes agglomérations françaises: Paris–Lyon–Marseille en 1891', *Annales Démographie Historique*, 27–41.

Chauviré, Y. and Noin, D. (1980) 'Typologie socio-professionnelle de l'agglomération parisienne', *Bulletin, l'Association de Géographes Français*, 467, 51–62.

Chazalette, A. (1980) 'Une ZUP qui vieillit mal', *Economie et Humanisme*, 255, 35–44.

Cheung, C. (1980) 'Contribution à l'étude de l'habitat individuel sur le rive droite de l'agglomération de Bordeaux', *Revue Géographique des Pyrénées et du Sud-Ouest*, 51, 71–84.

Chevalier, L. (1950) *La Formation de la Population Parisienne au XIXᵉ Siècle*, Cahier de l'I.N.E.D. No. 10 (Paris: P.U.F.).

Chevalier, L. (1973) *Labouring Classes and Dangerous Classes in Paris During the First Half of the Nineteenth Century*, trans. F. Jellinek (London: Routledge and Kegan Paul).

Chombart de Lauwe, P. H. et al. (1952) *Paris et l'Agglomération Parisienne*, 2 vols (Paris: P.U.F.).

Clark, J. R. (1977) *Turkish Cologne: The Mental Maps of Migrant Workers in a German City*, Michigan Geographical Publications No. 19.

Clark, W. A. V. and Avery, K. L. (1978) 'Patterns of migration: a macroanalytic case study', in Herbert, D. T. and Johnston, R. J. (eds), *Geography and the Urban Environment: Progress in Research and Applications, Vol. 1*, pp. 135–96 (Chichester: John Wiley).

Claval, P. (1981) *La Logique des Villes: Essai d'Urbanologie* (Paris: Litec).

Clerc, P. (1964) 'Vue rétrospective sur la migration provinciale à Paris', in Pourcher, G., *Le Peuplement de Paris. Origine Régionale. Composition Sociale. Attitudes et Motivations*, Cahier de l'I.N.E.D. No. 43 (Paris: P.U.F.).

Clerc, P. (1967) *Grands Ensembles, Banlieues Nouvelles: Enquête Démographique et Psycho-Sociologique*, Cahier de l'I.N.E.D. No. 49 (Paris: P.U.F.).

Cobb, R. (1980a) *The Streets of Paris* (London: Duckworth).

Cobb, R. (1980b) *Promenades* (Oxford: Oxford University Press).

Coppock, J. T. (ed.) (1977) *Second Homes: Curse or Blessing?* (Oxford: Pergamon).

Coppolani, J. (1977) 'La population de Toulouse en 1975', *Revue Géographique des Pyrénées et du Sud-Ouest*, 48, 9–32.

Corbin, A. (1971) 'Migrations temporaires et société rurale au XIXᵉ siècle: le cas du Limousin', *Revue Historique*, 246, 293–334.

Cortie, C. (1972a) 'Patterns of external migration in Amsterdam classified by location', *Op Grond van Cijfers*, 8, 43–54.

Cortie, C. (1972b) 'Migration within and around Utrecht: a testing of some of

Burgess's hypotheses', *Tijdschrift voor Economische en Sociale Geografie*, **63**, 315–30.

Cosgrove, D. (1982) 'The myth and the stones of Venice: an historical geography of a symbolic landscape', *Journal of Historical Geography*, **8**, 145–69.

Costa, P., Lando, F. and Zanetto, G. (1980) 'Rinnovo urbano e trasformazioni sociali nel centro storico di Venezia', *Sistemi Urbani*, **2**, 385–410.

Crew, D. F. (1979) *Town in the Ruhr: A Social History of Bochum, 1860–1914* (New York: Columbia University Press).

Cribier, F. (1975) 'Retirement migration in France', in Kosiński, L. A. and Prothero, R. M. (eds), *People on the Move: Studies on Internal Migration*, pp. 361–73 (London: Methuen).

Cromar, P. (1980) 'Labour migration and suburban expansion in the north of England: Sheffield in the 1860s and 1870s', in White, P. E. and Woods, R. I. (eds), *The Geographical Impact of Migration*, pp. 129–51 (London: Longman).

Curl, J. S. (1970) *European Cities and Society: A Study of the Influence of Political Climate on Town Design* (London: Leonard Hill).

Dahya, B. (1973) 'Pakistanis in Britain: transients or settlers?', *Race*, **14**, 241–77.

Dalmasso, E. (1978) 'Tertiarization et classes moyennes à Milan', *Villes en Parallèle*, **2**, 169–76.

Damais, J. P. (1974) 'Essai d'approche socio-géographique du problème des logements anciens en milieu urbain: "rénovation" et "réhabilitation" au Havre', *Annales de Géographie*, **83**, 284–318.

Dandri, G. (1978) 'The evolution of the Italian housing situation from 1951 to 1978', *Review of the Economic conditions in Italy*, **32**, 137–52.

Dang, R. (1978) 'Qui habite les quartiers de Lille-Roubaix-Tourcoing?', *Profils de l'Economie Nord – Pas-de-Calais*, **3**.

Darroch, A. G. and Marston, W. G. (1971) 'The social class basis of ethnic residential segregation: the Canadian case', *American Journal of Sociology*, **77**, 491–510.

David, J. (1971) 'L'évolution d'une commune suburbaine de l'agglomération grenobloise', *Revue de Géographie Alpine*, **59**, 141–8.

Davies, M. L. (1973) 'The role of land policy in the expansion of a city: the case of Stockholm', *Tijdschrift voor Economische en Sociale Geografie*, **64**, 245–50.

Davies, M. L. (1976) 'The social and economic impact of suburban expansion in the Stockholm region', *Tijdschrift voor Economische en Sociale Geografie*, **67**, 95–101.

Davies, W. K. D. and Lewis, G. J. (1973) 'The urban dimensions of Leicester, England', in Clark, B. D. and Gleave, M. B. (eds), *Social Patterns in Cities*, pp. 71–86, Special Publication No. 5, Institute of British Geographers.

Davis, K. (1955) 'The origin and growth of urbanization in the world', *American Journal of Sociology*, **60**, 429–37.

De Bertier de Sauvigny, G. (1977) *Nouvelle Histoire de Paris: La Restauration, 1815–1830* (Paris: Hachette).

Deffontaines, P. (1966) 'L'inmigration française en Catalogne et à Barcelone', *Estudios Geográficos*, **27**, 561–78.

De Lannoy, W. (1975) 'Residential segregation of foreigners in Brussels', *Bulletin, Société Belge d'Etudes Géographiques*, **44**, 215–38.

De Lannoy, W. (1977) 'De woonsegregatie van sociaal-economische groepen in de Brusselse agglomeratie', *Bevolking en Gezin*, **2**, 195–211.

De Lannoy, W. (1978) *Sociaal-Geografische Atlas van Brussel-Hoofdstad/Atlas Socio-Géographique de Bruxelles-Capitale*, Studies en Documenten 11, Centrum voor Bevolkings- en Gezinsstudiën, Ministerie van Volksgezondheid en van het Gezin (Antwerp: De Sikkel).

Den Draak, J. (1966) 'De woonfunctie van de Utrechtse binnenstad', *Tijdschrift voor Economische en Sociale Geografie*, 57, 179–85.

Den Draak, J. (1967) 'The diminishing residential function of the inner city', in University of Amsterdam, Sociographical Department, *Urban Core and Inner City*, pp. 213–25 (Leiden: E. J. Brill).

Deneux, J-F. (1981) 'Les îlots de la couronne de Paris. Approche méthodologique du contenu social', *Villes en Parallèle*, 4, 43–59.

Deplancke, M. and Vandermotten, C. (1978) 'Croissance urbaine et structure foncière péri-urbaine. Le cas de Bruxelles au XIXme siècle', *Revue Belge de Géographie*, 102, 43–50.

De Smidt, M. (1979) 'Hoe buitenlandse werknemers in Utrecht worden geïsoleerd', *Bouw*, 14, 23–5.

De Terán, M. (1961) 'El desarrollo espacial de Madrid a partir de 1868', *Estudios Geográficos*, 84–5, 599–615.

Dickinson, R. E. (1961) *The West European City: A Geographical Interpretation* (2nd edn) (London: Routledge and Kegan Paul).

Dion, R-M. (1974) 'Effets des processus volontaristes dans la formation d'une région urbaine: Nancy et les plans d'aménagement et d'extension dans la première moitié du XXe siècle', *Revue Géographique de l'Est*, 14, 245–312.

Döpp, W. (1968) *Die Altstadt Neapels: Entwicklung und Struktur*, Marburger Geographische Schriften No. 37.

Doré, A. (1972) 'Le peuplement d'un quartier neuf de Dijon: la Fontaine d'Ouche', *Revue de l'Economie du Centre-Est*, 14, 204–18.

Drewe, P. et al. (1975) 'Segregation in Rotterdam: an explorative study on theory, data and policy', *Tijdschrift voor Economische en Sociale Geografie*, 66, 204–16.

Dubesset, P. (1971) 'La population tuberculeuse dans l'agglomération lyonnaise', *Revue de Géographie de Lyon*, 46, 91–116.

Dubois, M. H. (1980) 'Une grande opération urbaine sous la second empire: le percement de la rue Impériale (rue de la République)', *Bulletin, Société de Geographie de Marseille*, 84, 47–56.

Duchac, R. et al. (1977) 'Facteurs urbains de l'adaptation des immigrés maghrébins: étude comparative de trois quartiers de Marseille', in *Les immigrés du Maghreb: Etude sur l'Adaptation en Milieu Urbain*, Cahier de l'I.N.E.D. No. 79, pp. 1–132 (Paris: P.U.F.).

Duclaud-Williams, R. H. (1978) *The Politics of Housing in Britain and France* (London: Heinemann).

Duncan, O. D. and Duncan, B. (1955) 'Residential distribution and occupational stratification', *American Journal of Sociology*, 60, 493–503.

Dupré, M. and Laferrère, M. (1977) 'Les immigrés maghrébins dans les établissements chimiques et métallurgiques de l'agglomération lyonnaise', in *Les Immigrés du Maghreb: Etudes sur l'Adaptation en Milieu Urbain*, Cahier de l'I.N.E.D. No. 79, pp. 287–326 (Paris: P.U.F.).

Dyer, C. (1969) 'Mobilité géographique de la population de Caen, 1911–1966', *Etudes Normandes*, 73, 11–15.

El Gharbaoui, A. (1969) 'Le prolétariat maghrébin immigré dans la banlieue nord-ouest de Paris', *Bulletin Economique et Social du Maroc*, 31, 25–49.

El Gharbaoui, A. (1971) 'Les travailleurs maghrébins immigrés dans la banlieue nord-ouest de Paris', *Revue de Géographie du Maroc*, 19, 3–56.

Elkins, T. H. (1968) *Germany* (London: Chatto and Windus).

Elkins, T. H. (1973) *The Urban Explosion* (London: Macmillan).

Erminero, C. and Peruzzi, W. (1962) 'Brevi osservazioni sull'immissione dei baraccati in un quartiere periferico di Verona', in Centro di Ricerche Industriali e Sociali di Torino, *Immigrazione e Industria*, pp. 353–66 (Milan: Edizioni di Comunità).

Esteva Fabregat, C. (1975) 'Ethnicity, social class and acculturation of immigrants in Barcelona', *Ethnologia Europaea*, **8**, 23–43.

Esteva Fabregat, C. (1977) 'Aculturació lingüística d'immigrats a Barcelona', in Climent, E. (ed.), *Treballs de Sociolingüística Catalana*, *1*, pp. 81–116 (Valencia: Impremta Nàcher).

Ettlin, W. and Hafen, W. (1978) 'Die Breite: Nutzung, Baustruktur und Grundeigentumsverhältnisse eines Basler Quartiers', *Regio Basiliensis*, **19**, 2–14.

Evenson, N. (1979) *Paris: A Century of Change, 1878–1978* (New Haven: Yale University Press).

Faccioli, M. (1978) 'Evoluzione storica dei processi di urbanizzazione nel quadrante sud-occidentale dell'area di Roma', *Notiziario di Geografia Economica*, **8**, 1–29.

Faure, A. (1978) 'Classe malpropre, classe dangereuse? Quelques remarques à propos des chiffoniers parisiens au XIXe siècle et de leurs cités', in Murard, L. and Zylberman, P. (eds), *L'Haleine des Faubourgs*, pp. 79–102 (Fontenay-sous-Bois: Recherches).

Federici, N. (1964) 'Aspetti sociali della mortalità infantile a Roma', *Statistica*, **24**, 79–94.

Fédou, R. (1980) 'Personnalité de la "Presqu'île" dans le Lyon médiéval', in *Lyon et l'Europe: Hommes et Sociétés. Mélanges d'Histoire Offerts à Richard Gascon*, Vol. 1, pp. 237–49 (Lyon: Presses Universitaires de Lyon).

Ferras, R. (1977a) *Barcelone: Croissance d'une Métropole* (Paris: Anthropos).

Ferras, R. (1977b) " 'Les autres catalans": le prolétariat urbain à Barcelone', *Revue Géographique des Pyrénées et du Sud-Ouest*, **48**, 191–8.

Ferras, R. (1978) 'Espace social et espace urbain à Barcelone', *Villes en Parallèle*, **2**, 177–86.

Fofi, G. (1970) 'Immigrants to Turin', in Jansen, C. J. (ed.), *Readings in the Sociology of Migration*, pp. 269–84 (Oxford: Pergamon).

Fontaine, C. (1977) 'Bruxelles: la bataille de la Marolle', *Urbanisme*, 162–3, 120–1.

Francescato, D. and Mebane, W. (1973) 'How citizens view two great cities: Milan and Rome', in Downs, R. M. and Stea, D. (eds), *Image and Environment: Cognitive Mapping and Spatial Behavior*, pp. 131–47 (Chicago: Aldine).

Freyssenet, M., Regazzola, T. and Retel, J. (1971) *Ségrégation Sociale et Déplacements Sociaux dans l'Agglomération Parisienne de 1954 à 1968* (Paris: Centre de Sociologie Urbaine).

Gabert, P. (1958) 'L'immigration italienne à Turin', *Bulletin, l'Association de Géographes Français*, 276/277, 30–45.

Gächter, E. (1974) *Die Demographisch-Sozioökonomische Struktur der Stadt Bern in Quartierweiser Gliederung*, Berner Beiträge zur Stadt- und Regionalforschung, No. 1.

Gächter, E. (1978) 'Untersuchungen zur kleinräumigen Bevölkerungs-, Wohn- und Arbeitsplatzstruktur der Stadt Bern', *Geographica Helvetica*, **33**, 1–16.

Gago Llorente, V. (1979) 'La oferta de nuevas viviendas en el área metropolitana de Madrid', *Información Comercial Española*, **548**, 109–27.

Galtung, J. (1971) *Members of Two Worlds: A Development Study of Three Villages in Western Sicily* (Oslo: Universitetsforlaget).

Gans, P. (1979) 'Das Entropiekonzept zur Ermittlung räumlicher Eigenschaften von innerstädtischen Wanderungsverflechtungen am Beispiel Ludwigshafen/Rhein', *Erdkunde*, **33**, 103–13.

Ganser, K. (1966) *Sozialgeographische Gliederung der Stadt München aufgrund der Verhaltensweisen der Bevölkerung bei Politischen Wahlen*, Münchner Geographische Hefte No. 28.

Ganser, K. (1967) 'Mobility, a feature of the residential function of the inner city', in University of Amsterdam, Sociographical Department, *Urban Core and Inner City*, pp. 210–12 (Leiden: E. J. Brill).

Garbagnati, B. (1962) 'L'immigrazione nei comuni della "Cintura di Torino": condizioni, problemi e conseguenze dell'imigrazione in Venaria Reale', in Centro di Ricerche Industriali e Sociali di Torino, *Immigrazione e Industria*, pp. 287–94 (Milan: Edizioni di Comunità).

García, A. A. (1977) 'El cinturón humano de Madrid', *Revista Internacional de Sociologia*, 22, 289–93.

Gaspar, J. (1976) 'A dinâmica funcional do centro de Lisboa', *Finisterra*, 11, 37–150.

Gastelaars, R. V. E. and Beek, W. F. (1972) 'Ecologische differentiatie binnen Amsterdam: een factor-analytische benadering', *Tijdschrift voor Economische en Sociale Geografie*, 63, 62–78.

Gastelaars, R. V. E. and Cortie, C. (1973) 'Migration from Amsterdam: a discussion of the movement of employment and residential population away from the municipality of Amsterdam', *Tijdschrift voor Economische en Sociale Geografie*, 64, 206–17.

Gastelaars, R. V. E., Heinemeyer, W. F. and De-Wijs Mulkens, E. (1971) 'Amsterdammers, hun woonplaats en beroepsniveau. Het dilemma Burgess-Hoyt' *Geografisch Tijdschrift*, 5, 409–21.

Gehmacher, E. (1974) 'A cost-benefit analysis of alternative immigration policies for Vienna', *International Migration Review*, 8, 165–80.

Geiger, F. (1975) 'Zur Konzentration von Gastarbeitern in alten Dorfkernen: Fallstudie aus dem Verdichtungsraum Stuttgart', *Geographische Rundschau*, 2, 61–71.

Gentileschi, M. L. (1977) 'La collettività italiana di Stoccarda', *Studi Emigrazione*, 47, 247–81.

Gentileschi, M. L. (1978) 'I lavoratori italiani indipendenti a Stoccarda', *Studi Emigrazione*, 51, 325–60.

George, P. (1967) 'Un difficile problème d'aménagement urbain: l'évolution des noyaux historiques – centres de villes', in Sporck, J. A. and Schoumaker, B. (eds), *Mélanges de Géographie Physique, Humaine, Economique, Appliquée Offerts à M. Omer Tulippe*, Vol. II, pp. 287–92 (Gembloux: J. Duculot).

Georgulas, N. and Markopoulou, A. (1977) 'Mixed uses in Athens urban area', *Built Environment Quarterly*, 3, 73–8.

Ghirardo, D. A. (1980) 'Mezzanotte in the Mezzogiorno: the urban problems of Southern Italy', *Journal of Urban History*, 6, 221–30.

Giannoni, M. (1976) 'Struttura sociale e demografica di Roma', *Studi Romani*, 24, 510–20.

Ginatempo, N. and Cammarota, A. (1977) 'Land and social conflict in the cities of Southern Italy: an analysis of the housing question in Messina', in Harloe, M. (ed.), *Captive Cities: Studies in the Political Economy of Cities and Regions*, pp. 111–22 (London: John Wiley).

Gisser, R. and Kaufmann, A. (1972) 'Sozialstruktur Wien 1961', *Der Aufbau*, 27, 242–84.

Gokalp, C. and Lamy, M-L. (1977) 'L'immigration maghrébine dans une commune industrielle de l'agglomération parisienne: Gennevilliers', in *Les Immigrés du Maghreb: Etudes sur l'Adaptation en Milieu Urbain*, Cahier de l'I.N.E.D. No. 79, pp. 327–404 (Paris: P.U.F.).

Goursolas, J-M. (1980) 'New towns in the Paris metropolitan area: an analytic survey of the experience, 1965–1979', *International Journal of Urban and Regional Research*, 4, 405–21.

Gozalvez-Perez, V. (1977) 'Distribución espacial de los inmigrantes', *Cuadernos de Geografía – Universidad Valencia*, 20, 87–95.

Grigg, D. B. (1980) 'Migration and overpopulation', in White, P. E. and Woods, R. I. (eds), *The Geographical Impact of Migration*, pp. 60–83 (London: Longman).

Grimmeau, J. P. and David-Valcke, A. (1978) 'Les cadres étrangers à Bruxelles', *Revue Belge de Géographie*, 102, 33–41.

Grönholm, L. (1960) 'The ecology of social disorganization in Helsinki', *Acta Sociologica*, 5, 31–41.

Grötzbach, E. (1978) 'Die Innenstadt von Hannover – Entwicklung und Struktur der City', *Jahrbuch der Geographischen Gesellschaft zu Hannover*, 185–201.

Guibourdenche, H. and Joly, J. (1979) 'Changement social et structures spatiales dans l'agglomération et les quartiers de Grenoble (1968–1975)', *Revue de Géographie Alpine*, 67, 257–79.

Guidicini, P. (1962) 'Note su modificazioni nella morfologia e nella struttura sociale in un quartiere urbano periferico destinatario di massimi flussi immigratori', in Centro di Ricerche Industriali e Sociali di Torino, *Immigrazione e Industria*, pp. 367–86 (Milan: Edizioni di Comunità).

Guillaume, P. (1972) *La Population de Bordeaux au XIXᵉ Siècle* (Paris: Armand Colin).

Guillon, M. (1974) 'Les rapatriés d'Algérie dans la région parisienne', *Annales de Géographie*, 83, 644–75.

Hajdu, J. G. (1978) 'The German city today: crosscurrents of readjustment and change', *Geography*, 63, 23–30.

Halsey, A. H. (1978) *Change in British Society* (Oxford: Oxford University Press).

Hammarström, I. (1979) 'Urban growth and building fluctuations. Stockholm 1860–1920', in Hammarström, I. and Hall, T. (eds), *Growth and Transformation of the Modern City*, pp. 29–47 (Stockholm: Swedish Council for Building Research).

Harts, J. J. (1978) 'Kleine gemeenten in een stadsgewest: een empirische studie van suburbanisatie van bevolking rond Utrecht', *Geografisch Tijdschrift*, 12, 351–61.

Haussmann, E. (1893) *Grands Travaux de Paris, 1853–1870* (3rd edn); reprinted 1979, 2 vols (Paris: Guy Didier).

Heinemeyer, W. F. (1968) 'De Amsterdamse binnenstad als centrum van attractie', in Heinemeyer, W. F., Van Hulten, M. H. M. and De Vries Reilingh, H. D. (eds), *Het Centrum van Amsterdam: Een Sociografische Studie*, pp. 9–68 (Amsterdam: Polak and Van Gennep).

Heinemeyer, W. F. and Gastelaars, R. V. E. (1971) 'Urban core and inner city in Amsterdam: processes of change in spatial structure', *Tijdschrift voor Economische en Sociale Geografie*, 62, 207–16.

Helvig, M. (1976) 'Den indre differensiering i Bergen sentrum og konsekvenser for bosettingen', *Norsk Geografisk Tidsskrift*, 30, 139–56.

Herbert, D. T. (1972) *Urban Geography: A Social Perspective* (Newton Abbot: David and Charles).

Herzog, A. N., Levy, L. and Verdonck, A. (1977) 'Some ecological factors associated with health and social adaptation in the city of Rotterdam', *Urban Ecology*, 2, 205–34.

Holzmann, G. (1971) 'Die Zuwanderung nach Wien', *Zeitschrift für Wirtschaftsgeographie*, 15, 117–19.

Holzner, L. (1970) 'The role of history and tradition in the urban geography of West

Germany', *Annals, Association of American Geographers*, **60**, 315–39.

Hook, J. (1979) *Siena: A City and its History* (London: Hamish Hamilton).

Horne, A. (1965) *The Fall of Paris: The Siege and the Commune, 1870–71* (London: Macmillan).

Howard, E. (1902) *Garden Cities of Tomorrow* (London: Swann Sonnenschein).

Huet, B. et al. (1975) 'Les centres historiques face au développement', *Architecture d'Aujourd'hui*, **46**, 1–74.

Hyldtoft, O. (1979) 'From fortified town to modern metropolis. Copenhagen 1840–1914', in Hammarström, I. and Hall, T. (eds), *Growth and Transformation of the Modern City*, pp. 49–58 (Stockholm: Swedish Council for Building Research).

Ioli Gigante, A. (1980) *Messina* (Rome: Laterza).

Jackson, J. H. (1981) 'Overcrowding and family life: working-class families and the housing crisis in late nineteenth-century Duisburg', in Evans, R. J. and Lee, W. R. (eds), *The German Family*, pp. 194–220 (London: Croom Helm).

Jackson, J. H. (1982) 'Migration in Duisburg, 1867–1890: occupational and familial contexts', *Journal of Urban History*, **8**, 235–70.

Jacquemet, G. (1975) 'Belleville aux XIXe et XXe siècles: une méthode d'analyse de la croissance urbaine à Paris', *Annales: Economies, Sociétés, Civilisations*, **30**, 819 43.

Jardel, J. P. (1967) 'La Bocca (Cannes). Géographie sociale', *Recherches Régionales*, **7**, 1–44.

Jobse, R. B. (1974) 'Bevolkingssamenstelling en -ontwikkeling in grootstedelijke nieuwbouwwijken: achtergronden en consequenties', *Stedebouw en Volkshuisvesting*, **55**, 354–66.

Johnston, R. J. (1971) *Urban Residential Patterns* (London: Bell).

Johnston, R. J. (1978) *Multivariate Statistical Analysis in Geography* (London: Longman).

Johnston, R. J. (1980a) *City and Society: An Outline for Urban Geography* (Harmondsworth: Penguin).

Johnston, R. J. (1980b) 'Xenophobia and referenda: an example of the exploratory use of ecological regression', *Espace Géographique*, **9**, 73–80.

Johnston, R. J. and White, P. E. (1977) 'Reactions to foreign workers in Switzerland: an essay in electoral geography', *Tijdschrift voor Economische en Sociale Geografie*, **67**, 341–54.

Joly, J. (1978) 'Structure sociale de l'agglomération et des quartiers de Grenoble', *Revue de Géographie Alpine*, **66**, 385–407.

Joly, J. (1979) 'Structure sociale des quartiers de Grenoble. Géographie des "couches moyennes"', *Revue de Géographie Alpine*, **67**, 5–28.

Jones, P. C. (1982) *The Segregation and Integration of Provincial and International Migrants in Lyon, France, 1962–1975*, unpublished Ph.D. thesis, University of Sheffield.

Josse, R. (1968) 'Routes, urbanisation et restructuration urbaine: un exemple dans la banlieue Nord de Paris', *Vie Urbaine*, **4**, 241–86.

Kain, R. (1981) 'Conservation planning in France: policy and practice in the Marais, Paris', in Kain, R. (ed.), *Planning for Conservation*, pp. 199–233 (London: Mansell).

Kaufmann, A. et al. (1978) *Sozialräumliche Gliederung der Österreichischen Grossstadtregionen. Kleinräumige Analyse der Wohnverhältnisse in den Stadtregionen Wien, Graz, Linz, Salzburg, Innsbruck, Klagenfurt*, Publikationen des Instituts für Stadtforschung No. 58 (Vienna: Jugend und Volk).

Kesteloot, C. (1980) *De Ruimtelijke Sociale Struktuur van Brussel-Hoofdstad*, Acta Geographica Lovaniensia Vol. 19.

Keyfitz, N. (1980) 'Do cities grow by natural increase or by migration?', *Geographical Analysis*, 12, 142–56.

Killisch, W. F. (1979) *Räumliche Mobilität*, Kieler Geographische Schriften No. 49 (Kiel: Geographischen Institut der Universität Kiel).

King, J. C. (1971) 'Housing in Spain', *Town Planning Review*, 42, 381–403.

King, R. (1976) 'The evolution of international labour migration concerning the EEC', *Tijdschrift voor Economische en Sociale Geografie*, 67, 66–82.

Kinsey, J. (1979) 'The Algerian movement to Greater Marseille', *Geography*, 64, 338–41.

Klamroth, H-B. (1974) 'Der Einsatz von Gastarbeitern im Ballungsraum Nürnberg', *Nürnberger Wirtschafts- und Sozialgeographische Arbeiten*, 18, 139–61.

Kouvelis, K. (1979) 'Description d'une nouvelle stratégie de rénovation – la rénovation avec participation de la population: le cas du quartier Kreuzberg à Berlin', *Espaces et Sociétés*, 30–1, 109–42.

Kreth, R. (1977) 'Sozialräumliche Gliederung von Mainz', *Geographische Rundschau*, 29, 142–9.

Kreuzaler, E. (1977) 'The Federal Republic of Germany as host country to foreign guestworkers and their dependents', *International Migration*, 15, 138–42.

Lacave, M. (1980) 'Stratégie d'expropriation et haussmannisation: l'exemple de Montpellier', *Annales: Economies, Sociétés, Civilizations*, 35, 1011–25.

Lamy, B. (1967) 'The use of the inner city of Paris and social stratification', in University of Amsterdam, Sociographical Department, *Urban Core and Inner City*, pp. 356–67 (Leiden: E. J. Brill).

Lando, F. (1978) 'La struttura socio-economica veneziana: un tentativo d'analisi', *Rivista Veneta*, 12, 125–40.

Laquerbe, J. (1967) 'La population des quartiers historiques de Montpellier', *l'Economie Méridionale*, 60.

Laurant, A. and Declercq-Tijtgat, A. (1978) 'Les migrations internes définitives relatives aux agglomérations de Bruxelles, Liège, Charleroi, Verviers et Namur', *Population et Famille*, 45. 73–132.

Laux, H-D. (1983) 'Structural and regional differences of natural population growth in German cities, 1880–1905', *Erdkunde*, 37, 22–33.

Lawrence, D. H. (1944) *Sea and Sardinia* (Harmondsworth: Penguin).

Ledrut, R. (1977) *L'Espace en Question ou le Nouveau Monde Urbain* (Paris: Anthropos).

Lemay, C. (1970) 'Les résultats de la rénovation urbaine d'un quartier du XIIIᵉ arrondissement de Paris', *Revue de Géographie de Montréal*, 24, 55–64.

Lerch, S. et al. (1972) 'Genève 1900–1970: évolution de l'habitat collectif par rapport au processus d'urbanisation', *Architecture d'Aujourd'hui*, 161, 16–20.

Leroy, E. (1971) 'La banlieue est de Paris: un sous-développement inéluctable?', *Urbanisme*, 122, 62–6.

Le Roy Ladurie, E. (1981) *Carnival in Romans*, trans. M. Feeney (Harmondsworth: Penguin).

Liang, H-H. (1970) 'Lower-class immigrants in Wilhelmine Berlin', *Central European History*, 3, 94–111.

Lichtenberger, E. (1970) 'The nature of European urbanism', *Geoforum*, 4, 45–62.

Lichtenberger, E. (1972) 'Ökonomische und nichtökonomische Variablen kontinentaleuropäischer Citybildung', *Die Erde*, 103, 216–62.

Lichtenberger, E. (1976) 'The changing nature of European urbanization', in Berry, B. J. L. (ed.), *Urbanization and Counter-Urbanization*, pp. 81–107, Urban Affairs Annual Reviews, Vol. 11 (Beverly Hills: Sage).

Lichtenberger, E. (1977) *Die Wiener Altstadt: Von der Mittelalterlichen Bürgerstadt zur City* (Vienna: Franz Deuticke).

Lieberson, S. (1963) 'The old–new distinction and immigrants in Australia', *American Sociological Review*, **28**, 550–65.

Lindemann, M. (1981) 'Love for hire: the regulation of the wet-nursing business in eighteenth century Hamburg', *Journal of Family History*, **6**, 379–95.

Logan, J. R. (1978) 'Rural–urban migration and working-class consciousness: the Spanish case', *Social Forces*, **56**, 1159–78.

Louckx, F. (1978) 'Linguistic ambivalence of the Brussels indigenous population', *International Journal of the Sociology of Language*, **15**, 53–60.

Lowder, S. (1980) *The Evolution and Identity of Urban Social Areas: The Case of Barcelona*, Occasional Papers Series No. 4, Geography Department, Glasgow University.

Lowenthal, D. and Comitas, L. (1962) 'Emigration and depopulation: some neglected aspects of population geography', *Geographical Review*, **52**, 195–210.

Lusso, G. (1978) 'Distribuzione delle residenze degli operai della FIAT in Torino', *Rivista Geografica Italiana*, **85**, 43–55.

Lyttleton, A. (1979) 'Milan 1880–1922: the city of industrial capitalism', in Brucker, G. (ed.), *People and Communities in the Western World*, Vol. 2, pp. 249–88 (Homewood, Illinois: Dorsey Press).

McClintock, H. and Fox, M. (1971) 'The Bijlmermeer development and the expansion of Amsterdam', *Journal, Royal Town Planning Institute*, **57**, 313–16.

McElrath, D. C. (1962) 'The social areas of Rome: a comparative analysis', *American Sociological Review*, **27**, 376–91.

McElrath, D. C. (1965) 'Urban differentiation: problems and prospects', *Law and Contemporary Problems*, **30**, 103–10.

McKeown, T. (1976) *The Modern Rise of Population* (London: Arnold).

Madge, C. and Willmott, P. (1981) *Inner City Poverty in Paris and London* (London: Routledge and Kegan Paul).

Mallet, F. (1967) 'Le quartier des Halles de Paris', *Annales de Géographie*, **76**, 1–28.

Martinez-Marí, J. M. (1966) 'La inmigración en el área de Barcelona', *Estudios Geográficos*, **27**, 541–6.

Matthiessen, C. W. (1972) 'Befolknings- og boligstrukturen i Københavns kommune belyst ved en principal-component analysis', *Geografisk Tidsskrift*, **71**, 1–19.

Matthiessen, C. W. (1973) 'Syntese af Københavns kommunes befolknings- og boligstruktur', *Geografisk Tidsskrift*, **72**, 57–63.

Matthiessen, C. W. (1976) 'Activity systems of the inner city of Copenhagen', *Geografisk Tidsskrift*, **75**, 70–3.

Maurice, M. and Deloménie, D. (1976) *Mode de Vie et Espaces Sociaux: Processus d'Urbanisation et Differenciation Sociale dans Deux Zones Urbaines de Marseille* (Paris: Mouton).

Meeus, B. (1974) 'De vreemdelingen te Brussel', *Gids op Maatschappelijk Gebied*, **65**, 677–91.

Meeus, B. (1975) 'De immigratie in de Brusselse agglomeratie', *Bevolking en Gezin*, **3**, 421–53.

Mérenne-Schoumaker, B. (1979) 'Les images perçues du centre-ville liégeois', *Bulletin, Société Géographique de Liège*, **15**, 5–27.

Metton, A. and Bertrand, M-J. (1974) 'Les espaces vécus dans une grande agglomération', *l'Espace Géographique*, **3**, 137–46.

Meyer, P. (1968) 'Mulhouse: le poids de l'histoire dans une structure urbaine', *Regio*

Basiliensis, **9**, 93–103.

Mik, G. and Verkoren-Hemelaar, N. (1976) 'Segregation in the Netherlands and Turkish migration: an explorative study of Turkish migrants in Rotterdam and Utrecht', in Abadan-Unat, N. et al. (eds), *Turkish Workers in Europe 1960–1975: A Socio-Economic Reappraisal*, pp. 253–83 (Leiden: E. J. Brill).

Mikkelsen, L., Reis, D. and Pereira Roque, J. (1976) 'La structure des âges de l'agglomération bruxelloise', *Revue Belge de Géographie*, **100**, 49–70.

Mohr, B. and Plattner, N. (1978) 'Demographische Prozesse und sozio-ökonomische Strukturen im suburbanen Raum von Freiburg i. Br.', *Berichte zur Deutschen Landeskunde*, **52**, 49–72.

Mols, R. (1965) 'La mobilité bruxelloise', *Bulletin, Société Belge des Etudes Géographiques*, **34**, 301–34.

Mols, R. (1966) 'La mobilité bruxelloise', *Bulletin, Société Belge des Etudes Géographiques*, **35**, 35–66.

Mols, R. (1968) 'Les Bruxellois, d'où viennent-ils?', *Revue Nouvelle*, **24**, 236–58.

Montes Mieza, J., Paredes Grosso, M. and Villanueva Paredes, A. (1976) 'Los asentamientos chabolistas en Madrid', *Ciudad y Territorio*, **2–3**, 159–72.

Moreau, G. (1967) 'Aspects géographiques et sociologiques d'une commune de la banlieue sud de Paris en 1966: Palaiseau', *Etudes de la Région Parisienne*, **14**, 9–24; **16**, 20–34.

Moreau, G. (1968) 'Dans une commune de la banlieue sud de Paris: essai de sociologie électorale – Palaiseau (1962–1966)', *Etudes de la Région Parisienne*, **17**, 23–9.

Müller, D. O. (1976) 'Luftbilder – Berlin (West) – Charlottenburg und Wilmersdorf zwischen Kaiserdamm und Villenkolonie Grunewald', *Die Erde*, **107**, 89–151.

Müller, D. O. (1978) *Verkehrs- und Wohnstrukturen in Gross-Berlin 1880–1980: Geographische Untersuchungen Ausgewählter Schlüsselgebiete Beiderseits der Ringbahn*, Berliner Geographische Studien, Vol. 4.

Mumford, L. (1961) *The City in History: Its Origins, Its Transformations, and Its Prospects* (London: Secker and Warburg).

Murdie, R. A. (1969) *Factorial Ecology of Metropolitan Toronto, 1951–61*, Research Paper No. 116, Department of Geography, University of Chicago.

Navarro Laguarta, L. (1968) *Mortalidad en la Ciudad de Zaragoza Durante un Siglo (1861–1960)* (Zaragoza: Institución 'Fernando el Católico').

Naylon, J. (1981) 'Barcelona', in Pacione, M. (ed.), *Urban Problems and Planning in the Developed World*, pp. 223–57 (London: Croom Helm).

Nelde, P. N. (1982) 'Conflit ethnoculturel et changement de langue à Bruxelles', in Caudmont, J. (ed.), *Sprachen in Kontakt: Langues en Contact*, pp. 37–57 (Tübingen: Gunter Narr).

Niemeier, G. (1969) 'Braunschweig. Soziale Schichtung und sozialräumliche Gliederung einer Grossstadt', *Raumforschung und Raumordnung*, **27**, 193–209.

Niethammer, L. and Bruggemeier, F. (1978) 'Urbanisation et expérience ouvrière de l'habitat dans l'Allemagne impériale', in Murard, L. and Zylberman, P. (eds), *L'Haleine des Faubourgs*, pp. 103–54 (Fontenay-sous-Bois: Recherches).

Ogden, P. E. (1977) *Foreigners in Paris: Residential Segregation in the Nineteenth and Twentieth Centuries*, Occasional Paper No. 11, Department of Geography, Queen Mary College, University of London.

Ogden, P. E. and Winchester, S. W. C. (1975) 'The residential segregation of provincial migrants in Paris in 1911', *Transactions, Institute of British Geographers*, **65**, 29–44.

Olives Puig, J. (1969) 'Deterioración urbana e inmigración en un barrio del casco antiguo del Barcelona: Sant Cugat del Rec', *Revista de Geografía*, 3, 40–72.

O'Loughlin, J. (1980) 'Distribution and migration of foreigners in German cities', *Geographical Review*, 70, 253–75.

O'Loughlin, J. and Glebe, G. (1981) 'The location of foreigners in Düsseldorf: a causal analysis in a path analytic framework', *Geographische Zeitschrift*, 69, 81–97.

Origo, I. (1963) *The Merchant of Prato: Francesco di Marco Datini* (Harmondsworth: Penguin).

Pahl, R. E. (1965) 'Class and community in English commuter villages', *Sociologia Ruralis*, 5, 5–23.

Pahl, R. E. (1970a) *Patterns of Urban Life* (London: Longman).

Pahl, R. E. (1970b) 'Introduction: minorities in European cities', *New Atlantis*, 2, 5–11.

Pailhé, J. (1978) 'Les transformations de la composition de la ville de Bordeaux', *Revue Géographique des Pyrénées et du Sud-Ouest*, 49, 11–28.

Paine, S. (1974) *Exporting Workers: The Turkish Case* (Cambridge: Cambridge University Press).

Paine, S. (1977) 'The changing role of migrant workers in the advanced capitalist economies of Western Europe', in Griffiths, R. T. (ed.), *Government, Business and Labour in European Capitalism*, pp. 199–225 (London: Europotentials Press).

Panieri, A. (1962) 'Aspetti dell'immigrazione nel comune di Bologna', in Centro di Ricerche Industriali e Sociali di Torino, *Immigrazione e Industria*, pp. 387–93 (Milan: Edizioni di Comunità).

Pappas, P. and Virirakis, J. (1972) 'Residents' activities and journeys to work', *Ekistics*, 33, 492–9.

Papy, L. (1972) 'Réflexions géographiques sur l'histoire de Bordeaux', in Brillet, M. et al. (eds), *La Pensée Géographique Française Contemporaine: Mélanges Offerts à Andre Meynier*, pp. 517–34 (Saint-Brieuc: Presses Universitaires de Bretagne).

Pattyn, M. and Van Eeckhoutte, Y. (1977) 'Ruimtelijke patronen van de sociale, economische en demographische differentiatie in de Westvlaamse steden', *Acta Geographica Louaniensia*, 15, 61–93.

Peach, C. (ed.) (1975) *Urban Social Segregation* (London: Longman).

Pedersen, P. O. and Rasmussen, P, (1973) 'Danske provinsbyers indre differentiering og differentieringen mellem danske provinsbyer', *Geografisk Tidsskrift*, 72, 49–56.

Petersen, V. C. (1976) *Boligområdepraeference i Århus – En Eksperimentel Undersogelse*, Skrifter fra Geografisk Institut ved Aarhus Universitet No. 35.

Piasentin, U., Costa, P. and Foot, D. (1978) 'The Venice problem: an approach by urban modelling', *Regional Studies*, 12, 579–602.

Picheral, H. (1969) 'Mortalité et quartiers à Barcelone', *Bulletin, Société Languedocienne de Géographie*, 92, 299–319.

Pinkney, D. H. (1953) 'Migrations to Paris during the Second Empire', *Journal of Modern History*, 25, 1–12.

Poinard, M. (1972) 'Les Portugais dans le département du Rhône entre 1960 et 1970', *Revue de Géographie de Lyon*, 47, 35–58.

Ponsot, P. (1980) 'Problème de la conjoncture urbaine: le cas de Séville, milieu XVIe–milieu XIXe siècles', in *Lyon et l'Europe: Hommes et Sociétés. Mélanges d'Histoire Offerts à Richard Gascon*, Vol. 2, pp. 211–21 (Lyon: Presses Universitaires de Lyon).

Popenoe, D. (1977) *The Suburban Environment* (Chicago: University of Chicago Press).

Poschwatta, W. (1978) 'Verhaltensorientierte Wohnumfelder. Versuch einer Typisierung am Beispiel der Augsburger Innenstadt', *Geographische Rundschau*, 30, 198–205.

Pourcher, G. (1964) *Le Peuplement de Paris. Origine Régionale. Composition Sociale. Attitudes et Motivations*, Cahier de l'I.N.E.D. No. 43 (Paris; P.U.F.).

Preston, S. H. and Van de Walle, E. (1978) 'Urban French mortality in the nineteenth century', *Population Studies*, 32, 275–97.

Prouvost, J. (1966) 'Le quartier de la Guingette à Roubaix', *Hommes et Terres du Nord*, 1, 52–8.

Pumain, D. (1976) 'La composition socio-professionnelle des villes français: essai de typologie par analyse des correspondances et classification automatique', *Espace Géographique*, 5, 227–38.

Putz, M. C. and Prié, N. (1975) 'Mobilité résidentielle et espace social: deux ensembles résidentiels H.L.M. à Rouen – Marin le Pigny et Les Sapins', *Cahiers Géographiques de Rouen*, 3, 43–61.

Pyle, G. F. and Rees, P. H. (1971) 'Modelling patterns of death and disease in Chicago', *Economic Geography*, 47, 475–88.

Råberg, M. (1979) 'The development of Stockholm since the seventeenth century', in Hammarström, I. and Hall, T. (eds), *Growth and Transformation of the Modern City*, pp. 13–26 (Stockholm: Swedish Council for Building Research).

Radford, J. P. (1979) 'Testing the model of the pre-industrial city: the case of antebellum Charleston, South Carolina', *Transactions, Institute of British Geographers*, 4, 392–410.

Ralite, J-C. (1969) 'Ville nouvelle de Lille-Est', *Urbanisme*, 114, 44–9.

Ranger, J. (1977) 'Droite et gauche dans les élections à Paris (1965–1977): le partage d'un territoire', *Revue Française de Science Politique*, 27, 789–819.

Rapoport, A. (1966) 'Some aspects of urban renewal in France', *Town Planning Review*, 37, 217–27.

Rapoport, A. (1969) 'Housing and housing densities in France', *Town Planning Review*, 39, 341–54.

Rasmussen, T. F. (1966) *Storbyutvikling og Arbeidsreiser. En Undersøkelse av Pendling, Befolkningsutvikling. Naeringsliv og Urbanisiering i Oslo-Området*, Samfunnsøkonomiske Studier 18 (Oslo: Statistisk Sentralbyrå).

Regni, B. and Sennato, M. (1973) 'Appunti sulle trasformazioni morfologiche della città di Roma dai programmi napoleonici al 1930', *L'Universo*, 53, 897–924.

Rein, D. B. (1982) 'Une attitude allemande face à l'évolution démographique', *Population*, 37, 113–30.

Rex, J. A. and Moore, R. (1967) *Race, Community and Conflict: A Study of Sparkbrook* (Oxford: Oxford University Press).

Ricci, G. (1980) *Bologna* (Rome: Laterza).

Riquet, P. (1960) 'Stuttgart. Reconstruction ou esquisse d'une nouvelle ville', *Annales de Géographie*, 69, 124–34.

Riquet, P. (1978) 'Clivages sociaux au sein des espaces urbanisés an Allemagne Fédérale', *Bulletin, l'Association de Géographes Français*, 444, 13–21.

Rist, R. C. (1978) *Guestworkers in Germany: The Prospects for Pluralism* (New York: Praeger).

Robson, B. T. (1969) *Urban Analysis* (Cambridge: Cambridge University Press).

Robson, B. T. (1975) *Urban Social Areas* (London: Oxford University Press).

Robson, B. T. (1979) 'Housing, empiricism and the state', in Herbert, D. T. and Smith, D. M. (eds), *Social Problems and the City: Geographical Perspectives*, pp. 66–83 (Oxford: Oxford University Press).

Rochefort, R. (1970) 'Grands ensembles et mutations des banlieues lyonnaises', *Revue de Géographie de Lyon*, **45**, 201–14.

Rochefort, R. (1977) 'Les enfants et adolescents dans l'agglomération lyonnaise en 1975: disparités et segrégations', *Revue de Géographie de Lyon*, **52**, 319–37.

Rochefort, R. et al. (1977) 'Les familles maghrébines dans la communauté urbaine de Lyon', in *Les Immigrés du Maghreb: Etudes sur l'Adaptation en Milieu Urbain*, Cahier de l'I.N.E.D. No. 79, pp. 133–237 (Paris: P.U.F.)

Rollet, C. (1982) 'Nourrices et nourrissons dans le département de la Seine et en France de 1880 à 1940', *Population*, **37**, 573–604.

Roncayolo, M. (1972) 'La division sociale de l'espace urbain: méthodes et procédés d'analyse', *Bulletin, l'Association de Géographes Français*, 395–6, 5–20.

Ronzon, J. (1979) 'Une exemple de ségrégation spatiale: la disparité dans la répartition scolaire des enfants de travailleurs immigrés dans la région stéphanoise', *Revue de Géographie de Lyon*, **54**, 127–57.

Roseman, C. C. (1971) 'Migration as a spatial and temporal process', *Annals, Association of American Geographers*, **61**, 589–98.

Rossi, D. (1959) *Aspetti dello Sviluppo Demografico ed Edilizio di Roma*, Istituto di Demografia dell'Università di Roma.

Russac, J-M. (1968) 'Réflexions sur la restructuration des centres urbains', *Urbanisme*, 106, 19–25.

Saint-Raymond, O. (1979) 'Problématique de l'évolution des quartiers anciens: contribution du cas de Toulouse', *Espaces et Sociétés*, 30–1, 57–69.

Salcedo, J. (1977a) *Madrid Culpable: Sobre el Espacio y la Población en las Ciencias Sociales* (Madrid: Tecnos).

Salcedo, J. (1977b) 'Segregación "dirigida" y pautas de asentamiento en el municipio de Madrid', *Revista Internacional de Sociologia*, **24**, 523–42.

Salgueiro, T. B. (1977) 'Bairros clandestinos na periferia de Lisboa', *Finisterra*, **12**, 28–55.

Sarracco, F. (1972) 'I quartieri geografici della città di Prato', *Rivista Geografica Italiana*, **79**, 185–207.

Sauberer, M. and Cserjan, K. (1972) 'Sozialräumliche Gliederung Wien 1961: Ergebnisse einer Faktorenanalyse', *Der Aufbau*, **27**, 284–306.

Saviranta, J. (1970) 'Der Einpendelverkehr von Turku', *Fennia*, 100/4.

Sbragia, A. M. (1979) 'Milan and public housing policy: a case of municipal initiative', in Romanos, M. C. (ed.), *Western European Cities in Crisis*, pp. 135–51 (Lexington, Mass.: Lexington Books).

Schaffer, F. (1972) 'Tendenzen städtischer Wanderung', *Mitteilungen, Geographische Gesellschaft in München*, **57**, 127–58.

Schenk, W. (1975) 'Ausländer, insbesondere ausländische Arbeitnehmer, in der Altstadt von Nürnberg', *Nürnberger Wirtschafts- und Sozial Geographische Arbeiten*, **24**, 221–34.

Schinz, A. (1968) 'Die Stadterneuerung in Berlin', *Raumforschung und Raumordnung*, **26**, 10–16.

Schnapper, D. J. (1976) 'Tradition culturelle et appartenance sociale: émigrés italiens et migrants français dans la région parisienne', *Revue Française de Sociologie*, **17**, 485–98.

Schnore, L. F. (1965) *The Urban Scene* (New York: Free Press).

Schorske, C. E. (1980) *Fin-de-Siècle Vienna: Politics and Culture* (London: Weidenfeld and Nicolson).

Schulz, P. (1975) 'Turks and Yugoslavs: guests or new Berliners?', *International Migration*, 13, 53–9.

Seger, M. (1972) 'Sozialgeographische Untersuchungen im Vorfeld von Wien', *Mitteilungen, Österreichischen Geographischen Gesellschaft*, 114, 291–323.

Selva, E. M. B. (1966) 'La condición social de los inmigrantes', *Estudios Geográficos*, 27, 547–60.

Sewell, J. H. (1976) 'Social mobility in a nineteenth-century European city: some findings and implications', *Journal of Interdisciplinary History*, 7, 217–33.

Sharlin, A. (1978) 'Natural decrease in early modern cities: a reconsideration', *Past and Present*, 79, 126–38.

Shaw, P., Halls, R. and Marlow, M. (1970) 'Functioning areas of the inner zone of Aarhus (Denmark)', *Journal, Durham University Geographical Society*, 12, 18–34.

Shevky, E. and Bell, W. (1955) *Social Area Analysis* (Stanford: Stanford University Press).

Short, J. R. (1978) 'Residential mobility', *Progress in Human Geography*, 2, 418–47.

Sick, W. D. (1979) 'Die innerstädtische Mobilität im Freiburg/Breisgau', *Stuttgarter Geographische Studien*, 93, 257–66.

Sidenbladh, G. (1975) 'Stockholm: three hundred years of planning', in Eldredge, H. W. (ed.), *World Capitals: Towards Guided Urbanization*, pp. 25–54 (Garden City, N.Y.: Anchor/Doubleday).

Sijbrandij, F. N. J. (1974) 'Stadterneuerung in Berlin am Beispiel Neukölln-Rollbergstrasse. Nachbetrachtung über ein soziographisches Fachgutachten', *Geographische Rundschau*, 5, 202–14.

Simmons, J. W. (1968) 'Changing residence in the city: a review of intra-urban mobility', *Geographical Review*, 58, 622–51.

Simon, G. (1977) 'Les Tunisiens dans l'agglomération lyonnaise', in *Les Immigrés du Maghreb: Etudes sur l'Adaptation en Milieu Urbain*, Cahier de l'I.N.E.D. No. 79, pp. 239–86 (Paris: P.U.F.).

Sjoberg, G. (1960) *The Pre-Industrial City* (Glencoe: Free Press).

Sola-Morales Rubió, M. D. (1970) 'Factorialización de características de un área suburbana', *Revista de Geografía*, 2, 159–86.

Sostres, J. M. (1966) 'Aspectos de la asimilación cultural de los inmigrados', *Estudios Geográficos*, 27, 607–24.

Soubeyroux, J. (1978) *Pauperisme et Rapports Sociaux à Madrid au XVIIIeme Siècle*, 2 vols (Lille: Université de Lille III).

Sporck, J. A. (1966) 'Evolution de la population liégeoise de 1947 à 1963 et sa répartition', *Bulletin, Société Géographique de Liège*, 2, 35–59.

Sprengel, U. (1978) 'Zur sozialräumlichen Differenzierung Hannovers – eine Skizze auf statistischer Grundlage', *Jahrbuch der Geographischen Gesellschaft zu Hannover*, pp. 125–47.

Steinberg, H. G. (1978) *Bevölkerungsentwicklung des Ruhrgebietes im 19. und 20. Jahrhundert*, Düsseldorfer Geographische Schriften 11.

Stephenson, G. V. (1972) 'Cultural regionalism and the unitary state idea in Belgium', *Geographical Review*, 62, 501–23.

Sutcliffe, A. (1970) *The Autumn of Central Paris: The Defeat of Town Planning, 1850–1970* (London: Edward Arnold).

Sutcliffe, A. (1981) *Towards the Planned City: Germany, Britain, the United States and France, 1780–1914* (Oxford: Blackwell).

Sweetser, F. L. (1965a) 'Factor structure as ecological structure in Helsinki and

Boston', *Acta Sociologica*, **8**, 205–25.

Sweetser, F. L. (1965b) 'Factorial ecology: Helsinki 1960', *Demography*, **2**, 372–85.

Talamo, M. (1962) 'L'inserimento socio-urbanistico degli immigrati meridionali a Torino', in Centro di Ricerche Industriali e Sociali di Torino, *Immigrazione e Industria*, pp. 185–219 (Milan: Edizioni di Comunità).

Taubmann, W. (1969) 'Die Innenstadt von Århus, I. Innere Gliederung aufgrund der Flächennutzung', *Kulturgeografi*, **110**, 333–66.

Thorns, D. C. (1973) *Suburbia* (St Albans: Granada).

Toesca, D. and Trojani, M-J. (1977) 'Le quartier Malausséna à Nice', *Recherches Régionales*, **17**, 1–43.

Traband, G. (1978) 'La ville comme "oeuvre" et la ville comme "produit". Un exemple: Karlsruhe', *Revue Géographique de l'Est*, **18**, 35–50.

Trebbi, G. (1978) *La Ricostruzione di Una Città: Berlino 1945–1975* (Milan: Mazzotta).

Trenard, L. et al. (1977) *Histoire d'une Métropole: Lille-Roubaix-Tourcoing* (Toulouse: Privat).

Tuppen, J. (1977) 'Redevelopment of the city centre: the case of Lyon – la Part Dieu', *Scottish Geographical Magazine*, **93**, 151–8.

Tuppen, J. (1979) 'New towns in the Paris Region: an appraisal', *Town Planning Review*, **50**, 55–70.

Van Amersfoort, J. M. M. (1982) *Immigration and the Formation of Minority Groups: The Dutch Experience, 1945–1975*, trans. R. Lyng (Cambridge: Cambridge University Press).

Van Amersfoort, J. M. M. and Cortie, C. (1973) 'Het patroon van de Surinaamse vestiging in Amsterdam in de periode 1968 t/m 1970', *Tijdschrift voor Economische en Sociale Geografie*, **64**, 283–94.

Vance, J. E. (1977) *This Scene of Man: The Role and Structure of the City in the Geography of Western Civilization* (New York: Harper and Row).

Vance, J. E. (1978) 'Institutional forces that shape the city', in Herbert, D. T. and Johnston, R. J. (eds), *Social Areas in Cities: Processes, Patterns and Problems*, pp. 97–126 (Chichester: John Wiley).

Van Ginkel, J. A. (1979) *Suburbanisatie en Recente Woonmilieus, II. Een Residentiëel-Geografisch Onderzoek in het Middengebied Randstad*, Utrechtse Geografische Studies 16.

Van Hulten, M. H. M. (1968) 'Minder én meer bevolking in de binnenstad', in Heinemeyer, W. F., Van Hulten, M. H. M. and De Vries Reilingh, H. D. (eds), *Het Centrum van Amsterdam: Een Sociografische Studie*, pp. 69–128 (Amsterdam: Polak and Van Gennep).

Vant, A. (1973) 'Centre-ville et antagonismes sociaux: l'exemple stéphanois', *Revue de Géographie de Lyon*, **48**, 5–44.

Vaudor, B. (1966) 'Saint-Marcel: aspects et problèmes d'une banlieue marseillaise', *Bulletin, Société de Géographie de Marseille*, **76**, 5–45.

Verbanck, W. (1975) 'Oriënterend onderzoek naar een relatiemodel voor binnensteden. Enige bevindingen bij de struktuur van de Gentse Kuip', *Bulletin, Société Belge d'Etudes Géographiques*, **44**, 323–54.

Verniers, L. (1958) *Bruxelles et son Agglomération de 1830 à Nos Jours* (Brussels: Editions de la Librairie Encylopédique).

Vidal, A-M. (1978) 'Rue Impériale, rue Nationale, rue Foch: l'haussmannisation à Montpellier', *Bulletin, Société Languedocienne de Géographie*, **12**, 1–10.

Vieille, P. (1978) 'Sociologie historique de Marseille, XIIème–XVIIème siècles. Tentative d'interprétation de la structure sociale d'un grand port méditerranéen', *Peuples Méditerranéens, Mediterranean Peoples*, **4**, 77–112.

Vince, l'abbé (1966) 'Les courants d'immigration vers la région nazairienne de 1954 à 1962 et l'émigration apparente', *Norois*, **51**, 534–41.

Waley, D. (1978) *The Italian City-Republics* (2nd edn) (London: Longman).

Warnes, A. M. (1973) 'Residential patterns in an emerging industrial town', in Clark, B. D. and Gleave, M. B. (eds), *Social Patterns in Cities*, pp. 169–89, Special Publication No. 5, Institute of British Geographers.

Weber, E. (1977) *Peasants into Frenchmen: The Modernization of Rural France 1870–1914* (London: Chatto and Windus).

Wehling, H-W. (1981) 'Subjektive Stadtpläner als Ausdruck individueller Gliederung städtischer Strukturen', *Geographische Zeitschrift*, **69**, 98–113.

Weise, O. (1973) *Sozialgeographische Gliederung und Innerstädtische Verflechtungen in Wuppertal*, Bergische Forschungen Vol. 11.

White, P. E. and Woods, R. I. (eds) (1980) *The Geographical Impact of Migration* (London: Longman).

White, P. E. and Woods, R. I. (1983) 'Migration and the formation of ethnic minorities', in Kirkwood, K. et al (eds), *Biosocial Aspects of Ethnic Minorities*, 7–22, *Journal of Biosocial Science*, Supplement No. 8.

Whysall, P. and Benyon, J. (1980) 'Urban renewal policies in central Amsterdam', *Planning Outlook*, **23**, 77–82.

Williams, R. (1973) *The Country and the City* (London: Chatto and Windus).

Williams, S. (1981) *Politics is for People* (Harmondsworth: Penguin).

Woessner, R. and Bailly, A. (1979) 'Images du centre-ville et méthodes d'analyse factorielle: le cas du Mulhouse', *Environment and Planning A*, **11**, 1039–48.

Wolcke, I-D. (1968) *Die Entwicklung der Bochumer Innenstadt*, Schriften, Geographischen Instituts der Universität Kiel, Vol. 28.

Woods, R. I. (1976) 'Aspects of the scale problems in the calculation of segregation indices: London and Birmingham, 1961 and 1971', *Tijdschrift voor Economische en Sociale Geografie*, **67**, 169–74.

Woods, R. I. (1978) 'Mortality and sanitary conditions in the "Best governed city in the world" – Birmingham, 1870–1910, *Journal of Historical Geography*, **4**, 35–56.

Woods, R. I. (1979) *Population Analysis in Geography* (London: Longman).

Wrigley, E. A. (1967) 'A simple model of London's importance in changing English society and economy, 1650–1750', *Past and Present*, **37**, 44–70.

Wynn, M. (1979) 'Barcelona: planning and change 1854–1977', *Town Planning Review*, **50**, 185–203.

Zanetto, G. and Lando, F. (1980) 'Mestre: analisi tipologica di una struttura urbana', *Bollettino, Società Geografica Italiana*, **9**, 213–55.

Index of authors

Abele, G., 9
Abellan Garcia, A., 70, 71, 72, 73
Abrahamson, M., 161, 171, 173, 195
Accame, G. M., 205, 207
Achilles, F-W., 17, 52, 195, 208
Adamo, F., 59, 84, 164, 196, 223
Adams, J. S., 144
Adler, S., 110
Agnelli, S., 161
Ah-Peng, Y., 102, 122
Allain, F., 227
André, R., 224
Anfossi, A., 83
Angenot, L. H. J., 137, 198, 199, 236
anon., 61, 95, 114, 224
Arena, G., 102, 115, 129, 237
Armengaud, A., 100
Arnaud, J-L., 66
Arnauné-Clamens, A-M., 169, 206
Åström, S-E., 29, 156
Atkinson, W. C., 99
Aubenque, M., 64-5, 66
Aust, B., 42, 206, 209
Avery, K. L., 146

Baillet, P., 196
Bailly, A., 186
Ballesteros, A. G., 61, 62, 90, 95, 137, 161, 236
Barou, J., 111, 122, 126, 129
Barrère, P., 112, 113-14, 118, 119, 129, 136, 198, 201, 208
Bassett, K., 36, 39, 160
Bastano, I., 53, 154, 157, 201, 236

Bastide, H., 63
Bastié, J., 28, 216
Beek, W. F., 159, 163, 173, 174-7, 236
Beijer, G., 83
Bell, M., 147
Bell, W., 170, 176
Bellettini, A., 53, 63, 65, 68, 69, 75, 89
Ben Sassi, T., 121
Bentham, G., 44, 168, 199, 202, 203, 210, 235, 237
Benyon, J., 210
Bergues, H., 66, 117
Beringuier, C., 206, 209
Bernhardt, E. M., 63
Berry, B. J. L., 48, 155, 212, 235
Bertrand, M-J., 185, 187, 236, 237
Bianchi, E., 186
Bilet, F., 208
Bird, H., 136
Blanc, M., 205
Bléry, J. P., 136, 139
Boal, F. W., 128
Bobek, H., 13, 15, 20, 24, 40-1, 43, 47, 59, 100, 136, 156, 236, 237
Bogaert-Damin, A-M., 26, 92
Böhm, H., 51, 53, 70, 145, 157, 177, 236
Böhning, W. R., 76-7, 99, 100, 112-13
Boleat, M J., 37
Bollerey, F., 48-9, 222
Bolos y Capdevila, M. D., 85-6
Bonneville, M., 52, 56, 146, 201, 215
Bontinck, I., 185, 220
Borde, J., 112, 113-14, 118, 119, 129, 136

Borris, M., 61, 105, 106–7, 111, 112, 114, 116, 117, 119, 131, 136, 146, 153, 236
Boyce, R. R., 145–6
Boyer, J-C., 169
Branchereau, J–P., 208
Braudel, F., 5, 7, 14, 15, 23, 27, 98, 99, 235
Breitling, P., 24, 49
Brown, L. A., 137, 144
Bruggemeier, F., 17–18, 25, 45, 47, 72, 136
Brunet, J-P., 216
Bruyère, J., 224
Burgel, G., 99, 153, 154, 161, 171–2
Burtenshaw, D., xiii, 3, 28, 41, 42, 51, 205, 235
Buzzi-Donato, A., 89

Calabi, D., 29
Cammarota, A., 31, 40, 46-7, 90, 210
Cano García, G. M., 90
Capote, C., 12, 55, 72, 90, 192–3, 197, 202, 236
Caralp, R., 213
Carlsson, G., 62
Carter, F. W., 77, 90
Carter, H., 68, 155
Cassou-Mounat, M., 129, 198, 201, 208
Castells, M., 47, 151, 205–6, 207, 210, 235
Castles, S., 100, 112
Ceaux, J., 126, 194, 237
Charles, G., 50–1 53, 70
Chatelain, A., 64, 78–9, 81, 95
Chauviré, Y., 162, 168, 169, 237
Chazalette, A., 219, 220
Cheung, C., 138, 224
Chevalier, L., 15, 19, 64, 77–8, 79, 80, 235, 237
Chombart de Lauwe, P. H., 151, 185, 236, 237
Clark, J. R., 111, 116, 117, 122, 187, 235
Clark, W. A. V., 146
Claval, P., 4, 6, 163, 235
Clerc, P., 50, 71, 78, 167, 218, 219, 220, 227, 236
Cobb, R., xiv, 79, 126, 184, 196
Comitas, L., 59

Coppock, J. T., 164
Coppolani, J., 202, 219, 223
Corbin, A., 76, 78
Cortie, C., 44, 60, 95, 102, 114, 117, 130, 133, 140, 224, 236
Cosgrove, D., 7
Costa, P., 139, 159, 161, 169, 203, 236
Crew, D. F., 16, 17–19, 81, 156, 235
Cribier, F., 95
Cromar, O., 75
Cserjan, K., 158, 162, 174–80, 182, 237
Curl, J. S., 3, 4, 22, 28

Dahya, B., 121
Dalmasso, E., 198–9
Damais, J. P., 54, 158, 222
Damas, H., 224
Dandri, G., 39, 41, 54
Dang, R., 163, 167
Darroch, A. G., 120
David-Valcke, A., 113, 122, 126, 128, 236
Davies, M. L., 229
Davies, W. K. D., 177
Davis, K., 14
De Bertier de Sauvigny, G., 15, 20, 26, 78, 125
Declercq-Tijtgat, A., 95, 223, 224
Deffontaines, P., 98
De Lannoy, W., 70, 71, 73, 107, 111, 118, 126–7, 133, 154, 157, 158, 163, 222, 235, 236
Deloménie, D., 168, 216, 217
Den Draak, J., 137, 169, 192, 195, 202
Deneux, J-F., 26, 44, 156
Deplancke, M., 223
De Smidt, M., 118, 130
De Terán, M., 23-4, 237
Dickinson, R. E., 1, 3
Dion, R-M., 8, 10
Döpp, W., 6, 15, 45, 48, 53, 156, 201, 206, 236
Doré, A., 71, 73, 219, 220
Drewe, P., 110, 112, 122, 130, 133, 168, 235
Dubesset, P., 66
Dubois, M. H., 28
Duchac, R., 112, 113, 118, 119, 129
Duclaud-Williams, R. H., 37, 38, 41, 44, 45

Duncan, B., 155
Duncan, O.D., 155
Dupré, M., 114
Dyer, C., 95

El Gharbaoui, A., 100, 114, 117, 118, 121
Elkins, T. H., 47, 115, 235
Erminero, C., 45
Esteva Fabregat, C., 85, 86, 88
Ettlin, W., 53
Evenson, N., 10, 25−6, 28, 30, 43, 50, 53, 64, 66, 170, 214, 218, 227, 231, 235, 237

Faccioli, M., 225, 232
Faure, A., 26, 45
Federici, N., 67−8, 237
Fédou, R., 4
Ferras, R., 12, 14, 15, 38, 40, 44, 45−6, 85, 86, 87, 90, 151, 168, 174−6, 226, 236
Fofi, G., 82
Fontaine, C., 207
Fox, M., 218
Francescato, D., 186
Freyssenet, M., 139, 154

Gabert, P., 77, 83, 84
Gächter, E., 94, 130, 159, 162, 173−7, 199, 236
Gago Llorente, V., 37, 52, 161
Galtung, J., 83
Gans, P., 145, 146, 236
Ganser, K., 144, 163, 184, 197
Garbagnati, B., 84
García, A. A., 219
Gaspar, J., 31, 192, 195
Gastelaars, R. V. E., 60, 157, 159, 163, 173, 174−7, 197, 224, 227, 236
Gehmacher, E., 95, 106
Geiger, F., 112, 113, 117, 122, 123
Gentileschi, M. L., 98, 106−7, 112, 113, 115, 121, 130
George, P., 196
Georgulas, N., 32, 185
Ghirardo, D. A., 161
Giannoni, M., 154, 237
Ginatempo, N., 31, 40, 46−7, 90, 210

Gisser, R., 53, 68, 71, 73, 95, 157, 162, 236, 237
Glebe, G., 131
Godard, F., 151, 205
Gokalp, C., 119
Goursolas, J-M., 38, 51, 230−1
Gozalvez-Perez, V., 89
Grigg, D. B., 15
Grimmeau, J. P., 113, 122, 126, 128, 236
Grönholm, L., 178, 184
Grötzbach, E., 195, 202, 206
Guibourdenche, H., 154, 165
Guidicini, P., 89
Guillaume, P., 15, 21, 64, 81, 99, 129, 235
Guillon, M., 99, 107, 113, 115, 119, 122

Hafen, W., 53
Hajdu, J. G., 10
Halsey, A. H., 152
Hammarström, I., 19, 48, 237
Hartmann, K., 48−9, 222
Harts, J. J., 228
Haussmann, E., 28
Heinemeyer, W. F., 186, 197
Helvig, M., 198, 199−200, 202
Herbert, D. T., 225
Herzog, A. N., 67, 159, 178
Holzmann, G., 59, 95
Holzner, L., 31
Hook, J., 6, 10, 14, 15
Horne, A., 23
Howard, E., 229
Huet, B., 205, 207, 208, 218
Hyldtoft, O., 15, 19

Ioli Gigante, A., 30, 31, 98, 156, 226

Jackson, J. H., 16, 17, 47, 50, 72, 81, 136, 235
Jacquemet, G., 194
Jardel, J. P., 168
Jobse, R. B., 51−2
Johnson, P., 161, 173, 195
Johnston, R. J., 36, 75, 77, 97, 110, 115, 120, 152, 155
Joly, J., 153, 154, 163, 165, 168, 223
Jones, P. C., 173−7
Josse, R., 218, 220, 221, 222

Kain, R., 207, 208
Kaufmann, A., 37, 48, 53, 68, 70, 71, 73, 95, 157, 162, 198, 236, 237
Kesteloot, C., 173−7, 236
Keyfitz, N., 15
Killisch, W. F., 55, 95, 137, 138
King, J. C., 37, 44
King, R., 100, 111
Kinsey, J., 177
Klamroth, H-B., 104, 112, 114
Kosack, G., 100, 112
Kouvelis, K., 80, 195, 197, 209, 210
Kreth, R., 162, 174−7, 182
Kreuzaler, E., 100

Lacave, M., 28
Laferrère, M., 114
Lampedusa, T., 5
Lamy, B., 186
Lamy, M-L., 119
Lando, F., 153, 159, 174−7, 178, 236
Laquerbe, J., 70−1, 155
Laurant, A., 95, 223, 224
Laux, H-D., 62
Lawrence, D. H., 14
Ledrut, R., 205
Leidlmair, A., 9
Lemay, C., 50, 195, 201, 208
Lerch, S., 25, 44
Leroy, E., 217
Le Roy Ladurie, E., 6
Lewis, G. J., 177
Liang, H-H., 19, 47, 80, 236−3
Lichtenberger, E., 2, 3, 10, 11, 12−13, 15, 20, 24−5, 29, 32, 33, 40−1, 43, 48−50, 55, 59, 100, 136, 153, 156, 166, 188, 209, 225, 226, 232, 235, 236, 237
Lieberson, S., 129, 130
Lindemann, M., 21
Logan, J. R., 168
Louckx, F., 92, 94
Lowder, S., 24, 37, 46, 159, 209, 218, 235, 236
Lowenthal, D., 59
Lusso, G., 84, 197
Lyttleton, A., 26, 81

McClintock, H., 218
McElrath, D. C., 161, 171−2, 237

McKeown, T., 64
Madge, C., 39
Mallet, F., 28, 196
Maréchal, L., 26, 92
Markopoulou, A., 32, 185
Marston, W. G., 120
Martinez-Marí, J. M., 87, 89, 220
Masini, A., 66
Matthiessen, C. W., 159, 163, 173, 174−7, 180−2, 204
Maurice, M., 168, 216, 217
Mebane, W., 186
Meeus, B., 91, 107, 112, 124, 127, 128, 135, 147, 236
Mérenne-Schoumaker, B., 186
Metton, A., 185, 187, 236, 237
Meyer, P., 215
Mik, G., 116, 117
Mikkelsen, L., 70, 112, 127
Mohr, B., 225
Mols, R., 79, 91−3, 107, 128, 137, 144, 224, 226, 227, 236
Montes Mieza, J., 46, 90
Moore, E. G., 137, 144
Moore, R., 36, 120
Moreau, G., 182, 222
Moseley, M. J., 44, 168, 199, 202, 203, 210, 235, 237
Müller, D. O., 29, 40
Mumford, L., 1, 3, 13, 14, 15, 22
Murdie, R. A., 172

Navarro Laguarta, L., 65
Naylon, J., 40, 46, 64, 89, 236
Nelde, P. N., 92, 125
Niemeier, G., 162, 167
Niethammer, L., 17−18, 25, 45, 47, 72, 136
Noin, D., 162, 168, 169, 237

Ogden, P. E., 79−80, 86, 90, 99, 107, 108, 114, 124−5, 235, 237
Olives Puig, J., 25, 53, 70, 86, 87, 89, 236
O'Loughlin, J., 105, 116, 120, 123, 131, 133, 136, 146, 235
Origo, I., 98

Pagnol, M., 184
Pahl, R. E., 68, 133, 223

Pailhé, J., 69, 139, 153, 154–5, 157, 163, 168, 198
Paine, S., 100
Panieri, A., 89
Pappas, P., 226
Papy, L., 14, 21
Pattyn, M., 173
Peach, C., 120
Pedersen, P. O., 159, 163, 171, 178
Perussia, F., 186
Peruzzi, W., 45
Petersen, V. C., 139
Piasentin, U., 199, 225
Picheral, H., 65–6, 236
Pinkney, D. H., 78
Plattner, N., 225
Poinard, M., 112, 114, 116–17, 118, 119, 121, 129
Ponsot, P., 14, 16
Popenoe, D., 51, 222, 229–30, 235, 237
Poschwatta, W., 192
Pourcher, G., 94–5, 236, 237
Preston, S. H., 20, 64
Prié, N., 71, 137, 138
Prouvost, J., 67, 194, 195
Pumain, D., 154
Putz, M. C., 71, 137, 138
Pyle, G. F., 63

Queneau, R., 184

Råberg, M., 9, 12, 23, 28, 237
Radford, J. P., 5
Ralite, J-C., 231
Ranger, J., 125, 153, 154, 182–3
Rapoport, A., 33, 201, 218
Rasmussen, P., 159, 163, 171, 178
Rasmussen, T. F., 225, 227, 228
Rees, P. H., 63
Regni, B., 12, 27, 28, 219, 222
Rein, D. B., 104
Rex, J. A., 36, 120
Ricci, G., 6, 10, 11, 14, 21, 27
Riquet, P., 44, 45, 162, 220
Rist, R. C., 100, 116, 117, 118, 129, 130, 235
Robson, B. T., 35, 36, 45, 135, 177
Rochefort, C., 184
Rochefort, R., 69, 70, 113, 130, 133, 138, 220, 222

Rollet, C., 20–1
Roncayolo, M., 154, 169
Ronzon, J., 111, 130
Roseman, C. C., 134
Rossi, D., 16, 55, 138, 144, 199, 202, 236, 237
Russac, J-M., 206

Saint-Raymond, O., 206
Salcedo, J., 90, 236
Salgueiro, T. B., 46
Sarracco, F., 218
Sauberer, M., 158, 162, 174–80, 182, 237
Saviranta, J., 225, 228
Sbragia, A. M., 38, 43, 44
Schaffer, F., 95, 136, 137, 138, 144
Schenk, W., 97, 130
Schinz, A., 202, 236
Schnapper, D. J., 121, 187
Schnore, L. F., 160
Schorske, C. E., 24–5, 40
Schulz, P., 107, 113, 236
Seger, M., 221, 224
Selva, E. M. B., 85, 86
Sennato, M., 12, 27, 28, 219, 222
Sewell, J. H., 19–20
Sharlin, A., 15
Shaw, P., 195, 197
Shevky, E., 170, 176
Short, J. R., 36, 39, 137, 160
Sick, W. D., 137, 138, 144, 145, 146, 236
Sidenbladh, G., 10, 28, 208, 212, 229, 230, 237
Sijbrandij, F. N. J., 209
Simenon, G., xiv, 82
Simmons, J. W., 135, 144
Simon, G., 112, 113
Sjoberg, G., 1, 5–6, 7, 13–14, 160, 213
Sola-Morales Rubió, M. D., 89, 178
Sostres, J. M., 85, 89
Soubeyroux, J., 5, 11, 15, 21, 23, 74–5, 237
Sporck, J. A., 61
Sprengel, U., 53, 131
Steinberg, H. G., 16–18, 30, 99, 236
Stephenson, G. V., 91
Sutcliffe, A., xiii, 12, 25, 26, 28, 29, 30, 41, 43, 52, 64, 66, 235, 237
Sweetser, F. L., 174–8

Talamo, M., 54, 84−5
Taubmann, W., 202, 203, 204
Thorns, D. C., 213
Toesca, D., 197
Traband, G., 9, 199, 202
Trebbi, G., 30, 51, 209, 218, 219, 220, 231, 236
Trenard, L., 18, 99, 231
Trojani, M-J., 197
Tuppen, J., 51, 196, 208, 230−1

Van Amersfoort, J. M. M., 100, 102, 130, 133, 235
Vance, J. E., 1, 5, 7, 213, 216, 235
Van der Meersch, M., 184
Vandermotten, C., 223
Van de Walle, E., 20, 64
Van Eeckhoutte, Y., 173
Van Ginkel, J. A., 37, 224, 228
Van Hulten, M. H. M., 70, 71, 149, 198, 199−201, 202, 236
Vant, A., 192, 198, 205
Vaudour, B., 227
Verbanck, W., 203
Verkoren-Hemelaar, N., 116, 117
Verniers, L., 15, 20, 25, 28, 43, 80, 92, 156, 198, 236

Vidal, A-M., 28
Vieille, P., 4, 6
Vince, l'abbé, 95
Virirakis, J., 226

Waley, D., 5, 6
Warnes, A. M., 164
Weber, E., 76, 164
Wehling, H-W., 186
Weise, O., 42, 166
White, P. E., 74, 75, 76, 81, 97, 100, 112, 116, 134
Whysall, P., 210
Williams, R., 163
Williams, S., 153
Willmott, P., 39
Winchester, S. W. C., 79−80, 86, 90, 237
Woessner, R., 186
Wolcke, I-D., 16, 17−19, 192, 202−3
Woods, R. I., 62, 63, 64, 74, 75, 76, 81, 87, 100, 112, 116, 134
Wrigley, E.A., 15
Wynn, M., 11

Zanetto, G., 153, 159, 178, 236
Zola, E., 18

Index of places

Aalborg, 159, 178

Aarhus, 27, 48, 59, 139, 159, 178, 204

Amsterdam: further reading, 236; history, 3, 10, 27; housing, 35, 37, 43, 44, 45, 52, 53, 117, 146, 159, 197, 218; inner-city, 70, 169, 186, 198, 199–201; migrants, 95, 98, 103, 108, 110, 114, 117, 122, 135, 136, 137, 142–4, 150; population growth, 15, 59, 60–1; social areas, 130, 157, 173, 174–7; social composition, 70, 159, 163, 169, 197; social protest, 210; suburban growth, 214, 223, 224, 228

Antwerp, 5, 15, 26, 48, 51, 52, 98, 105, 123–4, 199

Athens, 14, 52, 57, 77, 82, 90, 99, 101, 153, 154, 161, 171–2, 226

Augsburg, 3, 192

Avignon, 98

Barcelona: commuting, 226; further reading, 235, 236; history, 3, 11, 12, 16, 23, 24, 29; housing, 40, 44, 46, 53, 218; migrants, 70, 77, 82, 85–9, 98, 101, 102, 217; mortality, 64, 65–6; population growth, 14, 15, 57; shanty-towns, 45, 46, 87–8, 89, 217; social areas, 87–9, 151, 159, 161, 167, 174–6, 178; social structure, 86

Bari, 3, 24, 51, 53, 58, 59

Basel, 11, 14, 23, 39, 43, 53, 62

Bergen, 198, 199–200, 202

Berlin: filtering, 197; further reading, 236; history, 7, 10, 15, 20; household size, 202; housing, 17, 19, 29, 39, 40, 45, 47, 118, 218; migrants, 18, 58, 80, 81, 98, 99, 103, 105, 107, 111, 118, 123–4, 128–9, 131, 135, 136, 137, 197; social areas, 220, 231; transport, 214; urban renewal, 30, 208–9

Bern, 39, 49–50, 94, 130, 159, 162, 173–7, 199, 236

Besançon, 50–1

Bilbao, 3, 24, 49, 57, 82

Birmingham, 63

Bochum, 16, 17–18, 30, 72, 156

Bologna, 3, 5, 6, 10, 11, 14, 21, 23, 27, 29, 36, 52, 53, 63, 65, 68, 69, 75, 89, 184, 207–8, 109, 210

Bonn, 53, 57, 58, 70, 145–6, 147, 148, 157, 177, 236

Bordeaux, 5, 14, 15, 21, 27, 36, 49, 64, 68–9, 81, 99, 103, 118, 129, 138, 139, 154, 157, 162–3, 198, 224, 236

Bremen, 3, 27, 105

Bruges, 14

Brunswick, 7

Brussels: age-structure, 71, 73, 112; further reading, 236; history, 23, 26, 27, 28, 202; housing, 32, 36, 49–50, 52, 71, 118, 158, 159, 196, 207; language, 91–4; migrants, 20, 70, 77, 79, 80, 91–4, 98, 103, 105, 107, 110, 111, 112, 113, 123–5, 126–8, 129, 130, 135, 144, 147, 148; population growth, 14, 15, 20, 61, 198; segregation, 122, 126–8, 156, 157; social areas, 154, 158, 163, 164, 167, 168, 173–7; suburban growth, 95, 214, 216, 223–4, 226, 227

Cadiz, 98
Cahors, 6
Cannes, 168
Catania, 52, 53
Charleroi, 95
Chicago, xiii, 63
Cologne, 3, 14, 18, 27, 30, 31, 39, 43, 58, 62, 72, 105, 135, 136, 141–2, 199
Copenhagen, 15, 25, 27, 36, 43, 52, 57, 61, 103, 135, 144, 159, 163, 164, 173, 174–7, 180–2
Cordoba, 5, 101

Dijon, 71, 220
Dortmund, 17, 30, 31, 72
Duisburg, 16, 17, 30, 58, 72, 81, 136
Dunkirk, 151, 205
Düsseldorf, 7, 10, 36, 38, 72, 123, 131, 204

Essen, 17–18, 30, 72, 136, 204

Florence, 5, 6, 7, 14, 27, 58, 101, 223
Frankfurt, 27, 47, 58, 59, 103, 104–5, 118, 130
Freiburg, 137, 138, 144, 146, 225

Gelsenkirchen, 18
Geneva, 23, 25, 36, 39, 49–50, 62, 98, 103, 109–10, 122, 123
Genoa, 51, 53
Ghent, 49–50, 52
Gothenburg, 9, 10, 39, 42, 59, 105, 108
Graz, 37
Grenoble, 49–50, 52, 57, 102, 103, 123, 163, 217, 223

The Hague, 3, 22, 39, 43, 51, 224, 228
Hamburg, 21, 27, 30, 32, 39, 110
Hanover, 10, 43, 53, 103, 131, 195, 202, 206
Le Havre, 30–1, 57, 158
Heidelberg, 10
Helsinki, 29, 38–9, 59, 156, 174–8, 184, 223

Innsbruck, 37

Karlsruhe, 9–10, 199, 202
Kiel, 51, 95, 103, 137, 138
Klagenfurt, 37

Lens, 49–50, 103
Letchworth, 229
Liège, 2, 11, 61, 95, 166, 186, 224
Lille, 18, 52, 102, 123, 163, 194–5, 231
Linz, 37, 70
Lisbon, 2, 15, 30, 31, 35, 45–6, 57, 82, 98, 99, 192
Liverpool, 203
Livorno, 98
London, 10, 13, 29, 30, 48, 64, 98, 99, 166–7, 203, 214
Ludwigshafen, 146, 148
Lyon, 4, 20–1, 28, 52, 56, 69–70, 81, 98, 103, 112, 114, 118, 121, 122, 123, 129, 130, 138, 146, 173–7, 196, 208, 214, 215

Madrid: further reading, 236; history, 3, 5, 10, 11, 12, 21, 23–4, 29; housing, 37, 48, 52, 55, 71; migrants, 62, 70, 74–5, 90, 101; population growth, 15–16, 57, 61; servants, 72, 192; shanty-towns, 45–6, 90; social areas, 161, 171, 173, 192–3, 197; suburban growth, 95, 219; transport, 214, 226
Mainz, 174–7, 182
Malaga, 46
Malmö, 36, 42, 51
Mannheim, 10
Marseille, 3, 4, 15, 19–20, 28, 30, 38, 51, 57, 66, 81, 112, 117, 118, 119, 129, 133, 184, 216, 226
Messina, 30, 31, 46–7, 52, 58, 90, 98, 101, 156, 226
Milan, 3, 6, 14, 15, 16, 26, 32, 52, 53, 81, 101, 102, 129, 186, 198, 214, 226
Montpellier, 28, 155
Mulhouse, 186, 215
Munich, 3, 7, 10, 51, 61, 62, 105, 144, 184
Münster, 27, 57, 58
Murcia, 90

Namur, 224
Nancy, 8, 10, 102
Nantes, 102, 103

Naples, 3, 5, 6, 15, 30, 45, 48, 52, 53, 58, 59, 101, 154, 156, 157, 167, 201, 206, 223, 236
New York, 32
Nice, 3, 52, 197
Nuremberg, 14, 27, 31, 104, 112, 114

Odense, 57, 159, 178
Oporto, 46, 49
Orléans, 231
Oslo, 36, 48, 51, 53, 61, 225, 227

Palermo, 3, 5, 14, 15, 53, 57, 58
Paris: further reading, 235, 236, 237; history, 10, 12, 23, 25−6, 27−8, 30, 59, 202, 125−16; housing, 35, 38, 39, 40−1, 43−4, 45, 48, 50, 51−2, 53, 117, 118, 119, 170, 195, 201, 218; migrants, 31−2, 76, 77−80, 81, 82, 87, 90, 94−5, 98, 99, 103, 105, 107, 108, 111−12, 114, 117, 118, 121, 123−6, 129, 187; population, 14, 15, 20−1, 64−5, 77, 199; segregation, 122, 123−6, 130, 156; social areas, 19, 139, 162, 167−8, 170, 182−4, 185, 186, 187, 193−4, 196, 208, 217; social structure, 153, 154, 169; suburban growth, 29, 38, 55, 203, 218, 220, 223, 229, 230−1; transport, 166, 214, 220, 221, 226−7, 228

Rennes, 51, 57, 102
Romans, 6
Rome: further reading, 236, 237; history, 5, 11, 12, 28, 161; housing, 53, 55, 202; intra-urban migration, 135, 138, 141−2, 144, 147−9; migrants, 101, 102, 129; mortality, 67−8; population growth, 14, 15, 16, 57, 58, 59, 199; shanty-towns, 45; social areas, 164, 167, 171−2, 185, 186, 222, 225, 232; transport, 214
Rotterdam, 30, 31, 36, 37, 39, 67, 110, 122, 130, 133, 159, 169, 178, 224, 228
Roubaix, 67, 99, 184, 194−5
Rouen, 31, 137, 138, 227
Ruhr, 16−19, 30, 81, 99, 215, 235, 236; *see also individual cities*

St Etienne, 120, 130, 192, 198
Salonica, 52, 57
Salzburg, 37
San Gimignano, 6
Seville, 3, 15, 27, 46, 48, 98
Sheffield, 75
Siena, 4, 5, 6, 10, 14
Stockholm, 2, 9, 10, 11, 23, 28, 29, 30, 39, 42, 43, 51, 61, 62, 105, 108, 110, 135, 136, 142−4, 196, 208, 222, 229−30, 231, 235, 236, 237
Strasbourg, 22, 52, 57, 98, 110, 122
Stuttgart, 10, 31, 61, 103, 105, 106−7, 111, 112, 114, 116, 117, 119, 123, 136, 146, 153, 204, 216, 236
Sunderland, 177

Tampere, 36, 57
Toulon, 27
Toulouse, 3, 28, 52, 122, 206−7
Tourcoing, 194−5
Tours, 231
Trier, 3
Trieste, 3, 53, 101−2
Turin, 30, 31, 53, 58, 59, 77, 82−5, 89, 101, 102, 114, 118, 161, 164−5, 193, 196, 215, 226
Turku, 36, 57, 61, 225, 228

Ulm, 95, 136, 137, 138, 144
Utrecht, 3, 27, 37, 49−50, 95, 118, 130, 137, 169, 202, 224, 228

Valencia, 3, 48, 89−90, 101
Venice, 3, 5, 6−7, 13, 14, 53, 98, 139, 153, 159, 161, 174−7, 178, 199, 203, 216−7, 236
Verona, 6, 27, 52
Vienna: further reading, 236, 237; history, 2, 5, 10, 11, 12−13, 23, 24−5, 28, 29; housing, 36, 37, 39, 40−1, 42, 43, 48, 49, 51−2, 53−4, 55, 158; intra-urban migration, 135, 136, 144, 149; migrants, 95, 99−100, 105−6, 108, 110, 111; population, 15, 20, 59, 61, 67, 68, 71, 73; segregation, 156, 157; social areas, 162, 164, 166, 174−80, 182, 188, 193; social structure, 12−13, 153; suburban growth, 221, 224−5

Welwyn, 229
West Berlin, *see* Berlin
Wiesbaden, 3, 58
Wuppertal, 42, 72, 166
Wurzburg, 30

Zaragoza, 65
Zürich, 27, 35, 36, 43, 59, 60, 61, 94, 104–5, 123–5, 135, 140, 142, 144, 197, 199, 223

Index of subjects

action space, 185–7
age-structures, 68–72, 112, 138–9

building regulations, 10–11, 29

commuters, 107, 223–8

density, housing and population, 33, 52–3, 201, 202–3
depopulation, inner-city, 53, 59–60, 61, 198–204

factorial ecologies, 173–82
fertility, 59, 62–3
filtering, 195–7
fortifications, 8, 22–7

garden suburbs, 222
gentrification, 33, 197, 208–10
grands ensembles, 44, 56, 217–21

haussmannization, 27–9, 33, 194
household size, 53–4, 71–2, 201, 202
housing, 17, 18–19, 28, 29, 33, 35–56, 84–5, 115–20, 122–3, 136–8, 143–4, 149–50, 156–7, 158–60, 177, 178, 194–5, 221, 224; age and amenities, 51–2, 117–18, 129, 159; allocation policies, 44–5; classes, 36, 158; employer-provided, 17–19, 42, 116–17; owner-occupied, 36–8, 55, 56, 119; preferences, 50–1; privately-rented, 38–42, 55, 71–2, 117–18; publicly-rented, 42–5, 55–6, 71, 116, 118–19, 166, 168, 217–19; types, 38, 47–52, 170, 229–30, 231;

industrial growth, 16–22, 27, 75–7, 82–9, 98, 100, 164–6, 213, 215–17

infant mortality, 67–8

journey-to-work, 166, 217, 220, 226–9

land ownership, 11–12, 28–9, 42, 205–6, 229
language use, 85, 86, 91–4
life-cycle, 68, 70, 72, 134, 137–9, 176–7, 178
lodgers, 47, 80–1, 135–6
lower middle class, 169–70, 221–2
lunch hours, 226–7

mental images, 186
middle class, 152, 154, 160–7, 180, 192–3, 221–5
migrant communities, 122, 129, 132–3
migrants, 15, 62, 66, 70, 72, 83, 85–6, 90, 91, 94–5, 108–15, 137–9, 186–7, 224
migration, 17–18, 19, 20–1, 33, 61–2, 74–150, 198; chain, 117, 120; distance, 145–6, 148; international labour, 77, 97, 99–108, 136; intra-urban, 129, 134–50; return, 121; rural-urban, 75–6, 77, 81, 131–2; seasonal, 78

models of urban form, 2, 12, 139–40, 160–1, 163, 187–9

mortality, 15–16, 20, 63–8

neighbourhoods, 184–6, 187, 229, 231

new towns, 230–1

population growth, 14–18, 20–1, 57–62, 78, 105, 194, 212, 223–4

power and control, 2, 3–14, 32, 205

refugees, 98–9, 105–6, 115

religion, 121–2, 177

rent control, 40–2, 136

repatriates, 107, 115, 119

residential structure, 151–90

segregation, 4, 13, 24–5, 29, 49, 79–80, 87, 92–4, 120–31, 132–3, 150, 155–8, 167, 168, 189, 224–5

self-employed class, 152–3, 157, 169, 175, 189, 192

servants, 72, 90 153, 169, 192–3

sex structure, 62, 72–3, 112

shanty-towns, 26, 31, 45–7, 87–8, 90, 118, 217

slum clearance, 199–202

social area analyses, 170–3, 176

social areas, 151–90

social mobility, 19–20

social modernization, 76, 83, 121

social pathology, 184

social protest movements, 168, 207, 210–11

social structure, 4, 5, 12–13, 18–20, 21, 86, 120, 152–5, 192, 230

suburban growth, 59–62, 95, 212–32

taxes, 26, 215–16

transport, 213–14, 220, 221

urban culture, 33–4, 163–4, 166, 184–5, 212–13, 221, 232

urban renewal, 194, 204–11

voting patterns, 182–4

working class, 167–9, 193–5, 215–21